SCREEN JESUS

Portrayals of Christ in Television and Film

PETER MALONE

THE SCARECROW PRESS, INC.
Lanham • Toronto • Plymouth, UK
2012

Published by Scarecrow Press, Inc.
A wholly owned subsidiary of The Rowman & Littlefield Publishing Group, Inc.
4501 Forbes Boulevard, Suite 200, Lanham, Maryland 20706
www.rowman.com

10 Thornbury Road, Plymouth PL6 7PP, United Kingdom

British Library Cataloguing in Publication Information Available

Library of Congress Cataloging-in-Publication Data

Malone, Peter.
  Screen Jesus : portrayals of Christ in television and film / Peter Malone.
     p. cm.
  Includes bibliographical references and index.
  ISBN 978-0-8108-8389-5 (cloth : alk. paper) — ISBN 978-0-8108-8390-1
(ebook)
  1. Jesus Christ—In motion pictures. I. Title.
  PN1995.9.J4M38 2012
  791.43'68232—dc23

                                                      2012014380

Printed in the United States of America

CONTENTS

FOREWORD

When I was invited to write the foreword to *Screen Jesus* I was extremely honored and proud. I have been fortunate to work with Peter Malone over many years in universities, small summer schools, retreats, and international conferences. Amazed at Peter's sheer knowledge of film—from who won which Oscars, when, and for which films to who starred, directed, or played a humble supporting character in whichever film under discussion—I once called him an Anorak. Peter, being Australian, wasn't familiar with this British expression for someone who gathers and retains endless information on some subject or other and was unsure whether or not I was being pleasant. I was indeed, being pleasant—nay, I have again and again found myself utterly bemused by and envious of his sheer ability of recall and his unparalleled knowledge of film and theology.

I have over the years watched generations of students from the college at which I lecture in film, myth, and spiritualities sitting in lecture halls, or in the more intimate setting of workshops, engrossed with Peter's enthusiasm for his subject and for the connections he makes between film story, mythic themes, human emotion, and spiritual approaches. Peter is a born movie buff, and that is one of the differences between his writing and that of many others who write about film in an academic environment. Peter is soaked in the stories we tell each other and is just as much at home with a piece of slapstick comedy, a rom-com, a weepy chick flick, a sci-fi adventure, or hanging out with the vampires and superheroes as he is with the more serious attempts of filmmakers to query, investigate, or interrogate the human condition. Many of my students studying for a media and film degree opt to study ideas of the sacred and the screen. They are well aware, as students of screenwriting and the creation of characters, that without offering a spiritual dimension to their characters' identities, there is no depth and therefore less hope of connecting with the audience at the kind of level that ensures people will want to see their films again and again. This is a question of the filmmaking craft, but it is also, of course, a commercial issue. Think of *The Green Mile* and *The Shawshank Redemption* with their exploration of goodness, compassion, and hope, or *Shirley Valentine* who, in direct close-up to the audience, asks, "Why do we have all these feelings and dreams if we get lost in all this life?" Such movies sell, and sell again, as each new generation discovers them and finds in them answers to their questions on life—or at least, better questions than perhaps they have, so far, been asking.

A prolific writer on film, Peter has contextualized movies such as these and others too numerous to count, such as *Kundun*, *Meet Joe Black*, *The Accused*, *Where the Heart Is* (in terms of the liturgy of the Mass), and *The Ten Commandments* (these in partnership with Rose Pacatte, FSP). His work on film and values continues to shine a light on how stories as varied as *Easy Rider* (1969) and the American comedy Jesse Peretz's *Our Idiot Brother* (2011) help us to ask questions of ourselves such as What is goodness? and Is goodness catching? Above all, in the age of that perhaps most enduringly popular movie character—the superhero—Peter's work on Jesus- and Christ-figures has enabled us to open up our understanding of the connections and distinctions between the two and how they connect with, and are distinct from, so many movie characters both superhero and those of us who try live with our feet on the ground.

Peter's 1988 book *Movie Christs and Antichrists* does not contain in-depth exploration of one or two films on the Christ-figure—others have done this to great effect, as has Peter as contributor to many such books. Rather, it offers us a long list of categories of Jesus-figures and Christ-figures through a creative, knowledgeable, and significant list of movies from a variety of genres, from Zeffirelli's *Jesus of Nazareth* to Polanski's *Rosemary's Baby*. I cannot overstate the boon this book has been to generations of film students, many of whom have no or very little introduction to theology. Many students whose culture is based on two thousand years of Christian theology, faith, and practice have been thoroughly impoverished theologically over the past thirty years or so. More and more young people have no background knowledge or understanding of how the past two thousand years of Christian thinking have shaped the world in which they live. They no longer know the stories that have informed our art, our literature, and even our comic book heroes from the early part of the twentieth century. These stories have not been their formation. Their delight, then, when they find it possible to read *Mad Max* through the character of a savior-figure that can be traced back to the New Testament—not Jesus as Mad Max nor Mad Max as Jesus but rather a mythic/spiritual identity of one who, as Peter describes it, "suffers in a mindlessly violent society and rescuer of victims and leader to safety in Paradise"—is one of discovery and encouragement to seek deeper and deeper meaning. Pop-culture saviors speak to the generations who have neither heard, nor are interested in hearing, the Gospel as spoken in church.

Screen Jesus, however, takes that earlier work to another level. As Jaroslav Pelikan did for our cultural understanding of Jesus through the centuries, Peter Malone has compiled a first-rate resource for everyone interested in the Jesus-figure in film since the first movie camera was directed at this subject. The book covers the whole spectrum of films, from Jesus in art to the early twentieth-century Jesus films to Jesus films through the decades; from categories such as Jesus in our world today to verbal Jesus-figures to Jesus and film beyond Christianity to the reverent and the bizarre, including documentaries such as *Searching for the Wrong-Eyed Jesus* (United States, 2005) and *What Would Jesus Buy?* (United States, 2007) to Jesus on YouTube and the new wave discourse on this panoramic subject after Mel Gibson's *The Passion of the Christ*. Peter also sends us to the main scholars in his field, such as Lloyd Baugh, Adele Reinhartz, W. Barnes Tatum, and others.

No one in the field of film scholarship is better suited to this subject than Peter Malone. No one else has taught and studied film and theology with the breadth and depth that Peter has. The sheer scope of his international interest in film is unique. He has traveled the world and been the honored guest at film festivals in the Philippines, across Europe and the United States, in Asia, in the Pacific Islands, and in the Middle East, including Iran. In his capacity of president of SIGNIS, the World Catholic Association for Communication, Peter has met with film scholars, filmmakers, and those who organize film events across the globe over the past few decades. He has been a film critic and commentator for diverse publications and broadcasting outlets across the world. Most of all, he has shared his passion for film and his film and theological scholarship with immense generosity. Peter has enthused generations in the subject of the screen Jesus and so has opened eyes and ears both to the "greatest story ever told" and the threads connecting that story with all the other stories told on celluloid into the digital age.

Above all, *Screen Jesus* offers us quite simply an engrossing read. Peter talks us through his scholarship with deceptive simplicity. This is a book not only to use as a reference when exploring resources for studying Jesus on screen but also to dip into for spiritual nourishment, combining as it does the sensitive reflections of one who loves movies but who walks a deeply spiritual path through the stories told in the medium that offers, as Jimmy Stewart said, "little tiny pieces of time we will never forget."

Maggie Roux
Communications and Media
Trinity and All Saints College
Leeds, UK

INTRODUCING THE THEME

H. B. Warner gliding soulfully through Jerusalem. Robert Powell speaking the Gospel parables with beautiful articulation. Jeremy Sisto dancing and splashing water on his disciples. Jim Caviezel enduring a scourging of sadistic brutality. Who is the real Jesus?

It is important to look at the major portrayals of Jesus on-screen over more than a century to see why millions of people worldwide have responded to the Jesus films and how these films have interpreted Jesus and the Gospel message.

However, it may also be useful to go back over the hundred years or more of these portrayals of Jesus with a second purpose. There have been distinctive phases of how Jesus could be presented and what was outlawed from the screen. The expectations of the generation that was in its teens in the 1940s when there were no Jesus films, only memories of Cecil B. DeMille's *The King of Kings*, are different from those who were in their teens in the 1950s and enjoyed *The Robe*, *The Silver Chalice*, *The Big Fisherman*, and *Ben-Hur*. Teenagers in the 1960s saw the remake of *King of Kings* while those in the '70s saw *Jesus Christ Superstar* and *Godspell*. In the late 1980s, they might have gone to see *The Last Temptation of Christ*. After a very quiet period during most of the 1990s, there was quite some Jesus-film activity at the beginning of the new millennium. American television made *Jesus* as well as *Mary, Mother of Jesus*. British and Russian animators created *The Miracle Maker*. The evangelical British *Jesus* of 1979 (The *Jesus* Project) was reissued to large audiences; dubbed into many languages, especially in India; and distributed by the Vatican to guests in Rome for the celebration of the Jubilee year, 2000.

And, of course, the early twenty-first century brought the unpredicted worldwide box-office and VHS/DVD phenomenon of Mel Gibson's *The Passion of the Christ*.

This means that it is possible to trace an outline of Christian spirituality as well as Christology as gauged by the Jesus films and audience response, especially in Europe, the Americas, and Western-influenced cultures.

At the beginning of the twentieth century, there was a devout piety as can be seen in the plaster statuary and holy cards, where Jesus is somewhat ethereal, almost tentatively incarnate. With the longer feature films of the silent era and the possibility of filming on location in the Middle East, audiences were able to gain a more realistic impression of Jesus in his historical and geographical context. To that extent, the Incarnation became more real. However, Cecil B. DeMille went back to the studio and the Gospel story was made an extravagant artifice with a solemn "holy" Jesus. And then Jesus disappeared from the popular screen for thirty-five years, in the 1950s his presence merely suggested visually.

With the 1960s, there was change. Jesus was impersonated by an actor. He was seen. He spoke. The reverential tradition prevailed in the American films, but Pier Paolo Pasolini wanted a more rugged, earthy, and earthly Jesus in the Italian *Il Vangelo secondo Matteo*. With the Jesus movement and the rock operas of the 1970s, Jesus was seen as a superstar. These images showed the humanity of Jesus. Franco Zeffirelli's *Jesus of Nazareth*, with its right blend of humanity and divinity, indicated that a human and divine Jesus was part of the consciousness of Christians around the world.

There was a veering toward an emphasis on humanity and its limitations and challenges with *The Last Temptation of Christ* in the 1980s, but by 2000, there was a renewed emphasis on the unity of humanity and divinity, especially in the made-for-television *Jesus* and *Mary, Mother of Jesus* (both 1999); the animation film *The Miracle Maker* (2000); and the full text of John brought to the screen with word and image in *The Gospel of John* (2003).

Audiences were challenged by *The Passion of the Christ*. Mel Gibson's emphasis on the suffering and its intensity appealed to an older piety and to cultures that were more emotional. Cooler blooded cultures found some sequences too much and lamented the lack of emphasis on the Resurrection. However, a newer generation welcomed the sense of a transcendent Jesus in the midst of his sufferings.

A review of the Jesus films also has the advantage of opening up the panorama of the developments in cinema: from the short one-reelers of the early silent era to the feature films of D. W. Griffith with immense sets but with fixed tripod camerawork and some tracking to the initial experiments with color tinting, the introduction of sound, color processes, wide-screen experiments, the age of the biblical spectaculars with huge screens and stereophonic sound systems, the influence of television and its styles, video production, and the transition to the digital era.

1

THE JESUS-FIGURE

We often use the terms *Jesus-figure* and *Christ-figure* interchangeably, but there is an immediate distinction to be made between the two. The lead was given by Malachi Martin in his entertainingly instructive book *Jesus Now*. He himself was particularly interested in the variations in Jesus-figures over the centuries and how art, religion, and popular piety were influenced by historical and social conditions.

- The Jesus-figure is any representation of Jesus himself.
- The Christ-figure is a character (from history, fiction, visual arts, poetry, drama, music, cinema) who is presented as resembling Jesus in a significant way.

The Jesus-figure can be presented in a "realistic" way or in a "stylized" way:

Realistic—Jesus as he was thought to be
Stylized—Jesus presented in contemporary or in deliberately "unrealistic" settings, or Jesus represented in any artistic way.

The Jesus-figure, which is the focus of this book, is any representation of Jesus himself: a crucifix, a statue of the Sacred Heart, a Roualt Jesus-clown, verbal descriptions as in the theological disputes in Umberto Eco's *The Name of the Rose*, a "Negro spiritual," the music of Bach's *St. Matthew Passion*, or Rice and Lloyd Webber's *Jesus Christ Superstar*.

One of the main difficulties with this kind of presentation of Jesus is that it has tended and still tends to be based on a fundamentalist interpretation of scripture—the reading of scripture as if written solely for the reader's present time and cultural references rather than looking at texts with the mentality of the time of the writer. This requires some knowledge of the Old Testament background and of biblical literary forms. It would seem that most of the representations of Jesus on-screen are based on literal readings of the Gospel texts with little awareness of their Jewish background. An exception will be Franco Zeffirelli's *Jesus of Nazareth*, which takes account of this history and spirituality.

It is necessary to note that Jesus-figures can be realistic or stylized. More accurately, all Jesus-figures are stylized. Any representation of Jesus as a thirty-year-old, first-century, Middle Eastern man might be realistic, but this is not how Jesus is generally represented. However, most artists seem to have in their minds that they are trying to represent Jesus "realistically." The work of Renaissance painters and the films of Cecil B. DeMille are presumed attempts at realism, despite the Umbrian backgrounds or the special effects. Cinema realistic presentation tends to rely on the well-known or classic visual portraits of Jesus. These presentations have tended to soften Jesus. It was Marxist Italian director Pier Paolo Pasolini who attempted to portray a rugged Jesus in the mid-1960s in his *Gospel according to St. Matthew*. It was an attempt to make Jesus more realistic and less a Hollywood concoction. *Jesus of Nazareth* offered the historical background and explanations to make Jesus more real.

Most realistic portraits are, in fact, quite stylized. Have we any real picture of Jesus "as he was"? The more closely the portrait of Jesus is based on a "scientific-spiritual" reading of the Gospels, the more realistic it will be. Zeffirelli with his *Jesus of Nazareth* has come closest so far, along with many sequences of Roger Young's *Jesus*.

Stylizing the image of Jesus happened immediately in the early Christian centuries with Jesus linked to the styles of Greek or Roman art as well as to politics—the Jesus All-Powerful of the Ravenna mosaics.

We are used to seeing Jesus in Italian settings in medieval and Renaissance art or listening to Handel's or Bach's sacred scores of Jesus' Passion, for instance. Though originally surprising or shocking, the stylistic presentations of Jesus visually and in music—*Jesus Christ Superstar* and *Godspell*—are now taken for granted. The film version of *Jesus Christ Superstar* made the link with the art tradition by including a collage of the suffering Jesus and the symbol of the paschal lamb at the climax of the Agony in the Garden.

The tradition of literal interpretation of the scriptures has also reinforced the belief that artists are presenting a realistic Jesus-figure. Pasolini's infancy stories are no more realistic than those of *King of Kings* or *The Greatest Story Ever Told*. They just look starker in black and white and in simpler locations (which are Italian, especially the high mountain of crucifixion, rather than Palestinian). Most of the popular screen Jesus-figures are based on literal, almost fundamentalist, readings of the Gospels.

Which means that almost all Jesus-figures are, in fact, stylized. The stylization might be more obvious to Western sensibilities regarding an Aboriginal Madonna and Child or an African Madonna and Child than in contemplating the work of artists like Raphael. But Raphael's seemingly realistic images are also stylized. The coming of Jesus as Superstar at the end of the 1960s and in the carnival and vaudeville atmosphere of *Godspell* shocked many devout people, believers or not, because they had come to believe that the Western art tradition was real and that it should be revered. Anything else was, as many claimed at the time, "blasphemous." But this highlighted how much the Jesus-figure had become stylized—and it freed artists of the 1970s and 1980s to be adventurous in the way they dared to portray Jesus. What would *Jesus of Montreal* be without *Jesus Christ Superstar*?

Many find the immediate impact of these figures too contrived, but they continue a respected art tradition where Jesus is placed in the art styles of the times.

THE FACE: JESUS IN ART

There is a valuable two-hour overview of the history of the image of Jesus in art, *The Face: Jesus in Art*, released in 2001. It was written by James Clifton, directed by Craig MacGowan, and photographed by celebrated cinematographer Dean Cundey. The narrators were Mel Gibson, Edward Herrmann, Star Herrmann, Stacy Keach, Juliet Mills, Ricardo Montalban, Bill Moyers, and Patricia Neal.

The history of the portrayal of Jesus was given in quite some detail—the origins, the catacomb frescoes, the Byzantine mosaics, Chartres, and northern Africa—with more detailed visuals and verbal descriptions of the work of Giotto, Raphael, da Vinci, Michelangelo, Rembrandt, Holman Hunt, Marc Chagall, and Andy Warhol, as well as popular faces of Jesus and Afro-American images, and a focus on Latin America, on Asia, and on the twentieth-century United States.

Since there is no actual visual portrait of Jesus, no verbal description of his appearance, artists have tried both realistic and stylized ways to show how divinity suffuses the humanity of Jesus and how idealized human beauty is the way to appreciating the divine.

Faces of Jesus in Film

One cinema source for reflection on the art tradition is the small number of film biographies of artists who have painted or sculpted Jesus.

More faces of Jesus in art can be found in Andrei Tarkovsky's portrait of the Russian painter and creator of icons *Andrei Rublev* (1967, but banned in Russia until 1971). The film shows the artist in his turbulent times as well as his painting and his interpretations of the face of Jesus. At the end of the film there are color images of Rublev's work.

Another example is *The Agony and the Ecstasy*, which is a strange film. Many people have thoroughly enjoyed it because of their interest in Michelangelo and their reading of Irving Stone's novel. Other people have thought it a most silly film. It is a section from Stone's novel and shows the central years of Michelangelo's career, especially in his clashes and confrontations with Pope Julius II.

Charlton Heston seems an odd choice to play Michelangelo. However, he does his best with his tradition of playing important historical characters. Rex Harrison is also an odd choice for Pope Julius II. He seems to suit battle sequences, but as pope he is a peculiar blend of Professor Higgins and Doctor Dolittle. His deathbed scene when he fights with Michelangelo and recovers seems particularly ludicrous with the choir changing from dirge to alleluia song. However, visually the film is most impressive.

In theaters, *The Agony and the Ecstasy* had a twenty-minute prologue showing in Panavision the most famous works of Michelangelo. This has been omitted in the television presentations of the film. Sets look beautiful, but there is some bathos in sequences where Michelangelo in the mountains of Carrara sees what looks like the ceiling of the Sistine Chapel in the clouds in the sky. Direction was by Carol Reed, who had made such excellent films in the 1940s and the '50s as *Odd Man Out* and *The Third Man*. Reed went to America and made a number of very average films, although in this time he won an Oscar for his direction of *Oliver* (1968). This is not the last word in film on Michelangelo.

El Greco (1966) is a moderately interesting biography of the painter and his life in Spain. His paintings are presented in some detail. The atmosphere of the times is recreated. While Mel Ferrer is somewhat stolid in the central role, the film does give an opportunity to see something of the painter within his surroundings and environment.

Caravaggio (1986) is the work of Derek Jarman. The film is a study of Caravaggio (Nigel Terry), emphasizing some fictional aspects by including references, visual and sound, of the twentieth century. The film is also a memoir—Caravaggio dying, attended by his mute servant, Jerusaleme. Caravaggio remembers his past on the Roman streets, being adopted by church figures, and being educated and commissioned to paint. The film shows Caravaggio's paintings, his use of light and shade, of colors, of live models for his works of art. Many of his paintings are pictured as live tableaux. The film can be seen as a chamber piece, not a Hollywood biopic or spectacular. It is a perception of Caravaggio, his personality, his art, and his times.

Caravaggio and My Mother the Pope, directed by Maureen Murphy (2011), is advertised as a three-hour film on Caravaggio's life and work, which included many Jesus paintings.

There have been numerous short films as well as many documentaries on Jesus in art.

2

BIBLICAL PORTRAITS OF JESUS

JESUS REDEEMER

One of the principal ways the New Testament presents Jesus is as Redeemer, the man amongst mankind who experiences their sufferings but who suffers on behalf of others, enabling them to be blessed, forgiven—to be saved.

The pattern of the redeemer-figure is established in the Old Testament. The key texts are those of the anonymous prophet of the period of Israel's collapse and exile in the sixth century BC.

The Hebrew people had experienced the worst events in their history, a time of infidelity to their God who had, they understood, pledged himself to them in a covenant of loving kindness and justice. The destruction of Jerusalem and the Temple, the loss of the Ark of the Covenant (the structure containing the Ten Commandments, their covenant law)—all was seen as The Day of the Lord, a day of doom (justice), but because of the fidelity of God, a day of hope (salvation). The majority of the population of the kingdom of Judah was taken into exile in Babylon.

This context of bitter experience is a context of suffering in which the redeemer-figure can emerge.

The anonymous prophet in the second part of Isaiah seems to be a literary hero, a personality who embodies the best qualities of Israel, and is depicted as a prophet and redeemer. He is presented in the traditional Servant Songs, which begin at chapter 42 of the Book of Isaiah. This figure is a character with a special mission and destiny. He is beloved by God, chosen, filled with the very spirit of God himself. His style is not that of power but of gentleness. If a flame is still smoldering, he will not extinguish it. If a reed is bruised, he will not break it. But this gentleness has strength and will enable true justice to be done, not only for his people but for those far beyond. He is described as a light of the nations (Isaiah 42:1–6).

This kind of figure, no matter how admirable, does not win acclaim from all. When people are challenged, when different values threaten an accepted way of life, reaction is hostile. So it was with the anonymous figure, who is also called the Servant. He is attacked emotionally and physically. But, with his sense of mission, he listens like a disciple to his God, and with his convictions, he holds firm. This leads to mockery, abuse, degradation, and death.

The image offered is that of the sacrificial lamb. However, the writer realizes that while those who see this "man of sorrows" are appalled, his willingness to endure the suffering is a jolt to those who watch. The Servant going to suffering and death is "a man for others."

The jolt, the challenge, can be what we might call an experience of grace for others, a change of heart (a repentance) that enables them to redeem the evil in their lives. The Servant is, therefore, a redeemer. While the Old Testament texts speak of his being acknowledged (glorified) by God, the emphasis is on his suffering and death: laying down of life for love and for the benefit of others (cf. Isaiah 52:12–53:12).

Readers of the Old Testament appreciated the servant-figure in connection with other suffering figures. Just prior to the exile, the most human of the prophets, Jeremiah, exercised a faithful ministry—but at great personal cost. Even the story of his prophetic call shows him as quite reluctant. He was not listened to. Crowds scorned him. The king literally cut up and burned the scrolls of his oracle. He was thrown into a pit. Yet ultimately he "committed" his cause to God.

There are powerful passages, called his "confessions," in which he berates God, threatens to sue him and take him to court; he laments the day he was born. Unlike the men of his day who found immortality in their children, Jeremiah was asked to be celibate. Yet he confesses that there is a fire in him that drives him on to be a prophetic redeemer (cf. Jeremiah 15:15–18). Prayers of suffering are found throughout the Psalms.

The other Old Testament figure of anguish and endurance is that of Job. He is described as God's victim. God allows one member of his heavenly court (according to the Old Testament mentality), Satan (the devil's advocate), to test, to plague Job. It is well known that Job did not curse God in any way. He suffered, though not silently, because he wanted to know why he suffered; he knew he was in no way a sinner despite the carping of his friends (or comforters!).

Job is the symbol of all those innocent victims, the endurers who have to acknowledge the mystery of human existence and throw themselves on the mystery of God's ultimate providence and love (cf. Job 3:1–26; 19:23–27).

These are the patterns for the New Testament presentation of Jesus. He is seen as Redeemer. While, like the Servant, he is beloved by God, he is baptized by John the Baptist among the repentant sinners in the Jordan. The Letter to the Hebrews highlights that he is "a man like us, with the exception of sin" (Hebrews 4:15), and that though ultimately he is raised and glorified by the Father, he knows human sufferings since he has endured them (Hebrews 5:7–10).

In Gethsemane, Jesus is ignored by sleeping friends, sweats blood, experiences agony and sudden fear, and is prepared to endure, like the Servant, the scorn of religious authorities who have continually tried to trap him. He knows the fickleness of the loyalty of friends and followers, the physical abuse and torture of his Passion, the seeming absence of and abandonment by God on his cross. He is the timeless image of the man of sorrows, the sacrificial lamb for others.

In the first letter of Peter, the author states directly that he sees Jesus as the redeemer-figure and quotes the Servant Songs of the Old Testament for his proof.

The pattern of Jesus as the man of sorrows, the man who died for humankind while forgiving his killers, has become part of the consciousness of Western culture. Believers and unbelievers alike have been able to draw on the experience of Jesus as a metaphor or as a symbol of the suffering that does not turn in on itself in despair or bitterness but is offered to others for support, courage, or endurance. The instrument of Jesus' death, the cross, has become the sign of this suffering for others.

This image of Jesus as Redeemer has become in the arts the reference point for stories of innocent sufferers, so that they can be understood as Christ-figures, redeemer-figures.

JESUS SAVIOR

In the New Testament Jesus is called Lord. After his living as a human being, like us—sin excepted—he was raised from the dead, the risen Savior who leads the way to joy, peace—the salvation of heaven.

The first striking Old Testament story concerns Abraham, the head of a large clan on the now Persian Gulf who, like many clans of the time (about 1800 BC), took part in nomadic migrations. Abraham's clan eventually settled in the land of Canaan, later Palestine, which became for them home, a promised land, rich and fruitful, flowing with milk and honey. Though much of it was arid mountain and desert, it was, nevertheless, their paradise homeland.

However, the reason for Abraham's migration was his experience of his God. He felt a sense of call, of destiny for himself and his descendants; not just the establishing of a dynasty, but a people responsible to their God and devoted to him, a "chosen" people. We remember that the early centuries of their history were marked by squabbles and bitterness, but also by joy and reconciliation.

After many of them stayed in Egypt for hundreds of years, they were oppressed by the pharaoh, made slaves, and, in a mass escape led by Moses, went out of Egypt into the desert, forming themselves into a people, exhilarated by liberation, on their way back home to the land of Abraham, a promised land that they saw as their inheritance.

Old Testament writers, listening to the stories remembered and repeated from these times and passed on orally for generations, realized that there was a deep religious meaning in these events. Their God had acted for them in their history. They were oppressed and needed liberating. He freed them, he saved them. They were a sinful people. He freed them from their sinfulness, he forgave them. They were a chosen people, and their God had pledged himself to them—to be just, loving, and faithful no matter how unfaithful his people were.

This union of God and his people, this covenant (with its laws, especially the Ten Commandments) became the sign of salvation. Old Testament personages were remembered and written of in connection with this covenant: leaders like Moses and Joshua, the judge Samuel, Kings Saul, David, and Solomon.

Needless to say, chosen people do not remain faithful. They turn away from their fidelity in personal sin, social sin, especially injustice. They need forgiveness and salvation. In the Old Testament history of Israel, the main figures who embodied this message of salvation were the prophets, a group who, intermittently, for over two hundred years, showed by their words, by their oracles, by their symbolic actions, and by their own lives that God was a saving God.

In looking at the religious experience and the messages of such diverse personalities as the rugged shepherd Amos, the tender Hosea, the statesman Isaiah, the reluctant and persecuted Jeremiah, and the exotic Ezekiel, we see God's fidelity to his people in offering his salvation.

It was little wonder that New Testament writers drew on covenant themes—and especially the experiences and words of the prophets—when they wanted to show that Jesus was a savior. It is the constant theme of the Gospels that Jesus was this kind of figure: a prophetic Savior.

A phrase that the Old Testament prophets used was "The Day of the Lord." For a while, the Hebrew people were presumptuous enough to think that this meant that God would sweep away all their enemies, and they would live in power, prosperity, and peace. (Many Zealots of Jesus' day still had the same hope and followed Jesus because of it but were disappointed when he was found not to be the restorer of the kingdom of Israel.) What the prophets really meant by "The Day of the Lord" was a day both of justice and salvation. There would be justice because the evil in the hearts and actions of the people would inevitably bring down on themselves some decay, moral weakness, and destruction. This was interpreted as the hand of the Lord striking them.

But The Day of the Lord was also the time for reassessment, a change of heart—repentance—a humble and more realistic attitude so that whatever the disaster and destruction, a renewed fidelity could carry the people through. They might only be few: a remnant. But they could be the foundation of a renewed growth. Prophets like Jeremiah and Ezekiel said that for people like this, God would take out their hard hearts (like stone) and put in hearts of flesh, making them a "fresh-hearted" remnant, people with "new heart." It would be a second covenant. We recognize this promise as the language of Jesus and of the New Testament.

The Hebrew people were not a nation of scholarly philosophers. Rather, they were imaginative, poetic, a people of experience, especially religious experience. The way they expressed themselves was in concrete rather than abstract language: new hearts, shepherds leading sheep to graze and rest, dry bones in a valley coming to life with flesh and becoming human again, fruitful vines, banquets of the best food and drink when those who are faithful are forgiven, healed, and gathered together to rejoice.

These images were developed over the centuries by many writers. For instance, David was a shepherd before becoming king; kings are seen as shepherds, bad kings being bad shepherds, good kings being good shepherds; the great king and, therefore, the good (best) shepherd is God himself, who listens to his sheep, guides them, and rescues them when they are lost. Jesus and the New Testament writers use these images for signs and symbols of salvation. They quickly became constant themes for Christian art, poetry, hymns. They still are. So many of Jesus' own stories rely on this kind of imagery for their impact and meaning.

Even the servant-figure of the Old Testament who willingly gave his painful suffering and his death for the sake of others, is spoken of, finally, in words of joy and exultation. Every redeemer-figure is, ultimately, a savior. That is why Jesus' Passion and death can be described so vividly in Old Testament language. But it is not a despairing description; there is hope.

The Christian meaning is death—and resurrection. J. R. R. Tolkien, author of *The Lord of the Rings*, created a fine word to describe this connection between Jesus' death and his Resurrection: eucatastrophe. The Greek word for "well" is *eu*. So for Tolkien (and for the Gospel writers)—for those who believe in salvation from God—suffering, which is real and painful, is, nevertheless, a eucatastrophe.

JESUS LIBERATOR

With the rise of basic Christian communities during the 1970s and 1980s, especially in Latin America and in the Philippines, pastors and theologians looked at the violent and oppressive societies in which they lived. They saw that going back to the basics of the Gospels, especially in small communities that celebrated and listened to God's word, would provide a spiritual and practical impetus in fighting for justice. However, many judged, rightly or wrongly, that this way of thinking was too strongly linked to Marxist philosophy and presuppositions (and so linked to his atheistic Communism), and proponents were condemned.

However, when one opens the scriptures and sees, for instance, the figure of Moses freeing his people from oppression (with some rather violent plagues and drownings in the Red Sea) and being the mediator of a covenant and law for the people, one sees a line that was pursued by Samuel and the prophets throughout Hebrew history. Moses was a liberator. Jesus, the new mediator and the new covenant, is also the Liberator: from oppression, from physical ailment, from the burdens of sin.

JESUS PRIEST, PROPHET, AND KING

In her article "Christ Figures in the Movies," Barbara Nicolosi makes a fine theological case for taking the lead from the Second Vatican Council's focus on the person of Jesus and his mission and ministry. He is described as Priest, Prophet, and King.[1]

While she goes on to give examples of Christ-figures, her focus on Jesus is significant for the Jesus-figures in film.

The Priest, she notes and refers to Romans 1, is someone who is a living sacrifice to save or improve the lives of a community. This is a facet of Jesus as Redeemer.

The Prophet seeks out the people of God who have lost their way and leads them back into the embrace of God; he reminds people who they are and recalls them to their vocation to be a holy people. This is a facet of Jesus as Savior, especially when the Gospels draw specific parallels with

Old Testament prophets in Jesus' teaching, miracles, or symbolic actions. In Luke 7, all of these are highlighted: he is the new Elijah, raising a son from the dead for a widow; the new Isaiah, telling the disciples of John the Baptist that healing signs accompany his mission; the new Ezekiel, who plays beautiful songs to signify God's coming; the new Hosea, who loves into forgiveness the woman who was the sinner in the city.

The King is the servant leader who unifies a broken and disrupted community, bringing peace and brotherhood, which Jesus did as he proceeded with joy into Jerusalem on a donkey and then more powerfully with his Spirit, which he breathed on his disciples in the upper room after his Resurrection. This is a facet of Jesus the Liberator.

JESUS "HOLY FOOL"

Dostoyevsky's *The Idiot* reminds us that there has been a long art and literary tradition of "holy fools." St. Paul in 1 Corinthians 1:18–31 knows that "the message of the cross is foolishness to those who are perishing, but to us who are being saved it is the power of God. . . . It was the will of God through the foolishness of the proclamation to save those who have faith." He goes on to say that Christ crucified is "foolishness" to the Gentiles even though he is the power and wisdom of God and that the foolishness of God is wiser than human wisdom and the weakness of God is stronger than human strength. In reminding the Corinthians that they were not wise by human standards, he tells them that God chose the foolish of the world to shame the wise.

There is a long biblical tradition of wise fools. We might think of Abraham bargaining and wheedling with God for the salvation of Sodom and Gomorrah for ten just men or Jacob laboring for seven years to win the hand of Rachel. Joseph, even in his prison cell, is the wise fool who interprets the dreams of his fellow prisoners. David's wife Michal considered him a fool as he exuberantly danced before the Ark of the Covenant.

We can interpret some of the prophets in this lineage: Amos being mocked in Bethel and ordered out of the city, Zephaniah rejoicing that his God was a dancing God, Jeremiah lamenting how he was despised and rejected, Tobit piously burying the dead against the law, and Daniel in the lions' den are images of God's fool.

Jesus himself can continually be seen as "foolish" for God: in his temptations in the desert, in experiencing the contempt of the Pharisees, in his mixing with tax collectors and prostitutes, in the popular stories he told, in the rumors spread by his enemies that he was possessed. The fact that he was betrayed by one of the twelve indicates foolhardiness in his choices.

It is in his Passion that we see images of Jesus as Holy Fool. Whether he is denied by Peter; scoffed at by Herod; ridiculed as the scourged and thorn-crowned king; standing like the suffering servant, silent before Pilate; or hanging on the cross abused by the religious leaders and the thief beside him—Jesus is portrayed as the Holy Fool. In his Resurrection, he is there for all to see as the one who transcends death, the risen Lord who is the wisdom and power of God.

NOTE

1. Barbara Nicolosi, "Christ Figures in the Movies," *Ligourian*, February 2003.

3

THE JESUS FILMS: THE EARLY
TWENTIETH CENTURY

Soon after the Lumiere brothers screened their first short films in Paris on December 28, 1895, the cinema phenomenon spread quickly right around the globe. And, one of the earliest focuses of screen presentations was the Bible, especially the New Testament and the Gospels.

After these recordings of the Passion plays, there quickly developed a distinct and popular genre, the life of Christ drama. In 1898, L. J. Vincent directed a Passion play for producer Richard Hollaman. It was promoted as a recording of the famous Bavarian Passion play but was actually shot according to a Salmi Morse screenplay in New York City. This two-reel black-and-white film appears to be the first life of Christ ever filmed.[1]

In 1900, the Salvation Army in Australia had created a program in Melbourne consisting of slides and film segments, explained by lecture, of scenes of the Gospel and the history of the early church. It was called *Soldiers of the Cross*. The Salvation Army continued with this kind of program for a decade. Many church groups did likewise.

The French film *The Pathé Brothers* (1995) offers a glimpse of what it was like to make the Gospel films in the 1890s and the early twentieth century (not without some comic touches). With the sets confined to a single space and with fixed tripod cameras, the actors could move from the cave at Bethlehem to Calvary in a few seconds. *The Pathe Brothers* shows both the filming of the Nativity as well as the Crucifixion—including some nonchalant behavior of cast and filmmakers rather less in keeping with the spirit of what they are filming.

One of the experiments of animator Georges Melies was an 1899 *Christ Walking on the Water*, showing the waves, a cloud forming, and Jesus emerging and miraculously walking on water.

14

Life of Jesus was originally made in 1902 by the French company Pathé, whose trademark rooster appears in every scene; an expanded colorized version is available on DVD. The film consists of tableaux-like segments, beginning with the Annunciation, as Mary puts down her jug of water to kneel before an angel to receive the news of the virgin birth. The film continues with the birth of Jesus, the star guiding the shepherds and the three kings, the Massacre of the Innocents, and the flight into Egypt. In the segment of the holy family in Nazareth, Joseph is shown cutting down a tree and teaching Jesus carpentry. Highlighted during Jesus' public life are his baptism, numerous miracles including the turning of water (which looks like milk) into wine, and his walking on or really coming up out of the water. The numerous events from Jesus' triumphant entry into Jerusalem to his Crucifixion and death are also shown. The film concludes with his Resurrection and ascension into heaven to join his father and the Holy Spirit. Although the film is more of a historical curiosity, the various segments, identified by placards, may be useful as illustrations in educating children about the important elements of Christ's life.[2]

Pathé also distributed *La Vie et la Passion du Notre Seigneur Jesus Christ* (1905), a thirty-minute (two-reel) dramatization of the Passion by Ferdinand Zecca. This film was included in the Vatican's list of forty-five films selected for attention to celebrate the centenary of cinema. The citation notes that the film was said to be very popular in its time and quotes a French historian, Georges Sadoul, on its "rudimentary" camera movements. The Pathé company produced *The Judas Kiss* in 1909 with Jesus, Judas, and John as central characters.

For more than twenty years, Passion play films and dramas of the life of Jesus or derived from the Gospel were made with great frequency and were very popular. Unfortunately, none of them exist today because of the corrosion of the materials on which they were filmed.

The Internet Movie Database (IMDb) has a page for Jesus as a character. It has a quite comprehensive list of Jesus in films (349 titles from film and television from 1897 to 2011, 27 for 2010–2011 alone). A number of short films are included from the first two decades of the twentieth century with links to basic information within the IMDb. A Google search reveals very little more than what is in the IMDb. Some films seem to be short biblical stories. Others seem to be moral stories, set in the present, with Jesus inserted into people's lives. Titles include *The Battle Hymn of the Republic* (1911), where both Abraham Lincoln and Jesus are in the cast list; *Though Your Sins Be as Scarlet* (1911), this time with Jesus, an angel, and the Scarlet Woman in the cast; and *The Holy City* (1912), a contemporary story where a character is named The Redeemer.

Jesus Christ Movie Star (1990), a quite comprehensive fifty-four-minute documentary produced by Britain's Channel 4 in conjunction with an Anglican group, traces the history of the Jesus film with a generous selection of clips and interviews. It traces the popularity of the biblical films in the early years, showing some scenes from the 1913 *From the Manger to the Cross*, filmed on location in Egypt. It also quotes from the actor who portrayed Jesus, "an upper-class Englishman called Henderson Bland," whose writings of memoirs on his playing Jesus were "in prose which aspired to the biblical." Many of these films were like holy cards or plaster statues coming to life. They offered poses and posturing rather than dramatizing the Gospel events. Another program, *E voi che dite che io sia: I Gesu del cinema*, produced in 1999 by ACEC (Associazione Cattolica Esercenti Cinema), thirty minutes, also contains a great number of excerpts from the Jesus films, especially several from Italy that are not available in other documentaries. More recently, Britain's Channel 4 screened *The Passion: Films, Faith and Fury* (2006), which has clips and interviews from the major Jesus films.

However, a very useful compendium of information about early representations of Jesus on screen can be found in *Religion in the Cinema*, by Ivan Butler. Some of the following information is gleaned from his chapter "Christ in the Cinema" (pages 33–54).

Butler notes the 1897 filming of *The Passion Play* in Horwitz. It was made by two American theatrical producers, Marc Klaw and Abraham Erlanger. It was followed in 1899 by another movie from producers R. G. Hollaman and A. G. Eaves, filmed on the roof of a New York building and using a narrator instead of captions. *The Passion Play* at Oberammergau was filmed in 1900, a rooftop *Passion* in France, and a 1906 *Passion* by V. Jasset and Alice Guy, where Golgotha was built at Fontainebleau. Butler notes that a gramophone was used to help the actors in their performances. Ferdinand Zecca was inspired by contemporary chromo-lithographs and made his rather longer film during the years 1902–1905. By 1908 Pathé produced a three-reel version of *The Life of Christ* in color. By 1914 it was expanded to seven reels.

The titles of other films of the period indicate audience interest and entrepreneurial skills: from France, *The Kiss of Judas* and *The Birth of Christ* (both in color) in 1909, as well as *Star of Bethlehem* in 1910 from Edison; from the United States in 1911, *Though Your Sins Be as Scarlet* (featuring Jesus and Mary Magdalene); from Italy in 1912, the second episode of four parts of *Satan: Or the Drama of Humanity* and *The Pilgrim*. Sidney Olcott, director of *From the Manger to the Cross*, directed *Ben-Hur* in 1908.

As a postscript to this indication of titles from the silent era, Ivan Butler concludes his chapter with a note of regret. Carl Dreyer had long planned a life of Jesus film and had finally received financial assistance from the Danish government but then he died. Another great of the silent era, the French director Abel Gance (*Napoleon*), had spent years trying to make a film of Jesus, but in 1949 the financing failed.

In 2000, a recently restored Italian film, *Christus*, was screened at the Venice Film Festival, an eighty-minute film shot in Palestine and Egypt from 1914 to 1916. Half of *Christus* was devoted to the Passion of Jesus. Many of the sequences are very moving, and it still amazes how so much action can be contained in a fixed frame and enhanced by judicious editing. The approach of the Magi with a large cast of their entourage is a single long shot in which the column of travelers snakes in its progress, filling the screen from top to bottom and from left to right. The films, of course, were silent.

Some scenes from the Crucifixion in *Christus* were used to telling effect in Marco Bellocchio's 2009 film about Mussolini, *Vincere*. After Mussolini was wounded in action in World War I, the hospital where he was being treated screens *Christus*, projecting it in a large format on the roof of the ward where he is.

This contemporary use of *Christus* by Bellocchio reminds audiences that the early appeal of Jesus on-screen was limited to action and a theatrical style of acting, exaggerating by sweeping gesture. Subtitle captions presented the words as well as some description of the action.

The interpretation of Jesus was reverent, often over-reverent.

CIVILIZATION

In the same year as D. W. Griffith's *Birth of a Nation* (1915), Thomas Ince made a strong anti-war film, seen as an allegory for pacifism—*Civilization* (which some commentators comment on as "slightly ludicrous" if "spectacular"). The hero, a submarine commander, refuses to fire a torpedo at a ship and is imprisoned for mutiny. His sub is destroyed and he dies, making his way through purgatory to heaven. However, the spirit of Christ enters into his body to work for the abolition of war.

It is difficult to find ready information about *Civilization*. The following comments indicate the scope and effect of the film.

> With American opinion divided over the European war in 1915, no
> fewer than three major motion pictures were conceived with anti-war
> messages in mind: J. Stuart Blackton's *The Battle Cry of Peace*, D. W.
> Griffith's *Intolerance* and Thomas Ince's *Civilization* the mythical king-
> dom of Wredpryd. *Civilization* begins with war spreading through the

land. Inventor Count Ferdinand (Howard Hickman) against the wishes of his pacifist fiancée (Enid Markey) agrees to commandeer a submarine against the enemy. When his sub blows up, the Count is rescued from eternal damnation by the spirit of Jesus Christ, whose soul enters Ferdinand's body. Ferdinand returns to life, convincing the King of Wredpryd (Herschel Mayall) that he, the king, has divine powers. But Jesus, using Ferdinand as his vessel, shows the king that no man is above the laws of God—and also gives him an up-close-and-personal tour of the bloody battlefield. The King realizes the error of his ways, and declares an end to the battle. Extremely popular during its first year of release (1916), *Civilization* disappeared from view the moment that the US declared war against Germany. Though its direction is often credited to producer Thomas Ince, *Civilization* was actually directed by committee: among its helmsmen were Walter Edwards, Raymond B. West, Reginald Barker, Jay Hunt, J. Park Read and David M. Hartford.[3]

INTOLERANCE

The best presentation of Jesus at this time was in D. W. Griffith's *Intolerance* (1916), the Gospel narrative being one of four stories of intolerance over the ages that were intercut throughout the film. While Griffith's film is extraordinarily sophisticated in terms of a three-hour epic made only twenty years after the Lumiere brothers' screenings, its picture of Jesus is more thematic rather than the depiction of a rounded character, showing him in episodes like the wedding feast at Cana or encountering the woman taken in adultery as well as in some brief shots of the way to Calvary and the Crucifixion.

Intolerance was subtitled *Love's Struggle throughout the Ages* and was described in theater terms in the credits as a play with acts. It opens and closes with a tableau of the mother gently rocking a cradle (the three Fates sitting behind her), "today and yesterday, endlessly rocking." While the three stories of Babylon, the St. Bartholomew's Day Massacre, and the contemporary 1916 story are treated at length, there are four sections on Jesus and the Gospel stories.

The first episode is entitled "Jerusalem." While it shows people going about their business near the Jaffa Gate, it also offers a glimpse of the house at Cana. Since the theme of the film is intolerance in all ages, we are introduced immediately to examples of the intolerant, the hypocrites among Pharisees (with a caption note that they gave the contemporary word its meaning). An exceedingly intolerant Pharisee (with reference to Luke's parable of the Pharisee and the publican, chapter 18) is shown ostentatiously praying and demanding that everything stops while he prays, including some workmen (and a rather toothless old man munching on his lunch).

The gentle rocking is seen once again—but with a caption that relates mother and child to "the Comforter out of Nazareth."

The other two Jesus stories in *Intolerance* come from John's Gospel. The first is the wedding feast at Cana (John 2:1–11). The festivities are shown with the first sop of wine offered to the bride. Jesus arrives in a stately manner, akin to H. B. Warner's style in *The King of Kings*. There is advice to be "harmless as doves" and doves are shown. But then a plaintively sorrowing Jesus is shown with the caption, "Scorned and rejected of men."

So, Jesus is filmed face-on as a character, but he is rather statuesque in both height and demeanor. His gait is slow, as is that of Mary, a rather swathed figure who now arrives. Mother and son touch lightly but do not embrace. As the celebration continues, the film offers a sudden editorial comment (which relates also to a group of women do-gooders in the contemporary story): meddlers "then as now" are upset with people having too much pleasure and revelry. But revelry is short lived as the "poor bride and groom suffer humiliation." Jesus' first miracle is announced—with another editorial comment that wine was "deemed" by the Jews as a fit offering to God and was therefore allowable. Jesus blesses the jars. The tasters go into action. Mary is happy. And Jesus indicates matters with arm gestures and pointed finger, again rather like a statue.

The final Gospel episode is that of the woman taken in adultery (John 8). The scene is introduced with the comment that these times had equally intolerant people as in all ages. Jesus must not have made a good impression with some at Cana because we are told that he is considered "a wine-bibber," and to prove the point, Jesus is shown at something of a rowdy banquet, sitting a little loosely and smiling.

But the episode is about the woman. She is dragged in by a stone-toting crowd, waving her arms in distress. Jesus sits away from them, writing in the dust, again displaying the pointed finger as the accusers leave. Jesus is sitting alone with the woman and distant from her—still pointing. She falls at his feet and he extends a hand of blessing. She goes off with an exuberant gesture.

And the film adds as it moves to the contemporary story, "How shall we find Christly example in our own day."

Toward the end of *Intolerance*, as the young man prepares for execution with the chaplain and receives communion while a car races a train to petition for a pardon, as the St. Bartholomew's Day Massacre intensifies, and as Cyrus besieges Babylon, a sequence of the way of the cross is intercut, first Jesus walking amid the crowds with a sign around his neck, then the jostling crowd as he carries his cross. Just before the young man is about to die, the film has a long shot, pale-red tinted, of the three crosses on Calvary.

The only precedents that Griffith had from the preceding twenty years of cinema were the short biblical plays. While he uses these techniques, he integrates them into a popular feature film.

It was difficult to identify with the Jesus on-screen except as a response to a tableau or to a pageant. Jesus was personality-less, going through familiar reverent movements and moments that were aimed at inspiring audiences. Jesus was often piously observed.

I.N.R.I. (CROWN OF THORNS)

After World War I, Robert Wiene, perhaps influenced by Griffith's *Intolerance*, made *I.N.R.I.* in which a condemned prisoner is told the life of Christ by the chaplain and scenes are acted out like a Passion play; it was reissued in 1934 as *Crown of Thorns*. There is some discussion about the surviving copies of the original film, but in 1999 a copy was found in Friuli, Italy, and in 2006 a copy was found in Tokyo. Some of the sequences were discussed in a 1949 article in the *International Film Review* by Charles Ford, who comments on the effective casting, which included Werner Krauss (the original Dr. Caligari) as Pilate, Asta Nielsen as Mary Magdalene, and Gregory Chmara as the "truly moving and tragic figure of Christ," although he notes that some critics considered the film as cold and that Wiene may not have been comfortable in filming a life of Jesus. Ford's view is that "it was the first purely artistic transposition of the Passion to the screen."

LEAVES FROM SATAN'S BOOK

In the aftermath of *Intolerance*, Danish director Carl Theodor Dreyer made a portmanteau film with three different stories linked by Satan's coming to earth to tempt the human race to sin and hell. The three stories were set in Jesus' times, the Spanish Inquisition, and the French Revolution.

In the first part of *Leaves from Satan's Book* (1922), Satan enters into the Pharisee who leads Judas to betray Jesus. The Jesus story runs for twenty-seven minutes and covers the betrayal of Jesus by Judas and the Crucifixion. The style is that of silent film, fixed camera, and theatrical performance—though Dreyer was to break through these conventions in later films (*The*

Passion of Joan of Arc, *Vampyr*). He had in mind to make a Jesus film but was unable to raise finances.

Within his limited running time, Dreyer includes a great deal of material. It should be said immediately that his Jesus is presented as might be expected, Dreyer drawing on the tradition of European art. He chooses (as have so many later directors) to portray the Last Supper according to da Vinci.

The screenplay keeps quite close to Gospel texts with Caiaphas, the cleansing of the Temple, Simon the leper, Lazarus, and a banquet with a harp player. Satan has the ears of the scribes and Pharisees—though he grieves when evil seeds take root because so many will be condemned to hellfire.

Jesus has overtones of Good Shepherd imagery, with hands joined and eyes raised. He is anointed by Mary at the banquet as preparation for his Passion. At the Last Supper, the apostles question him. He raises his eyes as he offers the chalice (and offers it to Judas, and there is an incident with the scattered crumbs indicative of Judas, his disrespect and betrayal of Jesus).

The Jerusalem setting is presented realistically. We see it as Jesus and the apostles walk to Gethsemane. But the agony itself, once again, relies on the art tradition.

Judas is referred to as "the devil's son," and he is the other focus of the story. He is shown as the keeper of the money and complains about the anointing of Jesus—and hears Jesus' rebuke that there will always be the poor. Judas, after the Last Supper, experiences anguish and despair. He has to control his will so that he will be strong in his betrayal. However, it is clear that he is doomed and is to die. He is described as God's chosen: "You are his tool." He kisses Jesus and takes the money.

This film is still in the early years of the portrayal of Jesus, and Dreyer has to draw on the two decades of short biblical films, the visual art tradition of Europe, and the Reformed theology and spirituality of his native Scandinavia.

NOTES

1. Michael Duricy, "An Analysis of Cinematic Presentations of the Virgin Mary from 1897 to 1999: A Theological Appraisal of a Socio-Cultural Reality" (licentiate thesis, University of Dayton, 2000).

2. Peter E. Dans, *Christians in the Movies: A Century of Saints and Sinners* (Lanham, MD: Rowman & Littlefield, 2009), 17.

3. Hal Erickson, "Plot," *AllMovie Guide: Civilization*, retrieved from Answers .com, www.answers.com/topic/civilization-film-1.

4

THE JESUS FILMS: THE 1920s AND CECIL B. DEMILLE

The year before the release of Cecil B. DeMille's *The King of Kings*, there was a very successful version of *Ben-Hur* (1925) directed by Fred Niblo. General Lew Wallace's *Ben-Hur* novel is subtitled *A Tale of the Christ*.

BEN-HUR

This silent version of *Ben-Hur* contains early sequences of the journey of Mary and Joseph to Bethlehem and Nativity scenes with a great emphasis on Mary and on the coming of the Magi. These scenes are intercut with the story of Judah Ben-Hur. The Nativity and other Gospel sequences are in two-strip color, including Jesus' triumphal ride into Jerusalem and a da Vinci re-creation of the Last Supper. With Jesus carrying the cross to Calvary, we see Ben-Hur trying to free Jesus (rather than, as in the 1959 version, offering him a drink of water) and Jesus urging him to let go of his sword and be a man of peace.

A sign of trends to come and unlike other Gospel films being made at this time, especially DeMille's *The King of Kings*, the actor playing Jesus is not shown directly face-on but, rather, he is offscreen except for, principally, a gesturing hand or arm. The rather artificially white and slender arm is seen emerging from the side of the screen—sawing at the carpenter's shop in Nazareth, giving Ben-Hur his cup of water, preaching the Sermon on the Mount, and healing Ben-Hur's mother and sister on the way of the cross. The thematic use of the arm and hand is made clear when a close-up of the hand being nailed to the cross is the main image of the Crucifixion. In the brief Last Supper sequence, modeled on da Vinci, Jesus' face, but not his raised arms and the aura of his halo, is obscured by Judas, who is seated at the front of the table.

THE KING OF KINGS

A revealing anecdote from DeMille's autobiography speaks of the director giving H. B. Warner, the actor portraying Jesus, a separate and secluded caravan on the set and even having Warner eat his meals alone so that he would not, as DeMille declared, lose the atmosphere of Jesus. This theology of the Incarnation seems to overemphasize the divine nature of Jesus. However, *The King of Kings* has many fine touches of the humanity of Jesus as well as the light of divinity.

H. B. Warner looks like many of the holy cards popular during this period. He is quite thin and austere in appearance, but he often has gentle facial expressions and glimmers of a smile. He is photographed with a glow, sometimes a halo around his head, sometimes the bright light of an aura around his person.

As with the short biblical films and Griffith's *Intolerance*, the silent film acting techniques frequently make Jesus more of a moving icon than a real character with personality. This is also emphasized by the scriptural references at the bottom of the screen captions and dialogue. DeMille also opts for an archaic style of dialogue of thous and ye's and "Verily, I say . . . ," which detract from any attempt to give Jesus a contemporary impact. The musical scores on the DVD release emphasize the reverence and solemnity of the Gospel stories.

This is what DeMille intended. His initial caption informs his audience that this is a story of Jesus of Nazareth. His next caption highlights Jesus' message and the command that the message go to the utmost bounds of the earth. The film is to be "a reverent part of that great command." DeMille had religious advisers present on the set of the film, and a daily Mass was celebrated by Father Daniel A. Lord, S.J.

Audiences might be taken aback when the first story, at some length and in color, is all about Mary Magdalene, her extravagant lifestyle, her clients, her being informed about Jesus, and her flamboyant gesture (and zebra-drawn carriage), "Farewell, we go to call upon a carpenter!" And, even then, we do not see Jesus but are introduced to Judas, described as an ambitious Zealot, eager for Jesus to throw off the yoke of Rome and then be appointed to high office.

It is only then that we see a blind child and the lame boy Mark ("destined to write a Gospel") seeking Jesus. Mary, the mother of Jesus, is seen also as a reverent figure, with the disciples, and releasing doves. It is she who leads the blind boy to Jesus. We hear Jesus say that he is the light but the camera becomes the eyes of the blind boy, blurred vision, gradually clearing so that the face of Jesus is seen. He smiles, a halo behind him. But immediately DeMille's sympathy toward the human Jesus is apparent. Jesus touches the boy, hugs him, lifts him up, and carries him. Peter is elated, Judas bemused.

And Mary Magdalene arrives to find the "vagabond carpenter." Jesus stares her down, saying, "Be thou clean." Special effects create a phantasmagoria of evil spirits coming out of Mary. As each emerges, the screen lists Lust (first), Greed, Pride, Gluttony, Indolence, Envy, Anger. And someone remarks, "He doth cleanse her of the seven deadly sins."

These opening sequences indicate DeMille's approach to the Gospels and his cinematic style. For 1927, the special effects work wonders (literally). The scope of the sets is reminiscent of *Intolerance* and there is a huge cast of extras. DeMille's direction often amazes as his fixed camera shots contain so many people and so much and varied action. All this is a context to make *The King of Kings* the greatest story ever told. It shows us that DeMille was conscious of Jesus' humanity and Jesus' divinity, and sometimes they fuse.

DeMille must also have been fond of the Gospel exhortations that we should become like little children and that we should welcome them. Jesus embraces children and smiles at them. Mark appears quite frequently, a reminder of how much Jesus was fond of children. He is at the hosanna welcome to Jesus, at the celebration of Lazarus' raising from the dead, and at the Resurrection apparition.

Judas is often at the center of the film, as when he tries to heal a possessed boy and fails. Jesus stretches out his arm (something he does frequently) and gives the cured boy to his father, then gives Judas a reminder about faith and its possibilities.

A surprising touch is having Jesus go to the carpenter's shop and exercise his skills at planning, even working on the making of crosses—though Warner looks as if his hands were never soiled nor his clothes ever dusty.

DeMille also uses evocative symbols throughout the film: Mary with doves, Jesus finding a lamb in the Temple and holding it while he tells the crowds his kingdom is not of this world, a dove flying to the chalice at the end of the Last Supper, the rooster crowing after Peter denies Jesus and Jesus looks at him as he weeps in dismay, a dog at the foot of the crosses on Calvary, doves and flowers (in color) after the Resurrection. There is a Star of David in the court of Annas and Caiaphas, and Pilate sits under a huge statue of a Roman eagle.

With Caiaphas presented as sinister (loving revenue more than religion) and putting Jesus to the test concerning taxes and tribute to Caesar, the story of the woman taken in adultery becomes an important part of the screenplay. A minion of the high priest comes to his master with news of

Jesus' preaching. The high priest determines to humiliate Jesus when the woman is brought to him and thrust violently to the ground. She is then taken through the busy Temple precincts and a scoffing crowd. Jesus' silent reply to the questions and to the accusations is to write in the sand. We are given close-ups of the words he wrote (in Hebrew). They are accusations against the accusers: "thief," "murderer," "adulterer." No wonder the accusers drop their stones and slink away. Warner's Jesus is surprisingly gentle with the woman, warmly but discreetly reaching out to her and touching her. She leaves, grateful.

The Last Supper is shown in the da Vinci mode and composition, although it is interesting to note how Judas avoids eating the bread and drinking from the cup. The Agony in the Garden is intercut with scenes of Judas and the chief priests (Judas walking veiled to avoid recognition). However, Matthew is shown sitting on a rock, writing or probably taking notes!

It is interesting to study the way the Passion is presented in the light of Mel Gibson's later treatment. The controversy about anti-Semitism in *The Passion of the Christ* also makes us look more closely at all the Jesus films. Caiaphas appears as more of a stereotype than any character in Gibson's film. DeMille also has one of the accusers of the woman taken in adultery refuse to bay for Jesus' blood, "Ye cannot bribe me, a Jew, to call for the blood of an innocent brother," though he does call for Barabbas' release and then is seen to shout against Jesus. At the Crucifixion, Caiaphas prays that God will not pour out his wrath on his people: "I alone am guilty."

The trial before Caiaphas has almost no captions. The trial before Pilate is filled with dialogue from John's Gospel and adds a lengthy intervention for Jesus by Pilate's wife. The praetorium scene is also interesting, with the casual mockery of the soldiers, Jesus' arms stretched high as he is scourged, a thorn crown picked and woven, robes, scepter, and a throne.

A caption announces "The Way of the Cross." Once again, the child motif is strong. A little boy tells his father that if he were a big man, he would help carry the cross. The father is Simon of Cyrene. Much of the Calvary action is familiar: the two thieves, the mockery, Mary and Mary Magdalene. However, the big DeMille touch is in the huge storm, mighty winds with people blown away, a spectacular effects quake leading to chaos.

The Resurrection scene is also in color, with Jesus emerging from the tomb like a statue. He greets his mother, and the familiar scene with Mary Magdalene's recognition follows. There is a return to black and white for the scene in the upper room where many events are crowded into the one sequence: Jesus' appearance to the apostles, then Thomas' experience of the hands and the side, the giving of the Spirit, the bequest to Peter to feed lambs and sheep, a farewell to his mother, and an ascension. This is the culmination of the 1920s experience of a screen "king of kings," Hollywood-style.

LE BERCEAU DE DIEU

Le berceau de Dieu (*The Cradle of God*, 1926) is a French religious fantasy, a silent film about a man who loses his faith after the death of his wife. The daughter of a poor family encourages him to meditate on the Gospels. The device for conversion is that he has a significant dream. He sees the whole of salvation history—with a large cast representing Old Testament figures from Adam and Eve on. John the Baptist and "Le Christ" are also in the cast list. The man's faith is renewed.

CHIZOME NO JUJIKA

By way of a note to this era, the title *Chizome no jujika* (*The Bloodstained Crucifix*) is added. It is included in the Jesus character list in the IMDb, with actor Tsumasaburo Bando (about whom there are many references but none to this film) playing a priest and also billed as Jesus Christ. Unfortunately, it is difficult to find material on this film of the silent era in Japan.

JESUS OF NAZARETH

Produced in 1928, this film is a straightforward presentation of Jesus at the end of the silent era. One criticism is that it looks very old-fashioned in visual style and performance. However, there is discussion as to the availability of this film and how it relates to earlier films about Jesus. Most sources simply repeat that it is "a dramatic re-creation of the life of Christ from the Annunciation to the Ascension."

5

THE JESUS FILMS: THE 1930s, 1940s, AND 1950s—JESUS' ABSENCE FROM THE MAINSTREAM AND EVANGELICAL JESUS-FIGURES

As it turned out, Cecil B. DeMille showed the last full film portrait of Jesus for almost thirty-five years. Perhaps it was this emphasis on the divinity of Jesus that led to the British censor, in the second decade of the century, to state that direct portrayals of Jesus were not desirable on-screen. Perhaps it was the consequence of this atmosphere of reverence but, after DeMille's *The King of Kings*, close-ups of Jesus' face disappeared from the commercial screen in English-language cinema for over three decades. As will be seen in a subsequent chapter, in the Spanish-speaking world, Mexico offered several Jesus films in the 1940s and 1950s.

THE WANDERING JEW

The legend of the Wandering Jew was relevant in the atmosphere of the rise of Nazism in the 1930s and world attitudes, and Christian attitudes, toward the persecution of the Jews.

Adapted for the theater by E. Temple Thurston, *The Wandering Jew* was filmed twice by British director Maurice Elvey—once as a silent film in 1923, then as a more lavish production in 1933 with German actor Conrad Veidt. *The Wandering Jew* offers a basis for discussion between Jews and Christians about its Jewish background, the Christian context, and how the film was interpreted in terms of anti-Semitism.

In the latter version,

> Veidt plays Matathias, a Jew of Palestine who is on the road to Golgotha when Christ is brought to crucifixion. When Matathias expresses a lack of concern for Christ's fate, Christ tells him, "You will remain here until

I return." Because of Christ's words, Matathias has been cursed with immortality. He cannot die, he cannot grow older, and he must periodically relocate to another community (and establish a new identity) so that nobody will notice that he never ages. The film is necessarily episodic: we see Matathias trying to blend into one community; then the narrative abruptly jumps ahead to another century as Matathias has relocated yet again.[1]

According to F. Gwynplaine MacIntyre, who comments on the Internet Movie Database (IMDb) blog,

> This film's strangest (and most interesting) aspect is the decision not to depict Christ directly . . . neither by image nor by voice. During the early scenes, Christ is apparently located just outside the right-hand edge of the film's frame; Veidt and the other actors turn in profile to the camera and stare at something offscreen. . . . When Christ speaks, we do not hear an actor's voice . . . instead, we see words (in a very ornate type font) superimposed directly in front of Veidt's face, spelling out Christ's malediction. There is an eerie glow from just beyond the frame, apparently representing Christ's aura.[2]

In addition, says MacIntyre, "Most versions of the Wandering Jew legend (including the classic science-fiction novel "A Canticle for Liebowitz") state that the Jew is still wandering, right up to the present day, because (so they claim) Christ has not yet returned." MacIntyre says it would have been interesting if this film had included an epilogue set in the England of 1933 in which the Wandering Jew is still alive.[3]

Another IMDb blogger says,

> The Middle Ages segment is the second one; it is followed by the Renaissance segment and finally the Spanish Inquisition, in which the Jew is burned as a heretic. . . . The decision to end the Jew's life in this period has to do with the period when the film was made, the early '30s, when the Nazis were once again asking "Are you a Jew?" and condemning people based on the answer. . . .
>
> The original story would be that the Jew is to wait "until Christ comes again," i.e. the Second Coming, the Last Judgment. The film script modifies this to "until I come to you again," and the plot shows us the slow progress of Matathias from a man who would rather see his beloved dead than alive with her husband, to an understanding of the Christian hope in life after death and a less selfish love (in the Italian story, where he decides not to kill his wife as a gesture of possession when she wants to become a nun), to an actual Christ-like role in the Seville sequence, where a whore defines her relationship with him as

that of Mary Magdalene to Christ. . . . So Christ "comes to him again" as he is being burned as a heretic.

Interestingly, his heresy consists of (1) blasphemy, in saying that Christ might be hard put to recognize his own, i.e. the inquisitors them-selves, since they are not Christlike, and (2) refusing to deny his Jewish-ness. Christ, of course, was himself brought before the High Priests on a charge of blasphemy. The film sort of finesses the problem of baptism (in the version I saw, there was no evidence of the Italian son's being bap-tized, but the friar says that he has gone to Heaven when he dies), which is what the Inquisitors are in principle asking Matathias to undertake.

However, the decision is presented to him not as being baptized in Christ but rather as denying his Jewishness, ceasing to be a Jew, and in the early '30s the ringing declaration—by a Christ figure, "I am a Jew!" must have been pretty strong stuff.

The end of another British film of this period starring Veidt, *Jew Suss*, is similar; Suss in fact has a choice to declare himself not Jewish, since in fact his father was a local aristocrat, but he opts to die a Jew, representing the people he grew up with. Both Suss and Matathias are heavy-duty sinners (lust, avarice, and pride to say the least) and their Jewishness is not "normalized" . . . but they redeem their sins by their concern for the poor, the outcast, and, in Jew Suss's case, specifically Jews in a pogrom situation.[4]

A postscript: In 1948, *L'Ebreo Errante* (directed by Goffredo Alessan-drini) starred Vittorio Gassman. It was an adaptation of the novel by Eugene Sue about the Wandering Jew. Gassman portrays Mathieu Blumenthal, a banker, who is arrested with some friends and is sent to a Nazi concentra-tion camp. He escapes from the camp with Esther (Valentina Cortese). He is prepared to sacrifice his life for the sake helping others.

GOLGOTHA

While there was no commercial Jesus film between *The King of Kings* and *King of Kings* from English-speaking industries, there was an exception in France with Julien Duvivier's 1935 *Golgotha*. The film was a ninety-five-minute drama, filmed in black and white in the Billancourt studios in Paris, with a prominent cast of French actors, including Jean Gabin as Pilate, Harry Baur as Herod, and Robert Le Vigan as Jesus. The score, by Jacques Ibert, is given credit prominence. It is all-pervasive, more modern than what came to be ac-cepted as "biblical scores." Duvivier's principal Jesus film precedents were the silent short films made for religious education purposes.

Given the fascism of the period and anti-Semitic feelings in Europe and in France (and, in fact, the explicit anti-Semitism of the star, Robert Le Vigan, during the war and his subsequent trial and imprisonment for fascist collaboration), it is surprising that the film was made. The blame for Jesus' death is laid directly at the machinations of the high priests. Judas is also a prominent and striking presence, disappointed with Jesus and his not rousing the revolution and in league with the priests.

Golgotha was also known in the United States as *Behold the Man* (Ecce Homo), from Pontius Pilate's words to the crowd when Jesus came before him, scourged and crowned with thorns. The action of the film takes place from the procession of palms as Jesus entered Jerusalem and finishes with post-Resurrection sequences. This means that Jesus does not preach, although he does declaim after the cleansing of the Temple that people render to Caesar what is Caesar's and his words are quoted during his trial. There are no miracles, though many sick are shown reaching out to him during the procession and on his way to Calvary.

Duvivier may have been influenced by DeMille in his choice of actor for Jesus and in directing him to display an almost complete otherworldliness in his performance, communicating directly with others more indirectly (except for his words to Peter about his denial and after the Resurrection, or in sending Judas from the Last Supper). There is a brief intimate moment when he meets Mary on his way to Calvary and he falls and she says, quietly, "My son." Otherwise, he stands and moves like an icon, stern, sometimes indicating feeling through his eyes or by gestures, as when he holds the whip above him after routing the buyers and sellers in the Temple.

Duvivier makes his point about Jesus being human but filled with divinity by not showing Jesus directly for almost twenty minutes into the film, heightening audience expectation. There are subjective point-of-view shots as the camera becomes Jesus' eyes as he looks at the waving crowds during the procession. Then the audience catches a glimpse of him. Finally, he becomes a character in the film. The audiences of the time may have expected this kind of aloof, rather silent Jesus, more an image from art than from life.

The rest of the treatment is "realistic." Shots of Jerusalem and the Temple are used extensively throughout the film, especially the inner courts of the Temple, the rooms of the Sanhedrin, the open courts before Pilate's palace, and Herod's court. This realism contributes to the impression that the film is trying to show the credibility of the situation; the people's expectation of a Messiah to rise up against Roman rule; the reaction of the high priests in protecting their own power, currying favor with Pilate, and wanting Jesus out of the way.

The sense of realism is enhanced by Duvivier's visual compositions—many close-ups of faces (and sometimes resting on a face for an unexpected length), the placing of faces at different angles, the camera turning from one face to another, or the framing of two or three faces together. By contrast there are a number of long shots—of Jerusalem, of Judas hanging himself, of Calvary. Sometimes there are overview aerial shots. The contrast of light and shadow is used to moody effect. Duvivier has drawn on art traditions but now makes the cinema versions of this art the beginning of a cinema tradition for Jesus films. Pier Paolo Pasolini's *Il Vangelo secondo Matteo* later developed these traditions.

The Jesus who emerges from this film is human but he is—at least in character, demeanor, hopes, and suffering—rather more than human. He enjoys the triumphant entry into Jerusalem but then immediately disappears from his followers, dampening their expectations of a revolt against the oppressors. He swings his whip in the Temple, sending tables flying and initiating a stampede of scurrying animals—some of this shown from Jesus' subjective point of view—then stands on a table brandishing the whip and declaiming to a crowd about the Temple being a house of prayer. He is shown reverently at the Last Supper (with a glimpse of preparation by his mother and the other women, the roasted lamb on the table), shot from outside the upper room through a frame, the tables in a square u-shape with Jesus at a corner (not quite da Vinci). He speaks about not drinking until he is in his kingdom. John asks who the traitor is and Jesus indicates Judas. He speaks directly with Judas and with Peter.

The Agony in the Garden is brief, with Jesus laying his head on a rock in anguish and then waking the sleeping apostles. It is very dark in Gethsemane when the soldiers come and Judas kisses Jesus. The drama is from John's Gospel when he questions the soldiers and some of them fall back. Judas is later seen wandering among rocks. He returns to the open square to throw back his thirty pieces of silver. Once the Passion narrative begins, there is much more reliance on direct Gospel texts: the silence before Annas and Jesus being slapped, the false witness (and the witnesses floundering with their testimony) about destroying the Temple and rebuilding it, the transferral to Caiaphas and the rending of his garments, and the declaration that Jesus has blasphemed (though the screenplay simplifies this to Jesus simply admitting that he is the Christ of God).

A great deal of attention is given not only to Pilate but to Pilate's wife, her advice to him in how to govern as well as her dream and sending him a message to be wary of condemning Jesus. There is a long Herod sequence where Jesus is silent and mocked by Herod and his hangers-on. Herod is presented bejeweled and somewhat effete (and he could have said, "Walk across my swimming pool"). Pilate questions Jesus about his kingdom and about truth, brings him before the crowd, says "Behold the man," releases Barabbas, and washes his hands at the forefront while Jesus is seen standing in the background. Pilate also writes the title of King of the Jews.

Jesus is scourged, but the audience sees only two short sets of blows, the rest being offscreen; the crowd counts as they gleefully watch through the bars of the prison, one woman then fainting. Jesus is mocked by the soldiers, crowned with thorns, and a white cloak put on his back.

All these Gospel sequences are familiar and presented quite directly. The way to Calvary is quite long in proportion to the rest of the film, with quick references to Jesus lamenting with the women of Jerusalem, Simon of Cyrene carrying the cross, and Jesus walking with a placard around his neck. As mentioned, Jesus meets his mother. On Calvary it is the same, the roping and nailing, the raising of the cross, the assurance to the good thief, and Jesus saying to John, "Behold your mother." Jesus forgives his killers and, offering himself to the Father, dies.

One of the features of *Golgotha* is the attention given to the Sanhedrin, its composition, the disputes, the role of this council in supporting Judas and his payments. Annas and Caiaphas certainly dominate the Sanhedrin and have access to Pilate. They are vindictive at Jesus' trials and rouse the crowd against Jesus. They are present at Calvary to see their plot through. They are seen covering their tracks with the soldiers and explanations after Jesus' burial. Duvivier also places a great deal of importance on the crowds—and there are frequent crowd scenes both in long shot and in close-up. The crowds rejoice with their palms. They gossip and spread news and rumors. They turn fickle, enjoy the scourging, and are vociferously compliant with the wishes of the high priests. They jeer and boo. They continue their mockery on Calvary.

Then *Golgotha* turns apocalyptic in the manner of Matthew's Gospel. The sky darkens except for lightning flashes. Clouds swirl. The earth shakes. The Temple rocks. The crowds flee. To this extent, Matthew's version of the Passion is the most filmic.

Duvivier gives attention to the Resurrection. The camera is inside the tomb, the stone is rolled away. The Resurrection sequences move more rapidly: The women seek Jesus and hear an angel's voice (feminine?). Jesus appears to the disciples on the road to Emmaus and they hurry back to Jerusalem. Jesus shows his wounds. Then the apostles are back at the Sea of Galilee where Jesus appears and asks Peter to profess his love and, with sheep visible, urges him to feed his flock. Then, surrounded, Jesus speaks the final words of Matthew's Gospel, for them to preach the good news. And he is gone.

There is a cinematic effect at the end as two crosses are carried down the hill, one left standing and then shown in close-up.

Given the status of the director—he was one of France's most important at the time—and the subject, it is surprising that there was not another Jesus film in Europe for another thirty years, until Pasolini.

THE END OF THE WORLD, LA VIE MIRACULEUSE DE THERESE MARTIN, THE LAST DAYS OF POMPEII, AND BARABBAS

The way of the cross to Golgotha is glimpsed in the 1935 *The Last Days of Pompeii*, which was produced in the aftermath of Cecil B. DeMille's saga of Nero and the early Christians, *The Sign of the Cross*. A young boy, Flavius, is healed by Jesus and becomes a disciple and an adult Christian. There is a chance encounter as Jesus goes to Calvary. However, the scenes with Christ (who is not visible on-screen except in a visionary way at the very end) relies on the massed choir effect. There are also some chronological difficulties as Pontius Pilate (Basil Rathbone) is present in 79 AD at the eruption of Vesuvius (and still mindful of his washing his hands of the death of Jesus), though tradition has it that he killed himself in the late '30s AD.

Jesus appears on the cross in a prologue to Abel Gance's science-fiction film *The End of the World* (1931). Initially, it seems to be a scene from Calvary, but the camera draws back and it is a stage version. There are some Jesus moments in *La vie miraculeuse de Therese Martin* (*The Miraculous Life of Therese Martin*), a 1930 version of the young nineteenth-century Carmelite saint directed by Julien Duvivier (*Golgotha*), where the suffering Jesus appears to Therese and the silhouette of Jesus carrying his cross appears on the wall of a church. A close-up of the emaciated Jesus, crowned with thorns is seen in *E voi chi dite che io sia: I Gesu del cinema*.

Alf Sjoberg made a film version of Par Lagerkvist's novel *Barabbas* in 1953. It had location photography in Israel and Rome. It was also in competition at the Cannes Film Festival. Comment was that it was removed from distribution when Dino De Laurentiis re-made it in 1961. Jesus is not a central presence in the story of Barabbas, but he is listed as a character in the cast. The themes of Jesus and Barabbas are made explicit in the subsequent version.

THE GREAT COMMANDMENT

In 1939 Rev. James K. Friedrich produced *The Great Commandment*, an eighty-minute feature set in 30 AD and focusing on life in a small village "between Jerusalem and Jericho" that was a center for Zealots. It was directed by Irving Pichel and starred some Hollywood actors, including John Beal and

Albert Dekker. The American accents make the film seem too contemporary for non-American audiences as does some of the dialogue ("Is this your idea of a joke?"). The musical score sometimes anticipates the scores of Miklos Rozsa for *King of Kings*. The film plays like an effective costume drama of the 1930s.

The initial information is about Pilate, his oppressive laws and imposition of taxes. The focus is on two brothers, one a hothead who wants revolution now and dies for it, the other a student of the scriptures under his authoritarian rabbi father who is looking for a strong leader. When the second brother hears of Jesus, he imagines that he will have an army and rid the country of Romans. He journeys to Galilee, meets Andrew, and listens to Jesus (especially texts from Matthew about taking up one's cross as well as the beatitudes). Jesus also heals a blind man. When Joel offers his sword and allegiance, Jesus tells him that those who live by the sword will perish by it. Befriended by Judas who persuades him that Jesus could be talked into revolt, he returns to his village where his father, skeptical and sneering, asks about the greatest law and is answered by the parable of the Good Samaritan. This response has a profound effect on Joel who, after the Romans massacre the Zealots, puts Jesus' teaching about loving enemies into practice by tending to the wounded centurion. The village is spared while Joel is interned for his own safety. When the centurion comes to free him, he has just put Jesus to death and is amazed that his life was saved by a disciple of the man he had crucified. There is a romantic subplot, which, after some tangles, leads to a happy ending.

Jesus is not seen on-screen. Rather, his preaching, healings, and parable are voiced offscreen by director Irving Pichel, because Joseph Breen, administrator of the Production Code, raised difficulties with a full-on presentation of Jesus. Although made only twelve years after DeMille's film, it shows the strength of cinema techniques developed during the 1930s and is more akin to the 1961 *King of Kings*. Jesus has a strong and dignified enunciation (with the use of "thee" and "thou" language), and although he is present only after an hour of the film, he and his message make an impact. The film was released in 1941.

THE LAWTON STORY, THE PRINCE OF PEACE, AND THE PILGRIMAGE PLAY

During the late 1940s and early '50s, some American church organizations did make feature films of Jesus. In the late '40s, *The Lawton Story* was filmed in Oklahoma. It showed how the citizens of Lawton prepared for a Passion play, its effects on their lives, and the play itself. (Scenes were later edited for *The Prince of Peace*, which had an international distribution amongst church groups.)

However, there was something of a breakthrough in screen presentations of Jesus in *The Pilgrimage Play* in 1949. It was directed in Hollywood by studio director Frank R. Strayer, who, in the late 1930s and early 1940s, made twelve Blondie films. However, *The Pilgrimage Play* was not a studio production, and it did not receive mainstream release. It was a filmed play of the life of Jesus, but what made it different was that Nelson Leigh played Jesus fully on-screen rather than a voice offscreen or the visuals being limited to a hand or an arm as in the biblical films of the 1950s. And it was made in color.

Leigh's Jesus is suitably serious, smiles slightly sometimes, but is played in the grand manner of the superior rabbi rather than in any more personalized way. The framework of the film is having Peter in prison recounting the life of Jesus before he himself is executed. The scenes are more like tableaux than action, and the screenplay consists of large chunks of the Gospels recited in a solemn way as if this is how Jesus spoke all the time. This image of Jesus would have corresponded to the devout theological perspectives of the period, an emphasis on the way that the divine influenced the human in Jesus. Another factor for those who saw the film when it was made is that this was the first talking Jesus in color. There was no precedent, and it was just over twenty years since Cecil B. DeMille's *The King of Kings* with its Jesus in silent film mode.

Audiences on the lookout for interesting differences in Jesus films will notice the strong emphasis given to the role and influence of Nicodemus, especially at Jesus' trial. Another feature of Jesus' trial is the calling of Judas as a witness, but Judas is excluded by Nicodemus, who quotes the law that someone who betrays another cannot give testimony.

The film has a great deal of Jesus' teaching, some miracles, a da Vinci–like Last Supper, and some grim moments of the Passion (though, of course, everything pales in the retrospect of *The Passion of the Christ*).

The emerging television programs in the United States began to dramatize biblical stories. An example is a 1952 Studio One performance of *The Nativity*, directed by Franklin Schaffner (who went on to win the 1970 Oscar for Best Director for *Patton*) and based on the Miracle Plays that were written in the Middle Ages and performed in marketplaces and churches. (Both *The Pilgrimage Play* and *The Nativity* are in the public domain and can be found on the Internet Archive.)

I BEHELD HIS GLORY

In 1952 James K. Friedrich produced a fifty-five-minute drama called *I Beheld His Glory* using a flashback device: a centurion (played by George Macready) is sent by Thomas to tell the story of Jesus (Robert Wilson) to a group of men. They have heard stories about him but do not really know the truth about him. The centurion tells the story of Jesus from his arrival in Jerusalem to his appearance after the Resurrection. The film includes the Last Supper; Jesus' arrest, trial, and Crucifixion; his words from the cross; and his appearance to Mary Magdalene. There was some criticism that the small budget meant some poor backdrops and scenic effects. Robert Wilson played Jesus face-on, in a way which would not be commercially acceptable for another ten years. *I Beheld His Glory* is an elaboration of a series of thirty-minute films on the Gospels.

THE LIVING CHRIST SERIES AND THE LIVING BIBLE SERIES

DVD technology has enabled contemporary audiences and students to see material prepared for church exhibition and for television release from the early 1950s. Particularly useful is *The Living Christ Series*, which led to *I Beheld His Glory*. It is readily available in the United States.

While mainstream audiences may find the films too devout and may remember Sunday school classes, the productions have a strong impact today on religious groups. As has been mentioned, the sets are limited, with a number of painted backdrops. The models of the Temple and of Jerusalem are obviously models. However, the text of the Gospels is used often quite effectively (though some of the performances make it sound somewhat stilted at times). There is a similar use of the text for *Jesus* (The *Jesus* Project) twenty-five years later. But, when the writers elaborate some of the Gospel episodes—say, the Magi's discussion with Herod (who has clearly not been briefed on the scripture passages the Magi quote), Herodias discussing politics with Herod Antipas and her plotting with Salome, or Peter explaining his denial of Jesus—the drama is solid and enhances both the text and the audience's understanding of the stories.

There are twelve episodes in *The Living Christ Series*.

Another limitation is the small budget and the limited camera work, although this is less of a difficulty for small-screen viewing. There are many close-ups and even more fixed camera shots that last for a long time. This tableau style means a concentration on dialogue and on verbal interchanges rather than on dramatic action.

This concentration is more noticeable with Robert Wilson's performance as Jesus. Up until that time, there were no real talking film comparisons, and Wilson and the filmmakers had to be pioneers in deciding how Jesus should look and sound on-screen. These films came a decade before Jeffrey Hunter as the first all-talking Jesus on-screen and in color.

Wilson brings great dignity and bearing to his performance, looking rather older than thirty to thirty-three years of age. He is very serious in demeanor but not unapproachable (as in the sequence where the centurion comes to beg healing for his sick—and surprisingly elderly—servant). It is the speechifying that makes him look and sound more like the Jesus of Sunday school expectation than a warm, live, and authoritative Jesus. Wilson declaims. Everything is an utterance (though the Cana encounter with Jesus' mother and turning the water into wine has more mellowness). He is obviously the master, the teacher, the rabbi, the healer. Wilson's performance suffers in comparison with performances of a range of actors that were to follow, but selections of *The Living Christ*'s presentation of Jesus are well worth a look.

While James Friedrich's company, Cathedral Films, made *The Living Christ Series*, Family Films made another series with similar intentions and style, *The Living Bible* (1952). Three years later Family Films made *Acts* and in 1957 an Old Testament series. The actor portraying Jesus in *The Living Bible Series* was Nelson Leigh, who had played Jesus in *The Pilgrimage Play* in 1949. There were twenty-four episodes, also available on DVD in the United States.

Catholic Father Patrick Peyton produced a number of films in Hollywood with film-star friends using the stories of the decades of the Rosary. The IMDb has some credits for these films, noting three episodes, but there may be some confusion in identifying the correct films here, mixing *The Living Christ Series* and *The Living Bible Series*. However, one of Father Peyton's episodes from 1951 is *Hill Number One* where a chaplain in the Korean War tells the Jesus story to his men and scenes are dramatized. (This episode now has some fame because James Dean appeared briefly as the apostle John.) The Family Rosary Crusade also made a feature on Jesus' Passion, *The Redeemer* (1959), directed by the son of Joseph Breen, Joseph Breen Jr. He also used the conventions of the time in not showing Jesus in close-up, relying on the voiceover technique, with Macdonald Carey speaking the Gospel words in the English version. The cast was Spanish.

It should be noted that the information gained from a Google search and from the IMDb is not always reliable. There seem to be some mix-ups between Family Films (*The Living Bible Series*) and Family Theater (Father Peyton's company). Bloggers also make comments on *The Living Christ Series* (made by Cathedral Films), complaining that some of the material was too Catholic (for example, on Mary and Jesus' infancy), assuming it was a Catholic production when in fact it was not.

DAY OF TRIUMPH

More ambitious was Friedrich's *Day of Triumph* (1954). The tradition for presenting Jesus on film was that of the popular art of the nineteenth century. This tended to be sentimental and romantic—even kitsch. Here Robert Wilson portrays Jesus fully—quite well at the beginning with a certain strength and ruggedness. As the film moves toward the Passion and Resurrection, he becomes more stolid and stilted (perhaps considered by the producers "holy").

As with *Jesus Christ Superstar*, Jesus does not appear centrally but the emphasis is on Judas. With the background of the Zealot movement in Palestine at the time of Jesus, Judas is presented as a Zealot and his betrayal of Jesus as a device to trigger off a Zealot revolution. This is certainly an interesting interpretation of Judas, who is presented generally sympathetically.

The film was codirected by Hollywood actor-director Irving Pichel and John T. Coyle (who had worked on *The Living Christ Series* and *I Beheld His Glory*), and the film features Lee J. Cobb as Zadok, Joanne Dru as Mary Magdalene, Mike Connors as Andrew, and Lowell Gilmore as Pontius Pilate. It also contains a blend of the expected celestial chorus piety with some vigorous sequences of Jesus and of the times of the origin of the New Testament.

HIMLASPELET

During the 1930s and in Hollywood in the 1940s, while directors did not make Jesus films, there were a number of entertainments with a spiritual dimension, allegories about encounters with God and with the devil, judgment, heaven, and hell: *Here Comes Mr. Jordan*, *Heaven Can Wait*, *The Devil and Daniel Webster*. In Sweden, Alf Sjoberg, who collaborated with Ingmar Bergman, made *Himlaspelet* in this same vein. A man's wife is suspected of witchcraft, and so he goes on a quest to vindicate her, including meeting with "Our Lord."

THE POWER OF THE RESURRECTION

This is an hour-long film made in 1958 by Harold D. Schuster, a noted Hollywood editor and director of many films (including the family favorite

My Friend Flicka) who was involved with Moral Rearmament at this time. By the late '50s, Hollywood had released *Quo Vadis*, *The Robe*, and *The Big Fisherman* and was about to release *Ben-Hur*. Audiences were becoming more familiar with commercial Jesus films. In *The Power of the Resurrection*, a young man is about to be executed as is Peter (played by Richard Kiley). To comfort him, Peter tells his own story with dramatization of Gospel episodes as well as the Passion of Jesus.

Kiley brings dignity to the role of Peter, showing the transition from ex-fisherman to brash apostle to spirit-filled preacher to elderly martyr. He also has a fine speaking voice. So does Jon Shepodd, who portrays Jesus very much in the same way that Robert Wilson did in *I Beheld his Glory*—traditional in appearance, dignified, and eloquent. Jesus appears in the Last Supper sequence quoting excerpts from John, as well as briefly in the trial scene and a strange Crucifixion scene—strange in the sense that the budget must have been small and the three crosses are filmed from the back as if from a room. However, with the title of the film, the post-Resurrection scenes are longer and stronger, with Jesus appearing to the apostles and confronting Thomas.

There is a device of an interrogator who talks with both Judas and Peter during the last week of Jesus' life. Judas is disappointed in Jesus' peaceful approach to the political situation. Peter, on the other hand, is enthusiastic about Jesus and describes the miracle of the loaves and fishes.

This film is very similar to those made by Father Patrick Peyton at the time for Family Theater (though these films were reticent in showing Jesus face-on as does *The Power of the Resurrection*).

THE BLOOD OF JESUS AND GO DOWN, DEATH

When *The Great Commandment* was filmed in 1939, it was a white American enterprise. However, two years later, a film was released that was produced by and for African Americans. It was *The Blood of Jesus*. Written and directed by its star, Spencer Williams (who achieved some fame with his later television series *Amos 'n' Andy*), it was an attempt to make specifically religious films, moral and morale-boosting films, for its niche audience. Anyone who has seen any representation of an African American funeral in a film will be familiar with the emphasis on the word of God, the preaching, and the highly participative hymn-singing shown in *The Blood of Jesus*.

The film opens with a sermon, processions, and a baptism by immersion of the central character, Martha (Cathryn Caviness). She tries to persuade her husband, Razz Jackson (Spencer Williams), who has been out hunting, to "get religion." Tragedy quickly ensues as Razz puts down his gun. It slips, goes off, and wounds Martha, who has been contemplating a picture of the Sacred Heart hanging in the bedroom (to the accompaniment of "Were You There When They Crucified My Lord?"). As she lies dying, there is talk of God's will and miracles, and her friends kneel by her bed (now to the accompaniment of "Give Me That Old Time Religion"). As she dies, we hear an organ and see processions of people walking toward the pearly gates. However, an angel with wings and dressed in white appears at Martha's bedside. She rises.

The main drama of the film is an interesting variation on a theology of death and judgment; that is, as a person dies, he or she is confronted by the choice between good and evil, to make a life choice. Martha makes her way to the crossroads (with quotations from the Sermon on the Mount in the background). She is exhorted to walk clear of temptation and beware the hypocrisy of false prophets. But, Satan appears (dressed rather ludicrously like a pantomime devil and performs accordingly, which detracts somewhat from the life choices). A well-dressed man arrives to take care of Martha; he has a new dress and shoes for her. It is Judas who is commissioned by Satan; "Do your stuff," as he cackles. The angel is still quoting Matthew's Gospel.

Martha goes to a club (with some extended scenes of dancing, an acrobatic dancer, some women of easy virtue putting cash into their stockings). Martha does not want to take a job in the club, which angers the boss. The beatitudes and the saying on the salt of the earth are heard as Martha looks at another picture of Jesus and prays, "May God have mercy on my soul."

Martha is chased as she runs away (to the accompaniment of "Run, the devil's behind you . . . leave him far behind"). At the crossroads she sees the sign with one way pointing "To Hell" and the other "To Zion." The sign becomes a cross, and a crucifix figure appears. But, the voice of Jesus confronts Martha's accusers with the words from John 8, challenging the innocent to cast the first stone. Martha crawls to the foot of the cross and prostrates herself (to the accompaniment of "Steal Away to Jesus"). Drops of Jesus' blood fall on Martha's face. She wakes, alive, feeling her face and gazing on the picture of the Sacred Heart. Razz and the neighbors rejoice (to the accompaniment of "The Good News Chariot's Coming").

The contemporary poster claims, "A mighty epic of modern morals!" While it is not that, nor is it so well acted or directed, it signifies a great deal about African American faith in these years and the perspective on Jesus' love, forgiveness, and the role of the Crucifixion and Jesus' shedding his blood to save the human race. This strand of American filmmaking is not well known and did not influence mainstream filmmaking. While the

1970s saw a number of crime thrillers in the *Shaft* vein, black directors did not really emerge in any serious way until the 1990s.

Go Down, Death was Williams' religious film of 1944, from the celebrated Negro author, James Weldon Johnson. This is much more of a melodrama in which a club boss plans to get rid of a devout preacher who is engaged to his cousin. The preacher has been condemning the club, so the boss sets the preacher up with three women who come into his house to tempt him (with sex and alcohol); two photographers are also lurking. The boss' mother supports the preacher and confronts the boss. She also prays, gazing at her late husband's picture on the wall (to the accompaniment of "Nobody Knows the Trouble I Feel"). The boss threatens her and she collapses and dies. (In the background of much of the film is Schubert's "Ave Maria.") There is talk, as in the previous film, of God's will, of being in God's hands. At her funeral, people praise the boss' mother: "God's eye was on Caroline and God's big heart was touched with pity." In the aftermath of the funeral and quotations from the Book of Revelation (to the accompaniment of "A Mighty Fortress Is Our God"), the boss hears the voice of his conscience challenging him and he goes berserk. He runs into a tree and collapses at "the gates of hell." The film has some special effects of Satan devouring a sinner as well as re-creations of last judgment scenes with a finale of "Glory, glory, glory . . . , merciful and mighty."

The theology here is very literal as is the reading of the scriptural texts, but both films reveal the African American experience that embraced Christian faith during the slavery era and that still pervades so much of that culture.

The Blood of Jesus was put on the National Film Registry in 1991.

NOTES ON OTHER TITLES

- *Le Chemin de Damas* (1952) is a film about the conversion of Paul, which includes his experience of Jesus on the road to Damascus.
- Records show that there was a documentary released in 1936 on the Portuguese shrine, Bom Jesus de Braga.
- British actor Walter Rilla directed a black-and-white version, seventy-five minutes, of the Westminster Passion, *Behold the Man!* (1951).
- Veteran documentary maker Robert J. Flaherty made a film of Bach's "St. Matthew Passion" accompanied by images from the art tradition illustrating the themes of the Passion (1952).
- *Kalbaryo ni Hesus* is the title given to ritual and dramatic reenactments of the Passion of Jesus during Holy Week in the Philippines.

American actor Jennings Sturgeon appeared as Jesus in a film of that name in 1952. The translation is *Passion of Christ*. Another film of 1952 from the Philippines is *Ang pagsliang ng Mesiya* (*Birth of the Messiah*).

- A tongue-in-cheek note could be made of the Don Camillo films from Italy in the 1950s, humorous stories by Giovanni Guareschi titled *The Little World of Don Camillo* (1952) and *The Return of Don Camillo* (1953), both directed by veteran French director Julien Duvivier, who had made *Golgotha* in 1935. The third, *Don Camillo and the Honourable Peppone* (1955), was directed by Carmine Gallone.

Fernandel played the Italian parish priest who clashed with the Communist mayor. As regards Jesus, Don Camillo had a dialogue relationship with Jesus, who spoke to Don Camillo from a crucifix. Since Don Camillo was always getting into scrapes and trying to explain himself to Jesus, Jesus had some very good lines (as when, after being rebuked by Jesus for bribing a football referee, Don Camillo kicks the ball straight into the confessional opening and Jesus calls out, "Goal!") Mario Adorf played Don Camillo in a British television series in 1981, and Terence Hill (better known for his comedy westerns of the 1960s and 1970s) directed a Don Camillo film and played the role himself (1983).

NOTES

1. F. Gwynplaine MacIntyre, "Lush Historical Fantasy," *Reviews & Ratings for "The Wandering Jew"* (blog), Internet Movie Database, July 31, 2002, www.imdb.com/title/tt0024750/reviews.

2. MacIntyre, "Lush Historical Fantasy."

3. MacIntyre, "Lush Historical Fantasy."

4. jshoaf, "Early Death of the Wandering Jew," *Reviews & Ratings for "The Wandering Jew"* (blog), Internet Movie Database, November 12, 2005, www.imdb.com/title/tt0024750/reviews.

6

THE JESUS FILMS: THE 1950s AND 1960s—MAINSTREAM IMAGES

In the mid-1950s, James K. Friedrich's company produced Frank Borzage's *The Big Fisherman*, the story of Peter (played by Howard Keel) based on a novel by Lloyd C. Douglas, author of *The Robe*. By this stage of the 1950s, Jesus is once again offscreen, with only the suggestion of his presence by his hand or his garments. In *The Big Fisherman*, Jesus heals Peter's mother-in-law. He also encounters Herod.

By the late 1950s, a decade in which biblical films became popular again, especially with the introduction of Cinemascope and other wide-screen processes used for all kinds of historical epics, Jesus was becoming more visible. In 1951 came the first of the major Gospel epics, *Quo Vadis*. The title comes from an episode in which Peter wants to leave Rome to avoid the persecution of the Christians. On the Appian Way, Peter encounters Jesus. Peter asks Jesus where he is going. Jesus replies that he is going into Rome to be crucified. Peter, of course, turns back. Since this is all shown by light and sound, there is no characterization of Jesus. (During Peter's preaching, there are some flashbacks to the Gospels, amongst them a Last Supper that is a re-creation of da Vinci's painting.)

There is a Crucifixion scene in *The Robe* (1953), but it focuses on the slave Demetrius (Victor Mature), who kneels at the foot of the cross thus allowing the audience to see Jesus' feet and his blood running down on Demetrius and on the centurion, Marcellus (Richard Burton), and the soldiers playing dice for Jesus' seamless robe; Marcellus gazes at the crucified Jesus while the camera cranes from the ground to just behind the crossbeam.

Other biblical epics of the early to mid-1950s were not Jesus films. They focused on biblical characters with an emphasis on fiction: *Salome* (1953), *The Silver Chalice* (1954), and an elaboration of the parable of the prodigal son, *The Prodigal* (1955).

It was in this cinema context that Jules Dassin, working in Europe because of the blacklist, directed a Greek film that foreshadowed the kind of film made thirty years later. His striking version of Nikos Kazantzakis' *He Who Must Die* (1958) is the story of a village putting on a Passion play. It is the 1920s and the Turks have occupied the town. A shepherd who stutters is chosen to portray Jesus, while the butcher who wanted that role is Judas. A crisis occurs when some uprooted people come to the town and the citizens resent them, persecuting them. The film becomes a Gospel allegory of what is happening in the town. Thirty years later *The Last Temptation of Christ* and *Jesus of Montreal* were released.

Before considering the English language and mainstream films that emerged during the 1950s, it is important to remember the Jesus films of the 1940s from Mexico. Spanish refugee to Mexico from the civil war, José Diaz Morales made *Jesus de Nazareth* in 1942. The cast list includes Jesus, Mary, the Magdalene, and the apostles as well as the Samaritan woman and the woman taken in adultery. Mexico had not taken the stand that Jesus could not be represented fully on-screen with *Maria Magdalena, pecadora de Magdala* (1946); *Reina de reinas: La Virgen Maria* (1948), edited from *Maria Magdalena*; and *El martir del Calvario* (1952).

MARIA MAGDALENA, PECADORA DE MAGDALA

After World War II, Mexico produced *Maria Magdalena, pecadora de Magdala*. It was less than twenty years since Cecil B. DeMille's *The King of Kings*, and DeMille's film may have served as model/inspiration for director Miguel Contreras Torres. *The King of Kings* opens with Mary Magdalene and features her as a central character. However, the film becomes more of a Jesus film as Mary experiences her conversion and becomes Jesus' most devoted disciple (the apostles, with the exception of Judas, relegated more to the crowd or the background).

Maria Magdalena opens in Egypt with a more or less irrelevant but spectacular episode in which a prince steals a jewel from a temple and flees to Israel. He becomes one of several of the Magdalene's clients (presented as suitors). Judas, dressed rather affluently, also visits her. She herself lives as if she were in DeMille's *Cleopatra*, having a palace for a rich and intelligent courtesan. The Magdalene becomes curious about Jesus, who passes by her house with a crowd and stops to look at her before moving on. She listens, unseen, to him speaking and then visits him. He preaches to her with reference to the Good Shepherd, and there is an exorcism, rather gently shown, in which inner Marys representing the deadly sins (lust being the last to come out of her) are imposed under Mary and are seen leaving her. From then on she wears modest dress, frees her slave, gives away her wealth, and is prominently present at Jesus' ministry.

The opening of the film has captions on respect for the scriptures and a note identifying Magdalene with Mary, the sister of Martha and Lazarus, which the Gospel does not do.

Jesus, played by Luis Alcoriza, at first seems quietly bland and somewhat passive, and looks like the Jesus of popular holy cards. At times he becomes a little more animated, even occasionally smiling. The thinking behind this representation of Jesus is that his divinity seems to demand that his humanity be restrained and dignified, quietly superhuman. This is shown as he simply lays on hands and heals the sick, then offers a pious raising of his eyes to heaven.

A nice touch is the Magdalene meeting Mary, the mother of Jesus, and their becoming friends, sharing in Jesus' ministry, though the Magdalene gets most of the close-ups.

Because the Magdalene is identified with Mary of Bethany as well as the anonymous prostitute of Luke 7, the film can visualize this chapter of Luke where Simon invites Jesus to a meal and the woman anoints Jesus' feet, enabling Jesus to speak of love and forgiveness. And the film can show Martha and Mary, almost in tableau, Mary sitting at Jesus' feet and Martha (uncharacteristically) standing by silent. As with most Jesus films, the raising of Lazarus receives attention. This time Mary gets the lines that Martha speaks in John 11.

Other Gospel episodes include Jesus drinking wine and dining with the tax collectors and prostitutes and being criticized by the religious leaders, the feeding of the five thousand with a substantial multiplication of loaves and fishes, Mary anointing Jesus' head at the meal at Bethany with Judas' criticism, some preaching, and the giving of the Pater Noster with Mary and then the crowds falling on their knees with Jesus who prays with his hands raised.

Judas betrays Jesus and the high priests discuss what they are to do to capture Jesus. A large Star of David is seen on the back wall.

The film gives quite some attention to the events of the last week of Jesus' life. The palm procession into Jerusalem tends toward a DeMille–style spectacle. The Last Supper is imitation da Vinci, though the apostles do join Jesus in a group embrace. With no women at the supper, the screenplay takes some time with an invented scene in which Jesus explains what is about to happen to his mother and speaks with the Magdalene outside the upper room. The Agony in the Garden and Jesus' arrest are more or less as expected as is the rather briefer scene of Jesus before Caiaphas—with a short interlude by the fire where Peter denies Jesus.

Crowds accompany Jesus to Pilate, again with the expected scenes and treatment: Jesus' silence; the leaders' denunciations; Pilate's questions; the scourging, thorns, and soldiers' laughter and mockery; the statement "Behold the Man"; Pilate washing his hands. The road to Calvary is longer, reflecting the traditional devotion and the Stations of the Cross: Jesus falling, a reluctant Simon trying to lift the heavy cross and helping Jesus, Jesus meeting not only with his mother but also with the Magdalene when he falls, Veronica and the image on her cloth. A difference from the usual treatment is that Jesus has a rope around his neck so that he can also be dragged by the soldiers.

The nailing and Crucifixion do not stand out, and Jesus on the cross is like traditional art. The leaders mock. The good thief is promised paradise. Jesus entrusts his mother to John. The soldiers throw dice for the robe. There is, however, a special look of love and a smile for Mary Magdalene as she tells him she loves him with all her soul—and some of his blood splashes on her face. Jesus says, in Latin, "Consummatum est" and dies. What follows is apocalyptic darkness, lightning flashes, thunder, eruptions of fire and quakes, seas heaving, and pagan temples and statues collapsing. A bewildered leader, with a Star of David behind him, proclaims Jesus as the Messiah. Then quiet and tranquillity takes over, and Jesus is lifted from the cross. At this point cinematically, Mary Magdalene is allowed a superimposed series of flashbacks to her encounters with Jesus.

The tombstone catches fire, and Jesus emerges from the tomb like an icon. But this is not the end of the film. The Magdalene goes to the empty tomb with oil and flowers and encounters the risen Jesus. The climax honors Mary as the first witness to the Resurrection (a point made in the initial captions) and has her preaching the good news, giving her testimony.

The credit for the adaptation and the story for Maria Magdalene is given to Medea de Novara, who played the Magdalene.

Two years later, Miguel Contreras Torres made a similar film, *Reina de reinas: La Virgen Maria*, with the same cast, another version of a Jesus film.

EL MARTIR DEL CALVARIO

As *The Robe* was being produced in Hollywood, Mexico released a full Jesus film, *El martir del Calvario*.

To modern eyes the film looks very old-fashioned, but when compared with its contemporaries, especially *The Pilgrimage Play* and *I Beheld His Glory*, it is very similar in its staging of the Gospel events. The events look particularly staged, and the limited sets look like sets. Camera movement is limited and action is within the often static frame. It does not look like Judea or Galilee. *El martir* is also similar in the way that Jesus is portrayed, very much like popular religious art in appearance and manner, an otherworldly aloofness that is sometimes mellowed by a slight touch or a slight smile. On the whole, Jesus is the Son of God and quite solemn, with a rhetorical style, a blend of preaching and declamation. It is really a one-note interpretation.

One different feature is the emphasis on Mary, the mother of Jesus, dressed like a holy card or as in a nun's habit. She features more than she does in the Gospels, Jesus visiting her in Nazareth, her presence at his preaching, and a rather longer encounter on the way to Calvary. She is at the foot of the cross but is seen in a striking long shot standing upright, holding on to the cross after Jesus has died.

In fairness to the Mexicans who produced *El martir*, there were principally silent presentations of Jesus as precedents, along with *Maria Magdalena, pecadora de Magdala* and *Reina de reinas: La Virgen Maria* (both of which are technically and imaginatively superior to *El martir*), and we do not know whether they saw the American evangelical films. *King of Kings* was still nine years away.

El martir is really a succession of Gospel episodes one quickly following the other without a sense of continuity of time or a sense of place except for the events of the last weeks of Jesus' life in Jerusalem. It opens with Jesus walking ahead of his disciples to the Sea of Galilee, which is followed by the miraculous draft of fish, the call of Peter and the other fishermen, the healing of the paralytic, the encounter with the rich young man, and the apostles asking what they would get. Then immediately Peter's mother-in-law is healed. This all seems to happen in one day. With a transition, Jesus is praying, crowds gather and Jesus delivers the beatitudes, the centurion asks for the healing of his servant, and Jesus is commissioning the apostles to feed the crowd. Jesus continues to bring out sizeable loaves from a small basket.

At this point, it seems that the whole film has been influenced by *Maria Magdalena, pecadora de Magdala*.

Some attention is given to the stories of Luke 4, but the setting is not in a synagogue as the Gospel tells us. Jesus is criticized, quotes Isaiah about the work of the Messiah, and then directly states that he is the Messiah. Jesus has previously visited his mother and explained his mission to her. The indignant crowd want to attack him, but he walks silently through them, only stopping to heal a blind boy and welcome the children (with a mellow touch of slightly hugging and holding them). This offers an occasion for Jesus to answer the questions of John the Baptist's disciples about who he is.

After what seems only a short walk, he is at Jacob's well and telling the Samaritan woman that he is the Messiah and suddenly encountering Martha, who tells him Lazarus is ill. This rapid succession of events without a grounding in the geography that even the Gospels spell out can be disconcerting—but, for an audience not versed in the details of the scriptures, it may not have mattered very much.

Suddenly, some DeMille–like episodes take place. The set for Mary Magdalene's house is rather more lavish—and her dress more suggestive. To complicate matters, the screenplay deviates from the Gospels by making Mary Magdalene the sister of Martha and Lazarus (which excludes the use of Luke 11, where Jesus visits the sisters and Mary sits listening to him). In other films, Mary Magdalene is wrongly identified with the anonymous prostitute who anoints Jesus in Luke 7. With a text about the Good Shepherd, Mary is instantly converted from her ways, sees a halo behind Jesus, and hears the words of forgiveness from Luke 7:50. This enables the screenplay to move on to the death of Lazarus (Martha and Mary reuniting) and the raising of Lazarus from the dead.

Judas has been foremost amongst the apostles (and wearing an earing and looking somewhat effete compared with the rugged others). Judas spurns the poor and is interested only in Jesus becoming king of Israel. He urges a procession of palms and is dismayed when Jesus rides the donkey and goes to speak with a group of poor by the city walls.

The rest of the film focuses on the events of Holy Week and the Passion. The film also introduces Caiaphas and Annas (with a huge Star of David on the wall). The high priests are shocked when Jesus gets a rope and clears the buyers and sellers out of the Temple, even hitting some of them with the rope. This is quite a spectacular scene compared with the others. Jesus confronts the high priests with his challenge "Destroy this temple and I will raise it in three days." With little warning, they bring in the woman taken in adultery and leave when Jesus challenges them to cast the first stone. The woman kisses the hem of Jesus' garments, but he does not raise her up or touch her.

Judas then receives his thirty pieces of silver and plans the betrayal of Jesus. The Last Supper is a da Vinci imitation with Jesus raising the bread and wine like a priest at Mass. After a few words about his going to the Father, Jesus and his disciples leave for Gethsemane. The Agony in the Garden and the betrayal are much as expected by now—except that Jesus sees a special effect chalice as he prays and has some blood drops on his forehead. There is also some dramatic swordplay in the garden and Jesus heals Malchus. The set for the Sanhedrin is, in fact, very large, a quite spectacular and crowded gathering. The witnesses speak. Jesus is silent. He is slapped.

Judas interrupts and makes a scene. Caiaphas leaves the dais, makes a long walk to Jesus, and judges him to have blasphemed.

The scenes with Pilate are comparatively short. The Jewish leaders stand outside the wall of Pilate's house. Jesus speaks with Pilate, is scourged (with, as in *The Passion of the Christ*, Mary watching), is crowned with thorns, is mocked with genuflections by the soldiers, and is then brought to Pilate, "Behold the Man."

Much more is made of the road to Calvary than in other films, perhaps reflecting Mexican devotion to the Stations of the Cross. The cross is very large, with its beam trailing in the dust of the road. Eventually, Simon offers to help Jesus (and seems to struggle to lift it despite his burliness, making us wonder how Jesus could carry it). Jesus meets his mother and speaks with her. Veronica wipes his face and is rewarded with the imprint on the towel. On Calvary, Jesus is nailed (with the camera showing the nails and Jesus' hand but then, with the loud sound effects, showing the face of Mary, then the other hand nailed, with the hammer coming down but the hand just below the bottom of the screen, relying on suggestion rather than full view). Scenes audiences would expect are included: the soldiers playing dice, the taunts of the leaders, the good thief, Jesus entrusting Mary to John, the sip of vinegar. When Jesus bows his head and dies, lightning flashes, and there are apocalyptic scenes of thunder, wind, rain, fire in the Temple, and the crowds battened down to the ground because of the elements. Jesus hangs on the cross. Judas is seen swinging from his own gallows.

Pilate gives permission for the body to be taken away, and Jesus is taken down from the cross, being seen in a long shot Pietà. There is a substantial procession to the tomb. Soldiers guard it. Light appears in the stone (exactly as in *Maria Magdalena*), and accompanied by Resurrection music, Jesus appears as a risen icon and "Gloria" and "Alleluja" are sung.

In many ways, *El martir del Calvario* is basic Jesus movie making—snatches of preaching, few miracles, no parables. But for an audience from a Catholic country with a Hispanic tradition, this film would have fulfilled the expectations of filmgoers at the time. And when, as has been suggested, it is compared with the evangelical and Catholic films of the time, there is not a great deal of difference. (The complete film can be seen on YouTube in twelve sections in Spanish, but there are no English subtitles.)

BEN-HUR AND JESUS' REAPPEARANCE

The most striking of the films that re-introduced Jesus on-screen, if only with partial view, is William Wyler's multi-Oscar-winning film of 1959,

Ben-Hur, subtitled *A Story of the Christ*. Jesus is seen from the back, walking in the hills, as well as up on a hill for the Sermon on the Mount. There are Passion sequences and the Crucifixion, but Jesus' face is always obscured, except for an angle shot of him on the cross. There are no close-ups.

However, Jesus appears in two significant and parallel sequences that emphasize his humanity and thus allow an audience to feel for him as a person and begin an identification process.

When Ben-Hur is arrested and sent to Rome, the chained prisoners march through desert landscapes, arriving at Nazareth. We see them through the open workshop window, noticing the arm of Jesus with a carpenter's tool. But it is when the captain refuses water to the parched Ben-Hur that Jesus appears, first as a shadow cast on Ben-Hur when he has sunk to the ground and groans, "God help me." Jesus gives him water and, then, with a close-up of his hand, he pours water on Ben-Hur's head and brow, gently and soothingly. Jesus strokes Ben-Hur's hair as he pours the water. This sequence has great emotional appeal. When confronted by the captain, Jesus stares him down and the captain withdraws, taking the prisoners on, while Jesus continues to gaze at them (although this is completely dramatized through the reactions of the captain and then of Ben-Hur, photographed over Jesus' shoulder, showing only the back of his head).

This connection is made several times during the film. When Ben-Hur rescues the Roman consul, Arrius, after the battle with pirates, Arrius gives him a cup of water before he drinks it himself. Later, when Ben-Hur meets one of the Magi, Balthasar, on his way to hear Jesus preach, they stop at a stream and Ben-Hur recalls the water incident at Nazareth. But, he is sad over the fate of his mother and sister and says that the water should have flowed into the sand. But the fulfillment comes during Jesus' walk to Calvary. Falling under the cross and in need of water, Jesus is comforted by Ben-Hur, who offers him water and recognizes Jesus as the stranger who once comforted him.

This is all part of a conversion experience for Ben-Hur, who later relates how he heard the Sermon on the Mount, followed Jesus to Calvary, witnessed his death, and understood that he had to let go of his bitterness and hatred. The screenplay also has Ben-Hur's mother and sister being healed of their leprosy and given life, at the very moment that Jesus dies.

Charlton Heston lent his voice to an animated film version of the story in 2003. Scott McNeil was the voice of Jesus.

PONZIO PILATO AND *BARABBAS*

In the wake of the production of *Ben-Hur* at Cinecitta studios in Rome, several other biblical spectaculars were filmed there. Two of these—*Ponzio*

Pilato and *Barabbas*—focused on the Passion of Jesus; like *Ben-Hur* these two are transition films, moving away from the absence of the face-on Jesus in the period between first *King of Kings* (1927) and Jeffrey Hunter's appearance in the second *King of Kings* filmed in 1961, the same year as *Ponzio Pilato* and *Barabbas*.

Ponzio Pilato was one of the hybrid films so popular in Italy with a cast of Italians and Americans. It was codirected by Italian Gian Paolo Callegari (a writer of many sword-and-sandal epics popular at this time) and American Irving Rapper. French star Jean Marais (from Jean Cocteau's films) portrays the governor on trial before Caesar, giving an account of his stewardship. The flashbacks of his rule in Judea culminate in the Passion of Jesus. He manipulates Judas into betraying Jesus, then judges Jesus, washes his hands of him, and orders him to be crucified. Jeanne Crain portrays Pilate's wife, disturbed in dreams about Jesus and his death. American John Drew Barrymore is Jesus and is said to have "acted" the role of Jesus, though he is generally seen from the back or, finally, at a distance on Calvary.

There are two different and distinctive moments in *Ponzio Pilato* that are worth noting and seeing. Jesus has been photographed from the back in a deep conversation with Caiaphas (Basil Rathbone), the high priest quietly trying to persuade Jesus to relinquish his mission. Then, he is suddenly shown in close-up—but only of his eyes. They are eyes with an intense and penetrating gaze. Not long afterward when Pilate has been examining Jesus before the crowd, he washes his hands. As he looks into the bowl of water, Pilate sees the same piercing eyes of Jesus and the water turns to blood, an interesting and imaginative cinematic touch.

The more ambitious and significant film is *Barabbas*, also from 1961. This was a huge production, by producer Dino De Laurentiis, with a cast of both Italians and Americans. The director was American Richard Fleischer, a more than competent director of many films of diverse genres. In *Barabbas* he made a fine biblical epic. The screenplay was written by celebrated playwright Christopher Fry, who had contributed (uncredited) to *Ben-Hur*. He adapted a Swedish novel by Nobel Prize laureate Par Lagerkvist, which had already been filmed in Sweden in 1953 by Alf Sjoberg. It was reported that the Swedish version was sidelined to make way for the De Laurentiis version. The musical score consists of repetitions and variations on the plainchant Kyrie Eleison.

The screenplay takes the briefly mentioned brigand Barabbas and weaves the story of a man bewildered by what he saw of Jesus' death, imprisoned for twenty years in the Sicilian sulphur mines, and then transformed into a champion gladiator—only to be tormented by the mystery of why he was saved and ultimately dying on the cross himself.

Jesus is seen far more clearly in the opening sequences of *Barabbas* than before. However, he is still presented as silent, someone to be observed with pity and dismay.

Barabbas opens with Pontius Pilate's dilemma: to condemn Jesus or to let him go free. According to the customs of Jewish law, Pilate could release a prisoner because of the feast of the Passover. However, the crowd, incited by the religious leaders, clamor for the release of Barabbas. Barabbas is a scoundrel robber rather than a Zealot. (A later set piece of an ambush and robbery after Barabbas fights and kills a fellow robber dramatizes this.)

Pilate is seen here as a strong leader, making his demands. Jesus is seen, but at something of a distance, as a living icon, backstage so to speak, dressed in white with two guards standing by him. He is then scourged, the visuals of which are rather different from the usual. Jesus is squatting, hands bound and tied to a short pillar. After the scourging he still squats but, when untied, falls to the floor. He is raised up to be crowned with thorns and mocked. Humiliated and tortured, he then stands exposed to the hostile mob. The art direction has relied on traditional paintings of the Passion for the manner in which Jesus is dressed in a red robe and crowned with thorns.

Barabbas (Anthony Quinn) is released, and as he ascends the steps from the dungeon, pushed out to unexpected freedom, he is momentarily blinded by the light. He has a blurred vision of Jesus standing there. The glare fades, and he sees the condemned Jesus—the framing and design are like a traditional painting. As Barabbas makes his way from the praetorium, ignored by the crowds, he backs into a cross—and out of the Gospel accounts and into biblical fictions like this film.

Soon, Jesus is seen being loaded with the cross and beginning his way to Calvary. The screenplay makes a dramatic contrast between the freed Barabbas and the condemned Jesus, his friends at the tavern welcoming him back declare that since Jesus claimed to be king, they should crown Barabbas. He is enthroned as a mock king, broom for scepter and bowl for crown. Surveying his drunken kingdom, he chances to look out the window just as Jesus is passing, bearing his cross to Golgotha, and stops, shocked.

Soon, the afternoon light darkens and Barabbas, stumbling, wanders toward the crosses on the hill. The sun is eclipsed, the people shudder, and many run away, but the light comes back. Jesus is dead, taken down from the cross. There is a Pietà tableau, the focus on Mary who holds Jesus (his head away from the camera). Mary then gazes at the bewildered Barabbas. Jesus is buried in the garden and the stone is rolled against the door. Barabbas and his friend, Rachel, watch. Rachel predicts that Jesus will be alive on the morning of the third day. Her description of the Resurrection is rather apocalyptic: light in the sky, a horn, music, and a giant spear appearing in the sky.

While the interpretation of the Passion is acceptable to more literal, even fundamentalist interpretation, the fictional framework and the emphases on the contrast between Jesus and Barabbas offer the possibility of a more symbolic reading (as in the Gospels themselves) of such phenomena as the eclipse. Christopher Fry's spare and reverent screenplay captures the spirit of the Passion narratives.

One of the features of *Barabbas* is its portrayal of early Christianity and the range of disciples that it presents. Audiences can gauge something of the way Christianity spread throughout the Roman Empire and the effect on men and women, especially those who were slaves and prisoners.

In the earliest sequences of the film, we are introduced to Barabbas' woman, Rachel, whose life has been transformed by Jesus. It is she who explains the death and the hope of Resurrection to Barabbas. She goes to the tomb early on the first day of the week and sees Jesus talking with Mary Magdalene but, like Mary, does not recognize him. Barabbas goes into the room mystified but soon takes a stance of skepticism.

However, Rachel's significance in the film is as a martyr. She speaks out about Jesus, and the crowd and the religious leaders threaten her. She is dragged to a pit/quarry outside the walls. A blind man is forced to give testimony against her and cast the first stone. The scene, straight out of the Acts of the Apostles with the death of Stephen, is martyrdom by stoning.

The death of Rachel is one of the reasons for Barabbas' desperate behavior with the robbers and the arresting soldiers. But Barabbas also visits the upper room and encounters Peter and some of the apostles. Peter is fiddling, mending nets. He explains something of who Jesus was and how they were to become "fishers of men" (a "serious joke," he says). However, Barabbas is skeptical and meets a kindred spirit in Thomas. He knows from Rachel that Jesus urged people to "love one another." Barabbas says, "And they crucified him for that?" This gives Peter the opportunity to explain Jesus as the risen Lord whose body, though real, has different qualities and powers from those Jesus had as he walked Judea.

More than twenty years after this, Barabbas encounters Peter the preacher in Rome and finds the strength and conviction to die, crucified, for the Jesus who had been the cause of his freedom and his years of imprisonment.

When Pilate had condemned Barabbas to the sulphur mines of Sicily, Barabbas had told Pilate that he could not die because Jesus had died in his place: "He has taken my death."

The Gospel narratives have excited the imaginations of artists and storytellers for two thousand years. *Barabbas* fits into this imaginative reading. It is historical fiction. Barabbas is mentioned only very briefly in the Gospels but his memory is still alive. Barabbas means, literally, "son of the father." It is most appropriate that he becomes a parallel/contrast for Jesus who is Son of the Father. The story of *Barabbas* is one of a chance for a new life, of atonement and redemption, of a personal salvation. It is presented in the form of a life journey, a life that should not have been lived beyond Good Friday, a life of pain and puzzlement to Barabbas, who could not understand why he had to live this life.

THE SIN OF JESUS

Any film with the title *The Sin of Jesus* is certainly to be noticed. However, this one is not available. Some details are found on the Internet Movie Database indicating that it was from 1961, ran for thirty-seven minutes, and included Julie Bovasso, Telly Savalas, and character actor Roberts Blossom in the cast. The director, Robert Frank, was born in Switzerland but moved to the United States where he worked as a photographer and then as a filmmaker; he worked with Jack Kerouac and Allen Ginsberg and later made a documentary about the Rolling Stones and adapted a story by Isaac Bashevis Singer. Ivan Butler comments in his *Religion in the Cinema,*

> The incredible story concerns a woman-servant in a hotel who is six months pregnant by the janitor. She has already had twins by him, and he now deserts her. She thereupon appeals to Jesus, who presents her with an angel-husband for four years, but stipulates that he must take off his wings before getting into bed. The woman gets drunk, and, heavy with child, rolls on top of the angel and kills him. Jesus is furious with her for smothering his angel, bawling at her with such Christ-like expressions as "You filthy scum!" Later He asks her forgiveness which she refuses. It is just conceivable that this farrago is intended to make some obscure comment after the manner of television "satire"—the question is how far offensiveness can sheer silliness can go before losing claim to even that dubious result. This is, at least, curiosity raising, especially when one commentator calls it "bleakly Bergmanesque."[1]

NOTE

1. Ivan Butler, *Religion in the Cinema* (New York: A.S. Barnes, 1969), 46–47.

7

THE JESUS FILMS: THE 1960s

I t is interesting that the two films that begin and end the thirty-five-year gap between full portrayals of Jesus on-screen are the two versions of *The King of Kings*. In retrospect it is not so surprising that the change in depiction came with the 1960s, the decade that saw more social change, especially in Western culture, than any other decade of the twentieth century.

KING OF KINGS

King of Kings returned to a direct presentation of Jesus on-screen. It received mixed reviews. *Time* magazine, taking its cue from a current popular series of horror films for younger audiences, headed their review with the journalese, "I Was a Teenage Jesus." It was also noted that the problems with the humanity and divinity had not yet been resolved: Jeffrey Hunter's armpits were shaved for the Crucifixion, a touch of sanitizing for one of history's most violent memories.

But with *King of Kings*, it was now possible to identify with the Jesus portrayed. Hunter, under the direction of Nicholas Ray, is a fairly straightforward Jesus, a Jesus of the masses, who preaches his good news, goes about speaking and doing good and is crucified for it. The straightforward spectacle of *King of Kings* could draw on the response of the mass audience.

Jesus Speaks

King of Kings was the first film in thirty-five years to use an actor to portray Jesus as a fully developed character in the Gospel drama, a Jesus who is seen face-on and in wide-screen color. It was the first time that a worldwide audience had heard a Jesus speak on-screen. And the accent was light American. This was a dramatic decision for the beginning of the 1960s. The option was made to show the key Gospel events while using the old Cecil B. DeMille recipe of including some sex and violence in a sacred context to entertain the mass audience. So, *King of Kings* has the Roman legions massacre Barabbas' followers and, of course, it has Salome perform her dance before Herod (PG rated at most).

King of Kings has echoes of the previous reticence about presenting Jesus on-screen. Early in the film, Jesus heals a lame man. What we see of Jesus is the enlarged shadow of his outstretched hand in healing gesture and the crippled man's hand straightening and strength coming into his limbs. At the very end of the film, when Jesus has spoken to the apostles at the Sea of Galilee (using the final words of Matthew 28), the fishermen's nets are stretched along the width of the screen and the lengthening shadow of Jesus forms a large cross on the shore.

But the producers were aiming at the world audience for their film, ordinary people, seeing and enjoying what is up there on the screen, appealing to the eye, in pageantry, costumes, and decor, and to the ear, with Miklos Rozsa's reverently epic score, a score that became something of the pattern for the biblical epic.

Performance

The cast, however, was not a top-billing cast. It was second rung, sturdy and reliable rather than inspired. This means that the action is presented quite straightforwardly and in scenes that were familiar enough to Christians. To cover a lot of the Gospel action, a narrator describes the background to the Gospels and a great deal of Jesus' actions as well as some motivation. The screenplay sometimes minimizes Jesus' on-screen time by letting other characters speak his words or relate his actions. So, Mary, the mother of Jesus, actually speaks the parable of the lost sheep to the prostitute who is looking for Jesus and is invited to eat with Mary at her table. The centurion, Lucius, who is attracted by Jesus and his teaching reads out a document to Pilate that includes a description of the feeding of the multitude.

Jeffrey Hunter's performance is, one might say, workmanlike rather than inspired. The director gets him to speak the Gospel sayings with mild strength and has urged him to pose with reverent gestures, especially outstretched, raised arms. In fact, the performance is more inspired when the screenwriters have invented scenes like the one where Jesus visits John the Baptist in prison. John drags himself up the sloping wall of his dark dungeon to the grille where Jesus reaches out to him. John grips Jesus' hand and asks for his blessing. But John can't sustain the grip and slides down to the floor again. There is no Gospel precedent and the episode has some creative feeling.

With Hunter's performance what you get is what you see. The Sermon on the Mount is on a high mountain with crowds to look down at, a picturesque but physically impossible episode. However, the screenplay has not used Matthew 5–7 as a complete or even a partial text. Rather, as Jesus walks amongst those on the side of the mountain, he engages in a Q-and-A session of the briefest and most direct kind. Successive questioners put familiar issues from other parts of the Gospel to Jesus—about the greatest law, about forgiveness. Jesus' answers, if listed, would form an outline compendium of his key teachings. This Jesus is very clear when he communicates. It is the same with other episodes in the film. With the voiceover explaining who the twelve apostles are, they file past the camera. When Jesus heals a demoniac, he sees him, approaches him, holds him, and heals him.

The Passion

There is similar clarity and simplicity with the Last Supper and the Passion, although there is an effective dramatic moment when Jesus announces that one of the apostles will betray him. There is a close-up of Judas' eyes and Jesus leans across the table and stares him out. At the table Jesus then simply breaks the bread and distributes it. He prays the traditional blessing over the cup of wine and passes it around.

Since Jesus is mostly silent during the Passion, the film shows the familiar events: Jesus before Pilate, mocked by Herod, crowned with thorns, carrying the cross and falling, meeting his mother and having his face wiped with a cloth, being raised on the cross. He does speak on the cross: his sense of abandonment by God, the forgiveness of the good thief, his committing himself to the Father.

To this extent, Jesus in *King of Kings* is a "no frills" Jesus. We know where we stand with him. We know what he says; we know what he does and we see him do it.

THE GREATEST STORY EVER TOLD

Only four years after the breakthrough film *King of Kings*—which saw actor Jeffrey Hunter portray Jesus fully, face-on and speaking, on-screen—1965 brought the big-budget, over-three-hour-version of the popular Fulton

Oursler book on the life of Jesus, *The Greatest Story Ever Told*. It was a long, star-studded version—the film in which John Wayne was the centurion who proclaimed, "This man was truly the Son of God" (drawling "Gaaad")—but it did not gain the popularity that was hoped for and it was not the commercial success that it was expected to be. Directed by veteran George Stevens, who had twice won Oscars for Best Director (1951, *A Place in the Sun*, and 1956, *Giant*), and filled with well-known actors in dramatic roles or in cameos, it had strong cinematic credentials.

A Somewhat Dour Jesus

The locations scenery is magnificent, but the Gospel texts, as rearranged for Max von Sydow's laconic and somber delivery, gives very little context for their profound meaning and so are lost in rhetorical speeches rather than characterization. There is little action filling the wide screen, too many static tableaux, and Jesus is generally shown with only a few people, something of a religious loner.

Why would a director want a thirty-five-year-old somewhat dour Swede, Max von Sydow, to portray a first-century Jewish man? While von Sydow's performance was dignified and at times stately, in retrospect (and maybe at the time), the major difficulty with *The Greatest Story Ever Told* was in this casting of him as Jesus. An acclaimed Swedish actor, best known for his roles in the somber and profound classics of Ingmar Bergman—like that of the knight in *The Seventh Seal* or the father in *The Virgin Spring*—he was tall and fair-haired, and he spoke accented English.

It is not the most moving performance in the history of cinema. It is an over-reverent portrayal of Jesus with the result being that Jesus speaks and acts in a particularly stilted manner. Von Sydow's portrayal contrasts strongly with the performances of some of the guest stars who act with conviction (like Claude Rains' Herod Agrippa and Jose Ferrer's Herod Antipas); of those who do star turns, getting more screen time than needed (Charlton Heston as John the Baptist); of those who do pious, holy card turns (Dorothy McGuire as Mary, mother of Jesus); and of John Wayne, in that famously ludicrous moment when he appears as the centurion at the foot of the cross.

Whether Stevens or von Sydow decided that Jesus should be introverted or whether screenwriter James Lee Barrett wrote the character of Jesus that way, Jesus comes across as introspective and quiet. A clue to this may be found in the screenwriting credit, over and above the Oursler book, to "radio scripts by Henry Denker," scripts for programs on the Bible written in collaboration with Oursler. The Jesus of *The Greatest Story Ever Told* is frequently the equivalent of a radio broadcast Jesus.

An Icon Jesus

The Greatest Story Ever Told was released the year after Pier Paolo Pasolini's *Gospel according to St. Matthew*. Pasolini's film also presents an introverted, introspective Jesus. In his conception of a Gospel film, Stevens is sometimes quite close to Pasolini: sparse use of words and of the Gospel text; Jesus presented as more of a loner than a mixer; Jesus having a sternness of manner and demeanor; Jesus presented with comparatively few people and rather small crowds; Jesus as standing among posed, still tableaux; Jesus as an utterer and an exhorter of Gospel truths. However, Pasolini's overall vision of his film and his perceptions of the inner energy and the impact of Jesus and the Gospel lead him to succeed where Stevens does not.

Introverted people gain energy for their outer life from their inner world. This seems to be what the von Sydow Jesus is doing. The film opens and closes with an icon of Jesus in a mosaic in the apse of a church. The icon represents von Sydow as Jesus. An icon is a sacred image that viewers contemplate. It is enigmatic in its artistic style so that when the viewer does contemplate it, meaning is supplied from the viewer's own experience of the subject. The viewer can read into the icon a personal experience. Stevens seems to be relying on this iconic-contemplative dimension to his portrayal of Jesus.

Jesus throughout the film often stands silent, gazing at people. He moves ahead of the group, perhaps conversing with one of his disciples, but always a tall, almost isolated leader. When he exhorts or gives a sermon, he is at a physical distance—and an emotional distance—from his listeners. It comes as quite a surprise when Jesus becomes really engaged with the world around him as he does when in the Temple and suddenly a rage bursts out of him and he violently overturns the money changers' tables and frees the pigeons from their coops.

Von Sydow does his best with the screenplay he has been presented with, but the detached introversion of his character seems to be the vision of Jesus of the writer and Stevens who co-wrote the screenplay. Their understanding of Jesus emphasizes his hidden divinity rather than developing his humanity. Their understanding of the Incarnation is that the humanity seems less important than the underlying divinity. The divinity is the inner world of Jesus; the humanity, the lesser outer world. The unspoken theological reasoning is that being in touch with his inner divinity, Jesus must be introverted.

Use of the Gospel Text

This theological view (which professional theologians could criticize as less than orthodox in not acknowledging the true and full humanity of

Jesus) affects the literal use of the Gospel texts for the screenplay. The writers, looking for dramatic impact of texts while still using verbatim the Gospel verses, do not appreciate the meanings of the stories of the Gospels and their significance at particular stages of Jesus' ministry. A glaring example is the treatment of Martha, Mary, and Lazarus. By ignoring the forthrightness of Martha and Mary in Luke 10 and having Lazarus center screen, they overlook the significance of Jesus and his relationship with women and having women as disciples. Martha and Mary stand at the side with little significance. When Lazarus dies, again the focus is on him, whereas John 11 gives the two sisters much stronger roles and focuses on Jesus telling Martha that he is the Resurrection and the life.

Even the impact of the Resurrection is interrupted as Jesus, before ascending into heaven, preaches to the disciples some verses from the Sermon on the Mount. Franco Zeffirelli and his screenwriters were far more skilled at this rearranging of Gospel texts for dramatic purposes in *Jesus of Nazareth.*

The consequence of this lack of exegetical know-how and the icon presentation of Jesus is that there is usually no context, dramatically or theologically, for Jesus' utterances, especially when he asserts his union with his Father and proclaims his divinity. These are isolated utterances and rely on the audience's knowledge of the story and claims of the Gospel and of some faith or understanding. For the actor it is particularly difficult to create Jesus as a character. He is continually presented as isolated, not only dramatically, but also theologically. And, so, he appears as a loner, mysterious but in no way magnetic enough as a personality to attract the disciples he does or to retain their loyalty. (David McCallum's Judas seems a far more attractive character and decent enough so that there is some sympathy on a feelings level for his disillusionment and betrayal.)

A Touch of Puritanism

Even when Jesus performs miracles, it is as if he is locked in his inner world. In the final cut, a great deal of time is given to his healing the cripple and the old blind man (played by Ed Wynn), who knew him at Nazareth and to whom he restores his sight. There seems to be very little empathy from Jesus toward these two—"your faith is weaker than your legs"—but the screenplay has them be extraordinarily loyal to Jesus, even turning the blind man into the man born blind from John's Gospel (chapter 9) and having him give testimony at Jesus' trial.

There is also a great deal of nonconformist primness, a touch of puritanism, in the film that cuts Jesus off from the tax collectors and prostitutes, who the Gospels tell us were so eager to seek his company. When Jesus is about to call Matthew (Roddy McDowall), his brother warns Jesus of what a terrible man he is: "He drinks, he swears, he gambles." It is feared that Matthew will "say something vulgar." Even when Jesus does not condemn Mary Magdalene when she is dragged before him, he quotes the law first and then Uriah lifts her and lets her go free.

The woman-taken-in-adultery scene is an important one in the film. Donald Pleasence as Satan is at hand to greet Jesus sardonically. Gossiping scribes and Pharisees are there. Carroll Baker plays the woman, wearing a bright red (scarlet?) dress, who is chased by the crowds and flung at Jesus' feet. As in *The Last Temptation of Christ*, this woman is fused with Mary Magdalene. Jesus solemnly asks what this is all about.

Jesus asks Mary if the accusation is true and she is ashamed. Jesus declares that she is guilty and picks up a stone. He makes the speech about the innocent casting the first stone. In fact, when no one takes up his offer, it is he (the innocent) who throws down the stone on the ground (and Mary flinches). Von Sydow's letting Mary go is articulated solemnly. It is Sal Mineo's disciple, Uriah, rather than Jesus, who helps the woman up and escorts her away.

All this has the effect of cutting Jesus off from ordinary people. He can walk through the midst of his audience as he walks through and away from the crowds on the screen. It means that his speeches, no matter how accurate the actual words of the Gospel are, make him sound rhetorical instead of personal and persuasive.

At times Jesus smiles—and it is a great relief. However, the smile tends to be wan rather than jubilant and Jesus does not laugh.

It is not suggested that the portrait of Jesus in *The Greatest Story Ever Told*, a strongly solemn portrait that runs the danger of seeming too aloof and of preaching down to people, cannot be commended. Rather, it is an example of an interpretation of Jesus that recognizes Jesus' inward-looking nature but holds it up as something of an ideal, as if this is the way to be sacred.

The version that we have was cut several times after the original, which was well over three hours running time, did not prove popular. Perhaps there was a fuller portrait of Jesus in the director's cut. However, what we have is George Stevens' understanding of who Jesus was and how he should be portrayed. But the greatest story ever told receives only a partial telling in this version.

ACTO DE PRIMAVERA

One of the most Catholic of world-status directors is the Portuguese Manoel de Oliveira (born in 1908 and still making films in 2011). He turned his attention to the Gospel story before the new spate of Jesus films. His contribution was the filming of a Portuguese Passion play, performed each year from a sixteenth-century text. Much of Oliveira's work was based on the fixed camera style from the silent era. Many of his films could be described as "talkfests." The filming of a Passion play would be congenial for him.

IL VANGELO SECONDO MATTEO

Around the same time in Italy, Marxist novelist and director Pier Paolo Pasolini found himself waiting in an Assisi hotel during a visit by the popular Pope John XXIII in 1962. He started glancing at his Gideon Bible, and having been urged by a friend to read the New Testament, he began with Matthew's Gospel and decided to film it, dedicating his film to John XXIII. When *Il Vangelo secondo Matteo* (*The Gospel according to St. Matthew*) was released in 1964, it received mixed reactions. It was welcomed by many Italian Catholics, and it won the International Catholic Film Organization award at the Venice Film Festival.

A Non-Hollywood Jesus

The Jesus of this film does not appeal to everyone, but there is a strong appeal to those who identify with a non-Hollywood Jesus. This Jesus appears as strong, intense, thirsty for truth and justice, willing to confront on principle and according to principles, a man of authority and conviction. Critics have noted that he rarely laughs, let alone smiles, but smile he does, especially with the response of children to him. Pasolini is helped by Matthew's Gospel being the most straightforward of the Gospels. And he uses the text as is, using it as a screenplay. This device, while being powerful, runs the risk of presenting the Gospel events over-literally, even in a fundamentalist way.

However, this is the film that critics and cinema buffs praise. Its black-and-white photography, use of classical and contemporary music, and absence of sentimentality (not sentiment—the southern Italian histrionics and hysterics of Pasolini's mother as Mary at the Crucifixion give the lie to that) make many consider *Il Vangelo secondo Matteo* the cinematic biblical masterpiece.

The European tradition of cinema representations of Jesus differs from that of the American tradition. The Europeans were more direct at the time when the Americans showed Jesus less directly, by suggestion or by showing Jesus from behind rather than face-on.

Austerity and Immediacy

The film was photographed in black and white. It used an austere style that became the mark of most of Pasolini's films. He used mountain locations, barren rock scapes, or the heights of southern Italy. He also relied on the faces and profiles of men and women who were gnarled and wrinkled by life, as well as the fresh faces of children. And his musical score was a mélange of classical pieces with contemporary music and included Negro spirituals and the African Missa Luba. This treatment of the Gospels found immediate favor with more critical cinema buffs who usually commented on how this unsentimental treatment was more powerful and persuasive than the familiar biblical epics.

Because Pasolini used the text of the Gospel as the screenplay, he gave the film an immediacy in its presentation of Jesus and his words and actions. However, the film is very literal in its approach, even fundamentalist at times, especially in its presentation of the infancy narratives. This means that the drama and the visualizing of the drama have to be found in the text. Pasolini rarely uses his own variations on the Gospel text.

However, he does achieve a great deal visually when he elaborates the Massacre of the Innocents. There is little in Matthew's text beyond the information about the Magi not returning to tell Herod where the child was, the fact that the killings happened, and the fulfillment text from Jeremiah. Pasolini dramatizes extensively, showing the malice of Herod, but with some excellent action sequences, he also shows the tactics of the solders almost dwelling on the cruelty of their slaughter. He seems to be passionate about these events.

The brief sequence where Judas hangs himself is also vivid.

The Passion

Jesus carries his cross to Calvary in scenes that are familiar. However, when Jesus arrives on top of the hill, Pasolini uses a device to make his Crucifixion more accessible to the audience. Pasolini shows, very graphically and with sound effects, one of the thieves being nailed to the cross, the nails being brutally hammered into his hands. He is then lifted and the cross dropped into a hole. We do not need to see this happening to Jesus. The impact of the nailing of the thief is powerful and appalling.

Pasolini also seems passionate about the death of Jesus, especially when he uses his own mother to portray the older Mary and having her lament at the foot of the cross with southern Italian gesticulation and grief. Pasolini then orchestrates some apocalyptic destruction of Jerusalem, with earthquakes and collapsing buildings to announce the death of Jesus.

Intensity

But, mostly, the Passion is felt in the intensity.

Since the text used is that of Matthew's Gospel, the screenplay is spare, direct, unvarnished. It has a great deal of teaching compared with the episodes of miracles, encounters, or parables in the other Gospels. The language, especially that of Jesus, is solely the Gospel text. While this is Pasolini's personal and personalized interpretation of Jesus, it shows Jesus as a man of authority, clear teaching, and unflinching idealism, but in many ways detached from the people around him.

Perhaps this is also due to the fact that Pasolini chose an amateur performer to be his Jesus, a Spanish law student, Enrique Irazoqui. His Jesus is intense, serious, sometimes smiling—especially with children or, strangely, when he seems to be besting the authorities in wordplay—but rarely laughing (he laughs with children). His is a strong personality. He has the courage of his convictions and communicates these convictions.

Jesus calls his disciples at the Sea of Galilee, and they immediately follow him. Soon he is striding across the fields, the disciples finding it hard to keep up with him. When some disciples want to go with Jesus, they ask if they can first bury their dead or say goodbye to their fathers. Jesus moves straight ahead, calling back to them, making his injunctions for absolute discipleship sound severe. He tells them that foxes have holes and the birds of the air their nests, but the Son of Man has nowhere to lay his head (Matthew 8:20).

Limitations and Strengths of Being Literal

There are also very literal sequences in the feeding of the five thousand. As with some of the Hollywood epics, Jesus asks his disciples about feeding the crowd. There are five loaves and two fish. Within moments, there are baskets and baskets of food, instant provisions. This scene is followed by Jesus walking on the water, presented in a very matter-of-fact way. Such presentation gives the audience images, but it offers no explanation or keys to explanation or interpretation. There is no biblical background offered that might situate the event within a religious or prophetic context. It is presented as in a succession of events in Jesus' life—he had breakfast, he walked on water, he taught on the mountain. Pasolini provides icon images but provides minimalist help for appreciating who Jesus is.

By way of contrast, Pasolini can hold his camera on faces for what sometimes seems an inordinate amount of time. Toward the end of the film, we see the disciples sleeping and then Jesus, awake and praying. He is photographed in close-up, the actor's face immobile, contemplating. We contemplate the face and draw our meanings from it (or read into it our own conceptions of Jesus at prayer). This shot lasts for thirty-nine seconds. Ten seconds is usually a long time in terms of focus and concentration on one image for the audience. But we pause and watch Jesus pray for thirty-nine seconds.

Then the film becomes brisk again. Jesus is hungry. He goes to a fig tree and takes a pole to poke through the leaves for figs. He does not find any. And, as fast as we have seen loaves and fish multiply, the fig tree withers.

The sequences tend to be brief and no time is wasted. Or, if it seems to be wasted, it is because Pasolini is once again filming his faces in close-up, making sure the audience has plenty of time to study the expressions. We are to understand Jesus in relation to the faces we contemplate.

The story of the rich young man is a case in point. Jesus has been denouncing Capernaum for its infidelity. The young man descends with a haughty air to where Jesus is standing in an open space. He leads donkeys carrying his wealth. The young man asks what he should do. Jesus urges him to keep the commandments and lists them when the young man asks which ones. Jesus looks at him and invites him to sell everything and follow him. The young man instantly looks downcast and turns to leave. Jesus goes on to say how hard it is for the rich to enter the kingdom of heaven.

Emotional and Intellectual

There are very few parables recounted in Pasolini's film. Rather, Jesus teaches more directly than indirectly by story (an exception being the polemical parable of the vinedressers killing the heir to the vineyard). Jesus declaims a great deal, uttering truth for people to hear or not hear, accept or not accept. Pasolini chooses open locations—hills, town piazzas, open fields—for Jesus' proclamations. And he uses many long shots of crowds listening or groups in tableaux.

On one occasion Jesus himself proclaims passages from Isaiah (about the Servant and his mission in chapter 42) as he walks through windswept fields. Pasolini's reading of Matthew's Jesus is that Jesus is demanding, is absolute, and requires unflinching discipleship.

One exception, and a significant one, from this literal dramatizing of the Gospel is in the Resurrection narratives. The women are at the center of the visit to the tomb and the search for Jesus, most particularly Mary Magdalene. Mary Magdalene is central in the four Gospels.

Pasolini, on the other hand, moves away from his austerely emotional and intellectual treatment of Jesus by choosing to place Mary, the mother of Jesus, as a focal witness to the Resurrection. It is she who is center screen, who receives the message of the angel, who is the first witness to the risen Lord. Whether it is because Pasolini used his mother in the role and wanted to feature her or whether he succumbed to the long Italian tradition of devotion to the Madonna, he seems to have indulged this devotion at the very end of his film.

Postscript: La Ricotta

One of the most effective satiric Christ-figures appears in Pasolini's short episode in *Rogopag*, made just before *The Gospel according to St. Matthew*. Called *La Ricotta* (*The Cream Cheese*), it was a satire in the filming of a biblical spectacular on a Roman hillside. The scene was the Crucifixion. The actors who posed for the typical baroque Pietà tableau could not have cared less about religion or Christ as they fooled about waiting for filming. They had even less regard for Christ's counterparts, the needy poor of Rome around them. The hungry poor man who plays the good thief eventually steals a poodle belonging to an actress, sells it, and with the money buys bread and a cream cheese with which he stuffs himself.

The scene is to be filmed in view of Roman celebrities and the press. The good thief rehearses his lines, "Lord, remember me when you come into your kingdom" and the answer of Jesus, "This day you will be with me in Paradise." After wolfing his food so greedily, waiting on the cross for the visitors to finish cocktails is too much for Cicco, the hero, and he dies. The director, played by Orson Welles, turns to the camera and remarks, "Poor Cicco, he had to die before we even knew he was alive." This is certainly a biblical message about Jesus and the marginalized.

EL PROCESO DE JESUS

El proceso de Jesus is a 1966 Mexican film (from a country that had produced several Jesus films in the 1940s and '50s) that opens with the call of Peter and Andrew and then moves to three decades after the death of Jesus. Peter, Barabbas, and others are on their way to Rome. The guard, Marcus, stops at a farm of his former commander, Pontius Pilate. In the basement, Peter recalls in flashback the Crucifixion of Jesus and his own denials. Pilate, with his wife, Claudia, then asks Peter whether Jesus was innocent or guilty. Further flashbacks show scenes of the life of Jesus, Cana, the raising of the daughter of Jairus. Claudia contributes to the memories as does Barabbas with his story of Mary Magdalene. Finally, Peter, who missed the last hours of Jesus, asks Pilate to recount his story. This final part of the film has great detail about Jesus' trial, his appearance before Pilate, going to Herod, the way of the cross, and the Crucifixion. (A fuller synopsis can be found in the Wikipedia account of the film.)

LE LIT DE LA VIERGE

While the title focuses on Mary, the mother of Jesus, this is a stylized Jesus film by French director Philippe Garrel, with Pierre Clementi as Jesus. The provocative aspect of the film is that the same actress (Zouzou) portrays both the mother of Jesus and Mary Magdalene. A Godard scholar writing on Godard and Garrel notes about the director and his film in this period,

> In the 1960s, Garrel was not alone in invoking Christ to combat the repressive forces of a police state. There was a renewed interest in Christ in Western culture, even while . . . the traditional customs were losing their hold. Inspired by representations of Christ with long hair, Christ was taken as a modern-day hippie rebelling against authority and the older generation. In this movie, Garrel was in synch with and on the vanguard of his peers. Within the Garrel circle, his identification with Christ was echoed by his actor, "When I met Philippe, . . . I told him: Let's do a film about the return of Christ." He made *The Virgin's Bed*, which is definitely a film about death. If Jesus returned today, he would be helpless before our world.[1]

This helplessness can be seen on the several clips available on You-Tube: his mother washing Jesus before his going on ministry, Jesus riding a donkey, pursued and mocked, and finally dragged from the donkey.

SON OF MAN

The best Jesus-figure to emerge from this freedom to portray Jesus on-screen and to show the humanity as well as the divinity of Jesus appeared on British television in the late 1960s. The writer was Dennis Potter, whose range of plays and writing for television and films included the allegory of the devil incarnate in suburban London, *Brimstone and Treacle*, and *The Singing Detective*. Potter's television play was later staged in the theater, and there was discussion at the end of the 1990s about a possible screen version.

The play was called *Son of Man*. Colin Blakely portrayed Jesus. The sequence that symbolized the alarm that more fundamentalist viewers experienced but that students of the New Testament and of theology appreciated was the Agony in the Garden. Potter puts into the mouth of Jesus a desperate questioning of God's will followed by his acceptance of it. This is what the Gospels tell us of the agony, which continues on the cross when Jesus experiences being abandoned by God and the writers put the opening words of Psalm 22 on his lips, "My God, my God, why have you forsaken me?" Potter's words were (spoken by Blakely in increasing speed and desperation), "Is it me? Is it me? Is it me?" Literalists accused Potter of blasphemy, of denying that Jesus was God and knew that he was divine. The response was that this was a psychological expression of fear and desperation, one that any person who knows their destiny can still express as bewilderment as to how and why they are at this step in their destiny. Twenty years later, this same kind of dramatizing of Jesus' agony was seen in *The Last Temptation of Christ*.

NOTE

1. Sally Shafto, "Artist as Christ/Artist as God the Father: Religion in the Cinema of Philippe Garrel and Jean-Luc Godard," *Film History* 14, no. 2 (2002): 142–57.

8

THE JESUS FILMS:
THE 1970s

Just over ten years after the straightforward presentation of Jesus on-screen in *King of Kings*, the 1970s produced not just one musical of Jesus and his Gospel message, but two.

JESUS CHRIST SUPERSTAR

Jesus Christ Superstar became one of the most talked about phenomena of the 1970s. The LP record was a great success on its release in 1970. The film version followed in 1973. The stage version was a popular extravaganza, a box-office success. The film seems to be one of the best ways of communicating the rock opera visually. One of the surprising facts about *Superstar* seen in retrospect is finding out that Andrew Lloyd Webber and Tim Rice were only in their early twenties when they composed *Superstar*.

The music became very popular over the years and merited discussion in its own right. The lyrics have led to religious controversy. The work was intended only as an interpretation of the last seven days of Jesus' life, not a biography, nor a Gospel; however, many religious commentators found fault with the whole concept of the work. They considered that there was such an emphasis on the humanity of Jesus that it did not give enough attention to his divinity. To many who were thinking theologically rather than artistically, the fact that the rock opera finished with the burial of Jesus and said nothing of his Resurrection rendered the work unsatisfactory as a representation of Jesus (a criticism leveled at Mel Gibson's *The Passion of the Christ* with its brief Resurrection sequence). These discussions were modified a little by the film's seeming attempt to take criticism into account and cater for the widest possible audiences.

At the end of *Superstar*, when the cast, back in their ordinary clothes, get into the bus to leave, Ted Neeley (who played Jesus) does not appear. As the musical score comes to its end and the camera focuses on the sun, at the base of the screen a lone figure moves in silhouette and is followed by sheep. The Good Shepherd is now alive again.

As a visual experience the film is excellent, offering us a performance of the rock opera on location in the grandeur and sometimes desolate beauty of the Judean desert. This means the emphasis is on the film as a performance rather than a "naturalistic" telling of the Gospel story. The musical style is that of the 1960s. Many of the lyrics are contemporary and the cast, as they arrive by bus, are dressed in the most casual of styles—sunglasses and long hair, remnants in the aftermath of the hippie period. They unload their props, which include scaffolding and guns. The locations are used most effectively as backing for songs and dances. The choreography utilizes the scenery for atmosphere and effect.

Judas

One of the original comments on *Superstar* was that it gave great (undue?) prominence to the character of Judas. This is certainly true of the film. There was a racial tension factor at the time because Judas, villain, was played by an African American. Judas looks at the group of actors in costume, clapping and dancing, while Jesus walks past and raises his arms like a statue for the title to come on-screen. Judas then tells us that his mind is clearer now and he wants to strip away the myth from the man, that Jesus now believes that all that is being said of him is true.

For much of *Jesus Christ Superstar*, we are looking at Jesus from Judas' point of view. Judas acts as a devil's advocate. We don't agree with it, but it is a continual challenge. This means that the rock opera in both style and content is working as a provocative interpretation of Jesus as both human and divine.

Judas recalls the beginnings of Jesus' ministry, "no talk of God then, we called you a man" and that Jesus was better as a carpenter. Now, there is "too much heaven on their minds." Everything for Judas is "much too loud"; he says, "It's all gone sour."

This contrasts with the crowds around Jesus and the frenetic, "What's the buzz? Tell me, what's a happenin'?" But Judas continues to criticize Jesus' friendship with Mary Magdalene and her ministering to him, saying that he should not befriend "a woman of her kind" and that she does not fit in with Jesus' teaching. He also complains about the fickle disciples. "They think they've found the new messiah—but they'll hurt you if they think you've lied."

Jesus

This is the background before Jesus comes center screen. The crowd is buzzing. Jesus sees they are fickle. A tall and burly Caiaphas asserts his authority with his chief priests, black robed and wearing high, somewhat mitered headgear and climbing outdoor scaffolding. The council refer to "blockheads in the streets" and chant in chorus, "He is dangerous." This leads into the Superstar motif and the crowd responding with "Hosanna." Later Pilate will be introduced, singing of a dream of a most peculiar man who is killed and hearing people laying the blame on him.

Mary Magdalene is the reassuring figure: "Try not to turn on to things that upset you. . . . Everything's all right, everything's fine." She offers imagery of soothing ointment and myrrh and relief: "Close your eyes and relax, think of nothing, forget all your troubles tonight."

With Simon the Zealot in a frenzy, Jesus replies in lamentation, part wistful, part resigned, "No one knows what power is, no one knows what glory is. No one understands at all." This is combined with the plaintive song of lament over Jerusalem itself. The image of Jesus is of a calm man feeling a sense of torment within, small in stature but ultimately commanding. His conclusion for his listeners is that "to conquer death you only have to die."

Jesus has appealed to Judas to understand, holding his chin, clasping his hand. But Judas is one who does not understand at all. When Jesus goes into the Temple, finds it a market (with some contemporary imagery of guns and money changing ownership), and then bursts into action, clearing out the buyers and sellers with a rock-opera scream, "Go!" "Get out," Judas looks on in puzzlement.

In anticipation of the Agony in the Garden musical themes, Jesus walks along, being accosted by lepers, and amid the crowd there's a growing excitement that leads to a frenzied clamoring for healing and a reaching out to touch Jesus for power to come out of him to them. Jesus is desperate: "There are too many of you. Don't push me. There's too little of me. Leave me alone." With the melody of the agony, this is another facet of the agony of Jesus—how to fulfill his Father's will and the demands that the crowds make on him.

The Music

While the incisive lyrics of Tim Rice can be repeated and their dramatic potential appreciated, it is difficult to convey the cumulative effect of the musical score and what it contributes to the sense and the emotion of

Jesus' experience. Rock beats followed by ballad rhythms, screams followed by restrained and low-key melodies mean that the character of Jesus, the traits of his personality, and the challenge of his moral dilemmas and decisions are not so much matters to be understood by the audience's mind; instead, the music draws us to identify with its moods and its power, so that the audience is drawn into an appreciation of who Jesus is and what his mission means. The music evokes sympathy that is meant to lead to empathy.

Mary Magdalene and Judas

As Jesus is almost ready for his final days, the focus returns to Mary Magdalene and to Judas. Perhaps the song that has a life of its own outside of *Superstar* is "I Don't Know How to Love Him." Within *Superstar* it has an enormous influence on how the audience thinks and feels about Jesus. As Mary recounts how Jesus attracts her, frightens her, bewilders her because of the love she feels for him, it is the same for the audience. While "he's just a man," the audience realizes what a man he is in terms of his deep humanity and his human uncertainties and the challenge that God is offering him.

Judas goes in the opposite direction from Mary. Pursued by tanks, evoking the way the Gospel story breaks time boundaries, Judas, in his disillusionment with Jesus and his inability to persuade him to change, sings that he is "damned for all time." As he offers to betray Jesus, he rationalizes that Jesus would not mind that he was there with the priests. Further rationalizations include "I don't need your blood money" and his motivations about money given to the poor. This is "a fee, nothing more."

Judas does not have as clear a vision as Caiaphas: "I see blood and destruction because of one man"—the consequence, "elimination."

Last Supper and Agony

Norman Jewison's staging of the Last Supper outside moves entirely away from da Vinci conceptions so prevalent in Jesus films. There is some edge of ambiguity in the lyrics as well as a sardonic comment on the apostles' vision of their vocation. While the apostles sing in a somewhat slurred style ("what was in the bread, it's gone right to my head"), they praise themselves that they always knew that they would be apostles, then retire to write the Gospels "so they'll still talk about us when we've died." Jesus, in the meantime, is already anticipating his Gethsemane experience: "For all you care, this wine could be my blood, this bread could be my body." In some films, Judas eats the bread; in others, he does not. Here he does. And this is the prologue to an emotional altercation between Jesus and

Judas, with Judas asking, "What if I remained and ruined your ambition?" and then challenging, "You want me to do it." Finally, Jesus utters another scream, "Get out." And Judas goes, flees.

The staging of the Agony in the Garden begins familiarly enough with Jesus alone and the apostles sleeping. However, for five minutes, Ted Neeley's performance comes into its own. Jesus sings as he climbs a mountain. He goes over the demands God is making of him, his weariness over the three years of preaching, healing, and toiling: "I only want to know." The pace quickens, the climb is more rapid. Jesus is more demanding, and at the top, we hear his most desperate and loud rock-opera scream: "Why should I die?" God is "far too good on how and when but not so hot on why."

After the outburst (and Jewison editing in a collage of classical art images of Jesus and the paschal lamb), the tone is restrained, quiet, resigned, and accepting of his fate with a deep commitment. Finally, "God, thy will is hard. You hold every card. Let me drink your cup of poison." But, it must come soon, "before I change my mind."

The apostles wake and drowsily sing, "What's the buzz? Tell me, what's a happenin'?" and Judas and the cohorts arrive and Judas betrays Jesus with a kiss.

The Passion

The actual Passion sequences are familiar enough, similar to other Jesus films. Episodes include the taunts at the house of Annas and Peter's denials. With Pilate and Herod as two of the main protagonists in the condemnation, each is given a signature song, Pilate's being a bitter monologue, questioning who Jesus is and why he has to condemn "someone Christ, King of the Jews." Herod, on the other hand, makes a mockery of Jesus, who refused even to speak to him. That is the cue for one of those lighthearted interludes to make audiences a little more relaxed before they are taken into the heart of the tragedy. Fatty Herod, with his tinted glasses and his effete courtiers and his invitation to Jesus to walk across his swimming pool, is always a showstopper. Then Jesus returns to the harsh reality.

In the meantime, Peter and Mary Magdalene sing a rueful ballad about discipleship, fidelity, and betrayal. It is the prayer of sinners and the prayer of repentance and hope: "Could we start again, please?"

Judas' Despair

Once again the focus turns to Judas. He reprises "Damned for All Time." Some of his lyrics now have a combination of self-pity and self-excuse: "I would have saved you if I could. . . . I have been saddled with the murder of you." He sings that he has been spattered with innocent blood and dragged through the slime and the mud. And, with a sad irony, he also sings, "I don't know how to love him. . . . I'll never know why you chose me. You have murdered me." And the chorus quietly chants, "Poor old Judas."

Flogging and Condemnation

As the camera tracks from Judas, it returns to Pilate's court, the crowd calling, "Crucify him. . . . We need him crucified"—an interesting lyric in view of subsequent discussions about blame and anti-Semitism. The rock rhythms start again and are maintained through the counting of the thirty-nine lashes that scourge Jesus. Pilate's sardonic lyric has him refer to Jesus as a misguided martyr. He washes his hands of Jesus and there is blood in the water.

Apotheosis

This is the moment of apotheosis. While *Superstar* has traditional images of Jesus going to Calvary and being nailed to the cross (sound effects of nails and of mocking laughter, the piano and the last words), the showbiz pizzazz takes over—and some might suggest to theologians that the lyrics and melody of the "Jesus Christ Superstar" song are a celebration of his Resurrection. Judas also experiences a resurrection and leads the singing and dancing. But he still taunts Jesus that had he been born later, he could have reached the whole nation. And the famous line, "Palestine in 4 BC had no mass communication." However, Jesus dying in *Superstar* is also triumphant.

This was all quite incongruous in the early 1970s, Broadway meets Calvary, so to speak. But, as time has gone on and audiences understand the conventions of the rock opera, they take this finale for granted. Jesus' death is not the end.

However, the film does end quietly, a tableau of Calvary and the crosses and people moving away. The cast quietly get back into the bus. Ted Neeley is not there—and we glimpse the shepherd and his sheep moving across the sun at the bottom of the screen.

JESUS CHRIST SUPERSTAR (2000)

While chronologically it belongs to the end of the twentieth century, the 2000 version is better discussed here. Authorized by Andrew Lloyd Webber and his Really Useful Company, it is the version that Lloyd Webber himself says he wanted to see. (The DVD edition has a long "The Making of *Jesus Christ Superstar*" section, with many interviews including Rice and Lloyd Webber.) Produced on the London stage and then on Broadway, this is a filmed version by director Gale Edwards.

Most of the comments on the 1973 film version are relevant here. The lyrics are basically the same as is, of course, the music. The differences are in the staging, the performances, and the interpretation of the lyrics. While Norman Jewison's version remains visually anchored in the 1970s period (flared trousers), the 2000 version appeals to contemporary audiences, but with its street gang costumes, it is also of its period.

Instead of the Judean desert, we have big sets on the Pinewood Studios stages. The action is confined to the sets and the camerawork is less stylized with flourishes of flair. There is a reliance on close-ups, which gives many of the interactions great intensity. This is particularly true of the Last Supper sequence, which is filmed inside (with overtones of the da Vinci table and positioning) and leads to quite a frenzied confrontation between Jesus and Judas that provokes a great deal of thought and emotion. It may not correspond to the Gospel narrative but it is a very interesting re-creation of a growing passionate fight between the two. Gale Edwards capitalizes on this by filming the *Jesus Christ Superstar* apotheosis with Jesus bent to the ground, carrying his cross to Calvary, looking in pained disbelief at Judas, who is far more aggressive and taunting than in the 1973 version. For these two sequences alone, the new version is worth considering.

The emphasis on Judas is even stronger than before. Rice says that he pondered what it would be like to see the events of Jesus' last week through Judas' eyes. Because of the use of close-ups, there is a pervading sense of Judas being present all the time. He is very often center screen. But he is also seen sometimes as sitting back, watching with growing disbelief and distaste how the crowds flock to Jesus and Jesus accepts it. While Glenn Carter (as Jesus) is a bigger man than Ted Neeley, his swept blond hair still reminds us of a surfie no matter how serious he is. (Glenn Carter is English; Jerome Pradon, as Judas, is French; Cavin Cornwall, as Peter, is black.)

The interaction between Jesus, Judas, and Mary Magdalene is like an emotional triangle, with Judas, especially, jealous of Mary and her friendship with Jesus. Mary even pointedly sings a verse of "I Don't Know How to Love Him" directed at Judas.

The setting has something of the overtones of the revolution as before. Slogans and graffiti of social unrest and pleas for peace are seen on the walls. Caiaphas, Annas, and the chief priests have their discussions around a large table in a boardroom. It has television monitors—so that, as they sing "He

Is Dangerous," Jesus appears on the monitors and the crowds sing, "Hosanna, hey J.C. won't you smile at me." The monitors are used as props for the *Jesus Christ Superstar* finale (where the devilish dancers and Judas are in red leather, the ensemble looking more like an imitation cabaret bar rather than Broadway; the military clothing has been designed to remind audiences of Darth Vader and his cohorts as well as *The Matrix*).

Audiences of both versions have compared the quality of voice, articulation, and performance of the two films, finding Rik Mayall's Herod a touch more sinister and subdued, Pilate's fascist uniform a surprise, Annas more whining, and Caiaphas even more basso than in 1973. The 2000 Mary Magdalene, Simon, and Peter compare favorably with their predecessors.

Norman Jewison's staging of the Agony in the Garden with Ted Neeley climbing a cliff was one of the most telling sequences in the film. Gale Edwards, by contrast, has Jesus inside, spotlighted and not moving from the one spot. It is a complete contrast, relying generally on a camera angle, from God's point of view, so to speak, and Jesus looking up as he sings in anguish.

Whether it be the 1970s, the 1990s, or the beginning of the twenty-first century, *Jesus Christ Superstar* is still a striking theatrical interpretation of the meaning of the Passion of Jesus.

GODSPELL

After a prologue with words about God as Lord and Creator, we see panoramas of New York City, and *Godspell*, written by and with songs by Stephen Schwartz, opens a performance of a cinema play of the Gospels and the story of Jesus.

Contemporary Disciples

New York City. A group of ordinary people are going about their daily work but are feeling frustrated: office workers, diner waiters, taxi drivers, ballet students, auditioning actresses, librarian at a photocopier. They all hear a sound of music that seems to reach only them. They follow the call, especially when a strange character appears to tempt them away from their day-to-day lives.

They all gather, go to a market where they change into odd clothes that have a carnival style. As they walk and dance to one of the city fountains, they sing, "Prepare ye, the way of the Lord." Another young man arrives, dressed like a gentle clown, and goes through a baptism ritual in the fountain. The "disciples" leap into the symbolic water and frolic. The stranger who calls them is a John the Baptist figure. The baptized young man is the Jesus-figure. John has preached about a baptism of fire and the spirit. The whole group sings, "God save the people."

The troupe then sing, dance, and joke their way through the Gospel stories, the baptized young man taking the role of Jesus, the others going from role to role and performing as a chorus. They tell parables, listen to the beatitudes, and re-enact miracles.

In a junkyard, they pick up props and paint their faces while Jesus speaks of not abolishing the law, saying that every command must be fulfilled. The style is vaudevillian, with car horns and honks, trumpet blasts, and drum sounds, leading to a mime of the parable of the Pharisee and the publican including some Afro-American-style preaching. With the message of reconciliation and loving your brother and sister (this was the era of hugging), the next mime is that of the unjust steward, a combination of chant, drama, and mime.

Mime is very important for the performance of *Godspell*. There is a slapping contest between John and Jesus leading to turning the other cheek and embracing, then a separation of sheep and goats. The parable of the Good Samaritan is narrated but the actors let their fingers do the walking and the talking for the characters. There is a later pantomime-style fight to illustrate "love your enemies."

Parables and Songs

Some of the parables are more elaborately staged. The troupe goes into an old theater. Onstage the parable of the prodigal son is told with burlesque hoopla, while on-screen it is illustrated in the style of a silent era Western film. At Lincoln Center, there is quite a show for the parable of the sower as each lot of seed is represented in a different flower bed and the characters mime what happens to the seed. Jesus' verbal explanation follows. For the story of the rich man and Lazarus, they take over locations to indicate hell and heaven with Abraham.

But *Godspell* is a musical. After "God Save the People," the group sings what became a very popular song, even hymn: "Three things I pray, to see thee more clearly, love thee more dearly, follow thee more nearly, day by day." During this they pack up their cart, clean up, tend plants, and paint their house. The tone changes when the Mary Magdalene character, with acknowledgments to Mae West, sings, "Turn back, O man, forswear thy foolish ways." This leads to a praise song, "O Bless the Lord, My Soul." It is performed onstage with the women as chorus girls.

In the outdoor theater, we hear the beatitudes. Each member of the cast has the opportunity to speak out a parable. It is the Baptist who says that they are blessed when people revile and persecute them—ominous for Jesus and his coming Passion.

But this sharing of parables leads to the most elaborately staged of the songs: "When you feel sad—it's all for the best." It begins as a soft-shoe shuffle with the Baptist and Jesus, moves into some patter lyrics, and after a panorama of the New York skyline, it moves to Jesus having a baton and providing John with one as they do a tap dance routine in Times Square.

After the parable of the sower, there are some moments of more quiet reflective time and the song is, "All good things around us . . . thank the Lord for all his love." Jesus refers to the lilies of the field. Then the energy starts up again with Jesus' words from the Sermon on the Mount about the law and the prophets, and the song breaks out with the words of Matthew 5: "You are the light of the world." Then, a change of scene, as they are all on a boat, working on the river.

It is almost time for the Passion. A strange monster, breathing fire and smoke and with a kind of wizard of Oz voice and overtone, raises the question of Jesus' authority and the Pharisees' dilemma about whether John's preaching was from God or merely human. The episode about the coin and rendering to Caesar and God follows, as well as the discussion about which is the greatest commandment. When the monster is exposed like the wizard of Oz, Jesus begins that fearsome attack on hypocrisy from Matthew 23: "Woe to you, scribes and Pharisees . . ."

Passion and Resurrection

Jesus quietly weeps over Jerusalem, sitting on the pier. The group is quiet and they sing the plaintive, "Where are you going? Can you take me there? By my side . . ." The actor portraying John the precursor now assumes the role of Judas the betrayer. As they now go back to the junkyard, they sing, "Build the city of man." Judas gets a loose door and places it on the ground so that it serves as the table for the Last Supper. They all look in the mirror and are daubed with red. Jesus speaks the blessing in Hebrew over the bread and over the wine and then lets Judas go: "The words are yours."

"On the Willows," a lament, is sung before the agony of Jesus. He says his heart is ready to break with grief. He asks the group to stay awake. They protest their support. He tells them that they will betray him three times. As with other Jesus films (such as the Jeremy Sisto *Jesus*), the three temptations appear here, though the Gospel places them at the beginning of Jesus' ministry. Judas and the police cars arrive. Jesus embraces him and clasps his hand.

The Passion sequences are comparatively brief. Jesus attests that he taught in the synagogues but was never arrested. However, Jesus is tied to the wire fencing in the junkyard, which serves as background for the Crucifixion with fluttering red ribbons as his blood. The Passion and death of Jesus is rendered in lament song, with Jesus singing and the group responding as chorus,

> O God, I'm bleeding.
> O God, I'm dying.
> O God, you're dead.

Jesus is alone on the cross with the lights and with the wind blowing.

The Resurrection is portrayed symbolically. Birds chirp. The sun rises. The group wakes up and takes Jesus' body down. As they carry it ritually through the city streets, they sing "Long Live God" which transforms into "Prepare Ye the Way of the Lord." They carry him further through the city and the crowds and finish by singing "Day by Day."

Godspell took the English-speaking world by storm in the early 1970s. It was performed everywhere, not only in theaters, but, later, in schools. It was part of the reaction to the "God Is Dead" movement in the United States during the mid-1960s. The questioning of the place of God in the world led, amongst other spiritual quests, to charismatic renewal and to a Jesus movement. At the same time, audiences were also flocking to theaters to see *Jesus Christ Superstar*. The film versions of *Jesus Christ Superstar* and *Godspell* both appeared in 1973.

While the film version of *Superstar* was well reviewed and received, *Godspell* was compared unfavorably with the theater experience. The film could not compete with the immediacy of the theater experience. As so much time has passed, *Godspell* is worth a look for its inventiveness in interpreting the Gospels, drawing on so many aspects of the American musical tradition as well as vaudeville (and its contemporary musical, *Hair*). The style is very much of its period, but it can be now viewed as historical rather than dated.

By setting the musical in New York City with workers abandoning their jobs as Jesus' disciples did and following a Gospel road, *Godspell* situates its Jesus-figure in a contemporary world. Jesus is not alien to modern problems in a modern world.

JESUS CHRISTUS ERLOSER

Although the film version of Klaus Kinski's one-man performance of *Jesus Christus Erloser* (*Jesus Christ Savior*) was not released until 2008, it belongs in content and style to the 1970s. The stock footage was edited by Kinski's biographer, Peter Geyer, and premiered at the Berlin film festival in February 2008.

On November 20, 1971, in Berlin's Deutschehalle, German actor Klaus Kinski (who was soon to appear Werner Herzog's *Aguirre, the Wrath of God* and later in Herzog's *Nosferatu* and *Fitzcarraldo*) presented his thirty-page verbal portrait of Jesus. The performance turned out to be disastrous with heckling and interjections, criticism of Kinski as a person and as a rich film star talking about poverty. There were gibes about his career in crime films and, finally, that he was a fascist. People shouted that they wanted their money back (ten marks). Kinski had a ferocious temper and hit back at the audience, inviting critics onstage. To one man who had said that Jesus was patient, Kinski shouted that Jesus also took up a whip to beat people and that is what he (Kinski) would do. Later in the night, another man came to the microphone and quietly denounced Kinski, saying that by their fruits you shall know them. Kinski started his act again but walked offstage a second time. He waited. The management asked those who had come merely to complain or protest to leave. Eventually, at about 2:00 a.m. an exhausted Kinski did his performance for the hundred or so people who remained.

Kinski is said to have worked on this project for a decade. He began it in the 1960s when there were very few Jesus films. His portrait is closest to that of Pier Paolo Pasolini's in *Il Vangelo secondo Matteo*. By the time Kinski performed in Berlin, the Jesus movement had led to *Jesus Christ Superstar* (Kinski proclaims that he does not see Jesus as a superstar) and *Godspell*.

It seems generally agreed that Kinski portrayed odd, even mad and obsessed characters on-screen, and that he was something like this in real life. For this performance he is dressed oddly in a flamboyant shirt with colored sleeves and purple pants. He had a frighteningly intense face, always serious. He had a powerful voice, and when he increased his intensity and volume, his rhetoric sounded not unlike Hitler's.

Kinski opens his description of Jesus as *Besugte*, "Wanted." He emphasises Jesus' revolutionary bent, his social consciousness, even his anarchic behavior and teaching. He gives a verbal outline, referencing distinguishing features as "scars on his hands and feet." He names different titles including Son of Man, Messenger of Peace, Light of the World. Nationality: none. He states that Jesus may have been parentless, that his mother may have been a whore, and that his father may have been a convict living in a commune. Jesus was a worker and wore no uniform. He welcomed everyone for company: prostitutes, junkies, bums, people on death row, and (a category he names several times) Vietnamese mothers. Kinski says Jesus was not a Negro, not a Communist, not of the Christian party, not a Protestant, not a Catholic, not present at party conventions, not a church Jesus. The church is people.

While Kinski speaks of love, his emphasis in fact is on Jesus and truth (much like Pasolini). He quotes Old Testament prophets about the blind seeing, the deaf hearing. Listening to and watching Kinski, one does think of Old Testament prophets. Were Amos to have preached Jesus' message, he may well have looked and sounded like Kinski. He keeps up the attack on the status quo, listing people who claim "Jesus is here." This includes the pope who, he says, asks Jesus about following him into eternity. Jesus responds with, "Shut up and follow me." He exhorts soldiers to throw away their uniforms. Kinski speaks to his audience, saying that anyone who has information about Jesus and his sedition should go to the police.

As regards the Gospel texts that Kinski bases his piece on, they are generally from Matthew's Gospel. He quotes the Sermon on the Mount especially concerning prayer and fasting, about giving away clothes, about not serving God and money (with some gibes at the Vatican and its treasures and palaces full of priests). He also refers to the story of the rich young man and the text about not worrying what you are to eat or wear. Needless to say, he draws on Matthew 23 with its "Woe to you . . ." warnings.

Kinski uses only one parable and it is from Luke. He speaks a variation on the parable of the man who built bigger barns but who was called by God before he could enjoy his wealth. Kinski has the man investing in many offshore banks (his equivalent of the barns).

Kinski alludes to only two of Jesus' encounters with individuals. The first is Jesus' forgiveness of the woman who was a prostitute in the city (Luke 7) and, of course, the woman taken in adultery (John 8). Throughout the performance, Kinski refers to his hecklers as "big mouths," and here Jesus suggests that the big mouths cast the first stone. He stays with John toward the end and makes reference to Jesus' sayings during the last discourse, especially about eternal life.

Peter Geyer introduces the end credits, but it is not the end of the film. He then shows the last part of the evening where Kinski describes the Passion. The camera focuses more on the reactions of the audience than on Kinski himself. Kinski's voice is subdued, even reverent. Previously, he had referred to Jesus not exploiting his body on crosses everywhere. Now, he describes Jesus' suffering and death, Jesus commending his spirit to the Father with questions about the meaning of his death yet affirming his readiness and that he has been dying for two thousand years.

While the performance comes from the 1960s and 1970s with particular references to wars and changes of the period, *Jesus Christ Erloser* can still strike many chords today.

PROCESSO A GESU/THE TRIAL OF JESUS

Celebrated Italian Catholic playwright Diego Fabbri (whose theater work includes a play, *The Inquisition,* and whose film-writing work includes a film on the Second Vatican Council and the story for Krzysztof Zanussi's 1981 film on John Paul II, *From a Far Country*) wrote *Processo a Gesu* (*The Trial of Jesus*), which was first performed in 1955. It was filmed for Italian television in 1968, directed by Gianfranco Bettettini, and a feature film was made in Spain in 1973, directed by Jose Luis Saenz de Heredia. While the title focuses on Jesus, the play is really a trial of the human race in the light of Jesus' message.

The translator of the play into English, Emanuel L. Paparella, comments,

> And what is this play all about? It is really a modern trial, an *in absentia* trial of Jesus and to a certain extent of the ancient Jewish people by modern Jews. Paradoxically, as the trial progresses, we come to realize that it is in reality the trial of a decadent technological rationalistic civilization against itself; that is to say, the trial of a civilization that has lost the ability to hope in the future and to conceive salvation and redemption of any kind, a civilization, stuck in the horizontal (the immanent) and devoid of the vertical (the transcendent) and unable to conceive the two together as "both-and," often given to apocalyptic scenarios of its own future destiny. The play had that powerful effect on me personally as I translated it.
>
> Behind this bleak assessment by Fabbri of the modern social phenomenon, there is Charles Péguy, an author who influenced Fabbri more than any other, and who had written that "Christianity is a life lived together so that we may save ourselves together." After reading the play one realizes that indeed while Pirandello is Fabbri's artistic inspiration, Charles Péguy is Fabbri's spiritual inspiration for the conception of an authentic Christian society: a society that finds its "raison d'etre" in communion and solidarity and is thus alone able to free Man from that deep solitude of spirit described by Vico as "the barbarism of the intellect" and afflicting post-modern Man in the third rationalistic cycle of Vico's ideal *eternal history.*[1]

THE MESSIAH

Unfortunately, Roberto Rossellini's 1975 portrait of Jesus, *The Messiah,* has not been widely seen. Rossellini emerged at the end of World War II as the great protagonist of Italian neorealism with *Paisan* and *Rome, Open*

City. During the 1950s, he made several brief but telling dramas with his then wife, Ingrid Bergman. However, from the 1960s, he devoted a lot of his attention to the screen studies of famous historical personages, especially philosophers and theologians, including *Socrates* (1971), *Blaise Pascal* (1972), *St. Augustine* (1972), and *Descartes* (1975). He also showed great interest in religious themes, already making his celebrated film about St. Francis of Assisi, *Francesco, giullare di Dio*, in 1950 and his austere *Joan of Arc at the Stake* in 1954. In 1959, he directed a television miniseries, *The Acts of the Apostles*. This is the artistic lineage of his *The Messiah*.

It runs for almost two and a half hours. It is not a biblical spectacular, which is not surprising given Rossellini's style. The cast are not well known and it is not full of crowd scenes. Rather, the screenplay stays close to the Gospel texts, relishing the power of words, but also of silences.

The significance of the title *The Messiah* becomes clear in a prologue of twenty minutes or more where Rossellini offers his audience an introduction to the Old Testament that includes the background of Moses and the Exodus, the fidelity and infidelity of the people to the covenant. There follows the settlement in Canaan and the establishing of the monarchy. An unexpectedly long section is devoted to the prophet Samuel, and in a conversation between Samuel and Yahweh, the nature and significance of the kingdom and its kingship is discussed—with visuals of the wars against the Philistines and the oppressive behavior of some of the kings. This is the heritage of the descendants of David and of the Messiah.

More time is given, before the appearance of Jesus, to the history of Herod the Great (more than the attention given to the Gospels' infancy narratives, although Herod's dealings with the Magi, a tableau of mother and child, and the slaughter of the innocents are there with indications of the flight into Egypt. The Roman response to the reign of Herod prepares the way for the power of Roman rule in Jesus' time. The question arises, what is the dramatic impact of so little time spent on the actual birth of Jesus?

While there are homely touches with scenes of Jesus as a boy in Nazareth, the pilgrimage to Jerusalem is featured, giving another opportunity for social and religious background to Jesus, this time the Jewish religious traditions in the Temple and the official sacrifices.

Mary comes more to the fore at this time, the human search for Jesus. But she appears throughout the film with some human touches, giving Jesus his cloak, rushing to the synagogue when Jesus preached, being at the Sea of Galilee, appearing in the various episodes of his public life, and being called by John at the time of his trial. At the end she hurries to the cross where she comforts Mary Magdalene. She shows peaceful resignation after Jesus has been taken from the cross (a brief Pietà scene). She is seen again at the tomb, her eyes raised to the sky to indicate Resurrection.

There are some surprises in Rossellini's treatment compared with other Gospel films. There is no appearance of the miraculous though there is talk about Jesus' miracles, an indication of the feeding of the crowd but no actual miracle sequences.

More focus is on John the Baptist and his strength, the vigor of his preaching, people repenting at the Jordan and his performing the baptisms; on Jesus appearing suddenly within this context and going straightaway to be baptized. John's disciples see Jesus and follow. John the Baptist exercises a prophetic function, his defiance of Herodias and his imprisonment in squalor where Herod visits him seems to lead to their growing friendship. The film includes the famous dance and Herod having John executed in front of the guests.

Popular sequences from Jesus' public life are included: Jesus naming Peter, Philip finding Nathanael, and Nathanael's encounter with Jesus; the buildup of disciples, fishers of men, going out fishing at his command; Jesus' arrival in Nazareth, reading the text, alienating the people of Nazareth, and their rejecting him; the many sequences on the road with his disciples, the personal touch in his relationship with them, his smiles and kindness to the children, the visit to the meal with the Pharisee and the woman who was the sinner in the city, the call of Matthew, and the reaction of the scribes and Pharisees. Jesus is shown as skilled in carpentry and doing his work, a blending of the ordinary, his sense of mission, his religious leadership, and his message.

For Rossellini, Jesus' words and message are important: the telling of parables such as the Good Samaritan, the weeds in the field, the wineskins. Jesus also prays and teaches the Lord's Prayer as they all kneel and pray. Jesus is seen thinking along the road and then speaking the Gospel phrases. The film offers a composite picture of Jesus' Gospel preaching.

The other principal feature is the hostility toward Jesus, the presence of the scribes and Pharisees, their rigid religious attitudes, the letter of the law. The Sanhedrin meets and plans, and Caiaphas makes his famous statement about one man dying for the nation. Contact is made with Judas but much is left to the audience's imagination.

Once Rossellini comes to Jesus, we see Jesus' initial joy at the procession with palms but the film soon moves to the preparation for the Last Supper, the arranging of the room, checking that all is well. Jesus speaks of Judas' betrayal and sends him out. For the Eucharist sequence and its sense of reverence, the camera follows the bread and the wine around to each of the apostles. Rossellini keeps Jesus' washing of the apostles' feet and its meaning, as well as his prayers after the supper. There is only a brief indication of Jesus' fear in his agony. The trial and Passion sequences show the familiar details: Jesus' face being slapped, the arraignment of the witnesses, John's explanation of what was happening. There is some buildup to the arrival of Pilate and his long descent from the battlements, then his interview and his puzzlement over Jesus, the reaction of the scribes and Pharisees, the freeing of Barabbas, the scourging, and shouts for crucifixion.

There follows a device of showing children singing and then the raising of the camera to show Jesus carrying his cross. The death scene is only brief: Mary and Mary Magdalene watching the undramatic but telling moment of Jesus' death.

In the aftermath, Mary anoints Jesus and preparations are made for his burial, then the tomb is sealed. The treatment of the Resurrection is also very brief: the mourners approach, they find the stone rolled back, and Mary lifts her eyes to the sky—the sky indicating that Jesus still lives.

As with so many of Rossellini's films, *The Messiah* might be described more as a cerebral portrait of Jesus and the meaning of his messiahship rather than an emotional portrait. Jesus is portrayed with feeling, but the director seems determined that his view of the Gospels and the mission of Jesus is one of an intelligent inquirer after truth.

A VIDA DE JESUS CRISTO

This production is a 1971 filmed performance of a Gospel play in the Brazilian city of Sao Roque, Brazil. Most of the members of the cast were nonprofessionals, although Fernanda Montenegro (the letter writer of Walter Salles' *Central Station*) appears in it.

THE GOSPEL ROAD

In 1976, Johnny Cash and his wife, June Carter Cash, produced a Jesus film, *The Gospel Road*. It mixed reverent re-enactment of Gospel episodes with music and some documentary styles. It included scenes of Jerusalem as well as commentary about social issues of the time. Intercut were re-creations of the Gospel story with the film's director, Robert Elfstrom, as Jesus. These sequences were done in the literal style, the baptism of Jesus having a special effects golden dove descending on Jesus.

THE PASSOVER PLOT

Exactly the opposite approach to the Gospels, especially the Crucifixion narratives, was taken in a film version of a popular book of the time by Hugh Schonfield, *The Passover Plot* (1976). In some ways this was a precursor to such books as *Holy Blood and Holy Grail*, which was a precursor of *The Da Vinci Code*. It is not as if the "well-researched" arguments were new. The theory that Jesus was drugged on the cross had circulated from the earliest church times (and was part of the hypothesizing in *The Inquiry* [1986]).

The rationalist arguments against Jesus and his claims and the Gospel stories included this theory that Jesus was drugged and did not actually die or that he died and the disciples stole the body of Jesus and made the Resurrection claims.

This film version (a United States/Israel coproduction) was given lavish treatment. It was directed by Michael Campus (*ZPG* and *The Mack*) and had a strong international cast. An unlikely actor was cast as Yeshua: Zalman King, maker of softcore films and television series (like *Two Moon Junction* and *The Red Shoes Diaries*). British actors Donald Pleasence (Pilate), Harry Andrews (Yohanan the Baptist), and Hugh Griffith (Caiaphas) were joined by Americans Robert Walker Jr. and Scott Wilson.

The context for the release of *The Passover Plot* in terms of other Jesus films was soon after *Jesus Christ Superstar* and *Godspell* and just prior to Zeffirelli's *Jesus of Nazareth*. The very literal Jesus of The *Jesus* Project would be released two years later and find worldwide popularity. At the time, *The Passover Plot* was moving against the tide of interest in Jesus. A twenty-first-century *Da Vinci Code* mentality would probably find it intriguing—and, perhaps, believe it.

JESUS OF NAZARETH

The 1970s produced an outstandingly successful portrait of Jesus, Franco Zeffirelli's *Jesus of Nazareth* (1977). Designed as a television miniseries, it was also re-edited for cinema release. It was filmed in English with an international star cast. The instant popularity of the film, its being dubbed into several languages, especially Spanish, both for Spain and, especially, for Latin America, led to its being screened all over the world and to Robert Powell becoming the best-known Jesus face everywhere.

Congenial and Attractive

Why did audiences respond so well to *Jesus of Nazareth*? Was it Robert Powell, his presence and his fine voice? He was certainly a strong reason for its success. Was it the cast and the attractive re-creation of the Gospel era?

A suggestion for the popularity of *Jesus of Nazareth* is that, overall, the interpretation of Jesus is very congenial. Perhaps it is a dominant presence of episodes from Luke's Gospel, with such sequences as the parable of the prodigal son in the context of Matthew's banquet or the episode of the sinful woman coming to Simon's house. Robert Powell personalizes his interpretation of Jesus. It is almost the opposite of what Pasolini does with his austere Jesus and the opposite of George Stevens' direction of Max von Sydow in being a speaking icon in *The Greatest Story Ever Told*.

Zeffirelli had far more screen time available for *Jesus of Nazareth* than previous Jesus films. It was a television miniseries running for eight hours. When it was later cut for cinema, it ran for two and a quarter hours.

A Gospel Screenplay

Zeffirelli collaborated with veteran Italian screenwriter Suso Cecchi D'Amico, well known and respected for her work with such directors as Luchino Visconti, and with British novelist Anthony Burgess, best known for *A Clockwork Orange*. Together Zeffirelli, D'Amico, and Burgess fashioned a screenplay that incorporated the key incidents of each Gospel but also provided a great amount of historical and social background, rearranging Gospel incidents much as the early Christian communities assembled the Gospels as we now have them. They created characters like the secretary of the Sanhedrin (played by Ian Holm) as a way of dramatizing the Gospel tensions. Even with familiar incidents they added dialogue that gave the events more psychological and dramatic credibility. For instance, with the story of the rich young man who approached Jesus, they have him repeat, hesitatingly and with puzzled intonation, Jesus' invitation to sell everything. And he leaves Jesus, continually glancing back, bemused but unable to stay.

The screenplay and direction, with a blend of "realism" and "naturalism," meant that any audience would not feel that the material was too much "above them." They could identify with the events and with Jesus himself.

In this way, Zeffirelli's Jesus is personalized far more persuasively than Jesus in other films. The audience appreciates Jesus as a human being with feelings and warmth as well as intelligence and strong will. Before Jesus appears at the river Jordan to be baptized by John, the first two-hour episode of the series has passed, offering the setting and the infancy stories. Peter Ustinov as Herod is given dialogue that explains the context of the birth of Jesus, the reign of Augustus, and the census that brings Mary and Joseph to Bethlehem.

The Annunciation to Mary (Olivia Hussey) moves away from a literal interpretation. Mary is in her home at Nazareth. Instead of a human figure of the angel Gabriel entering, she is surrounded by light, suggestive of an experience of God's presence and her consent to the conception of Jesus. Sequences of life at Nazareth are developed, especially in having Jesus grow up as a traditional Jewish boy and celebrate his Bar Mitzvah.

Reshaping the Gospel Events

While Robert Powell is often framed on-screen like an icon and has been directed to gaze at the camera as if seeing through mere surfaces, he is still a powerfully human Jesus. *Jesus of Nazareth* serves as a powerfully feeling interpretation of Jesus, especially in looking at sequences that come from Luke's Gospel.

Zeffirelli, Burgess, and D'Amico follow the example of the Gospel communities in reassembling incidents and teaching for their own purposes. They introduce Judas as listening to Jesus preach on the hillside, drawn to Jesus but wondering. When he does finally approach Jesus, Judas speaks of his credentials, his ability to speak many languages and to translate, his being a manager. All the while, Jesus sits with his eyes closed, contemplating, seeming not to listen. When Judas asks, "Will you have me?" Jesus turns to look at him and quietly says, "By their fruits you will know them" and allows him to become a disciple.

The writers have characters meet, like Jesus and Barabbas. It is to Barabbas also that Jesus will give the teaching that those who live by the sword will perish by it. And on the way to Calvary, Nicodemus, the Pharisee sympathetic to Jesus who came to him under cover of darkness and who will help bury Jesus, speaks the voiceover of the fourth servant song, which sees the fulfillment of Messianic hopes—Jesus led like a lamb to the slaughter, dying for our sins. That the text is spoken by Laurence Olivier, who played Nicodemus, enhances the recitation.

Two Banquets

But the scope of this rearranging of events is even larger. A useful way of focusing on this dramatic technique and its effect of showing Jesus the person is to examine two banquet sequences. The first is that of the call of Matthew and Jesus dining with tax collectors and prostitutes (in episode two); the second is the meal at the house of Simon the Pharisee (in episode three).

The first banquet is a celebration of the call of Matthew. Zeffirelli gives it a setting in Capernaum. Peter is angry. He is on the shore of the Sea of Galilee with Andrew and other apostles. The target of his anger is Matthew, who has been collecting taxes from him, extorting money from them. The fact that Jesus could contemplate going to eat with Matthew and his friends is too much to take. Peter refuses to go.

Others warn Jesus on his way that usurers and whores are forbidden to enter the synagogues. Jesus tells them clearly that he has come not to call the just but sinners. The first glimpse of the party looks like a shot of grotesque and effete characters from a Federico Fellini film. But there is a hush and a change when Jesus enters, and Matthew, deeply moved by Jesus' presence, welcomes him as a rabbi. Jesus is offered a cushion and sits comfortably with the guests.

The masterstroke for Zeffirelli is in showing Jesus respond to a request to speak to the group and having him offer to tell them a story. And it is that of the prodigal son. Jesus sits as he tells the tale with verve (and Powell's beautiful diction and enunciation), but he gets up as he warms to the episode where the father runs to meet his returning son. Jesus mimes an embrace as he speaks of the son kissed by his father. While the parable is being spoken, Peter has come to the door. The camera focuses on him during the story, moves to Matthew, and shows us the guests who were identifying with the son.

At the conclusion, Peter, who has been shown as being quite moved, looks at Jesus and Jesus at Peter. He comes into the room and embraces Jesus. Matthew comes forward. They gaze at each other. Jesus brings them together and they embrace. The parable, though directed in the Gospel of Luke at the scribes and Pharisees, is depicted in the film as being fulfilled when Jesus' own disciples are no longer resentful and unforgiving elder sons. Peter then asks Jesus the question about how often he should forgive; the answer—seventy-seven times (Matthew 18:21–22, Jerusalem Bible translation).

The second banquet is the familiar meal in which Jesus has been invited by Simon the Pharisee to dine with him but, as appears later, has not been offered the ritual courtesies of greeting and washing on his arrival.

The screenplay of *Jesus of Nazareth* prepares the audience thoroughly for this sequence. Soon after the parable of the prodigal son we are introduced to the prostitute figure of the Gospels. She is here identified with

Mary Magdalene. Young men taunt her at her home. A client, as she helps him to dress as he leaves, tells her about Jesus, those he mixes with, his teachings of mercy. He, a merchant, has seen Jesus many times and is impressed by his consistent teaching. Mary is skeptical; men are forgiven, but women are not.

After this Jesus speaks on the mountainside and the people are impressed by his teaching. Among those sitting on the grass listening are several religious leaders, including Joseph of Arimathea. Joseph is impressed, while a companion wonders whether this teaching is too radical. Another suggests that they invite him to dinner to expound his teaching.

The scene of the woman taken in adultery is quite disappointing. Robert Powell looks more as if he is going through the motions and offering quite a conventional and basic interpretation, not nearly as nuanced as in other sequences. For the spirit of a humane Jesus and a Jesus who was in deep communion with the Father, the sequence in which Anne Bancroft is Mary Magdalene (here being identified as the woman who was a sinner in the city of Luke 7:36–50) has far greater depth.

Because James Mason (as Joseph of Arimathea) and Anne Bancroft have powerful screen presence, the sequence when Mary intrudes on the banquet in Simon's house is one of the most powerful in the film.

As Jesus sits and the hosts argue about the excessive freedom of what Jesus teaches compared with the rigidity they feel is necessary for them as a chosen people of God, Jesus looks wearied and disappointed by their righteousness. He buries his head in his hands. He examines a piece of fruit. He warns them not to judge. They proclaim that they understand what he is saying, but will ordinary people?

Jesus stops the conversation and asks Joseph of Arimathea what is the teaching found in the scriptures about the law. Joseph responds with "love of God," and Jesus says he is not far from the kingdom of heaven. But he goes on to stress love of neighbor as well. And Simon exclaims, "But who is my neighbor?" Instead of the parable of the Good Samaritan following, as it does in Luke, there is commotion outside and Mary Magdalene bursts in, weeping, and carrying an alabaster jar of ointment. She weeps, her tears falling on Jesus' feet, and she wipes them with her hair.

Powell acts this sequence full of the wonder and compassion that we might expect of Jesus. He plays it as though he were performing this scene for the first time, without rehearsal. He enables us to see him thinking through this situation and his response to the woman. Simon complains. But Jesus raises a hand to cut him off. He looks at the woman and we realize the forgiveness of God in Jesus. He says, "Your sins—and I know they are many" are forgiven, the reason being that she showed great love. She is to go in peace. This wonderfully embodies the compassion, love, and forgiveness of Jesus.

Jesus of Nazareth is the culmination of the development of the Jesus-figure on-screen, the attempts at realism, the different stylized images. Zeffirelli and his writers and Robert Powell have given us a strongly feeling and emotional Jesus.

JESUS/THE *JESUS* PROJECT

In 1979, a film simply called *Jesus* was released. Directed by English directors Peter Sykes and John Krish, and starring British actor Brian Deacon, it was backed financially by some evangelical religious groups. It pales in comparison with Zeffirelli's version. Once again, it uses Luke's Gospel and some of John's as screenplay, thus often offers the bare bones of the incidents and hurries from one event to another. Jesus is personal and personable but is caught in the narrow framework of the straightforward, often literal, Gospel text.

Even though *Jesus* was made after *Jesus of Nazareth*, it harks back to the style of the earlier films like *King of Kings*. It also uses a narrator to move events along, especially since the film has a relatively brief running time.

Brian Deacon's performance is less stiff than that of Jeffrey Hunter. Deacon's Jesus is more human and more humane. It is easier to identify with him in his human nature, simply Jesus as the title indicates rather than the divinely human King of Kings. This change within the twenty years or less between the films indicates how, during the 1960s and '70s, the spirituality of mainstream churches had moved closer to a more personalized relationship with Jesus in his humanity.

Literal Use of the Gospel Texts

The film also uses the Gospel texts (especially Luke and John) as screenplay. The immediate advantage of this is that the words are familiar as well as the events, and so audiences can respond quickly and appreciate what is happening. It's the Gospels come to life. However, it should be said that there is a danger of an over-literal reading of the text. And there is also the danger of a fundamentalist reading of the Gospels.

This is especially true of the sequence of the temptations in the desert. The devil is visualized literally as a snake, slithering and hissing through the rocks, in his encounter with Jesus. However, when the battle of the scripture texts between the devil and Jesus is heard, the devil's voice is one of the plummiest-toned, most beautifully enunciated English voices you could hear. Jesus is usually seen and heard as a middle-class Englishman, but the devil has moved to upper class!

A way of seeing the literal and immediate appeal of this film is to take a ten-minute segment of the film and list how many events are shown in such a short space of time. Commercial television screenings of the film highlighted this. For example, in one segment between commercials, Jesus goes out into the desert and experiences the temptations of the devil, including being shown a vision of the kingdoms of the world and being taken to the top of the Temple to look at Jerusalem; he goes to Nazareth, meeting people in the marketplace, praying in the synagogue, reading from the text of Isaiah, declaring how it is fulfilled in him, being criticized in Nazareth, and walking away from the people as they wanted to throw him over the hill; he goes to Capernaum, where the crowds at the shore hear his preaching of the parable of the Pharisee and the publican; he puts out to sea with Peter, where they experience the miraculous draft of fish and then their being pulled to land; Peter declares his unworthiness and hears Jesus' call—and then it was time for another set of commercials!

Small Details Rather Than Drama

The conception of this film is particularly direct with its plain presentation of text, images, and action. Where it is enhanced, especially for the viewers who want images of the Gospels, is in a number of small visually effective details: before Jesus is tempted to turn stone into bread, he stumbles over a rock, picks up a stone, and examines it before tossing it away; in Nazareth, he greets a small child who smiles up delightfully at Jesus and they exchange "hellos" (the only non-Gospel words in this whole segment); Jesus wears his prayer shawl in the synagogue and puts it over his head as he unrolls the scroll; the boat in which Jesus is sitting and preaching rocks with the waves.

Where it is less successful is in the drama. The danger with the rapidity of the action is that it is not dramatically credible. This is especially true of the sequence in the synagogue where Jesus' critics stand and attack him almost before he has finished saying that the prophecy is being fulfilled. He is instantly hustled to the brow of the hill and almost as instantly, he calmly walks away.

A Project in Process

The film was financed by evangelical church groups and the plain and direct portrayal of Jesus is congenial to this ethos.

The film was re-released in the later 1990s as if it were a new film. It found an appreciative audience. With the evangelical zeal behind the production, it has been dubbed into many languages throughout the world, over a dozen in India alone. It is interesting to know that the Vatican distributed copies of *Jesus*, in many different languages, to all the pilgrims visiting Rome in 2000 for the year of Jubilee—although the scene of the temptations was edited out, at least in the English-language version (but it is present in the commercial DVD release).

It is sometimes referred to as The *Jesus* Project. In fact, it is still a work in progress. In the early years of the first decade of the twenty-first century, it was edited to forty-two minutes and a twenty-minute segment was added that showed life in Palestine at the time of Jesus through children's eyes. It was distributed as *The Story of Jesus for Children*.

In 2007, some sequences were edited into *Jesus*, showing him and his actions from a woman's point of view. Produced in English, it was translated into Arabic for women's audiences in the Middle East (screened in Nazareth, March 14, 2007). This version is Jesus witnessed by Mary Magdalene. (This film also serves as a counterbalance to the picture of Mary Magdalene from *The Da Vinci Code*.)

The project was financed by Campus Crusade for Christ International. For more information and seeing the evangelical dimensions of the crusade, especially using the film, see the Life Agape website, also Come and See: The Christian Website from Nazareth.

JESUS, EL NIÑO DIOS; JESUS, MARIA Y JOSÉ; JESUS, NUESTRO SEÑOR

Director Miguel Zacarias made three features on Jesus, especially his early and unknown life, in 1969–1972. They were made in Mexico in a Hispanic style. The adult Jesus was played by prominent Hispanic actor Claudio Brook, who had appeared in several of Luis Bunuel's films, especially his religious-oriented films of the 1960s: *Viridiana, The Exterminating Angel, Simon of the Desert*, and *The Milky Way*, associating the actor with religious themes and critique of religion and the church.

The films were re-edited in 1986 with the title of *La vida de nuestro Señor, Jesucristo*. Commentators note that the television channel Univision has a custom of showing the 1986 version or a succession of the first films, especially at Christmas and Easter.

Jesus, el niño Dios

Unlike *Jesus, nuestro señor* and *Jesus, Maria y José*, *Jesus, el niño Dios* is not available on YouTube. The other two are there in their entirety, Spanish version with no English subtitles.

Jesus, el niño Dios is the story of Jesus' birth and his early years in Egypt. A still shows Mary with the infant Jesus, who is working a miracle. This kind of storytelling takes us into the realm of the apocryphal Gospels of the early Christian centuries where imagination took over from the authentic Gospels and supplied generally nice stories about Jesus and his hidden life. They tended to make Jesus a wonder worker from an early age, some of the stories being "cute," others showing Jesus with a touch of the vengeful—striking bullying boys blind. While the appearance is definitely very human, Jesus the child, the emphasis is on divinity through the miracles.

Jesus, Maria y José

Jesus, Maria y José takes up the story of Jesus childhood in Egypt. One point to make about this film is that while the focus is clearly on Jesus, Mary plays a rather subsidiary role while Joseph receives far more attention than he does in the Gospels. To that extent, the film is interesting in its imagining of the relationship between Jesus and Joseph, who appears (as the scriptures and later prayers suggest) as a "wise and just man." He is also quite middle-aged and grey.

The film opens in the deserts of Egypt with Jesus playing with a boat—and crying when some boys steal it. A kind Egyptian, Amroth, befriends Jesus. This playful (and crying) Jesus is then seen finding a stray and scraggy dog, petting it, and, one for the apocryphal Gospels, blessing a bowl of water for the dog, causing it to turn into milk as Jesus lifts his eyes to heaven.

Joseph meanwhile is working as a carpenter and is brought the design of a cross. He and Mary discuss it but Joseph decides not to build crosses. It is at this stage that the angel appears (rather kitschy with very feathery wings and hands crossed). The holy family leave Egypt with soldiers in pursuit but they turn back. There are also soldiers in Nazareth when they get back, Nazareth looking rather like a Mexican village.

Life in Nazareth is quite domestic. Joseph makes a hoop for Jesus and the dog. Jesus is training the dog to walk on its hind legs and then jump through the hoop. These are unforeseen aspects of the Incarnation. However, Jesus also has to learn good manners. The local teacher, Caiaphas, is irritated with Jesus interrupting, calling him insolent, and instructs Jesus always to put his hand up when he wants to ask a question, a lesson Jesus learns well as he is forever putting his hand up throughout the film, prompting a weary response from Caiaphas. Jesus excels, of course, in the synagogue (with its Star of David) and questions Caiaphas as to why God's chosen people should be subject to Rome. He explains to the nonplussed Caiaphas that, despite Jewish reticence, there are many names of God in other languages (and quotes the Latin, Deus), and is then dragged by the ears through the town to Joseph and expelled from the synagogue. Joseph is amazed that Jesus can quote the scriptures in Hebrew.

The screenplay makes some assumptions about Jesus and the people he met as a child. Joseph does carpentering work on boats and so Jesus witnesses Peter and Andrew in dispute with a local woman about payment for fish. He cheats more than a little by making Peter's fish weigh more on the scales than they do! Jesus lifts his eyes to heaven then draws a fish in the sand. Judas also makes a brief appearance.

At home, Jesus does carpentry work and has lessons in reading the scroll of Isaiah.

His cousin, John, the future Baptist, then comes for a visit (with the dog immediately growling). The boys become friends and wander the town eating melon, an opportunity for the film to show details of life in Jesus' Nazareth: the forge, the glassblowers, the potters. They see the boys of the town who play games with fights. This is not for Jesus, who has some clay birds that the others want and chase Jesus and John with stones. John tries to sell the clay birds, but the other boys break some and steal the others. Jesus lifts his eyes to heaven, and the birds come to life and fly off.

After some other incidents in Nazareth—Jesus helping a woman with water, the master of scripture giving Jesus a scroll—it is time for the pilgrimage to Jerusalem. Jerusalem is a crowded city, and the Temple is filled with buyers and sellers and animals for sacrifice. Jesus quotes the scriptures, and his family is mocked by the Judeans because of their Galilean accent. Jesus attacks them verbally for insulting Joseph, "an old man, my father." He also frees the bird that Joseph had bought for sacrifice.

But it is the intellectual discussions in the Temple that attract Jesus. He stays behind to listen to the talk about the Torah. He questions the scholars and eventually finishes on the podium, gesticulating like a teacher, discussing the nature of prudence and other virtues. Though Joseph, Mary, and John have discovered that Jesus is missing, have searched for him in Jerusalem, and have found him in the Temple, Joseph and Mary are not so upset but rather are proud of Jesus and his abilities. Interestingly, Mary in her concern has entered into the male area of the Temple.

Back home, Joseph and Mary realize that they cannot teach Jesus anything more, and so he is to go off with John to learn more. Jesus is sad and cries. Sad also is the death of the dog, which he and John bury. When it is time to leave, the accompanying scholar tells them to take no luggage. Joseph says that his greatest task has been caring for Jesus. Mary is sad. As Jesus goes with John, he takes only a cross, reflects on it, sits astride a donkey, and, once again, lifts his eyes to heaven.

Jesus, María y José is popular biblical storytelling, mixing Gospel with imagination and a piety that wants to capture the sentiment of a human childhood with the awe of the divine coming from Jesus in word, gesture, and some homely miracles. It is a mixture of sophistication and simplicity.

Jesus, nuestro señor

Miguel Zacarias then made his film about the adult Jesus, *Jesus nuestro señor*, with Claudio Brook.

Brook is a tall Jesus, dark with something of a severe though lived-in face, but sometimes able to break into a smile. His gestures are those solemn hand and arm movements that are captured in statues of Jesus, especially those of the Sacred Heart. His way of speaking and preaching is often of the stating, declaiming style, not unlike Max von Sydow in *The Greatest Story Ever Told*, which had been released only a few years earlier.

The film opens with a brief recapitulation of the previous two films: the edict for the census, the journey to Bethlehem for Mary and Joseph, the inn, the Magi, some texts quoted from Matthew with references, the coming out of Egypt. The film then moves to thirty years later.

The Baptist is in the desert, preaching and baptizing by the Jordan. He is also being criticized for his preaching. When Jesus arrives (dressed familiarly like the statues), John recognizes and acknowledges him but Jesus asks to be baptized and water is poured over his head on the bank of the river. Once again, there are quotations from the Gospels. A dove appears and flies to the top of an overlooking cliff. Jesus is seen praying on high rather like the statue in Rio de Janeiro.

Attention shifts to the Baptist's confrontation with Herod. His court is brightly colored. John confronts Herod, and Herodias makes a long speech of denunciation. Salome is there. Later, she will perform her dance, rather suggestively in costume, flesh, and choreography, at some length. One difference here is that when the head is brought in on the dish and laid on the floor, Herod gazes at John, whose head swivels and the open eyes stare at Herod.

In the meantime, Jesus has gone out into the desert for the forty days. He is in the dark and silhouetted against the sky when Satan appears through a sandstorm, seen from the back and wearing a Dracula-like cape and collar. They exchange the texts from the Gospels as Jesus rebuts Satan. On his return, Jesus speaks with his mother, using the parable of the vindictive workers in the vineyard who attack and kill the owner's son to explain his mission. This is followed by a very detailed calling of each of the twelve apostles by name, the four fishermen at their nets, Philip a builder with his friend Nathanael, and Matthew collecting the taxes. Judas is seen after the episode of Jesus reading in the synagogue and then healing a man possessed.

The main part of this portrait of Jesus is a series of episodes. At Cana, all is bright and colorful, everyone clapping hands to the music and dancing, and Jesus is very agreeable, changing the water into wine. Jesus seems to walk past a blind man without noticing. He then responds to the man's call, touches him, lifts him up, and responds to the charges that he heals on the Sabbath (with the argument that his opponents would rescue a donkey on the Sabbath).

As might be expected, Mary Magdalene gets a great deal of attention. She is blonde, dressed in blue, and goes to meet Jesus. They talk and he ousts the demons from her, naming the seven deadly sins. After he raises the son of the widow of Nain from the dead, Jesus dines with the Pharisee and the Magdalene anoints him (with the insertion of Judas' criticism about the waste of money from the story of Mary of Bethany anointing Jesus).

Jesus cures the paralytic, encounters disciples who want to follow him, and reminds them that foxes have holes but the Son of Man has nowhere to lay his head. As with most of the Jesus films, the feeding of the five thousand seems to be photogenic, and the multiplication of the loaves is quite extensive. Jesus preaches during this multiplication. The apostles have some of the leftovers when they are in the boat on the lake and see Jesus walking on the water. They are afraid but the lake seems sufficiently calm and still. Jesus follows this with preaching the beatitudes. Lazarus is raised from the dead.

With the advent of Jesus' last week, we see Caiaphas (backed by the seven-branch candlestick rather than a Star of David) alarmed about Jesus. His fear is heightened by the procession of palms into Jerusalem and Jesus immediately getting the whip (which he wields vigorously then thrusts away) and cleansing the Temple of buyers and sellers.

Some miracles and preaching are inserted at this late stage: the raising of the dead son (from John 4), the raising of Jairus' daughter, some preaching from the Sermon on the Mount, the confrontation with the authorities about payment to Caesar, followed by the case of the woman caught in adultery. Cecil B. DeMille, in *The King of Kings*, had Jesus write the sins of the accusers in the sand; this time Jesus confronts them face-to-face and tells them their sin. He then welcomes children and, rather strangely, tells them the parable of the prodigal son and also denounces the Pharisees (from Matthew 23). Jesus is made to be very busy just before his death.

The Last Supper (da Vinci again) includes the new commandment of love, the discussion about the washing of the feet, and Judas going to betray Jesus. The bread and wine sequence is very solemn, and Jesus is seen to distribute communion, the bread with the wine by intinction.

The Passion sequences are rather familiar: Gethsemane, Peter's denial, the court of the high priest (rather small), Pilate and the discussion about kingship, Pilate's wife warning him about Jesus, and a rather longer visit to Herod, who wants him to do some changing of wine and water.

Jesus is mocked by the soldiers, then crowned with thorns and scourged. Barabbas is freed and Pilate washes his hands. As with the other Spanish films, the cross is very large and Simon is unwilling to help and finds it very heavy. Jesus speaks to the women of Jerusalem on the way to Calvary, and Veronica wipes Jesus' face. Blood drops appear, then a special effects full face of the suffering Jesus.

The tableau at the foot of the cross is the usual one, Mary and John and the Magdalene, though the Magdalene stands almost embracing the cross. The soldiers play dice, but Judas hears the nailing. He prays, then hangs himself, the camera having Judas in the forefront and Jesus on Calvary in the background. The old blind man whom Jesus had given sight to is also on Calvary and asks why this is happening to Jesus when he could work such miracles.

It is dark and when Jesus dies, thunder and lightning appear. The film uses the text from Matthew where graves were opened and the dead wander the streets.

There is a Resurrection sequence bypass. The happy apostles (except for Thomas) rejoice at the news that Jesus is risen and that the world is saved. Thomas expresses his doubts and Jesus appears. He promises to be with them—and gives Peter the opportunity to affirm his love for Jesus after the denials. Jesus also promises him that he is the rock on which the church is built, a particularly Catholic touch. As Jesus ascends (too literally), the apostles watch and devoutly recite the Lord's Prayer.

Jesus, nuestro señor was made in the early 1970s. Mexico did have a tradition of films showing Jesus even when the English-speaking world did not. This film seems to be a mixture of that Mexican tradition with the appearance of Hollywood interpretations of the Gospels in the previous decade, *King of Kings* and *The Greatest Story Ever Told*. *Jesus, nuestro señor* illustrates a Hispanic piety, a literal reading of the Gospels but using the imagination to make the episodes dramatic.

PROCESO A JESUS

A Spanish film of 1973 in which a group of Sephardic Jews want to re-enact the trial of Jesus to determine the whether there was enough evidence to condemn him to death.

TELEMOVIES

The late 1970s saw two telemovies with Mary, the mother of Jesus, as their subject: *The Nativity* (1978) with Madeleine Stowe and John Shea, which received good reviews and *Mary and Joseph* (1979) with Blanche Baker and Jeff East, which did not. However, teenage audiences, even in the 1990s, responded better to *Mary and Joseph* than to other New Testament films precisely because of the soap opera treatment and the portrayal of Mary and Joseph kissing and behaving more like recognizable teenagers, part of their experience.

Robert Foxworth and Anthony Hopkins were in *Peter and Paul* (1981), a telemovie that has Paul visit Peter after his conversion, with Peter spending time with Paul and vividly explaining to Paul his experience of Jesus, a powerful verbal portrait. This is well worth listening to (as are the renditions of extracts from Paul's epistles spoken by Anthony Hopkins).

An Italian production, *San Pietro*, appeared in 2005 with Omar Sharif as Peter.

The most ambitious was a Jesus film based on a popular book by Jim Bishop, *The Day Christ Died*, focusing on Jesus' Passion and the meaning of his ministry. It had several religious advisers and consultants, including an expert on Christian-Jewish studies, Eugene Fisher, and the head of the National Catholic Office for Motion Pictures, Jesuit Father Patrick O'Sullivan. Some thought that the film did not put enough emphasis on the divinity of Jesus—a touch strange since one of the cowriters was James Lee Barrett, who so emphasized the divinity of Jesus in his screenplay for *The Greatest Story Ever Told*. Chris Sarandon received poor reviews for his portrayal of Jesus.

Sunn Classics in the United States was turning many American classics into telemovies and making a number of documentaries. Their Gospel documentary was *In Search of the Historical Jesus* (1980), which discussed the historicity of Jesus, while John Rubinstein was Jesus in some dramatizing of Gospel scenes.

LIFE OF BRIAN

For some audiences interested in Jesus-figures on-screen, the 1970s did not end peacefully. The Monty Python group released *Life of Brian* (1979), a parody of biblical epics and a whole range of issues from unionism to feminism.

The Monty Python group satirize the biblical and the Roman epic film and take hilarious shots at terrorists, unionists and committees, and feminists. They also send up jingoistic Christians and the mindless following of Christ.

However, Brian's life echoes that of Jesus in many episodes and incidents (and doubtless some may be offended), but Jesus is respected and the film is not blasphemous (as some have feared). One's taste for Python comedy will determine how hilarious the film will be. The satire serves to remind us how over-seriousness leads to eccentric pomposity—personal, social, political, and religious.

Where *Life of Brian* intersects with the life of Jesus (as envisioned by the biblical spectaculars) begins with the representation of the visit of the Magi. The three kings are directed to Brian's mother, Terry Jones as a harridan mother, who vents her cranky mood on them. They make a rapid exit only to see the genuine stable and crib up the street and quickly make their way there. This is a parody of the opening sequences of *Ben-Hur*.

Later, crowds go to listen to the Sermon on the Mount. This time the parody is on the equivalent sequence in the 1961 *King of Kings*, a vast plain and mountain where the milling throng could not possibly hear anything Jesus had to say. Eric Idle starts to chatter on a neighboring mountaintop and is shushed. People start to ask what Jesus actually said. Someone mistakes "Blessed are the meek" for "Blessed are the Greeks." The Python joke concerns the peacemakers. The listeners hear "Blessed are the cheesemakers." An aristocrat snobbishly informs them that this proclamation is not to be taken literally but is meant to refer to industry in general.

There are other episodes during Jesus' life, though he is offscreen. Michael Palin leaps around as a leper who has been unwillingly and unwittingly healed and has lost his begging livelihood. The humor about Jesus is oblique but targets divisions in Christianity when people pursue claiming that he is the Messiah. This gives rise to the well-known quotation from the film. Brian's mother insists that he is not the Messiah; "He's just a naughty boy."

Some of Brian's followers get possession of his shoe. Others get his gourd. This leads to factional rivalry—all in the name of following the Messiah.

This kind of parody is what the Pythons do so well. There is a send-up of stonings of sinners, especially with the exclusion of women, so that the women have to don beards, deny that they are women, and try to shout with deepened voices. There are parodies of the Zealot groups in Judea, especially in their willingness to sacrifice Brian to their cause.

Which leads to the most controversial part of *Life of Brian*: the Crucifixion scene. This section raises an interesting question as to what kind of sense of humor Jesus has, what kind of sense of humor God has. An automatic response is that God would be proper, even prim, suggesting irreverence in the film. Yet, we need to look at the range of Old Testament stories, the Hebrew sense of humor, from puns, to bargaining with God (Abraham did), to cantankerous prophets like Jonah sulking because God did not destroy Nineveh as he threatened and the people repented when Jonah preached.

Eric Idle jokes with the distributor of the crosses, a very precise and genial public servant played by Michael Palin. He suggests he has received freedom, but then tells the truth that his fate is crucifixion. Brian has been arrested and is being crucified along with many other victims (including the aristocrat from the Sermon on the Mount). While we immediately think of the Crucifixion of Jesus, the narrative moves away from the parallel to the Gospels and concentrates on the farcical aspects of the revolutionaries who are mouthing platitudes and then abandon him. The suicide squad arrive—and kill themselves. In line with the parody and the satirical intent of the film, Eric Idle leads the singing of the now renowned, "Always Look on the Bright Side of Life."

In the documentary *Jesus Christ Movie Star*, there is an excerpt from a 1979 British television debate about the film and the accusations of blasphemy. Malcolm Muggeridge and Anglican Bishop Mervyn Stockwood are critical of *Life of Brian*. John Cleese defends it. Malcolm Muggeridge sees the film as a direct mockery of the Crucifixion. John Cleese does not. Muggeridge also states the film is ephemeral and will soon be forgotten. This did not happen.

Response to the humor of *Life of Brian* depends very much on the viewers' senses of humor and cultural sensibilities. Many Americans did not find it funny at all. On the other hand, audiences who were brought up on British irony and understatement, Australians for instance, enjoyed it thoroughly.

By offering an alternate Messiah and following the Gospel outline— with the real Jesus somewhere up the street—the Pythons' ironic humor was useful in clarifying what the Gospel epic could do and where its limitations were. As one director of a religious film office replied when asked what he thought of *Life of Brian*, "I laughed unashamedly."

One might have thought that with the productions of the 1960s and 1970s, the transition from suggestions of Jesus to full-character portrayals, and the introduction of quite stylized Jesus-figures and a controversy over possible screen blasphemy, that there was nowhere to go. And until the late 1980s, that seemed to be the case, except for some television interest in the New Testament.

OTHER TITLES

- By the late 1960s, smaller films and television programs (like the British *Son of Man*) began to show Gospel sequences or introduced the figure of Jesus into contemporary moral stories. This was a period when Moral Rearmament, for instance, produced religious, ethical films. (*The Crowning Gift*, 1967, about a soldier remembering war sacrifice with Michael C. Gwynne, was a fifty-minute feature produced by Religious Films and distributed by the Rank Organization, its founder J. Arthur Rank having a religious background.) This was to continue during the 1970s.
- With *The Devils* (1971), Ken Russell led the way in presenting religious motifs and themes, and even the person of Jesus, in ways that were, at the least, unusual, and for many, weird and bordering on blasphemous.
- One of the earliest filmmakers to take advantage of this change of attitude by filmmakers and by some of the public was John Waters (better known later as the director of *Hairspray* and *Cry Baby*). His 1970 *Multiple Maniacs* used a cast he would use regularly in these years for shock (and/or challenge) reasons. A comment on the religious themes of *Multiple Maniacs* highlights this.

  The key to understanding this, John Waters' most profound film, is a understanding of its Roman Catholic content and allusions. Divine's long interior monolog inside the church, essentially a long meditation on being different, the Way of the Cross, and the crucifixion scene are all keys to the film's message. Notice that the actors who play the Way of the Cross and crucifixion scenes are the same ones who played in the Carnival of Perversions which opens the movie. And who plays Christ? The heroin addict. Now Waters doesn't use these actors again just to save on budget. The meaning is clear: those people that you smug, suburban do-gooders rejected and made fun of are Christ and his followers. Remember that Christ didn't hang out with sanctimonious, middle class people, but rather with whores, fallen women, the sick, the rejected, the stigmatized, the sinners. Waters draws the parallels very clearly, but most people view the film in such a middle-class way that they can't see Divine and Waters' troupe of hippie- weirdos as allegorical Christ figures. The real giveaway to this interpretation is the actual text of St. Francis's late medieval Way of the Cross which Waters quotes verbatim in the film. And of course, did you ever think about the literal meaning of "divine." Poor, abused Divine's symbolic sacrifice at the claws of Lobstora is yet another variation of the Passion theme. A very literary film indeed.[2]

NOTES

1. Emanuel L. Paparella, "Diego Fabbri's The Trial of Western Civilisation," *Ovi*, April 20, 2009, www.ovimagazine.com/art/.

2. wlb@gol.com, "A Very Spiritual Film," *Reviews & Ratings for "Multiple Maniacs"* (blog), Internet Movie Database, April 7, 2002, www.imdb.com/title/tt0067454/reviews.

9

THE JESUS FILMS:
THE 1980s

In the 1960s, Italy had provided a breakthrough presentation of Jesus on-screen with *The Gospel according to St. Matthew*. The 1970s were strong with the works of Roberto Rossellini and Franco Zeffirelli. With *Jesus of Nazareth* and *Jesus* (The *Jesus* Project), screen portrayals of Jesus seem to have reached a peak. What would be left for the 1980s? Martin Scorsese had tried to make *The Last Temptation of Christ* in the early 1980s but succeeded only in 1988. A breakthrough came from Canada with *Jesus of Montreal*. In the meantime, Italy produced a Jesus film with a difference: Jesus did not appear; rather, he was talked about. It was Damiano Damiani's 1986 *L'inchiesta* (*The Inquiry*), filmed in English with two American and one English leads.

THE FOURTH WISE MAN

In 1985, Father Bud Kaiser, the Paulist producer of the religious *Insight* programs on television (240 episodes from 1960 to the 1980s) and later producer of *Romero* and the Dorothy Day film *Entertaining Angels*, made a telemovie about one of the wise men (Martin Sheen) who never got to Bethlehem—*The Fourth Wise Man*. Based on a story by Henry Van Dyke, *The Other Wise Man*, it had been made for television in both 1957 and 1960. This version was written by Tom Fontana, who had much televi-sion experience, especially with *Homicide: Life on the Streets*. He also wrote the film *Judas* for Paulist Productions. Director Michael Ray Rhodes also worked for Paulist Productions and made *Entertaining Angels*. Martin Sheen portrayed the earnest young Magus, Artaban, and Alan Arkin was his continually complaining servant, Orontes. Veteran Hollywood actors (and Sheen's sons Ramon and Charlie) filled out the cast.

The film is a Jesus film. He is the goal of the Magi's journey. His message is put forward. He is glimpsed with Mary and Joseph going into Egypt as Artaban and Orontes arrive in Bethlehem unaware that the king they seek has just passed them. Later, Jesus appears, at a distance, for the way of the cross and the Crucifixion. His words from the cross are heard, but more importantly for the story, he appears to Artaban. The voice of Jesus is provided by James Farentino.

Artaban is presented as a Christ-figure. Already on the way to Bethlehem, he stops to aid an injured stranger (echoes of the Good Samaritan). He shields a young mother in Bethlehem, saving her child by giving one of the jewels that he had in his possession after selling everything he owned to seek the Lord (and one of the jewels is a pearl of great price). Artaban and Orontes spend years in Egypt searching for the king. Orontes even sets up a man to claim that his four-year-old son is the child they are looking for—but the father is not too good at remembering the details of the gifts they received from the Magi. Waylaid by villagers who are thieves and prostitutes, Artaban helps a sick girl and tries to heal a blind boy but does not. A day with the villagers turns into a week, months, thirty years. The unwilling Orontes writes letters to Artaban's Magus father, commenting on what life has been like and the decisions of his son.

Artaban also stays to help the villagers become self-sufficient; irrigate, grow, and harvest crops; and even start again when jealous neighbors set the crops alight.

When the blind boy visits Jerusalem, he encounters the crowd hailing Jesus with palms. He learns what Jesus does and he himself is healed (offscreen). He takes the news to Artaban. Even Orontes, when he hears that Jesus is to be executed, goes to the village to tell Artaban. Together they try to enter the praetorium but are refused—only to hear the sound of the scourging and the mocking soldier talking about Jesus' "coronation." Artaban collapses. He still presses on, following Jesus carrying his cross, glimpsing him at a distance. But, even then, Artaban cannot reach Calvary. The daughter of a merchant Magus, who has visited Artaban in the village to tell him of his father's death, is now bankrupt because of the destruction of his ships. The Magus is killed and his daughter taken for sale to repay the debts. Artaban buys her freedom with his pearl. He hears Jesus' words of abandonment and then his committing himself to God in death.

Artaban is dying, a sense of failure in his mission. At this moment, Jesus himself appears (seen only from the back as in *Ben-Hur*). He reveals himself to Artaban who is sad that he has no more gifts to offer Jesus. The screenplay has Jesus speak the words of Matthew 25 about feeding Jesus, clothing him, and visiting him in prison. Artaban is astonished and declares that this did not happen. Jesus tells him that this is his gift, himself, because when he did this for others, he did it to Jesus himself. Artaban joyfully repeats this for Orontes—and dies happy. And Orontes goes back to the village to continue to help.

L'INCHIESTA

Director Damiano Damiani, whose directing career reached from 1947 to 2002, is best known for thrillers. His eclectic films include *La Noia*, a version of Alberto Moravia's novel *The Tempter*, with Glenda Jackson, and *Amityville II: The Possession*. He was not an obvious choice for *The Inquiry*. Vittorio Bonicelli had collaborated on the screenplay for *The Bible: In the Beginning* and the miniseries *Moses the Lawgiver*. He adapted a story by veteran Italian screenwriter Suso Cecchi D'Amico, who collaborated with Luchino Visconti on many of his films and wrote Zeffirelli's *Brother Sun, Sister Moon*.

The premise of *The Inquiry* is that Tiberius is disturbed by what he hears about Jesus of Nazareth and his message and sends Taurus (Keith Carradine) as his special envoy to hold a special inquiry about the death of Jesus and to find his body. Pontius Pilate (Harvey Keitel) is suspicious and anxious about his position. He has become more and more estranged from his wife Claudia Procula (Phyllis Logan), who herself had been disturbed in dreams at the time of Jesus' condemnation.

Taurus is self-confident, objective, and thorough. He is a true and loyal Roman, a rational man—"Resurrection is not contemplated by Roman law." He interviews a number of witnesses: the woman who touched the hem of Jesus' cloak; a man who had been told the story of the Emmaus walk by one of the disciples; and someone who knew Cleopas, who takes Taurus to the Last Supper room and informs him of Judas' betrayal. Cleopas also takes Taurus to visit to Gethsemane, where Taurus puzzles over the proposition that God had pre-ordained the betrayal of Jesus and his suffering. Taurus also visits Nazareth, trying to find Jesus and sees Jesus' mother, despised by her neighbors, working in her garden.

A false corpse is brought to dispel the Resurrection claim, but it is denounced by Mary Magdalene. Taurus examines the body, interviews the centurion Longinus, and sees that the broken legs and the pierced side were recent wounds to the corpse. A soldier testifies that Jesus' legs were not broken because he was already dead. Pilate and the military have failed in this attempt to disprove the Resurrection. Taurus questions him about fraud. Pilate is concerned with what is politically viable.

One of the important features of *The Inquiry* is that the screenplay raises many of the age-old objections to the Resurrection. It presents the plausibility of alternate theories. But it also presents the plausibility that the disciples of Jesus had witnessed something extraordinary, that Jesus had risen, and they were telling the truth.

When Taurus visits the tomb of Jesus with Claudia Procula, the story of the sleeping soldiers is told, with the officer saying that they should have been sacked for such dereliction of duty. The theory that the disciples stole the body is also put forward. When Taurus hears that Jesus was seen in both Jerusalem and Emmaus and knows the distance between the two places, he wonders about a twin or a double.

When Zealots attack Taurus, his servant Marcus steps in and is stabbed to death. Taurus attends the crucifixion of one of them—which gives the audience the opportunity to appreciate what happened to Jesus. Taurus watches, waits hours, and finally blocks his ears to the cries of the crucified man. The Crucifixion issue is further developed, and the theory that Jesus was not dead on the cross, the swoon theory, is dramatized. Two magicians who had entertained Taurus on his arrival suggest that they can prove that Jesus did not die. He gives them permission to allow the dying man some water. He drinks. Soon afterward he dies. However, two hours later he revives because he had been given a drug that induced catalepsy. Jesus could have been drugged, taken down from the cross, and revived.

This experience gives Taurus more confidence and takes away some fear that he was feeling. He had been listening to so many of Jesus' words, hearing of so many of Jesus' deeds, puzzling over the beatitudes and the exhortation to love your enemy. He now realizes that these words of gentleness were a mask to cover ideas of rebellion, undermining the occupying Roman forces and their morale, making it easier to revolt.

Finally, Taurus is so intent on his mission and is convinced that Jesus is still alive and hiding with Mary Magdalene in Galilee that he dons a disguise and travels incognito to Galilee. He meets disciples talking realistically about Jesus being alive. One suspicious guide threatens to kill Taurus but is prevented when Taurus quotes Jesus' words of nonviolence. Taurus is given directions to a remote village where Mary Magdalene lives. He encounters a young girl only to discover that she is a leper and this is a colony. When Taurus finally meets Mary, thinking that at last his mission is accomplished and still puzzled why she and the disciples at Emmaus did not recognize Jesus at once, she explains that since that morning she has never seen him. He lives in people's hearts.

A last twist is that, because Taurus can quote Jesus' words, the crowds think he is Jesus and press 'round him for cures. For some mad moments, he agrees to heal, then comes to his senses and flees. A soldier finds Taurus wandering in the desert and takes him to Pilate, who abandons him. The soldier offers him a sword so that he can kill himself. As Taurus rubs his hand along the blade, he muses that this edge symbolizes the power and ethics of the empire. He realizes that Tiberius knows that with people accepting the words of a crucified man, the world is already changing. His final words to the soldier, asking him to assist him in death, are, "Thrust me into the mystery."

The audience, bringing its presuppositions about and knowledge of Jesus, is offered a great deal to reflect on as Jesus' words are repeated, the stories of what he did are retold, and the different possibilities, logical and illogical, secular and faith-filled, are presented in this dramatic form of the Roman inquiry.

There was a remake in 2006, *L'Inchiesta* (*The Final Inquiry*) with Daniele Liotti as Taurus and an international cast that ranged from Dolph Lundgren to F. Murray Abraham. Ornella Muti is Mary Magdalene. Enrico Lo Verso is Peter. The scope seems to have been extended because Max von Sydow is listed as Tiberius and Saul of Tarsus appears in the list of characters. Both Mary and Jesus appear in the cast list. It was directed by Giulio Base, who also appears as Lazarus.

THE COTTON PATCH GOSPEL

The Cotton Patch Gospel is a video recording of a Passion play (1985) that was staged in Georgia. Musician Tom Key, with the backing of four musicians, re-enacts the Passion of Christ in a southern United States setting with contemporary bluegrass songs composed by Harry Chapin.

AD

AD (1985) was a twelve-part miniseries from Vincenzo Labella and Anthony Burgess; Burgess had also written *Moses the Lawgiver* and *Jesus of Nazareth* for television. *AD* begins with the Resurrection (and a sequence of the road to Emmaus with Michael Wilding Jr. as Jesus) and continues through the early decades of Christianity. As with *Jesus of Nazareth*, it has a star cast. It was directed by Stuart Cooper.

JESUS—DER FILM

Jesus—The Film is a monumental feature film in 35 episodes, shot on Super8. The individual episodes retell the story of the New Testament and were made by a total of 22 filmmakers from East and West Germany in 12 months. The project's own history follows the story of Jesus Christ recruiting his apostles. The film's creator Michael Brynntrup is a central and controversial figure of Berlin's vivid independent community. His transgressive obsessions, as well as his capability to smuggle miles of Russian Super8 film-material through East-West customs, gathered a group of believers around him. Individuals and groups from various art factions filled the holy frame, inspired by the Dadaistic idea of an "ecriture automatic." From one to another, they passed ideas, material and actors, including Michael Brynntrup himself as the title character.[1]

ST. JOHN IN EXILE

St. John in Exile is a 1986 taping by director Dan Curtis (the *Dark Shadows* television series, *Winds of War, Our Fathers*) of a theatrical production. Dean Jones as John the evangelist speaks his witness to Jesus.

UN BAMBINO DI NOME GESU

In 1987, writer-director Franco Rossi directed a miniseries titled *Un bambino di nome Gesu* (*A Child Called Jesus*), an imaginative and speculative story of Jesus in his infancy and childhood being separated from his parents, who are persecuted by an evil servant of Herod. While it focused on the early years of Jesus' life and the unknown years before his baptism, the miniseries did include scenes with the adult Jesus, played by twenty-one-year-old Alessandro Gassman, son of Vittorio Gassman. Prominent European stars Irene Papas, Pierre Clementi, and Bekim Fehmiu were featured. The screenplay was written by Vittorio Bonicelli, who had written *The Inquiry* the year before.

In 1985, Rossi had made a miniseries of *Quo Vadis* with Max von Sydow as Peter and Klaus Maria Brandauer as Nero.

THE MASTER AND MARGARITA AND INCIDENT IN JUDAEA

Pontius Pilate is a principal focus of *The Inquiry*. He is also the central figure in another imaginative interpretation of the Gospel story, Mikhail Bulgakov's *The Master and Margarita*. Before considering this adaptation of Nikos Kazantzakis' *The Last Temptation of Christ*, some attention needs to be given to Bulgakov (1891–1940, son of a professor of theology).

Bulgakov wrote his novel in Stalin's Russia. It was thought that he burned the manuscript. However, his wife had preserved it. Within the story's broad scope—Satan visiting Moscow of the 1920s and 1930s and entering debate about literature and society—is a different dramatization of some of the events of the last week of Jesus' life. Bulgakov calls him Yeshua Ga Notsri. Ga Notsri has a meal with Judas of Keriot, who asks him about his teachings. He is brought before Pilate, and despite Pilate's admiration for him, he is condemned to death. He is crucified.

The Master and Margarita has been adapted for the screen several times. Celebrated Polish director Andrzej Wajda made a version for West German television, screened in 1972: *Pilatus und andere—Ein film fur Karfreitag* (*Pilate and Others*). This film consisted of the Pilate and Yeshua episodes. Several prominent Polish actors were featured, including Wojciech Pszoniak as Yeshua (he was to be a sinister Robespierre in Wajda's *Danton* ten years later) and Daniel Olbrychski (star of Wajda's bitter story of the Napoleonic Wars, *Ashes*, from 1965).

Also in 1972 an Italian/Yugoslav production of *The Master and Margarita* appeared. In 1989, there was a Bulgarian version. After the collapse of the Soviet empire, the Russians were able to make their own interpretation in 1994. However, the producer prohibited its release. Ten years later, it could be seen in a four-hour version and a cut-down version running two hours. A new Russian eight-hour television series was screened at the end of 2005.

The Yeshua episodes featured in a sixty-minute television film for channel 4 in the United Kingdom in 1991. It was called *Incident in Judaea*, written by Mark Rogers and Paul Bryers and directed by Bryers. John Woodvine had the central role of Pilate. Mark Rylance was Yeshua.

The film opens with Jim Carter dressed as Afranius, the head of Pilate's secret service in Rome, informing the audience about Bulgakov himself, how he was Stalin's favorite author, how his manuscript disappeared, and how his wife saved it. Afranius then moves into the action, at first a seemingly diabolical figure and then key to the action after Yeshua's death.

Woodvine's Pilate is a dignified official who finds Jerusalem hot, chaotic, and impossible. However, he is loyal to Tiberius and values his career. Yeshua is brought before him. Rylance's Yeshua seems, at first, a simple fool, and Pilate treats him as a vagrant stirrer, calls him a tramp. He is gently spoken and immediately addresses Pilate as "good man." For this he is lashed. Pilate is continually troubled by a blinding headache but nevertheless is bemused, then intrigued by this strange little man who speaks Greek and who complains that a reformed tax collector, Matthew, follows him around, writing down all he says. Pilate had already consulted Herod after

Yeshua was arrested, but Herod's view is that the laws of the Sanhedrin should be followed and Pilate alone has the power to execute. He orders Yeshua hanged.

But, the discussion on truth follows. Here, Jesus is not silent. He denies inciting the crowds to destroy the Temple. Rather he wants a new temple of truth to be built; "What is truth?" Yeshua knows Pilate's headache pain, concentrates, and heals him. He knows that Pilate is lonely; the only affection he feels is for his dog. Pilate's wife is absent from this story.

Bulgakov's idiosyncratic speculations about Jesus include familiar Gospel events but offer quite different perspectives. Yeshua's triumphal entry into Jerusalem has been reported. Yeshua says that there was only Matthew. The only witnesses testifying against Jesus are Dismas, Hestas, and Barabbas, but their testimony is that of thieves. Yeshua surprises Pilate by declaring that there are no evil people in the world and that is what he has preached.

The conversation veers toward the centurion in attendance. He has been wounded and scarred in battle, a fight in which he was rescued by Pilate. Pilate makes a great deal of his courage. This is dramatically important since Yeshua will repeat that the only mortal sin is cowardice.

When Yeshua is charged with disloyalty to Caesar, there is a flashback to a meal a few nights earlier where Judas (also a good man), who was interested in and curious about Yeshua's ideas, asks his views on the power of the state. Yeshua states that any kind of power is a form of violence against the people. The state will wither and then there will be no need for power. Justice will prevail. At the end of the meal, Yeshua is arrested.

At this point, we lose sight of Yeshua. Pilate summons Caiaphas to talk about the release of the Passover prisoner. Caiaphas and the Jewish authorities argue with Pilate, hostile toward Barabbas, especially in view of sending Yeshua, "a peaceful philosopher," to death. For Caiaphas, Yeshua is a demagogue, inciting people against religion, a profaner of the truth. Pilate announces Yeshua condemned to Golgotha.

The Crucifixion sequence is brief: Yeshua squatting on the cross, rain with the storm that had been anticipated beating down. The water spout runs with blood—and Pilate drops his bowl of wine, which also runs red.

Afranius now appears to reassure Pilate that Yeshua is dead. He explains how Yeshua thanked those who took his life and said he does not blame them. It is now that we hear Yeshua's statement that cowardice is one of the worst of the mortal sins—Afranius refers to Yeshua's look, his stare, his puzzled smile. Pilate orders a secret burial, that there be no remains.

The story then returns to Judas. Pilate's ambiguous talk veils his desire that Judas be quietly killed before Yeshua's friends do it—they had planned to throw back the thirty pieces of silver into the high priest's house to stir up trouble. Judas is set up by Afranius, who persuades the married Lisa with whom Judas is in love to come that night to Gethsemane. When Judas arrives, he is set upon and killed.

Yeshua appears to Pilate in a dream. He has that same look (and appears in the vein of Holman Hunt's *The Light of the World*). He repeats his saying about cowardice. Pilate is glad that Yeshua is not dead. But Yeshua tells him that the two of them will always be remembered together—remember me, remember you, in the same breath.

Now Matthew appears. Afranius has reassured Pilate that Judas is dead. Pilate slyly suggests that Judas may have committed suicide, that many rumors would be circulating. Afranius agrees, and happily accepts Pilate's offer of career advancement with him. Matthew is angry, has stolen a baker's knife to kill Judas, and is shocked when Pilate claims he has killed Judas.

Pilate wants to see Matthew's manuscript—again the words about cowardice. The manuscript also contains Jesus' words saying there is no death. Pilate offers Matthew a job as librarian in his palace at Caesaraea, but he refuses. Pilate quotes Yeshua against him, that Yeshua would have taken a gift and Matthew is a cruel disciple not to follow. The only gift that Matthew asks for is a new, clean parchment.

The film ends with Yeshua appearing again to the sleeping Pilate, reminding him that they would always be remembered together.

Yeshua is a good and sincere man. However, there is no developed context for his claims and his mission. He is a good individual, betrayed and condemned to death. The story presupposes a knowledge of the Gospel stories and Jesus' claims. Bulgakov sees Jesus as a Christ of culture rather than a Jesus-Savior of faith.

THE SEVENTH SIGN

The Seventh Sign is a thriller from the late 1980s, but is more reminiscent of films made in the 1970s after *The Exorcist*. Demi Moore is the pregnant heroine; Michael Biehn, her husband. Jurgen Prochnow broods as the messenger—who turns out to be Jesus Christ in his Second Coming. There are special effects, but the film relies more on atmosphere as well as quotations from the Book of the Apocalypse, with a sense of impending doom. Myths from Jewish tradition are also used.

The film opens in Haiti where a mysterious stranger walks to the beach, opens a seal of a book, and throws it into the water, which begins to boil. In Israel a village, possibly Sodom, turns to ice. This is the beginning of the apocalyptic times when humans will destroy themselves and the earth. It is also a time of God's wrath. With quotations from the scriptures, including Joel and the Book of the Apocalypse, and their very literal interpretation, we have the ingredients for a religious and occult thriller. *Rosemary's Baby* and *The Omen* come to mind with the pregnant mother, Abby, who may be about to give birth to an antichrist.

The mysterious stranger asks to board with Abby. He tells her stories of the past, of destruction, and of doom to come. His name is David but he is also Jesus. While he draws on the Christian scriptures, he also draws on Jewish mythology about the Guf, a place for souls about to be born, with stories and images of sparrows. At this time Guf is empty. Abby becomes more and more depressed about giving birth and is suicidal. Ultimately, she believes that her soul can be given to her child as it is born.

There is a lot of dialogue on these issues. The film also includes a Vatican emissary and a tormented priest, the embodiment of evil; a centurion and the gatekeeper of Pilate, who struck Jesus on his way to death and, according to the legend of the Wandering Jew, is to roam the earth until the Second Coming of Christ, whom David confronts; and events that are interpreted as signs.

However, David is revealed at the end to be Jesus himself, the light, the lion and the lamb, and there are flashbacks to Roman times and to Jesus and his death—and the question is raised whether Abby is the reincarnation of the woman who offered Jesus water during his Passion.

THE LAST TEMPTATION OF CHRIST

Thirty years before *The Last Temptation of Christ*, Jules Dassin had filmed one of Nikos Kazantzakis' novels, *He Who Must Die*, another story of the putting on of a Passion play, this time in a Greek village, and its effects on the people in the village and the paralleling of characters with those of the Gospels. In 1988, Kazantzakis received not only fame but notoriety.

The Last Temptation of Christ is not a Gospel portrait as such. It is a speculative portrait, a "fiction" grounded in the Gospels. In fact, it is probably a more effective treatment of Gospel narratives than the popular spectaculars of the past. This Palestine is rough, gritty, and dusty; it serves to situate its characters in a more "realistic" past. The film draws on information about customs of the period (from dances and celebrations at wedding feasts to the appearance of prostitutes like Mary Magdalene and their brothels) and suggests an "authentic" atmosphere. One of the difficulties for non-American audiences is the American accents for Jesus, the apostles,

Paul, and all figures except for Pontius Pilate, the foreigner, played by David Bowie with his English accent—reminding us that all portrayals of Jesus speaking English (or Italian) with any accent are stylized.

But, what is important for this film and where it became the target of criticisms of blasphemy is the presentation of Jesus as "human" and not "perfect." However, *The Last Temptation* might be seen as illustrating the saying from the Letter to the Hebrews that Jesus was like us in everything with the exception of turning away from God in sin. He is presented as tormented by the burden of his mission, struggling with accepting what God is asking of him. This comes to a head in the famous temptation scene, the temptation to ordinariness: that Jesus had done enough; that he could fittingly come down from the cross, recover from his Passion, marry, settle down, have a family, live to a ripe old age, and go to his reward. The setting for the temptation is Jesus being mocked on the cross, experiencing being forsaken by God, and hallucinating about this possibility of not dying and of living this alternate life. But the hallucination includes a dispute with Paul about the need for Jesus to die on the cross for his followers to believe in his preaching; and the apostles finally come to his bedside to tell him that his opting out was too easy and not what they expected. Jesus goes back on the cross. These reflections on the Incarnation have greater depth than the usual biblical films.

Members of the mainstream churches, used to appreciating the scriptures in their context and applying the techniques of literary criticism, found this Jesus-figure arresting and thought provoking. It was members of the fundamentalist churches who were stuck on their literal interpretation of the Gospels—which becomes a literal misreading of so much of the text, isolating it from its spiritual heritage in the Old Testament and from its emergence in the Greco-Roman world of the first century AD. It can be noted that Kazantzakis wrote in earthy and colloquial Greek, drawing on vivid imagery to dramatize his points; Paul Schrader and Martin Scorsese have followed this lead by incorporating earthy symbolism, for instance the motif of blood, even to a literal "sacred heart" taken from Jesus' breast and Peter's eating the bread of the Last Supper with blood dripping from his mouth. Thus *The Last Temptation* is a singularly personal film from Scorsese, interpreting the Gospel figure of Jesus for the questioner and searcher of the twentieth century, believer and nonbeliever alike.

Protest

The Last Temptation of Christ was released in 1988. However, it had been in preproduction in the early '80s, which means that it belongs in conception to the period of *Jesus of Nazareth*. Robert De Niro was Scorsese's choice to play Jesus. However, the finances for the film were not forthcoming. When eventually it was made available, De Niro was over forty and the role went to Willem Dafoe. When, finally, the film was made and released, it was a decade later and the times had changed.

The hostile reaction to *The Last Temptation of Christ* came before the film's release. Many conservative groups in the United States claimed that the film was blasphemous because it showed Jesus marrying and his sexual activity. Another fear at the time was that it also had homosexual overtones. Reference was made to a first draft of the screenplay, specifically Jesus in his relationship to John the Baptist, and the nature of the kiss at Jesus' baptism. (It seems that a reference to Isaiah 6 and the burning coal searing the prophet's lips before he could preach was misread in a homosexually suggestive way.) Demonstrations were held around the world and a petition was put to Universal Studios to destroy the negative.

On release, the film did moderate business. There were some initial vociferous protests at cinemas. And then the film went to video release. However, it seemed to be mainstream Christians, as well as director Scorsese's many fans, who appreciated the film and what it was trying to do. Scorsese received an Oscar nomination for Best Director. The novelist, Nikos Kazantzakis, was a member of the Greek Orthodox Church.

A Speculation about Jesus and the Last Temptation—to Give Up

Many of Kazantzakis' co-religionists took a dim view of his novel. Kazantzakis said that he was writing a novel based on the Gospels, not a Gospel. This allowed him the literary permission to speculate on Jesus' character, the events of his life and death, and his motivation.

The last temptation itself was not, as many protesters believed, a sexual temptation, but the temptation to ordinariness. In the famous final half hour of the film, Jesus is hanging on the cross. The soundtrack fades indicating that Jesus is losing consciousness of what is around him. The angel from the temptations in the desert comes to tell him that he can get down from the cross, that he does not have to die. God thinks that he has done enough. Jesus can now come down and live an ordinary life. He can marry (a sexual encounter is shown in a brief long shot), have a family, and live quietly at Nazareth. But Paul visits and complains to Jesus that he, Paul, is preaching a Christ crucified and that Jesus should have died on the cross. The remaining apostles visit Jesus in his old age and urge him to get back on the cross.

Jesus comes back to consciousness on Calvary. He has been tested and tried, "tempted" (in the words of the Letter to the Hebrews) as we all are except that he did not turn away from God. He did not sin.

The temptation was to give up his mission in life.

An "Everyman" Jesus

Between *King of Kings* and *The Last Temptation of Christ* there was only a quarter of a century, but by the 1980s, audiences were not satisfied with a plain presentation of Jesus of the Gospels, with the Gospel as screenplay. Audiences were more prepared to think and feel through the experience of Jesus.

The Jesus of the film, played by Willem Dafoe, is a Gospel "everyman" figure: he is uncertain about himself but knows that he has had an experience of God that demands of him that he go out, preach, teach, mix with ordinary people, and offer them deep hope and salvation.

Kazantzakis wanted to write, not a Gospel, but a fictionalized reflection on Jesus and the Gospels. This is the declared intent on-screen at the start of Martin Scorsese's version based on the screenplay by Schrader, "this fictional exploration of the eternal conflict." This is a dramatized meditation on Jesus Christ and the meaning of his life and death.

Scorsese brought an Italian American sensibility to the film—he had spent a little time in a junior seminary thinking of becoming a priest—and his film shows something of the flamboyant emotional and earthy (and bloody) piety of Italy: Jesus rips his heart out and holds it like a picture of the Sacred Heart; when the apostles eat the bread and drink the wine at the Last Supper, blood flows from their mouths (overtones of vampire films and the drinking of blood from flesh) to bring home Jesus' saying, "Unless you eat my flesh and drink my blood . . ."

On the other hand, Schrader is from the Midwest and declares that he has a strong Puritan and Protestant background (echoed in many the films he has written and directed, such as *Hardcore* [1979] or *Affliction* [1998]). Harvey Keitel's Judas or Harry Dean Stanton's Paul (slaying Lazarus in his Saul days of persecuting zeal) seem to be of particular interest to Schrader with themes of sin and guilt as well as the last temptation, the temptation to give up on one's vocation and choose ordinariness.

Yet, Kazantzakis was writing for ordinary Greeks in a Cretan-toned Greek, portraying for them a down-to-earth and ordinary Jesus who struggled with his God while he was called to greatness.

A Jesus "Out There" but Also a Tormented Man

While there is a great deal of interiority in the Jesus of *The Last Temptation*, he is also a person who is "out there," with people, finding the energy to go on with his mission in his awareness of his God, but more so in his preaching, his teaching, his Gospel of love, and his dealings with the people he encounters.

For many in the 1980s this seemed too much of a radical re-thinking of Jesus, too human a Jesus. To fundamentalist Christians it seemed blasphemous. During the latter months of 1988, it became a cause celebre with demonstrations at Universal Studios with demands that the negative be burned, official church denunciations, and picketing of cinemas screening the film all over the world.

The initial impression of Jesus is of a man caught in the eternal conflict of good and evil, of faith and disbelief, of wanting to serve God but also wanting to flee. Jesus hears voices. He is called by name. He stands in his carpenter's shop with his arms outstretched along one of the crosses that he had made. He is a cross maker who carries the crosses for the Romans to the place of execution. Yet, his experience of his call terrifies him: "God loves me. I want him to stop loving me. I make crosses so that he will stop."

For many audiences who wanted their Gospels simple, this tormented Jesus could not be the Son of God. Yet, this is a poetry of doubt reminiscent of the poems of the nineteenth-century Jesuit Gerard Manley Hopkins, a poet who was not denying his faith but suffering in it. He entitles one of his sonnets "Carrion Comfort," in which he imagines God as a lion mauling him. And in his torment, in another poem of anguish, he cries, "No worse there is none."

However, while the film begins with this introverted experience of Jesus and symbolizes it with his struggle with the serpent and the lion in the desert, it begins to show Jesus moving out into his mission. The catalyst for this is his friendship with Judas. As written by Schrader and played by Keitel, this is one of the most credible characterizations of Judas on-screen. Judas is a Zealot who has been sent to kill Jesus because of his collaboration with the Romans. He does not. Rather, he is drawn to Jesus and many of the best conversations about Jesus' mission are those between Jesus and Judas.

Jesus' first moving out amongst people is his following of Mary Magdalene, a friend from his past who now despises him. She spits on him as he carries his cross. He waits amongst her clients all day, and finally, taunted by her, he begs her forgiveness, "Thank you, Lord, for bringing me where I did not want to go."

The reprieve from death from Judas, the forgiveness of Mary Magdalene, his confronting his fears in the desert free Jesus from the worst of his grim introspection and enable him to be open to the outer world, to the world of people. As yet, he cannot love them, rather he feels sorry for him.

Responding to People in Ministry

But the way that Jesus' ministry develops in the film is his response to people. Perhaps the key segment in this regard is when he comes across a vicious group stoning Mary Magdalene.

This is 1988; the filming done in the dust and desert of Morocco, the cast authentically unwashed, Mary with tattoos. She is literally dragged before Jesus and the crowd start throwing rocks—which looks quite realistic as Mary, played by Barbara Hershey, flinches and cowers.

Dafoe's Jesus is a soul-searching prophet, finding his ministry. He stops the vicious crowd. He says he does not want this. They counter that they want it, Peter even arguing that Mary goes with Romans on the Sabbath and, therefore, she deserves to die. Someone throws a stone at Jesus. Jesus continues challenging them (Zebedee, especially, who says he has nothing to be ashamed of—but is shamed by Jesus and does not cast the stone). This is a vigorous, even wild, Jesus, fearless and uncompromising in acting out his mission. But, he is tender in raising Mary and escorting her away.

Moment by moment, the audience can see Jesus being transformed. He now knows what he must do. He speaks to them with an exhilaration and a joy that makes his face glow. He tells them that he is the one who is to come. He utters teaching that traditionally comes from the Sermon on the Mount. He tells them stories like the parable of the sower in which the seed scattered is love, love everywhere in the world.

As if to consolidate this, Scorsese and Schrader take Jesus to Cana and the wedding feast. The miracle of changing water into wine is a low-key event: Jesus keeps insisting that the jars not far away are wine, while the steward argues they are water until he tastes the wine. After that there is music with Jesus dancing, almost leaping; smiling, almost laughing; enjoying the celebration. This is one of the best screen images of an extraverted Jesus in itself, but also in the way it contrasts with his tormented introspection.

The other significant figure for Jesus is John the Baptist. Andre Gregory looks the part of the wild prophet. His message is one of fire but also of the axe. When branches are rotten, they need uprooting or have the axe taken to them. Jesus is so impressed by the power of what John preaches that he too begins to preach the axe. His ministry shows the eternal conflict that the prologue spoke of, the paradox of the seed of love and the justice of the axe.

The Hallucination, Then Final Commitment

The main section of the film in which Jesus might be interpreted as more outgoing than usual is within the hallucination sequence that is the visualizing of the last temptation itself, the last half hour of the film. The "temptation" begins when a young girl (an angel of darkness in the form of light) tells Jesus that the Father is satisfied with his willingness to die but that is all that is required of him. He can come down from the cross. He does.

Jesus then returns to Nazareth and a completely ordinary life. He marries Mary Magdalene. He fathers children. On Mary's death, he marries Martha. His life is normal. He ages like an ordinary man and comes to his deathbed. It is at this stage that the apostles come and, angry that he had misled them and their expectations, demand that he go back on to the cross.

One presumes that most people would agree that this life is the normal way for men and women to function. It makes the world go round. But, there is always the challenge of the inner world. Wholeness is found by going within. And this is what *The Last Temptation* dramatizes in Jesus. If he were to stay at the level of what is ordinary, what is normal, he would have abdicated the mission that God was calling him to. He must rediscover the call within and go back on to the cross and die. He does.

JESUS OF MONTREAL

Jesus of Montreal (1989) takes us back to the earliest Jesus films, theatrical re-creations of the Gospel (including the 1900 performance of *The Passion Play* at Oberammergau). The Gospel sequences are a play within a play. Denys Arcand presents Daniel, his central character, as a Christ-figure, a figure closely resembling the Jesus he enacts in the Montreal Passion play. This is also a return to earlier Jesus films, especially Griffith's *Intolerance*, where the contemporary 1916 story with its young man caught up with gangs and being condemned in court is juxtaposed with the Jesus story.

Jesus and Daniel Coulombe

Jesus of Montreal is far more complex, using the obvious references to the Gospels as well as more subtle allegorical references (especially with

Daniel's death, his being welcome only at a Jewish hospital, the keeping his memory alive by his friends and followers and their theatrical performances). We are in the realm of more intuitive subtleties with *Jesus of Montreal*. Daniel and Daniel's Jesus are dreamers. In the play, while Jesus heals and tries to save Peter from sinking, he also confronts. His treatment of his followers is compassionate and strong. But there is always an air of mystery and vision.

A Canadian writer-director, Arcand is on record (in the documentary *Jesus Christ Movie Star*) as saying it is impossible to make a film about Jesus because we know nothing about him. Arcand had a French Canadian Catholic education and has reacted against it. Nevertheless, he has made one of the most admired of the Jesus films in *Jesus of Montreal*. Perhaps his skepticism about Jesus and his critical reaction against Catholicism have sharpened his creative powers because he has brought Jesus to the screen vividly, with provocative stimuli, to understand the meaning of Jesus' life and message as well as to show the Gospel relevance to today's world.

A Passion Play

The actual sequences of the Montreal Passion Play where the Gospel scenes are re-enacted take up only twenty-five minutes or so of a film that last for almost two hours. Arcand is interested in the meaning of the play and of Jesus, so the film is useful as an example of a more intuitive and contemporary interpretation.

The context of the production of the play within the film is important. We are taken into the theater world of Montreal of the 1980s, to a performance of a Gogol play, to the gossip and chatter of the arts and media world, to a studio for the dubbing of pornographic films, to the auditions for slick commercials, to the actors who struggle for jobs while they wait tables.

Daniel Coulombe (the dove) is a gentle but enigmatic actor who seems to have disappeared after winning awards at drama school. His hidden life is the subject of speculation: vague wonderings about how long he was away, whether he had traveled the East and studied or just gone underground. Whatever his background, he has now been chosen by the university, which sponsors a now forty-year-old tradition of performing a Passion play to rewrite and restage the play. He does a great deal of research, including examining more recently discovered esoteric documents from the Dead Sea and elsewhere that speculate about Jesus, his origins, his legitimacy, and his being the adoptive son of a legionary. The immediate authority he answers to is a priest who loves theater and who is having an affair with an actress.

Half an hour into the film, we see the play, with Daniel in the role of Jesus, the Christ-figure portraying the Jesus-figure. The presentation of the play and of the Gospel events and words is the opposite of a straightforward presentation. There are spoken introductions to the play inviting the audience to share the speculations. Possibilities about Jesus are presented first.

Gospel Themes

As we see the play begin, we are immediately in the middle of the Passion. Jesus is before Pilate. The spoken text comes mainly from John 19, amplifying the discussion about Jesus' kingship and Pilate's inquiry about truth. There is also a lengthy discussion between Pilate and the religious leaders about the significance of Jesus' death and Pilate's loyalty to Rome. Pilate tells Jesus that he will suffer although he is innocent. It will be a short suffering, and Pilate adds an aphorism, "In the harshness of life, the ability to die is man's gift."

But the play does not continue with the Passion. The audience shown watching the play is invited to move to various locations with the cast (whom we see changing costume and makeup). A mini-lecture on representations of Jesus in early Christian art follows as do images of a Byzantine Jesus. There is speculation also about Jesus as a magus, a miracle worker like many in his time. This is a prelude to the dramatization, quite stylized, of a selection of miracles. Jesus heals the blind; raises the daughter of Jairus to life, using the Aramaic words "Talitha kum"; walks on the water and rescues Peter as he doubts and begins to sink. In a particularly moving sequence, Jesus multiplies the loaves but hands the bread to the actual audience to share and eat.

In a delightful interruption to the performance, an African woman rushes out of the crowd to kneel at Jesus' feet and proclaim her love for him. Daniel stands silent, doing nothing, but the pragmatic security man takes the woman, who huffs indignantly, back to the crowd and then indicates that the actors should continue. She tries again later but with just as little success. However, the dramatizing of the attractiveness of Jesus and the crowds rushing to him when they were not supposed to are a strong Gospel theme.

As Jesus hands the bread to the audience, he recites a selection of teachings—often from the Sermon on the Mount, sayings about the heart being where one's treasure is, about inviting the poor to dinner—and poses the question to the disciples as to who people say Jesus is.

Passion and Death

But then it is back to the Passion with Jesus being scourged and being offered myrrh to drink—and another mini-lecture about crucifixions in history. The next sequences are particularly physical and direct: Jesus being stripped naked, being carried naked to the cross by a soldier, being brutally set on the cross and nailed. As Jesus squats on the cross, the lecture continues with more information about the stifling heat and the crucifixion victim being suffocated.

As Jesus is being buried, a particularly intuitive voiceover is heard, Hamlet's "To be or not to be" soliloquy, which takes on striking meaning with this Gospel association.

Arcand's treatment of the Resurrection is quite powerful. Although Jesus is not seen, the angel runs triumphant the length of a bright blue-lit tunnel and announces that Jesus is risen, has been doubted, but has been seen and touched.

The play ends with some more reflections from the actors, a final homily for the audience on loving one another and on finding the self within, and a final blessing of peace.

A Contemporary Jesus-Figure

For those used to the standard biblical film of Jesus, this presentation is refreshing and insightful. It is a more intuitive dramatization, a more intuitive interpretation, a drama by association of Gospel events and of historical and cultural allusions and explanations. Arcand contrasts this wisdom with the vapid talk after the play, the media gush, the ponderously sonorous philosophizing, the actor who has missed all the meaning and is concerned about a part in a miniseries, the equivalent chatter of people walking down Calvary hill on that first Good Friday.

The drama does not find favor with the priest-producer who fears that authorities will not like its tone and its speculations. He demands that they return to the tried-and-true forty-year-old piously rhetorical text. In a repeat performance of the play, the cinema audience is shown only a brief sequence of a minute's duration. It is Jesus denouncing the Pharisees in the harsh condemnations of Matthew 23.

Finally, Daniel is arrested for assault and destruction of property after he has smashed cameras and recorders as one of the actors is asked to strip by lewd sponsors and a demanding woman producer (whom Daniel violently slaps) for her audition for a beer commercial (the cleansing of a modern temple). The police come for Daniel during the performance when he is, in fact, dying on the cross. While one of the arresting officers compliments him on the play and the performance, others demand that the play be allowed to finish. The security guard nonchalantly tells them that they know the ending. He dies and rises. However, brawling breaks out. A brawny defender of the play bashes into the cross; Daniel falls and the wood of the cross crashes onto his head.

This symbolic cause of Daniel's death is the focus of the allegorical sequences of *Jesus of Montreal*. Arcand has contemporary stagings of Gospel episodes. It was these that also made a great impact when the film was first released. The smashing of the media equipment is obviously an equivalent of Jesus cleansing the Temple of the money changers as well as a defense of a woman being humiliated by authorities. The picking of the actors for the play is a choosing of disciples (with the pornography industry standing in for prostitution in the past). Audiences were also struck by the suavely smooth face and tone of Daniel's lawyer, especially when he tempts Daniel to deals and they look over the city from an upper story of a skyscraper.

There is no room for Daniel at the Catholic hospital (and its curt staff) but there is at a Jewish hospital. Daniel temporarily recovers from the blow and preaches apocalyptic sayings in an underground railway station. But when he does die, his heart is given in transplant for the life of someone else. In the meantime, his friends gather and decide to perform in the future, keeping his memory and his spirit alive.

Jesus of Montreal depicts familiar Gospel sequences and brings them to life. But it does far more than this. It explores the meaning of Jesus and the Gospel. It gives us Daniel as an enigmatic, gentle, and compassionate but strong Christ-figure. And it relates the Gospel to contemporary issues and challenges.

JEZUS KRISZTUS HOROSZKOPJA

As the Cold War came to an end and Communism was about to collapse, celebrated veteran Hungarian director Miklos Jancso made a film with the provocative title *Jesus Krisztus Horoszkopja (Jesus Christ's Horoscope)*. He uses the Jesus reference to make social and political points. His central character's name is finally revealed as Joseph Kafka, focusing on impersonal bureaucracy, the Stalinist and Soviet-dominated past, and the loss of personal identity. Kafka has relationships with three women and may or may not have committed a murder. One of the women tries to check on who he is and the police say that there is no record of his existence. It is here that Jancso brings in the Jesus reference: the woman is told that their computer cannot prove that Christ existed. Jancso is quoted as saying that the title is impossible: "According to the Church, Jesus Christ could not have had a horoscope, because then the position of the stars would have determined his fate, and not God's will." Jancso has made abstract films with metaphysical implications.[2]

NOTES

1. hm, "Plot Summary for *Jesus—Der Film* (1986)," Internet Movie Database, www.imdb.com/title/tt0400553/plotsummary.

2. Grahame Petrie, "The Tyrant's Waltz," *Kinoeye* 3, no. 4 (March, 3, 2003), www.kinoeye.org/03/04/petrie04.php.

10

THE JESUS FILMS: CINEMA FREEDOM AND IMAGES OF JESUS

During the 1960s and its movements for freedom, some philosophers and theologians wanted a moratorium on the use of the word *God* and some asked, along with a *Time* magazine cover, "Is God dead?" However, it was also the era of a charismatic spirituality and a renewal of charismatic prayer in the mainstream churches. It was also the era of "Jesus movements."

JESUS-FIGURES INSERTED INTO COMMERCIAL FILMS

But, the cinema freedoms of the 1960s, including the acceptability of showing Jesus on-screen, led to Jesus becoming a minor but significant character in a range of films. The range of Jesus-figures indicates how filmmakers have felt freer to use "sacred" images to dramatize (illustrate or critique) their characters and values.

JOHNNY GOT HIS GUN

In the United States, Dalton Trumbo's antiwar film *Johnny Got His Gun* (1971) had Donald Sutherland as Jesus appearing in the hallucinations of Great War amputee Timothy Bottoms, driving a steam-train engine through his nightmares or sitting guard over him.

A CLOCKWORK ORANGE

There is a disturbing episode in Stanley Kubrick's *A Clockwork Orange* (1971), where Alex has fantasies about Jesus—that he is participating in Jesus' Passion, whipping him and making him suffer.

THE RULING CLASS

A striking playing with Jesus-figures in a satirical context came in Peter Medak's 1973 *The Ruling Class* starring Peter O'Toole. An insane member of the British aristocracy, O'Toole's character spends a great deal of his time on a mantelpiece, arms extended as in crucifixion. He sees himself as Jesus on the cross. However, he is treated by a psychiatrist and is eventually proclaimed cured. He might appear normal, but he has switched from Jesus to be Jack the Ripper.

THE DEVILS

The most controversial of the directors using this Jesus device was Ken Russell. Russell, dubbed by journalists as the British "enfant terrible" of his day, appears on the dust jacket of John Baxter's biography, large as life in sloppy clothes, grinning from a cross, crowned with thorns. Arresting and bizarre images of Jesus recur in the lives and dreams of Russell's characters, in *Mahler*, *Tommy*, and *Lisztomania*, but more explicitly in *The Devils* (1971), which dramatizes weird religious fantasies of the repressed superior of the convent (Vanessa Redgrave) in Loudun, France, 1634. She saw the parish priest (Oliver Reed) as Jesus, walking toward her on the water and coming down from the cross to passionately embrace her as Mary Magdalene during the recitation of the rosary.

By the late 1980s, Ken Russell's talent had veered into more camp excess. He was in his post-Catholicism period. *The Lair of the White Worm* (1989) was based on a Bram Stoker story and dealt with pagan rituals, myths, and occultism, giving Russell an opportunity to introduce an actor playing Jesus and have him attacked by the dragon-snake of the title.

These films allowed filmmakers a greater scope for the portrayals of Jesus, like that of Jean-Luc Godard's controversial allegory of Mary, Joseph, and Jesus as ordinary people today in *Je Vous Salut Marie* (*Hail Mary*). It is still difficult to realize that there is a distance of only nine years between *King of Kings* and *The Devils*.

THE MILKY WAY

Veteran director Luis Bunuel had already been using religious and Catholic themes as the targets of his critique, *Nazarin, El*, and the Last Supper parody in *Viridiana*. He made *The Milky Way* (1969), in which his pilgrims on the way to Compostella enter into the Gospel stories: Jesus about to shave and a statue-like Mary urging him to keep his beard, Jesus at Cana and discussions about him laughing.

By this time in his career, Bunuel was back in his native Spain after some decades and prolific filmmaking in Mexico. The story is told that he said, "Thank God, I'm an atheist." However, he had a Dominican friend, a friar who had denounced *Viridiana*. Bunuel shows here a great knowledge as well as a satiric appreciation of the Christian/Catholic tradition. The pilgrims encounter a great number of heresies and discuss transubstantiation, the equality between good and evil, Gnosticism, the Inquisition, and hell—with a flash to the Marquis de Sade.

CAMMINA, CAMMINA

Even a devout Catholic director like Ermanno Olmi used the pilgrimage as a source of satiric critique of Christianity. In his *Cammina, cammina* (1982), he re-enacts the journey of the Magi in Italianate style. He uses it as a symbol of various attitudes toward discipleship. Some of the pilgrims refuse to go. Others grumble and are critical. Some drop out, while others persevere in order to see a miracle. It throws light on the attitudes of the people toward the Jesus they want to find.

FROM A FAR COUNTRY

Quite a different tone is found in Krzysztof Zanussi's biography of Pope John Paul II, *From a Far Country* (1981), which focuses on the pope's early years. The film opens with a ten-minute sequence, set in 1926, when the pope was a boy of five, almost six, in Holy Week. The village of Katowice re-enacts the Passion, its own Passion play. The film shows the devotion of the people, beginning with a formal bath and washing of the man who was to portray Jesus. He is then solemnly dressed in Jesus' clothes and brought out to the people, and the cross is laid on his shoulder. He makes his slow and painful way to Calvary. Solemn religious music accompanies Jesus and the following crowd. The little Karol Wojtyla watches the pageant with his father. This kind of Passion play is seen as an expression of faith and a reinforcing of faith.

HISTORY OF THE WORLD: PART I

Mel Brooks also parodied the da Vinci Last Supper with John Hurt as Jesus in *History of the World: Part I* (1981), the film in which Brooks, as Moses, comes down from Mt. Sinai with three tablets of stone, stumbles, and drops one of them and it shatters. Moses quickly improvises, changing his fifteen commandments to "these ten commandments." There is also a sequence of the Spanish Inquisition in which nuns take off their habits and dive into a swimming pool as if they were in an Esther Williams musical.

The Last Supper sequence is brief. Jesus and the apostles are sitting at tables and Mel Brooks himself plays the waiter/manager and wants to ask whether they will be paying together or on separate checks. When the waiter hears about the betrayal, he calls out "Judas" but it is something to do with the meals. When Brooks says, "Jesus," Hurt looks up and responds, "Yes," to which Brooks responds, "What?" and a verbal routine follows. Finally, Leonardo da Vinci comes in speaking with an Italian intonation. When he sets up his easel, he realizes that he has only backs of those sitting at the table near him. He gets them all to move together and poses them in the famous positions—except that Mel Brooks is there standing behind Jesus and smiling. It was a flip farce, potentially (and actually for some) offensive, but the work of a comic writer mocking religious pretensions.

History of the World: Part I was released two years after *Life of Brian*.

BAD LIEUTENANT

In the early 1990s, there appeared what was to become a key film in theological discussion about cinema and dealt with sin and despair—*Bad Lieutenant* (1992). Reference was made to the opening of Psalm 130: "Out of the depths I cry to you, O Lord, Lord, hear my voice." Such films show the human condition in all its ugliness and desperation: men and women crying out in agony without knowing whether anyone, human or divine, can hear their voice. We know that life is a search for God and that many search in byways rather than highways and find themselves, not infrequently, in dead ends. The portrayal of these searches may be ugly, but they are still searches for the transcendent and for God.

Bad Lieutenant is a strong and disturbing film from Abel Ferrara. Ferrara's career has focused on urban stories, violence in crime, sin, and the possibilities of salvation. He has a stark style, both realistic and stylized, which is not in the smooth Hollywood vein; he offers characters and situations with extraordinary bluntness, leaving the audience to do their work. *Bad Lieutenant* is a portrait of a corrupt policeman, his descent into the hell of drugs, alcohol, sexuality, gambling, and disregard of family, coworkers, and the law. However, he is confronted when a nun is raped in a church.

During the graphic rape sequence, the camera moves to the image of the crucified Jesus at the back of the altar of the church. The crucifix comes alive (actor Paul Hipp). It is clear that Ferrara believes that the nun's assault and suffering are akin to, even part of, the sufferings of Jesus.

The lieutenant is desperate for the nun to name her assailants. They are young men from the neighborhood and she refuses the lieutenant's request. She says she has forgiven them. This questioning takes place on the sanctuary steps of the church. He cannot understand her forgiveness. Yet, this is a last chance for him. He begins to howl as he squats on the aisle floor, a primitive, even primal, howl. He then bursts into a cursing of God, repeated shouting to God, "Fuck you." The lieutenant is truly in the depths. But he experiences a hallucination of Jesus (like the pious art of the nineteenth century), the same Jesus the audience saw while the nun was raped. The lieutenant demands of Jesus, "Where were you?" He acknowledges his sinfulness, that he is "weak, so fucking weak." And then, weeping and howling he cries, "I'm sorry" and repeats it as he crawls toward the apparition of Jesus down the aisle, a desperate prayer out of the depths. He comes to and is kneeling at the feet of the church caretaker. (These images of Harvey Keitel and statuary are reminiscent of his first film role in Martin Scorsese's first feature *Who's Knocking at My Door?* [1968], where he goes into the confessional and the church icons and images are shown us in a three-minute collage.)

CERCASI GESU

The scene: a boardroom, up to date and flashy—a marketing presentation. The board members, male executives, including some nattily garbed clerics, discuss business in their assured way. Some nuns, back from the table, sit demurely attentive. Onto the screen flashes an Identikit slide, a young man, curly hair, curly beard. You might momentarily mistake him for Jesus. But, no. It's not a mistake. The board's talk is of charisma, media image, and research for U.S. presidential election candidates. The board is searching for a marketable Jesus. This is evangelization by media, a publication of the

Gospels with live photography of Jesus, Jesus in action. The head cleric has a candidate who matches the Identikit, a hitchhiker he picked up on the autostrada, a man just released from an institution. This, of course, is only a film. And it is called *Cercasi Gesu* (*Looking for Jesus*; 1982), directed by Luigi Comencini. It is an offbeat presentation of a Jesus-figure of the 1980s.

The central character is a genial man named Giovanni, looking a bit like a contemporary Jesus with his curly hair and beard. After being discharged from a mental institution, he is given a lift by a modern priest who happens to be in charge of the publication of a *Life of Jesus*, illustrated by photos of a Jesus-lookalike. Giovanni meets the computer requirements for a Jesus face that would attract the public. He agrees to do the job and he is scrubbed, coiffured, and groomed for maximum photogenic appeal. However, he upsets his mentors (except the simple priest assigned to look after him whom, Giovanni realizes, they look down on): he intervenes in a press conference but is silenced, finally banging out an extemporaneous ballad on the piano about his deals and his being silenced for the benefit of the journalists.

Behind the scenes, he resembles Jesus in his caring for a drug-addict mother who squanders the money he gives her, for a terrorist who has befriended him—and he allows children to play in places forbidden for playing. The parallels are not made particularly subtly, but they are done very nicely, humorously, and with some important ironic points about the church and the living of the Gospels.

THE FAVOUR, THE WATCH AND THE VERY BIG FISH

You may not expect to see Jesus on-screen in a film titled *The Favour, the Watch and the Very Big Fish* (1992; directed by Ben Lewin), but it is also central to discussion of the 1980s and 1990s. The plot is not dissimilar to that of *Cercasi Gesu*. Bob Hoskins plays a photographer commissioned to illustrate the life of Jesus with photos of Gospel tableaux for a religious dealer. Parallel with this plot is another involving a young woman and her concern for a melancholic Jewish pianist, played by Jeff Goldblum. He is arrested and spends some time in jail, emerging with long hair and a beard—the perfect candidate for the model of Jesus. He accepts. But he is quite cantankerous on set, although a perfectionist about the actual photographs. In a park, he is literally mistaken for Jesus and requested for miracles. When he agrees to pray and lay hands on a blind boy, he closes his eyes devoutly, as do the women who request the healing, and the boy is accidentally hit on the head with a flying ball. He recovers his sight. The film looks at the consequences for the pianist, who begins to believe in his healing gifts, and for people who think he is Jesus, finally walking on water. And so, the film pokes satiric fun at faith and religiosity.

The Jesus-figure in these films is a cultural vehicle for alerting audiences to authentic religion, genuine living out of Gospel principles compared with the phoniness, the hypocrisy of so many professed Christians and their practice.

LEON THE PIG FARMER

In this 1993 British comedy, directed by Gary Sinyor and Vadim Jean, a London Jew who is an estate agent discovers his biological father is a pig farmer—which leads to the breeding of kosher pigs. There is a painting scene in which the artist spends time painting portraits of Jesus using live models.

11

THE JESUS FILMS:
THE 1990s

With such a wealth of material from the 1970s and the creative burst at the end of the 1980s, the question for the 1990s was whether anything new or creative could appear. The 1990s were marked by the effect of the video revolution. Many local groups made their own films, amateur and professional. It was at the end of the decade, with the impending millennium, that studios and production companies moved again into Jesus films.

LA BELLE HISTOIRE

La belle histoire (1992) is perhaps influenced by *Jesus of Montreal* and the idea of having the Gospel story alive in contemporary times. French director Claude Lelouch (who won an Oscar for his *A Man and a Woman*) presents three stories with the same characters. The hero of the 1990s story is a gypsy named Jesus (Gerard Lanvin). The heroine is his childhood friend Mary (Marie-Sophie L). However, they also appear in a story set in Gospel times, paralleling the familiar narrative. Lelouch sees this as a beautiful, recurring story. (Others have interpreted it as reincarnation.) The film, which runs over three hours, was not a success at the box office.

THE VISUAL BIBLE: *MATTHEW, ACTS*

The Visual Bible project was begun in 1993 with *Matthew*, directed by Regardt van den Bergh. It was filmed in South Africa. Once again the whole text of the Gospel is seen and dramatized. It is seen as a sympathetic interpretation of Jesus, lightened by a little horseplay (as in Roger Young's 1999

Jesus with Jeremy Sisto). As played by Bruce Marchiano, Jesus is particularly cheerful, often grinning and laughing (perhaps sometimes unexpectedly as at the Sermon on the Mount), but he also has a pronounced American accent compared with most of the other characters, like Peter, who speak with a South African accent. This is not exactly the Jesus of Matthew's Gospel. While he does welcome the children and urges his disciples to do likewise, the Jesus of Matthew tends to be straightforward, a no-nonsense Jesus, a no-frills Jesus. Pier Paolo Pasolini certainly took this view in his classic version.

The film opens with an old Matthew (played by Richard Kiley) reminiscing about his life and using a nonbiblical text as an explanation of his background in Capernaum as a tax collector and giving witness of how Jesus was the longed-for Messiah, the fulfillment of the Law, the Prophets, and the Psalms. He is then seen dictating to two scribes what was to become the Gospel. This device is used throughout the whole film, the action moving backward and forward from visualizing the Gospel story to details of Matthew's life: his home, his friends, other children, walking in the hills, day sequences, and night sequences. As a welcome dramatic variation, Matthew also voices some of the sayings of Jesus, alternating with Bruce Marchiano. Richard Kiley has a clear diction and speaks Jesus' words as well as the narrative with a strong gravitas.

With the film using the complete text of the Gospel, audiences know the story and its development and can be checking with a printed text as the film proceeds. The film also has the Bible references as subtitles on-screen as the narrative develops.

The film gets over the detail of the genealogy by showing Matthew at work as he names the ancestors. The transition is then to a young, smiling Joseph who hesitates on seeing the pregnant Mary. An interior voice speaks the words of the angel, Joseph at first blocking his ears. The infancy narratives move rapidly at this stage, showing an affectionate Joseph with the baby Jesus. The Magi come to a bustling Bethlehem and then visit Herod and experience quite a dramatic questioning. They come and offer their gifts and then return. The massacre of the innocent children is always dramatic, and there are the usual soldiers, swords, and babies here—as well as a very sad Matthew telling the story. When Herod dies, Mary and Joseph are lit as the angel gives them a voiceover message to return to Nazareth.

Jesus makes his first adult experience, all smiles already, while the Baptist is at the Jordan (with more of a British accent) preaching to some passive listeners and some rather fat Pharisees. John clasps Jesus' face and Jesus nods, is baptized by immersion. This version does not show a dove at all, and Matthew describes the voice from heaven. Matthew also supplies the voice of Satan for the temptations in the desert, alternating with a very weak Jesus' responses and rebukes after forty days of fasting.

The limitations of Gospel text as screenplay now become more apparent as events move dramatically and quickly: Jesus calling the fishermen apostles, immediate healings—although this Jesus is vigorously charming with children and the elderly. The charm continues through the key chapters, 5–7, with the Sermon on the Mount. There is a whole lot of laughing going on—with the statements on salt and other images, like the plank in the judgmental eye—and Jesus standing with hand on hip or moving briskly around. However, with the Lord's Prayer, Jesus becomes quite serious.

Matthew 8 contains a series of miracles including close-ups of Jesus' concern for the leper and the centurion riding in on horseback. With the storm on the lake, Jesus is very wet but there are guffaws of relief when the storm is calmed. What follows is a mixture of preaching, affection for the children, the raising of Jairus' daughter, and the kindly bending down to the woman with the hemorrhage who wants to touch the hem of Jesus' cloak. As the screen scenes move from the Gospel back to Matthew and then to Jesus, the locations for Jesus' activity are varied: at the lake, with children, around a campfire, in the cornfields where they are caught picking grain on the Sabbath by the spying Pharisees, and in the synagogue where Jesus heals the man with a withered hand after being interrogated superciliously by the religious leaders.

Matthew 13 is a long chapter containing many parables and explanations. Jesus teaches from a boat. While it is not in the text as such, the film shows Mary Magdalene listening to Jesus behind a grille as he speaks of judging people by their fruit. The film also adds its own detail to the swirling dance of Herodias' daughter and the head of John the Baptist on the platter.

As the film goes on, Jesus becomes more vigorous, yelling at the fearful disciples who thought he was a ghost walking on the lake. At the beginning of chapter 15, we are surprised to see him laboring in a field, shirtless.

Jesus takes pity on the plea of the Syrophoenician mother for her daughter's health and on the crowds (very large), grinning while multiplying the loaves and fishes. With Peter's profession of faith in chapter 16 (extremely South African sounding), they are on the move, Jesus laughing as he promises the keys of the kingdom to Peter and hugging him even as he says, "Get behind me, Satan" when Peter hopes to protect Jesus. The vision of Moses and Elijah at the Transfiguration is rather literal, although the experience itself is a climbing one, up the mountain.

At this stage, with eleven more chapters to go, the film heightens some of the activity: walking through a flock as Jesus talks about the shepherd and the lost sheep, the rich young man coming on horseback and riding off dejected, seeing laborers in the vineyard, Jesus hopping on a wagon to talk about marriage and divorce, Jesus holding up a child to illustrate who was greatest in the kingdom of heaven—and Jesus and the apostles indulging in horseplay under a waterfall. Jesus riding into Jerusalem receives enthusiastic crowd acclaim, and the whipping of the buyers and sellers in the Temple is in slow motion. An interesting variation is the story of the unjust steward with Peter and Jesus acting it out in action and in word.

In moving toward the Passion, Matthew has a number of parables and preaching about apocalyptic times. The parable of the talents is visualized. The anointing of Jesus by Mary is the moment when Judas is introduced as a specific character, although it is several of the disciples who criticize the waste of money with the expensive oil.

The Passion sequences are treated more familiarly—though, for a change and relief, the Last Supper is not modeled on da Vinci. In Gethsemane, Jesus gasps, cries, weeps. The pain of Jesus in the Passion is suggested by his extremely bruised and battered face. There are close-ups of Jesus' face when he is nailed. A glimpse of Mary, not in the text, is added.

Jesus' final cry is more of a scream, and Matthew's voice emphasizes the apocalyptic imagery on-screen. Jesus is seen being taken down from the cross in a silhouette. For the last chapter, Matthew describes the Resurrection rather than the film dramatizing anything. What is seen is Jesus encountering the Magdalene and raising her up and the guards being bribed to say that the body was stolen.

At the end, with his exhortation to go out to the nations, preach the good news, and baptize, Jesus looks out at the audience, walks, and looks back, smiling and beckoning everyone to follow him as a choir sings "Alleluia."

This version of Matthew comes from an evangelical perspective. Its aim is to present Jesus as a credible and sympathetic human being who is on a mission from God. While some aspects of the Gospel are presented literally, it is still an interpretation of the text and the filmmakers have tried hard not to have the audience feel that they are bogged down in a great deal of serious preaching. In that, it succeeds, helped immeasurably by Kiley's dignified but attractive reading of the text as well as in the surprise of Marchiano's Jesus smiling and laughing so much.

The next project was a film version of the Acts of the Apostles, simply called *Acts*. It runs for 183 minutes and covers the whole text of the New Testament book. Jesus does not appear very much after his ascension in the first chapter. He is played by Bruce Marchiano, from *Matthew*, once again very cheerful as he was in the Gospel film. Jesus' appearance is limited in the Acts of the Apostles to his being seen in Galilee by the disciples and his ascension into heaven, which is rendered quite literally here. Peter is played by James Brolin and Paul by Henry O. Arnold, an actor and writer of religious-oriented films, including *The Second Chance* and a documentary on Billy Graham. The director was again South African, Regardt van den Bergh.

Acts uses the device of the older Luke (Dean Jones) remembering his life and recalling the events, the same technique as was used in *Matthew* with Richard Kiley as the older Matthew.

The third installment of the Visual Bible was *The Gospel of John*, an ambitious project that will be considered later.

THE GOSPEL ACCORDING TO JESUS

This film is a 1995 production with selected Gospel readings by well-known Americans, including Maya Angelou, Deepak Chopra, Judy Collins, Andrew Greeley, Tim Robbins, and Susan Sarandon, followed by discussion and theological reflection.

THE REVOLUTIONARY: PARTS I AND II

Another venture in the mid-1990s was a two-part film on the public life of Jesus, the first focusing on his preaching, the second on his miracles. Written by Joyce Marcarelli, who had written a number of religious documentaries, and directed by Robert Marcarelli, who was to direct *The Omega Code*, it was produced by Paul Crouch Sr., who founded the Trinity Broadcasting Network (TBN), which promotes more evangelical programs and films, many with an immediate apocalyptic perspective. British actor John Kay Steel portrayed Jesus.

The TBN also produced two concert films in the mid-1990s, featuring a large array of artists and the actor Danny York. TBN tends toward a strong patriotism as well as an evangelical interpretation of the Bible, which grew more apocalyptic as the millennium approached. The two concert films indicate the tone: *The Glory of the Resurrection* and *The Glory of America* (both 1996).

MARY, MOTHER OF JESUS

While *Mary, Mother of Jesus* (1999), directed by Kevin Connor, is a Mary film, the portrayal of Jesus is significant and substantial. Made with the millennium in mind (as was the telemovie *Jesus*, which will be discussed in the next section), it was screened on American television in 1999. Mary is portrayed by Danish actress Pernilla August (who, ironically, in the same year appeared as the mother of Annikin, later Darth Vader, in George Lucas' *The Phantom Menace*).

The initial focus is, of course, on Mary in Nazareth, the Annunciation, the visitation, Joseph's acceptance of her pregnancy, the census in Bethlehem, and the birth of Jesus (with both shepherds and the Magi, who have met Herod and then avoid him), the Massacre of the Innocents and the flight into Egypt. Mary, it should be said, is what they call "feisty," a strong-minded girl who defies the Romans, witnesses the death by stoning of a woman caught in adultery, and speaks her mind to Joseph—she's a strong role model for her son.

Jesus himself appears as a boy on the way back from Egypt. The screenplay posits many years in Egypt. Jesus has a touch of precocious awareness about him as he asks his parents about the law of an eye for an eye. This is emphasized with his being lost in Jerusalem and his discussions with the religious leaders. He tells his parents, "I thought you would know where to find me!" Zechariah, Elizabeth's husband, comments to Mary and Joseph how wise their son is.

However, back in Nazareth, there is some inventive storytelling. Mary tells her son the story of the Good Samaritan and, later, he will tell her that he knows how to teach with the stories she told him. However, the local kids think he is stuck up and fight him, giving him a bloody nose. Jesus does not retaliate.

When he grows up, Jesus is more popular, especially in his carpentry work and satisfying his customers, allowing them to pay when they can.

There is also the death scene for Joseph. Elizabeth comes to visit and Jesus looks on quietly and thoughtfully. As Joseph dies, he tells Mary, "Everything he is—you made him what he is."

The rest of the film shows us Mary and Jesus in the Gospel episodes where they appear together. Christian Bale portrays Jesus in quite a low-key performance. He is strong minded, not immediately prone to smiles or laughter, a serious man who accompanies his mother to the Jordan and, at her encouragement, is baptized and recognized by John as well as by some of those who will become the twelve apostles. He also quietly tells his mother that he must go away to the desert to prepare himself for his mission. He says he heard God's voice when he was a boy in Jerusalem and now he has to go away for God's guidance. Mary did not accompany her son during the forty days and forty nights, so we just see him returning, ready to preach and with some disciples.

The key Gospel story of Mary is that of the wedding feast at Cana. It is dramatized in the familiar way, quite straightforwardly with Jesus hesitating—and his mother not hesitating. She knows her own mind and her son's. In a lighter touch, they join in the dancing. Mary is also present when, as in Luke 4, Jesus goes back to Nazareth to read from the scroll— but the screenplay takes the text further and Jesus speaks the words from John 6 about being the bread of life. He receives the same contempt: that they know who he is, his parents and family, and Mary who is there in the synagogue.

The other Gospel story is that where Mary and others want to see Jesus while he is preaching and he declares that those who believe are his mother, brothers, and sisters. We observe this from Mary's point of view, outside the area where Jesus is teaching. While Mary realizes that Jesus includes all his followers as his disciples, one of them takes what he said very much amiss. Then Jesus comes out and embraces his mother.

The Passion is presented briefly and rather quickly. Jesus speaks to his mother, after riding the donkey into Jerusalem, about the journey that both he and she have been traveling. There is a glimpse of Jesus before Pilate, but the focus is on Jesus carrying the crossbeam, like a halter, and falling. In these sequences, Bale's face expresses intensely what Jesus is going through. After the nailing, there is the brief word from John 19 entrusting Mary to John's care.

Jesus speaks the words of forgiveness, that his mission is finished, and then he commends his spirit to his father. When he is taken down from the cross, his mother cradles him. After the Resurrection, he appears to his mother, distant and on a roof where he appears glorified. He does not speak but disappears from view.

This portrayal of Jesus draws on the tradition of Jesus films. However, Bale's quiet dignity makes us wonder what he would have been like in a full Jesus film.

OTHER MARY FILMS

Two other Mary films appeared in the mid and later 1990s. The first was French, *Marie de Nazareth* (1995). Veteran French director Jean Delannoy, who had made respectful films about Bernadette of Lourdes, *Bernadette* (1988) and *La Passion de Bernadette* (1989), took up a suggestion of John Paul II to make a film on Mary like Franco Zeffirelli's *Jesus of Nazareth*. There was no budget for a project that size, and Delannoy was ageing (eighty-six to eighty-seven while filming, though he died in 2008 at the age of one hundred). Jesus appears more as infant and child. The film is rather pious in its presentation of Mary, then begins to move more rapidly toward the end and the Crucifixion, relying somewhat on familiar images of the Passion and tableaux (again, perhaps because of time and budget constraints).

The other film was an Italian drama on Mary, with a theological conundrum in its title, *Maria, figlio del suo figlio* (*Mary, Daughter of Her Son*), playing on physiology and sanctification. It is an almost three-hour telemovie, covering the whole of Mary's life according to the Gospels and some of the apocryphal Gospels with Israeli model turned actress Yael Abecassis as Mary and Australian model Nicholas Rogers (only two years younger than Abecassis) as a conventional Jesus.

A 2002 film, *Mary and Joe*, directed by John Hamilton, portrays a contemporary Jewish couple in New York City who are parents waiting for the coming of the Messiah and whose experience parallels that of the Gospel Mary and Joseph. Hamilton had World Vision and Rotary amongst his clients for film and video production. With this humanitarian background, he also lectures in cinema at the Christian college Azusa Pacific University in Los Angeles County.

As of this writing, *Mary, Mother of Christ* (working title, *Myriam, Mother of Christ*) has been in pre-production since 2009. The script is by Barbara Nicolosi and Benedict Fitzgerald (writer of *The Passion of the Christ*). Camilla Belle has been cast as Mary. A high-powered cast includes Jessica Lange, Al Pacino, Jonathan Rhys Meyers, and Peter O'Toole.

JESUS (UNITED STATES, 1999)

At first, *Jesus* (directed for American television by Roger Young, who made several of the telemovies on Jewish scripture characters like Joseph) might seem like a throwback to the 1960s, another attempt at "realism." However, it benefits from the influence of the stylized images of Jesus during the 1970s. This is immediately evident as the film opens with contemporary battle scenes that startle the viewer. In fact, it is a dream (or vision) that Jesus has, a kind of recurring dream that takes him into the future, glimpsing the sin and evil of the centuries—Crusades, World War I, and so on—for which he must sacrifice his life. The most striking use of this stylization is in the sequences of the temptations in the desert, with images of contemporary poverty and hunger, and the Agony in the Garden with even more detail of the Crusades, the burning of a witch, as well as Jesus and Satan walking through the gunfire in a bombed town. In the desert a scarlet woman first appears and taunts Jesus with his human condition, inviting him to empty himself of his divinity, of his Father. Jeroen Krabbe then appears playing Satan dressed in a black suit and, again, offering Jesus tempting modern visions of power that resonate with a contemporary audience. He tells Jesus it has only just begun. He returns even more vengeful for those scenes at the Agony in the Garden.

Contemporary and Relevant

This Jesus film is an attempt to make the Jesus story contemporary and relevant.

The screenplay also gives a great deal of time to the Roman background of the times, with Pontius Pilate (Gary Oldman) center screen along with G. W. Bailey as Livio, a smiling but sinister courtier, adviser, and spy who runs between Herod and Pilate, ingratiating himself into their confidence. He is able to explain the Palestine situation to Pilate, as well as the situation with Caiaphas and the Temple, the Zealots, and the "Messiah." In an intriguing link between the two parts of the miniseries presentation, Livio indulges Pilate and his guests in a piece of theater poking fun at Jesus cleansing the Temple of the buyers and sellers (which has just preceded it). In this brief sequence, the attitude of the contemptuous Romans who heckle, laugh, and catcall is arrestingly communicated. Pilate leads the jeering. By the time of Jesus' entry into Jerusalem, Livio is much more serious, advising Pilate to kill Jesus, acting as counselor to Herod during Jesus' visit to him. Finally, at the foot of the cross, Livio's malice is complete: on hearing Jesus say that they know not what they do, he retorts, "We know exactly what we're doing, Messiah. We're killing you."

With the creation of Livio as well as Caiaphas' assistant, Jared, writer Suzette Couture takes a leaf out of the screenplay of *Jesus of Nazareth*, benefiting by introducing fact-based fictitious characters who can provide necessary information for the audience and heighten the conflict and drama.

Jesus' Humanity

The striking feature of this Jesus is his humanity. Jeremy Sisto (only twenty-four during filming) plays Jesus as a genial, very charmingly genial, man prone to emotions including anger, but someone who is able to joke, to laugh heartily (and splash his companions at the fountain), to dance at the wedding feast of Cana, and to be good company as well as a charismatic leader. His version of the Sermon on the Mount is an interactive lesson—Jesus offers a beatitude idea and individuals in the crowd ask questions or make suggestions. Some of them are jokey and Jesus seems to be enjoying himself, laughing and responding, a little in the vein of a stand-up comic who is a good teacher. This Jesus is able to gauge people's reactions very well and can move seamlessly from humor to serious instruction or exhortation.

This is a breakthrough from presentations of Jesus that seem afraid to let him be seen smiling, let alone laughing. This film also works on the premise that Jesus is consciously aware of his divinity. Jesus is seen to pray, to refer matters to his Father. This is presented solemnly in the raising of Lazarus (where, unfortunately, the dialogue attributed to Martha and Mary in John 11 is reversed; in fact it is to Martha, not Mary, to whom Jesus reveals he is the Resurrection and the life). The screenplay's overall ability to combine humanity with divinity should please theologians.

The television style uses plenty of close-ups of Jesus. Sisto adopts a quiet tone, almost underplayed at times, as in the scene where he is left alone with the woman taken in adultery. Mary Magdalene has witnessed Jesus' behavior and is stunned. Jesus sees her and invites her to follow him. She protests that she is free. Jesus casually and quietly says, "You're not free." And then in a comfortably conversational way adds, "But, you could be." Later, Mary says that his father would be proud of him. "Which one?" asks Jesus. "Both."

The celibacy issue is nicely handled. Mary of Bethany is in love with Jesus. Martha and Lazarus act as matchmakers. Jesus' dialogue explaining that his call in life must be without Mary is brief, compassionate toward her, but quite convincing.

Many episodes are omitted, including miracles and parables. Some that are included are unexpected. The calming of the storm after the walking on water is a bit literal visually but the point is made about little faith and Jesus puts his arm around Peter as they return to the boat. Also included is the encounter with the Syrophoenician woman. After Jesus agrees to heal her daughter, the disciples question whether he should be healing foreigners. Jesus remarks, "If I can learn, so can you."

A Credible Jesus

The selection of episodes means that the makers of this Sisto *Jesus* have read the potential audience correctly. For believers, this is not only a credible Jesus; it is a pleasing Jesus that they can relate to. For the devout, it is a nicely effective shock to appreciate this "real" Jesus. Robert Powell charmed audiences with his presence, his down-to-earth dignity. Jeremy Sisto makes his audience more comfortable in the presence of Jesus and able to make the transition to his "godliness" more readily.

The film also gives a great deal of attention to Mary, the mother of Jesus, played with dignity and calm by Jacqueline Bisset, a beautiful and mature woman. We see her at Nazareth with Joseph, who is kind with a touch of the crusty, as when he wonders why of all women Mary was chosen and keeps muttering "angel?" We see Mary waking Jesus up and then giving him the gifts of the Magi. She goes with him in his mission, reassuring him when he has moments of anxiety or doubt. She also befriends Mary Magdalene (whose conversion experience and discipleship are accurately but unobtrusively developed). Mary accompanies Jesus in his Passion, and we see her in Pietà tableau (with Andrew Lloyd Webber's *Requiem* on the soundtrack).

Passion and Resurrection

A lot of running time is given to the final week of Jesus' life, the triumphant entry into Jerusalem and Caiaphas consulting the Sanhedrin, reminding those who witnessed the raising of Lazarus, that it could be a fraud, that the dead do not rise (as a Sadducee, he did not believe in resurrection). Caiaphas also discusses the issue with Pilate and with his close assistant, agreeing that it is better for one man to die for the whole nation. Meantime, there is a powerful scene in which Judas makes his case in the upper room for Jesus to lead the revolution. Jesus' failure is the trigger for his betrayal, though he tells Peter after Jesus is arrested that he hoped Jesus would be stirred to anger and help the people rise up against the Romans.

The Last Supper sequence is quiet by comparison, very reverent with a touch of the da Vinci seating. It is in the Agony in the Garden and the return of Satan that the drama picks up intensity. Jesus says that he must face his death as a man, and falls on his face on the ground: "I am afraid I can't endure this." Satan tells Jesus that this is the final act, that there will be no reprieve from the Father. Satan also relishes his sadistic description of crucifixion and the slow suffocation. Jesus' answer is that in his death, "through me God will reveal his love for mankind." While Satan condemns God as "heartless," asking Jesus what kind of God would allow such poverty and war, Jesus offers him the answer about God giving us choice, the gift of free will, that God is not a dictator. "So this is what they choose," Satan retorts.

Finally, Jesus tells Satan that he will not die alone. He will be with his Father and "those who want to will find in me the strength to love to the end."

While the Passion narratives are dealt with in a familiar enough way, some of the visuals of the blood-spattered and crowned Jesus anticipate *The Passion of the Christ*. The same is true of the hammering of the nails, where Jesus really screams in pain; the pulling of the ropes to raise the cross; and the icon of Jesus on the cross.

The end of the film has delighted many audiences with its unexpectedness. The apostles dispute the death and Resurrection, with Thomas particularly vocal. He tells Mary, the mother of Jesus, that he wants to believe but "my mind won't let me." He needs to see. Mary Magdalene has seen Jesus in the garden and hugs him; as a consequence, instead of saying "Do not touch me," Jesus says, "You must let me go," a more telling and layered translation. Jesus acknowledges them all, quietly says that he will be with them, and walks out of the room.

And, here is the delight. Jesus walks out into the contemporary world. He is wearing casual clothes, his long hair cut in a more modern style. He strides out and greets the children who come running to be with him. And off he goes, carrying one, the others playfully clinging, with a gentle rock song over the scene and the final credits. It makes quite an impact.

JESUS (FRANCE, 1999)

Another Jesus film was released in 1999 but was not widely seen outside of French-language territories. It was simply called *Jesus*. It opens with Jesus' baptism and follows through his public life until the Passion and Crucifixion. The screenplay is based on a book by Jacques Duquesne, *Jesus: An Unconventional Biography*. In the film, directed by Serge Moati, which runs for 106 minutes, Jesus experiences doubts and struggles about his identity and his sense of mission. He is played by Arnaud Giovaninetti.

I GIARDINI DELL'EDEN

There has always been interest in Jesus' hidden life, from age twelve and the episode in the Temple until his baptism. Hindu writers speculate that he went to India. The Glastonbury myth (as explained in Julien Temple's elaborate documentary *Glastonbury* [2006]) has him traveling to Britain with his uncle, Joseph of Arimathea, with the Holy Grail eventually coming to Glastonbury to be associated with Arthurian legends.

Alessandro D'Alatri's 1998 film *I Giardini dell'Eden* focuses completely on this period, and has Jesus traveling east rather than west. The following is the description in the movies2.nytimes website:

> Alessandro D'Alatri directed this Italian drama about Jesus Christ, covering his childhood, adolescence, and early adulthood, an 18-year span not chronicled in the Bible. The film uses names of the period instead of names given in the Bible. The adult Jeoshua (Kim Rossi Stuart) reflects

on past events—his journey into the desert, baptism, acceptance into the Essenes' community, Jewish life in Galilee, his yeshiva studies, education from his father Josef, and his spiritual growth. After seeing slavery, crucifixions, the stoning of an adulteress, and brutal Roman soldiers, Jeoshua turns to God for answers, leaves the village, and is betrayed by his friend Aziz (Said Taghmaoui), who leaves him to die in the desert. Issues such as carnality bring Jeoshua in conflict with the Essenes, yet he speaks out on behalf of the Essene David (popular Italian singer Lorenzo Cherubini). Journeying forth once more, Jeoshua rejoins his cousin Jochannan, later known as John the Baptist, who recognizes Jeoshua's link to God. Shot in the Moroccan desert by lenser Federico Masiero, the film combines chants, vocals, and Middle Eastern–styled music by Pivio and Aldo De Scalzi.[1]

D'Alatri actually published a book on Jesus' hidden years which amplified his views on his choice of this period for making a Jesus film. He argued that Jesus was a literate man, familiar with Aramaic (his spoken language) and Hebrew (the language of the scriptures) as well as indications that he was familiar with Greek and could speak to Pilate in Latin. His role in reading in the synagogues and his familiarity with the scriptures confirms for D'Alatri that Jesus was a rabbi. He also suggests that this was a family tradition and that Joseph was also a rabbi—and rabbis had trades so Joseph was a rabbi carpenter.

D'Alatri also argues for Jesus traveling during those years. After all, he had been in Egypt as a baby and in Jerusalem at twelve. The main routes from through Galilee went south as well as going to the east. With the traditions of Jesus traveling to India, he points out that Jesus had ample time for a journey which took a few months to arrive in India and the same to return.

When D'Alatri considers Jesus' spoken words—after all in 4 BC there was no mass communication, so Jesus continued the oral tradition in teaching—reflect that range of people and situations that Jesus had seen at first hand: prodigals in exiles, kings with wedding feasts, laborers, vineyards, and fields of wheat. D'Alatri would claim that all his speculations in the film are grounded on Gospel texts.

THE MIRACLE MAKER

The Miracle Maker is a different kind of development for the Jesus film. After the "realism" of the 1960s and 1970s, the "stylization" of the rock operas, and the issues of the '80s like *Last Temptation* comes a puppet film with animated flashbacks, a more simple presentation of the Gospel stories, and with visual art flair.

With technical developments in the field of animation, especially with computer graphics, animated biblical films with both Old Testament and New Testament stories are proliferating. Prior to *The Miracle Maker*, some animated films had some success. The 1982 U.S./Japanese coproduction *Time kuoshitsu: Tondera House no dai boken* (*The Flying House*) was a series in which children encountering a scientist are transported to the lands of the Bible and experience the stories, including that of Jesus. *Yesu* is a 1998 animation version of St. Matthew's Gospel from Taiwan, South Korea, and Japan.

The puppet sequences, the major part of *The Miracle Maker*, were produced in Russia. The two-dimensional sequences were drawn in Wales by companies that had worked on animated short films of Shakespearian plays. The voices, with the exception of William Hurt as Jairus, are British. The puppets combine touches of realism with a sense of performance. They look Semitic, except for Pilate and the centurion. The settings are quite lavish and give a feel for the period and the land of Jesus.

A group of expert advisers from many churches contributed to the film, including Archbishop Rowan Williams of Canterbury, who was bishop of Monmouth at the time.

The two-dimensional animation via the flashbacks (the Nativity, finding Jesus in the Temple) as well as the use of some symbols (the temptations in the desert, the raising of Lazarus, the Agony in the Garden, and the Emmaus journey) and stylized parables (especially the houses built on sand and rock and the Good Samaritan) make a significant contrast to the three-dimensional puppetry. Jesus' words are spoken by Ralph Fiennes, who presents him as a strong-minded, genial young man with more than a touch of humor. He speaks the parables and teachings beautifully and clearly and brings powerfully anguished emotion to such scenes as the Agony in the Garden.

This is a very accessible and credible Jesus. Its particular appeal is to children, but most adults would appreciate and enjoy this telling of the story. Tamar, the daughter of Jairus and Rachael, is ill and cannot be cured. The decision to put Tamar and her parents to the fore as disciples and recipients of the miracle where she is raised to life means that this is a child's view of Jesus and his message. The audience sees Jesus through Tamar's eyes throughout the whole film. This device pays off dramatically.

Tamar sees a carpenter at work in the city of Sepphoris and is fascinated by him, especially in his defense of Mary Magdalene, a wild-eyed mad woman who haunts the town. When the foreman tries to lash her,

Jesus intervenes. When Jesus begins his public ministry, Tamar sees him again. The doctors give her no hope but her mother trusts that Jesus will heal her. Jairus is more cautious. He and his friend Cleopas go to the banquet hosted by Simon the Pharisee, and Jairus is overwhelmed by Jesus' kindness in receiving Mary. He calls Jesus to his daughter. From then on, Tamar is always at Jesus' side. She and the family are at the Last Supper (at an adjoining table). It is to Tamar that Jesus reveals that there are many mansions in his father's house—something she confides to another little girl on the mountain just after Jesus ascends to heaven. She is shocked when Jesus is arrested. Then, she and her parents follow Jesus to Calvary and are at the foot of the cross. Tamar even helps with placing Jesus in the shroud. The two disciples on the road to Emmaus are Cleopas and Jairus (who have sent Tamar and her mother on ahead for safety), so Tamar is the first to recognize Jesus in the breaking of the bread. And, she is there at the Ascension. *The Miracle Maker* is Tamar's view of Jesus.

The outline of the story is the familiar one. After his work in Sepphoris, Jesus leaves his work in the carpenter's shop at Nazareth, explains to his mother (who remembers his loss in the Temple as well as his birth and the visit of the Magi) that he must be about his Father's work.

He is baptized by John and is tempted in the desert. This is creatively shown in two-dimensional animation with an ordinary looking man as the devil who reappears at the Agony in the Garden, taunting Jesus to escape, opening up a path through the trees for him to pass through; the devil's voice is even heard briefly taunting Jesus on the cross. Stronger from the resistance to temptation, Jesus encounters Andrew and preaches the parable of the house built on the rock from Peter's boat. There is a huge haul of fish when Peter and Andrew go out to work.

Jesus has also healed Mary of Magdala and defended her when she came to Simon the Pharisee's house. The Pharisees are hostile as is Herod, whom the religious leaders consult. Pilate rules in the name of Caesar. Barabbas is a rebel but his friend, Judas, goes with great hopes to join Jesus.

Jesus has friends like Mary and Martha and enjoys visiting them (and later raises Lazarus from the dead). He heals the paralytic when people take away the roof. He comes to heal Tamar at Jairus' request (healing the woman with the hemorrhage on the way). Jesus enters Jerusalem triumphantly, clears the Temple, tells the story of the Good Samaritan, and urges his disciples that to be great they have to be like children.

Disappointed that Jesus will not rise up against the Romans, Judas betrays him. After his Last Supper, Jesus agonizes in the garden. Judas betrays him with a kiss—the scene has Jesus come alone through the apostles. It is only after the kiss that the troops appear. Peter, who has proclaimed his loyalty to Jesus, draws his sword quite violently but Jesus heals the wounded servant. Jesus is brought before the high priest and before Herod and Pilate, who finds no cause to condemn him. However, the people plead for Barabbas' release and Jesus is crucified.

After he dies, his body is taken down and buried but Mary Magdalene, who is shown wandering the streets grieving, finds him in the garden. Though it is not in the Gospels, Peter sees Jesus as do Jairus and Cleopas on the road to Emmaus. Thomas is presented as a forthright doubter but then a devout believer. Jesus promises to be with his disciples until the end of time. He then ascends to heaven.

While *The Miracle Maker* shows the whole public life of Jesus, a substantial amount, up to a quarter of the film, is given to the Passion of Jesus. The response of the disciples means that the entry into Jerusalem is a culmination of Jesus' ministry. Judas interprets it wrongly, that it is the beginning of the rebellion, and so betrays Jesus in disillusionment.

The Last Supper is also portrayed well, with the apostles at a table with Jesus, a bit da Vinci–like (where Jesus can walk to the end to talk with Judas and advise him to go to do what he must), but with other disciples at other tables. The Agony in the Garden is very effectively drawn in two dimensions with the symbol of the chalice appearing to Jesus, and Satan taunting Jesus in his torment about God's will.

Jesus could not be apprehended in public because of the reactions of the people (this is well dramatized in the discussion about the tribute to Caesar, which also dismays Judas), so, Judas has to identify him in the dark.

Though brief, the film shows us the response of the high priests and their question about the Messiah, the spurning of Jesus by Herod, and the previously supercilious Pilate coming around to see Jesus as no menace. But he is threatened as being disloyal to Caesar, and he washes his hands of everything.

One of the distinctive features of *The Miracle Maker* is the inclusion at some length of the walk to Emmaus. The screenplay uses the full text, which brings home to the audience the meaning of the Resurrection rather than simply presenting the fact of the Resurrection.

The Miracle Maker had more impact with its television screenings, with over eighteen million viewers watching it on network television in the United States on Easter Sunday in 2001.

GLI AMICI DI GESU

Called *Close to Jesus* in the United States and *The Friends of Jesus* internationally, this is a series of four films for television, directed by Raffaele Mertes, the cinematographer of the series of films of Old Testament characters, distributed by Time-Life. Mertes also directed the *Esther* film as well as *The Apocalypse* (with Richard Harris), which he also wrote.

There are four films in the series of friends of Jesus: *Joseph of Nazareth*, *Thomas*, *Judas*, and *Mary Magdalene*. Several of the cast carry over into the other films, like Mathieu Carriere as Pilate. Jesus in played by Danny Quinn, son of actor Anthony Quinn. The films are speculative dramas based on the Gospel narratives.

The *Mary Magdalene* film invents a great deal: that Mary was divorced by a wealthy husband from Magdala; that she took up with a Roman centurion who then rejected her; and that when she is welcomed at Herod Antipas' court by Herodias, she becomes the companion of another commander and engineers the death of her former lover.

Jesus has a few appearances. Mary attempts to drown herself but is rescued by Jesus and the apostles on the lake. She later glimpses him healing. However, she had seen John the Baptist at the Jordan and is distressed at his imprisonment. John sends her to Jesus to ask whether he is the one to come (Luke 7), and she brings back Jesus' reply to John. She engineers an attack on Magdala in which the young son of the slave Joanna dies. Grief stricken, she gives up hope, but Jesus arrives and saves the boy. The main scene with Jesus is Simon's banquet, where Mary weeps and wipes Jesus' feet with her hair. What follows is a very, very brief distant glimpse of Calvary and Mary's comment about Jesus' death and Resurrection.

Jesus is quite conventional in appearance and action, very American sounding with a somewhat reedy voice (as has the Baptist). There is a genial compassion in the close-ups of Jesus at Simon's house.

KRISTO

With the 1990s offering the technology for local industries and local groups to produce their Jesus films, the Philippines made the 1996 *Kristo*, directed by Ben Yalung.

This is an "indigenized" Jesus. He fits into the life and customs of Filipinos in the north of Luzon. While there is great fidelity to the Gospel texts, some of the familiar stories are adapted to the experience of the local people.

For instance, during the staging of the wedding feast at Cana, it is not water into wine that is the center of the miracle. Rather, the drink that the wedding guests enjoy is the local tuba, which derives from coconuts. The costumes of the bride and groom, of the master of the feast, and of the guests are what locals would wear to such a ceremony. The dancing is also local. (However, in something of a nod to the historical narrative, the Roman soldiers seemingly standing guard at the wedding are wearing recognizably Roman costumes.) In keeping with piety, Mary looks younger than Jesus himself. For the rest, the details of John 2 are dramatized in both word and action, with Jesus played by popular actor Mat Ranillo III and looking a commanding figure with strong screen presence, eminently loved by the camera.

This is also evident in the beatitudes sequence. It does not take place on a mountain. Rather, Jesus walks about like a teacher instructing and inspiring a rather smaller group of disciples and followers. Again, there is fidelity to the text. However, Jesus and the apostles have changed costume and are wearing the simple daily garb of the locals, with Jesus and the disciples all dressed the same. The temptations sequence is also quite striking, in a Filipino sand-and-hills setting.

This Jesus film screened in Philippine cinemas and appears on television. It is easily recognizable as part of the tradition of the Jesus film of the West but is distinctively Filipino to make the Gospel relevant to its intended audience.

In an interview with Walden Sadiri (the *Manila Bulletin Online*), Ben Yalung gives some background to his approach to religious filmmaking:

> This kind of film has been his life's mission ever since he became a more devout follower of the Roman Catholic life. According to him, when he converted from being a man of the world to a man who keeps up with God's teachings, he has decided to use his talent in retelling through film the messages of God. To his credit were other religious films like Ama Namin, Kristo and Divine Mercy.
>
> For Ben Yalung, his vision of doing religious films began after he graduated as a member of Oasis of Love Batch 6 in 1989. He was then the Head Servant of Oasis. From doing action films he decided that it was time to praise God by doing religious films. "Making money was far from my mind when I made this film. Even with my other religious films I never thought about money. I just wanted to preach through these movies and I have a better medium through film. Making these films is my commitment to the Lord. If ever it makes money then why not so I can produce more. My target is to make a film on the Acts of the Apostles which will be the sequel to *Kristo*. I just hope to be able to make a film for Holy Week every year."[2]

In fact, Yalung made some religious films, including one on the Divine Mercy. His 2005 film *Birhen ng Manaoag* focussed on the Virgin Mary and miracles and included scenes with Jesus.

NOTES

1. Bhob Stewart, "*The Garden of Eden* (1998): Review Summary," *New York Times*, movies.nytimes.com/movie/173732/The-Garden-of-Eden/overview.

2. Walden Sadiri, "'Birhen ng Manaoag,' a Mission for Filmmaker Ben Yalung," *Manila Bulletin Online*, telebisyon.net/balita/Birhen-ng-Manaoag-a-mission-for-filmmaker-Ben-Yalung/artikulo/85930/.

From the Manger to the Cross. Director, Sidney Olcott, 1912. General Film Company/
Photofest, © General Film Company

Civilisation. Director, Thomas Ince, 1916.
Triangle/Photofest, © Triangle

Intolerance. Director, D. W. Griffith, 1916. Triangle Film/ Photofest, © Triangle Film Company

Ben-Hur. Director, Fred Niblo, 1926. MGM/Photofest, © MGM

The Great Commandment. Director, Irving Pichel, 1939. 20th Century Fox/Photofest, © 20th Century Fox

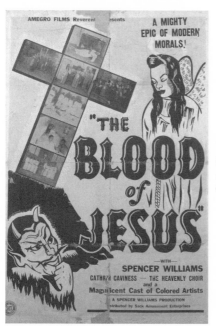

The Blood of Jesus. Director, Spencer Williams, 1941. Sack Amusement Enterprises/Photofest, © Sack Amusement Enterprises

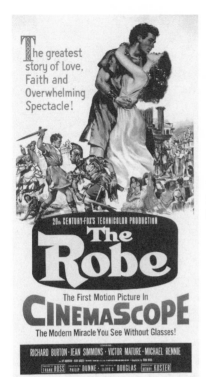

The Robe. Director, Henry Koster, 1953. 20th Century Fox/Photofest, © 20th Century Fox

Ben-Hur. Director, William Wyler, 1959. Metro-Goldwyn-Mayer/Photofest, © Metro-Goldwyn-Mayer

King of Kings. Director, Nicholas Ray, 1961. Photofest

Il Vangelo secondo Matteo. Director, Pier Paolo Pasolini, 1964. Continental Distributing Inc./Photofest, © Continental Distributing Inc.

The Greatest Story Ever Told.
Director, George Stevens, 1965.
UA/Photofest © United Artists

Godspell. Director, David
Greene, 1973. Columbia/
Photofest, © Columbia Pictures

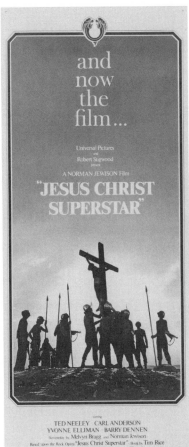

Jesus, Christ Superstar. Director, Norman Jewison, 1973. Universal Pictures/Photofest, © Universal Pictures

The Gospel Road. Director, Robert Elfstrom, 1973. © 20th Century Fox

The Passover Plot. Director, Michael Campus, 1976. Atlas Fim Corporation/Photofest, © Atlas Film Corporation

Jesus of Nazareth. Director, Franco Zeffirelli, 1977. NBC/ Photofest, © NBC

The Day Christ Died. Director, James Cellan Jones, 1980. CBS/Photofest, © CBS

The Last Temptation of Christ. Director, Martin Scorsese, 1988. Universal Pictures/ Photofest, © Universal Pictures

Jesus of Montreal. Director, Denys Arcand, 1988. Orion Classics/Photofest, © Orion Classics

Jesus. Director, Roger Young, 1999. CBS/Photofest, © CBS

The Gospel of John. Director, Philip Saville, 2003. Photofest

The Passion of the Christ.
Director, Mel Gibson, 2004.
Newmarket/Photofest, ©
Newmarket Films

The Book of Daniel Television series, 2006, NBC Photofest. © NBC

12

THE JESUS FILMS:
THE TWENTY-FIRST CENTURY

THE BODY

Interestingly, the first film of the new millennium to touch on the subject of Jesus is a problem story rather than a life of Jesus. Jonas McCord's *The Body* is a popular entertainment film that raises age-old apologetical questions about Jesus and the Resurrection. It is the material of *The Passover Plot* or *The Inquiry* (the former of which prejudged the issues of the Resurrection, while the latter raised familiar questions with interest and respect).

The body of the title is that of a man from the time of Jesus, which is found by a Jewish archaeologist (Olivia Williams) who thinks that the bones could be those of Jesus. Here we have the key question of the Resurrection for Christians. Jesus rose physically from the dead so the tomb has to be empty. There can be no body. (Theologians and scripture scholars have tended to say that there are more important thematic questions as to what Resurrection means in terms of Christology and redemption.)

The film is also a political thriller, so Palestinian and Muslim groups take an interest in what could upset the religious status quo and cause unrest. Israeli authorities have both political issues in mind. The archaeologist is Jewish, so traditions of hostile Jewish-Christian relationships could surface. Israel also has to deal politically with the rest of the world, with pro-Israel lobbies and anti-Semitic groups. Needless to say, the Vatican takes a strong interest and sends a priest-scholar (who has a secret agent background, Antonio Banderas) on a mission to prove that the body is not that of Jesus. A priest who has lost his faith (Derek Jacobi) is tormented by the discovery and its consequences.

This gives the screenplay much opportunity to include dialogue about Jesus as a person, about his sufferings and death, about the meaning of the

Resurrection. Jesus does not appear at all—nor are the bones those of Jesus. They are ultimately recognized as the son of a prominent Jew who leaves an inscription, a prayer that his son will be received just as Jesus was. But, the film does raise old questions in a contemporary context, which enables the audience to reflect on the body, the risen body, and the consequences for faith.

JUDAS

Originally titled, *Judas and Jesus*, this film focuses on Judas himself with Jesus being a significant presence but having more of a supporting role. It was made by a Catholic television company managed by the Paulist congregation who had made the Insight series for television and films such as *The Fourth Wise Man* and *Romero*. It was written by Tom Fontana, one of the creators of *Homicide: Life on the Streets* and *Oz*. It was directed by a devout Catholic, Charles Robert Carner. Paramount Television did not screen it when it was ready for release in 2001 but did broadcast it in early 2004 in the wake of the success of *The Passion of the Christ*.

Johnathon Schaech gives quite an impressive performance as Judas, the angry Zealot who believes that Jesus is the man to lead the Jews to revolution against the Romans, but who cannot quite commit himself as a disciple, who betrays Jesus and kills himself, feeling betrayed by Jesus.

On the other hand, television actor Jonathan Scarfe, is a smiling, "modern" Jesus, a kind of Californian surfie Jesus who does not always come across as a sufficiently strong and powerful presence, able to command commitment or loyalty from his followers. The producers were right in taking Jesus' name out of the title and focusing on Judas.

While the prevailing American accents (especially with Jesus and Pilate and, to a lesser extent, with Judas and Caiaphas) would not cause problems for American audiences, they do for non-Americans. Mary, however, and most of the apostles have British accents. The American accent sounds too contemporary for a story set in a particular historical period. In addition, the dialogue includes many contemporary American idioms that are understood but not used by non-Americans. This makes the film sound anachronistic rather than relevant. Pilate says that he hopes Jesus "will stay out of town." There are such phrases as "I'll pass," "I figure," "What d'ya say?" and ". . . , right?" and Herod (British accent) says of John the Baptist, "What a pain in the arse."

Be that as it may, Schaech is strong enough and many of the re-created Gospel scenes are powerful enough to offer some insights into the Gospel story.

Judas is presented as the son of a crucified Zealot (in a field of many crucified Zealots), embittered while still a boy, growing up resentful of the Romans, looking for a Messiah who will not "roll over" to the Romans. He has become a wine seller—though his mother says he was born for better, a visionary like his father. He does not mince words about the priests handing over money to the soldiers for extra taxes for Pilate. When he hears of John the Baptist, he goes to the Jordan where John assures him he is not the Messiah. His first glimpse (and the audience's) is of an angry and yelling Jesus overthrowing the buyers and sellers in the Temple. Judas is impressed and invites him to a meal, where Jesus is sorry, saying that no one is changed by yelling or anger or being deprived of their livelihood. When the disciples arrive, Judas says that they should not be treated like peasants. "We are peasants," says Jesus.

There follows a love-suspicion-hate relationship on the part of Judas toward Jesus. When he is mugged in the streets of Jerusalem and his house raided, Judas escapes to Galilee where he is welcomed by Jesus, although the other disciples are aware of his dark side and wish that Jesus would send him away. However, Jesus likes Judas—"I wish you could see in yourself what I see." The screenplay gives Jesus the opportunity to preach to small groups the gist of the Sermon on the Mount, which Judas criticizes. Judas, now in charge of finances (Jesus saying he is no good at this), suggests that they charge for cures, something that Jesus abhors. Jesus trusts in providence and refers to the lilies of the field and God's care of them. When Judas persuades Jesus to give the apostles his powers to heal, Judas interprets this as raising an army. And Judas fails to heal, while the simple James succeeds by opening his heart and praying the Our Father.

Jesus is grieved by the news about the arrest of John the Baptist. There is an interesting scene where Judas asks Mary in her kitchen about Jesus' father and finds her account of the Annunciation hard to accept.

Caiaphas, a strong figure in the film, has kept in touch with Judas and asks him to spy on Jesus, suggesting that the powers that be would support Jesus as long as he led no protests or demonstrations. After Jesus raises Lazarus and singles out Peter as leader, Judas becomes more disillusioned, thinks that Jesus is "lame" because of his melancholy. Caiaphas tells him that one man's betrayal is another man's salvation.

The rest of the film—apart from Judas' mother dying and Caiaphas suggesting that Jesus could raise her (and giving the thirty pieces of silver for the funeral)—goes according to the Gospels. Jesus celebrates the Last Supper, experiences the Agony in the Garden. The Passion sequences are brief, and Jesus is spotlighted in his appearances before Caiaphas and before Pilate. There is some melodrama as Pilate's wife, who up till now has been complicit in the plotting, especially about the staging of Barabbas' release, has her nightmare and rushes to warn Pilate to free Jesus.

Jesus is nailed to the cross, is lifted up, speaks some of his last words (also saying, "This was my destiny"), and dies. The sky darkens; the soldiers run; Mary holds Jesus, Pietà fashion; and a choir sings an Agnus Dei. The film ends with its Judas focus as three apostles cut down Judas and take him away for burial. They pray for Judas: "This is what Jesus would have wanted."

SAINT MARY

Saint Mary is a film version of an eleven-part miniseries of the same name produced in Iran at the beginning of the twenty-first century (114 minutes cut down from eleven 45-minute episodes). It is based on the stories of Mary in the Koran and in Islamic tradition and produced in Iran. The comparison between this story and the Gospel stories holds its own fascination, but it is all the more challenging for a dialogue between Christians and Muslims concerning Mary and the understanding of Jesus as Prophet and Messiah. This discussion could serve as a prologue for even deeper dialogue about the status of Jesus himself as portrayed in the 2005 *The Messiah*—retitled in 2007, *Jesus the Spirit of God*, also a product of the Iranian film industry—which invites theological reflection about the humanity and divinity of Jesus, his role in Christianity, and his place as a great prophet in Islam. *Jesus, the Spirit of God* will be considered later.

As with so many films about Mary, including Jean Delannoy's 1995 *Mary of Nazareth* and the 2006 *The Nativity Story*, *Saint Mary* culminates with the birth of Jesus with very little of a screen Jesus.

Saint Mary puts Mary at the forefront of the religious community of Jerusalem in her day. In 16 BC, Herod, who has collaborated with the Roman occupation of Judea, suffers from nightmares about the coming of a Messiah. However, Hannah, wife of the prophet Imran, gives birth to a girl, Mary. She is dedicated to life in the Temple under the care of her cousin, Zechariah. There is a great deal of dispute as to a female living in the Temple, so her own small house is built on to the Temple. Mary, even before she is ten, is devout and has the gift of healing (mirroring the miracles of her son).

Later, she is favored by God, even to mysteriously receiving gifts of fruit and grapes out of season. At the same time, Elizabeth is pregnant and Mary visits her as she gives birth. Mary becomes pregnant, and bewildered but trusting in God, she goes out into the desert to give birth under a palm tree, which suddenly bears fruit. There is no mention of Joseph or any father. When she returns carrying the baby Jesus, the leaders and the people turn against her for her sins and want to kill her (mirroring her son).

In the meantime, the wise men (from Persia/Iran) visit Herod to ask where the Messiah is to be born. They explain the prophecies of two thousand years and calculate the place for the birth. Herod acts in the same way as he does in Matthew 2 but sends his guard to search for the child and kill this rival king of Judea.

The climax of the film—and an extraordinary scene for a screen Jesus—has a religious leader asking the baby to justify his mother. And the baby does. He speaks out words of praise for Mary as well as explaining his role as God's prophet.

Saint Mary is similar in many points to Luke 1, especially with Zechariah in the Temple, Elizabeth's pregnancy, and the birth of the Baptist and Mary's visitation. It is not so similar to Luke 2, which relates Jesus' birth in Bethlehem. However, the parallels between the film and the Magi story in Matthew 2 are strong.

For Western audiences it would come as a surprise to see an Islamic film about Mary and even more of a surprise to see *Jesus, the Spirit of God.*

MARIA, MAE DO FILHO DE DEUS

In this Brazilian tale (2002), a mother takes her daughter to the hospital and, to put her at ease, recounts the story of Jesus and Mary and the Gospels.

THE APOCALYPSE

The Apocalypse (*L'apocalisse*, 2002) is part of the series of principally Old Testament stories filmed in Italy from the later 1990s (including *Abraham, Joseph, Moses, Jeremiah,* and *David*). Richard Harris, in one of his final roles, plays the aged John the apostle on Patmos. The emperor Domitian has proclaimed himself a god and Christians are being persecuted. They want John to come to the community in Ephesus to strengthen their resolve. The screenplay creates a fictional story (along the lines of *Quo Vadis*) about the son of a general who is a Christian and a young woman he is in love with. This subplot provides scenes of prisoners in the quarries of Patmos, Roman oppression, and an escape attempt and allows for John to do Jesus-like things in caring for the prisoners.

This is the context for some mystical visions that form the core of the Book of the Apocalypse. In them, there are brief flashbacks to the Crucifixion and, when John sees a man flogged, a flashback to Jesus' scourging. Within the visionary sequences, a glorified Jesus is seen with the 144,000 saved in their white robes. He is pictured reading the names of those written on the scroll. There are many lamb images, especially of the lamb that is slain.

The Apocalypse provides an opportunity for Richard Harris to give moving renditions of passages from John on love and to voice key apocalyptic sequences like those of the four horsemen, the breaking of the seals, and the coming down of the New Jerusalem.

THE GOSPEL OF JOHN

A new but traditional version of the Jesus story, *The Gospel of John*, premiered at the 2003 Toronto Film Festival. It was directed by British filmmaker Philip Saville, written by veteran John Goldsmith, and narrated by Christopher Plummer. The director says that the film follows the text itself; "every single word is there." However, it is also referred to as part of the series The Visual Bible (whose *Matthew* and *Acts* appeared in the mid-1990s and were considered earlier).

The Gospel of John offers a visualization of the complete text of the Gospel. It uses a contemporary translation, *The Good News Bible*, and avoids exclusivist masculine language. It is also careful to give the historical context of the clash between Judaism and Christianity in the first century and to offer nuances with its translation of "The Jews." When Jesus challenges the religious leaders, the translation used is "the Jewish authorities."

Narrative and Drama

The narrative is spoken, to great effect, by Christopher Plummer. Since there is a great deal of dialogue in the Gospel, many characters such as John the Baptist, Mary at Cana, Peter, and Philip have speaking parts. This is the case for the Samaritan woman at the well, the man born blind, Martha, and Martha's sister Mary. And, since so much of the Gospel is monologue by Jesus himself, much of the meaning has to be communicated by actor Henry Ian Cusick as Jesus.

Before the long discourses of Jesus begin in chapter 5 after the healing of the lame man in the pool at Bethzatha, the narrative takes time for many pauses. This works to great dramatic effect. The audience, which is looking at Jesus, at the other characters, at the settings, and at the action, has plenty of time to respond to what is going on. In fact, the pauses help us appreciate the inherent drama in the text. Later, the continuous discourses make heavy demands on the listener (as they do in liturgical readings). The screenplay sometimes "opens up" the images to give the eye and the imagination something to focus on as well as the words. In a visual medium, this can ultimately be distracting as the audience's attention goes to the images rather than concentrating on words and meanings. This is particularly true of the last discourse of Jesus (chapters 14–17).

The film was immediately released in the southern states of America, perhaps its natural home with its more literal presentation of the Gospels. This is one of the major difficulties of filming the Gospel of John. It is not a particularly "literal" Gospel. Rather, it is a narration of some of the "signs and wonders" that Jesus performed so that through them, "he let his glory be seen" and "his disciples believed in him." This is said specifically of the changing of water into wine at the wedding feast of Cana (2:1–11). How to visualize the story while highlighting its "mystical" meaning over its "realistic" tone? This is something that the film does not really attempt—though, strangely, one moment where this kind of potential is shown is in the conversation between Jesus and Nathanael (1:43–51): when Jesus tells Nathanael he saw him under the fig tree, we see a flashback to Nathanael's moments of contemplation under the fig tree, divine light shining through the leaves with Nathanael in rapture. Generally, the film stays with a literal and realistic picture of events.

Signs and Wonders

The first two chapters work quite well. As Christopher Plummer speaks the prologue, we see images of the sun and the spreading light as well as the daily lives of people—who do not recognize Jesus, the Word of God made human, who is glimpsed first through shadow and an overhead tracking shot of his walking toward the Jordan. The Baptist scenes are effective as drama, building up to Jesus' own baptism (with close-up of the face of the immersed Jesus rather than any voices from heaven or literal doves). The calling of the disciples is well edited, very filmic, with action filling in detail during the pauses between the speaking of the actual words of the text. This is also true of Cana, where Mary is seen as a dignified, very matronly figure. Drama goes into action as the text stops and vigorous scenes of Jesus clearing the Temple of buyers and sellers visualize the text.

Chapter 3 and the discussion with Nicodemus introduce the Gospel text as a dialogue. The conversation style helps the audience appreciate the talk of being born again. This continues very well in chapter 4 with Jesus meeting the Samaritan woman at the well. The conversation is both serious and ironic, the woman parrying Jesus' comments with a wry smile. She is an interesting and engaging personality. As naturalistic conversation, it does not (and cannot) quite work, especially when the woman moves the conversation to specific religious matters about prophecy and worship on Mt. Gerizim and Jesus introduces discussion of the Spirit of God blowing where it wills.

Discourse

The difficulty in filming the complete text of John comes to the fore in the second part of chapter 5. After Jesus heals the cripple at Bethzatha, he moves into discourse. Jesus roams, the camera roams to convey a sense of action and drama, but the text is meditative. It is the same with the long chapter 6 on the bread of life. The feeding of the five thousand and the walking on the water take the audience back into drama but then there is more discourse on the bread of life. The hostility of many of the disciples to this teaching gives the discourse some edge.

Discourse is the main focus along with controversy with the religious authorities about the authenticity of Jesus' teaching and claims from chapter 7 to chapter 12. These are interrupted (welcome interruptions) by the story of the woman taken in adultery, which is treated quite straightforwardly according to the text, although Jesus shows a winning and smiling side as he sends her off without condemnation and the urging to sin no more (chapter 8). The story of the man born blind (chapter 9) is one of the best dramas in the whole Gospel with quite a number of speaking parts (which is how it is best communicated in liturgical reading).

The scene shifts from the Temple to the man washing at the pool of Siloam, back into the Temple, then to the Sanhedrin where the man and his parents are interrogated by the chief priests and Pharisees. This confirms in the viewers' minds who Jesus' antagonists are, especially Caiaphas.

An advantage of images is that they can be filmed as background to Jesus' sayings. He walks amongst sheep in chapter 10, the Good Shepherd chapter. In chapter 15, during the last discourse, he can walk through vines in a vineyard on his way to Gethsemane and speak of his being the true vine. Chapter 11 is another dramatic example of the signs and wonders, the death and the raising of Lazarus, the narrative giving a setting for Jesus telling Martha that he is the Resurrection and the life. This continues in chapter 12 with the banquet at the house of Martha, Mary, and Lazarus, with Mary's washing Jesus' feet with ointment and wiping them with her hair. At last we see Judas and hear his comments about selling the ointment for the poor. He gives a particularly arresting tone to his uttering three hundred denarii—it will not be long before he accepts thirty.

The Last Supper, the Last Discourse, the Passion

Chapter 12 is the preparation for the Passion: Caiaphas making his statement about one man dying for the good of the nation; Jesus saying about the grain of wheat dying in the ground before it produces fruit; Philip bringing the Greek visitors to see Jesus; Jesus saying he will draw all people to himself when he is lifted up; the roll of thunder that seems like the voice of God approving Jesus. Once again, the camera combines movement and contemplation as Jesus speaks and the crowd listens.

With John's version of the Last Supper, the emphasis is not Eucharistic (that has been the topic of the long chapter 6). Rather, this is at last Jesus' hour to be glorified and for him to glorify the Father (foreshadowed in the changing of water into wine at Cana). Jesus' key action at the supper is the washing of the disciples' feet and announcing the new commandment of love by which all would be known as his disciples: to love one another, just as Jesus himself loved. Judas goes out—and it is night.

For chapters 14–17, the long discourse of Jesus after the supper and his final prayer for his disciples, screenwriter and director chose to take it out of doors before the indications given at the start of chapter 18 of how they went through the Kedron valley to Gethsemane. Jesus and the disciples are on the way almost immediately. An interesting feature is that Mary Magdalene is present all the time, receives some close-ups as she listens to Jesus, and receives an individual blessing along with the other apostles.

The discourse can then be broken, visually, by the walk through the vineyard, through the tunnels of Jerusalem to the garden. When the screenplay gets too word heavy, there are many flashbacks, in fact, recapitulating the whole film. Intercut at once is the procession of soldiers and the crowd led by Judas toward Gethsemane. This gives the film a dramatic drive just when the text slows to mystery and mystical contemplation and prayer.

In the aftermath of *The Passion of the Christ*, most Passion dramatizations might seem somewhat slight. In John's Gospel, chapters 18–19, Jesus is scourged (here there are nine lashes some of which we see) and crowned with thorns, but when Pilate does bring Jesus out to the crowds, there is not much blood visible, some spatterings on Jesus' face that look more the result of makeup than torture. The core of the Passion narrative is the dialogue with Pilate, which is presented dramatically, and the release of Barabbas as the crowds call out for Jesus to be crucified. Jesus' death is presented reverently. Mary appears briefly at the foot of the cross, along with John

and Mary Magdalene. The pace of Jesus' dying goes with the Gospel text
and is brief—with attention given to the piercing of Jesus' side.

Resurrection

After the burial by Nicodemus and Joseph of Arimathea, the Resurrection narrative of chapter 20 moves quickly as well, apparitions to Mary,
the eleven, and then to Thomas. There is a longer treatment of the added
chapter 21, which again has narrative interest and moves outdoors to the
Sea of Galilee and the apostles fishing, Peter swimming to shore to Jesus.
The threefold profession of love is presented rather quietly, all seated
around the breakfast fire. When they all rise and Peter's death is foretold,
there is a momentary visual flash forward showing Peter's death while the
image freezes on John as the final words of the Gospel are spoken.

Watching *The Gospel of John* in one sitting is very difficult since it is
so long. While the visualizing of some of the Gospel narratives is helpful—
and Cusick's Jesus combines the traditional style of dignified stature more
than a cut above ordinary people with the more recent emphasis on genial
humanity—so much of the Gospel is meditative, long reflective passages.
The film is probably best seen, not in one sitting, but rather in sections, so
that the audience has time and powers of concentration to appreciate it.
The individual scenes could well be presented as the reading of the Gospel.
One of the strengths of an actor like Cusick speaking the discourses of Jesus
is that he speaks them with acting flare, intonations, and pauses, bringing
them to life and meaning better than the usual proclaimer of the Gospel.

THE PASSION OF THE CHRIST

The world and the film industry were surprised (the industry was astonished) by the commercial popularity of Mel Gibson's *The Passion* with
Jim Caviezel as Jesus. It focused on the last twelve hours of Jesus' life and
drew both on the Gospel texts as well as the writings of a German mystic
favored by Gibson, Anne Catherine Emmerich, who, from her prayer (her
"visions") gave detailed descriptions of what she saw of the Passion. Gibson
opted for Latin and Aramaic dialogue, wanting the audience to focus on the
visuals of Jesus' suffering.

Anti-Semitic? Too Sadistic?

The immediate response from some Jewish scholars as well as Catholic
(basing their comments on a draft of the screenplay) was that the film was

anti-Semitic. This raised issues both of how John's Gospel spoke of "the Jews" and their responsibility for Jesus' death and of the Matthew text (27: the "blood curse" on the Jews present and their descendants). The long traditions of Christians accusing Jews of being "Christ-killers" played their part in the debate. While the Catholic church apologized for the long persecutions and anti-Semitism in a Second Vatican Council document (1965) and Pope John Paul II visited the wailing wall in 2000 and inserted his own prayer in a crevice, questions about Jesus' death as being part of God's plan and how the Jewish religious leaders of the time and the Romans, with Pontius Pilate, fit into this plan, continue to be raised.

While Gibson continued to work on editing the film during 2003, several of the religious leaders who saw versions of *The Passion* thought that it was not anti-Semitic but that many audiences would find the visual depictions of Jesus' suffering and death too vivid and disturbing.

For over a year before the release of *The Passion of the Christ*—on Ash Wednesday, February 25, 2004—there was worldwide discussion and quite some controversy based on the apprehensions about how the film would be made as well as on sensitivities about Jewish-Christian history, anti-Semitism, and current dialogue between Judaism and the churches, especially in the United States.

The Passion of the Christ had been a long-cherished project of actor-director Mel Gibson. Gibson's Catholic affiliation and his support of traditional Catholicism, with the influence of his very outspoken father, was another controversial factor in the discussions. Early screenings of *The Passion* as a work in process offered opportunities for church leaders and Christians involved in media to see the actual film, offer their opinions, and dialogue with Mel Gibson. There seemed to be a general consensus that the film was not anti-Semitic. Some Jewish leaders and reviewers like Michael Medved spoke positively about the film. Several heads of Vatican offices saw a show-reel of the film and spoke in favor of the film, including Archbishop John Foley, head of the Pontifical Council for Social Communications, and Cardinal Dario Castrillon of the Congregation for the Clergy, who issued a statement urging all priests to see the film. Cardinal Walter Kasper received comments from Jewish leaders and issued a statement that the Vatican at large was not recommending the film and that any recommendation would depend on people seeing the completed film. This was the stance of many religious leaders in the United States, including the American Bishops Catholic Conference.

Early Christian-Jewish Antagonism

As regards the Jewish-Christian issues and the explicit language about the Jews in the Gospels, especially that of St. John, it is important to realize that the more formal, "official" antagonism between Christians and Jews emerged in the early decades of the second century. The Gospels of Matthew, Mark, and John emerged from Jewish communities. Luke's Gospel draws strongly on the Jewish scriptures, interweaving biblical references and motifs throughout the text. The clash between Jesus and the religious leaders of his time was a clash within Judaism, a religious controversy about the Messiah (of which there were a number in this period) and Jesus' claims. Disciples who became Christians accepted his claims. Many religious leaders amongst the priests and the Pharisees did not. There were other converts like Paul, who was proud of his Jewish heritage and who took a strong stance about disciples of Jesus not being bound by details of Jewish law. It has been difficult, given the centuries of antagonism and the experience of repression and persecution of Jews by Christian, and Catholic, communities to enter into the context of Jesus' time and the mentality of the period.

Biblical Background

The Passion of the Christ draws its narrative from each of the four Gospels, for instance, the quake and the rending of the Temple from Matthew, the fleeing young man from Mark, the women of Jerusalem (here, Veronica and her daughter) from Luke, and the Pilate sequences on truth from John. This linking of incidents in one narrative is the way in which the Gospel stories were remembered and written down. There is some material drawn from the later legendary stories and apocryphal Gospels (Veronica and her veil, Desmes the "bad" thief).

One of the difficulties that films of the life of Jesus encounter, especially from scholars and theologians who are not versed in the techniques and conventions of cinematic storytelling, is that they sometimes tend to be critiqued and judged as if they were actual Gospels. They are found wanting at this level and dismissed or condemned. This is a danger for *The Passion of the Christ*. It needs to be reiterated that this is a film and that the screenplay is a "version" of the Gospel stories with no claim to be a Gospel.

This use of the four Gospels means that there are different perspectives on the Jews of the time in each Gospel. Matthew's Gospel presupposes detailed knowledge of the Jewish scriptures and sees Jesus as the fulfillment of prophecy—hence the more "apocalyptic" scenes at his death. Mark and Luke look on from the outside, Luke writing for readers familiar with Greek and Roman ways of storytelling. John's Gospel from the end of the first century echoes the roots of Christianity in Judaism but acknowledges the growing rift.

The screenplay is able to combine Gospel incidents into a coherent narrative of the Passion with selected flashbacks to Jesus' infancy and life at Nazareth. The action of the Passion is intercut with brief scenes of Jesus' fall as a child and his mother picking him up, his making a table in the carpenter's shop, his relationship with his mother, and his playful sprinkling of her with water as he washes his hands. These are the screenwriters' inventions in the spirit of the Gospels. There are also flashbacks to Mary Magdalene's past where she is combined with the woman taken in adultery of John 8:1–11, to Peter and his protests of loyalty, to the Last Supper. There is a flashback to the palm welcome of Jesus to Jerusalem during the heckling of the crowd on the way to Calvary. There is dramatic development of characters like Pilate and his wife, Simon of Cyrene, the centurion, the good thief, and the thief who reviles Jesus (with retribution seen in the form of a vicious crow attacking him). Of interest is the portrait of Satan, the Tempter, who appears early as an androgynous character, visual suggestions of female but male voice, growing more obviously feminine as the film progresses and finally appearing at the Crucifixion (with a visual technique reminiscent of William Wallace seeing his loved one at his execution) carrying a child. Once again, this is imaginative license in interpreting Jesus' being tempted and tested.

As with most Jesus films, much attention is given to Judas. His motivations are not made explicit in the film. It relies on audience knowledge of Judas. The film portrays his action in Gethsemane and subsequent dismay and return of his thirty pieces of silver. It introduces a theme of children meeting Judas and taunting him as he goes to his death.

Theological Background: The Humanity and Divinity of Jesus

The Passion of the Christ generally follows the approach to the person of Jesus used by the Synoptic Gospels, a "low" Christology, a focus first on the humanity of Jesus and moving toward an awareness of his divinity. When the film uses John as a source, it reflects that Gospel's "high" Christology, the presupposition in the narrative that Jesus is divine and expresses this divinity in word and action. The Synoptic approach is seen in the flashbacks of incidents before the Passion as well as in the main events of the Passion, the Agony in Gethsemane, the treatment of Jesus by the Sanhedrin and Herod, the scourging and crowning with thorns, and the way of the cross and the Crucifixion itself. The Johannine approach is found in Jesus' declaration of his being the Son of Man at his trial (which is also in the Synoptics) and the discussions with Pilate about truth and about Jesus' kingdom.

This means that, theologically, the film presents the perennial teaching that Jesus, in his person, was both human and divine in nature.

The humanity of Jesus is often presented in a striking manner: Jesus working in Nazareth; the experience of deep human pain in his agony, scourging, falling on the way to Calvary; the nailing and his experience on the cross. It is there in his dignity at his trial, in his composure with Pilate and Herod. The film also highlights Jesus' human anguish of soul and sense of abandonment in his agony and on the cross, along with his profound surrender to the Father.

While the Jesus of cinema is usually slight and slender in build, Caviezel is big and strong, with some girth, a credible carpenter and a solid man. This makes the film's Jesus more real than usual.

Theological Background: The Resurrection

Some commentators criticize a film that focuses on the Passion for its meager treatment of Jesus' Resurrection. (This was a criticism in the 1960s and 1970s of *Jesus Christ Superstar*.) Theologically, the Passion makes sense only in the light of the Resurrection.

While Mel Gibson's film wants to immerse its audience in the experience of the Passion, the final sequence has the stone rolled over the tomb. The stone is rolled away, the cloths wound around Jesus' body are seen collapsing and the camera tracks to Jesus in profile, sitting in the tomb as a prelude to his risen life. These are the images with which the audience leaves the theater. The Resurrection, presented briefly, is still the climax of the Passion.

Theological Background: The Eucharist

There are flashbacks to the Last Supper during the Passion, especially to Peter protesting that he would not deny Jesus and to Jesus washing the disciples' feet.

One of the major theological strengths of the film is the insertion of the Eucharistic scenes of the Last Supper during the nailing and the lifting up of Jesus on the cross. As Jesus offers the bread as his body, we see the body that is painfully broken and given for us. As he offers the wine as his blood, we are only too conscious of the bloodletting, blood poured out for us. Jesus tells his disciples that there is no greater love than laying down one's life for friends—and we see it in its fullness. He tells them to celebrate the Eucharist so that his Passion and death will be present to them.

In this way, the screenplay highlights both aspects of the Eucharist: the celebration of the meal and the sacrifice of Jesus.

The Place of Mary

Mary has a strong presence in *The Passion of the Christ*. She appears as a woman in her forties, striking rather than beautiful. She appears in two flashbacks. Her demeanor is serious. She says very little. With Mary Magdalene and John, she follows the Passion and the way of the cross without any of the histrionics that characterize a number of portraits of Mary, especially Pier Paolo Pasolini's mother in *The Gospel according to St. Matthew* (who was more like a real Jewish mother, it was suggested by a Jewish mother, than Mary played by the Jewish Maia Morgenstern). At one stage, she wipes the blood of Jesus on the praetorium floor after his scourging. She kisses his bloody nailed feet. The bond between mother and son is suggested several times by significant eye contact rather than words. The request for John to take care of Mary is included. After Jesus is taken down from the cross, she holds him in a Pietà tableau. She gazes intently at the camera and at the audience as the camera withdraws from the scene.

Most audiences should be satisfied with the portrayal of Mary. Those who find some of the cinema representations of the past too much like holy cards or plaster statues will appreciate a more biblically grounded Mary.

Realism and "Naturalism"

One of the principal intentions of the director and his co-screenwriter, Benedict Fitzgerald, is to immerse audiences in the realism of the Passion of Jesus. Caviezel was chosen to play Jesus; the only other name performer is Italy's Monica Bellucci as Mary Magdalene. Caviezel was the same age as Jesus when the film was shot. As mentioned earlier, he is a believable human Jesus, a big, solid workingman who was able to stand up to the terrible sufferings of the Passion before he died.

One of the controversial aspects of the film was the early decision to have the film's dialogue in Aramaic and Latin with no subtitles. The language decision was followed through and works well, but we needed the subtitles, many of which are quotations from scripture. But, there is no distraction in hearing anachronistic American or British voices and accents. Rather the audience hears what conversation was like in those days. It is helpful to be reminded that Jesus spoke Aramaic and not English!

A useful distinction to be made is that between "realism" and "naturalism." The latter refers to filmmaking that portrays action as it is, home movies being a popular example, as is footage shot for newscasts. Realism is filmmaking that helps audience have a genuine feel for what is happening on the screen, as if it were real. A number of cinematic devices, such as the style of different compositions for the screen, the types of shots, and the pace of the editing can be used to give this impression of realism.

Mel Gibson has opted for much of his film to be naturalistic. He has plenty of time available and is in no hurry to take us away from the picture of Jesus' suffering. Perhaps a number of people in the audience will find the scourging (in two grim parts) too much to watch. This is a matter for sensibilities and sensitivity as well as cultural differences. With most of the characters being portrayed in a naturalistic way, the action seems authentic. However, Gibson is able to use cinematic devices that alter perceptions, helping us to realize that we are seeing a particular version of the Passion, as all of us do when we listen to the Passion narratives and use our imaginations. He frequently uses moments of slow-motion filming to make us dwell on a particular moment. He uses a musical score with a wide range of orchestral and choral tones.

This naturalism is seen in the confrontation in Gethsemane, at Jesus' trial, with the scourging and the crowning with thorns, and, especially, during the way of the cross as Jesus struggles with the cross, falls with thudding impact, is nailed, and the cross is raised. The stylization is seen in the close-ups, with the differences in lighting (Gethsemane blue, the confined space of the high priest's court lamp-lit, the broad daylight of the way of the cross), in the framing of the characters with memories of the traditions of Christian painting, in the lighting and some of the tableaux, in the passing of time as Jesus hangs on the cross, in his death and the apocalyptic aftermath, and in the intimations of the Resurrection.

This offers a credible picture and understanding of Jesus. Gibson has introduced some effective elements to reinforce this. For instance, in the garden, Jesus is hit in the eye and from then on and during the trial, he has the use only of one eye; when Jesus is able to open his injured eye, Gibson makes a great deal of his ability with eye contact—with Pilate, with his mother, and with John at the foot of the cross, simply looking at Jesus and nodding as he agrees to care for Mary.

Dramatically, familiar Gospel characters are briefly developed, which helps the narrative: Peter, Judas, Pilate, Pilate's wife, Simon of Cyrene, Herod, and the two thieves crucified with Jesus. Veronica is introduced as she watches Jesus pass and wipes his face with her cloth—but Gibson shows restraint by letting us see her holding the cloth and, if we look closely, suggestions of the outline of Jesus' face can be glimpsed. The Roman soldiers are also vividly dramatized: the brutes at the scourging with their sadistic commander, the drunken soldiers mocking and brutalizing Jesus along the way and on Calvary, the more sympathetic centurion. The key figure who has powerful dramatic impact in every Jesus film is Judas. The taunting of the tormented Judas and the children pursuing him to his death is dramatically effective.

The Passion of the Christ offers a credible, naturalistic Jesus whose sufferings of body and spirit are real. At its release, it was difficult to predict what impact it would have on those who are not believers. For those who believe, there was the challenge of seeing pain and torture, which are easier to read about than to see, but there was also the satisfaction of experiencing familiar Gospel stories in a different way.

After a Year

One of the interesting features of re-viewing the film a year and more after the initial controversy is that the film seems stronger. Sensitive to the criticisms that the film was anti-Semitic, many thought that the appearances, especially of Annas and some of the Sanhedrin, seemed like caricature villains (though they are less obvious than in some of the better-known Jesus films). This does not seem to be the case upon subsequent viewing. Trying to hear whether the "blood curse" of Matthew's Gospel was spoken by the leaders and the crowd, we hear only a murmur, no distinct words.

Mel Gibson responded to comments during 2004 that *The Passion of the Christ* was too brutal and bloodthirsty for some audiences and many potential viewers said that the reports of the visual violence influenced their decision not to see the film. Gibson recut the film so that it was six minutes shorter. More accurately, he "trimmed" his film with the hope that it would find the audience who did not see it originally and that it would receive a lower age classification this time, making it accessible to younger audiences. In fact, the British Board of Censors, which gave the film an 18+ rating in 2004, gave the recut version a 15+ certificate (whereas 15+ was the classification given to the original version in Ireland).

In fact, the recut version seems very little different from the original cut. The alternate images of Mary during the scourging and the lessening of the loud impact of the whips means that this sequence, though still very strong, does not seem quite so "over the top." The way of the cross seems unchanged—except for a lessening of the impact of the crow's attack on the unrepentant thief.

Reception in Other Countries

The film was screened in many Asian countries. As might be expected, it was very popular in the Philippines, the Catholic country of Asia, a country with a Hispanic religious tradition that has followed the devotional aspects of Catholicism with great emotion, even passion. In some areas, there are vividly physical re-enactments of Christ's Passion. This audience has very little difficulty in responding straightforwardly to the strong presentation of Jesus' suffering.

However, the film was successful in unexpected areas. It broke box-office records in Dubai, where the population is 85 percent expatriate, many from the Philippines but also from Sri Lanka, India, and Pakistan. Lebanon was another country where it drew large audiences.

In Hong Kong, where the Catholic Audiovisual Office prepared the Chinese subtitles, it was showing on twenty-seven screens during Easter weekend 2004. The distributors limited the screenings in Bangkok to six (with the Catholic office again preparing the subtitles) but they were immediately booked out, and so another four performances (with discussion following) were permitted.

The situation was different in neighboring Malaysia where the religious and legal climate did not permit public screenings. Audiences watched the film on pirated copies—pirating is something of an industry in this part of the world.

Issues of anti-Semitism are not prevalent in most countries of Asia.

The film, as might be expected, was very popular in Latin America. It was very strong in Brazil with its population near to that of the United States. Once again, the Hispanic and Iberian religious traditions and sensibility mean that audiences are immediately "on the wavelength" of this kind of film. The violent sequences do not seem out of place as they do in more reserved European cultures. Rather, audiences identify with the experiences of Jesus and his suffering. It was said in the 1970s that South America was the region where Franco Zeffirelli's *Jesus of Nazareth* was most popular. Many church leaders were supportive of the film.

One difficulty that emerged in Western comment was that the theology and spirituality underlying the film were inferior to those of more developed cultures, which sounds somewhat patronizing, even colonialist.

Europe was the region of the world where there was the greatest diversity in response to *The Passion of the Christ*. It was well received in Eastern European countries, especially Poland. Perhaps it was a heritage of religious persecution in the twentieth century that led audiences to identify more with the sufferings of Jesus. Opinion differed in Western European countries. Italy, Spain, and Portugal saw strong audiences. However, in France, there was a mood of hostility toward the film: American, religious, violent. In Germany and Benelux, the violence was considered far too much for its audiences, and the film was disliked by critics and some religious leaders, although many popular audiences went to see it. It was more successful in Ireland and, despite generally hostile criticism in Britain, *The Passion of the Christ* was top of the box-office chart for two weeks. Release was spread out through Europe—earlier in Lent in Italy, capitalizing on fervor, later in Lent in Britain, where it caught religious interest as Holy Week approached.

Different Christian groups in Europe contributed to an appreciation of the film from a religious standpoint. A German Protestant group prepared a book of reviews reflecting the wide range of opinion. In England, a group prepared a booklet of questions and answers about the film and about the Gospels. It was distributed at many of the cinemas screening *The Passion of the Christ*.

The issue of the violence of the film and the brutality depicted has caused a great deal of media debate and prevented a number of people seeing the film, fearing they would not be able to watch and bear the violence. Had the film been about any other person but Jesus, would the film have been made like this and allowed to be shown?

Practically everyone who saw *The Passion of the Christ* in 2004 felt compelled to mention the scourging and its brutality whether they admired the film or not. In retrospect, it seems somewhat strange that so much comment was made on what people saw in those nine minutes and comparatively little on the flashbacks, which were so well placed to give a wider perspective on Jesus' personality as well as his ministry and which, in dramatic terms, relieved the intensity of the torment.

The sight of blood has varying effects on different people. There are some robust sensibilities that are not so disturbed by it. Blood has been part of their history. There are other sensibilities that are more fastidious about the sight of blood. This seems to be the case in Western Europe where there has been a tradition for some decades to enforce tighter controls on depictions of violence (in contrast with a more liberal attitude toward the depiction of sexual behavior). Mel Gibson's career came into focus in this regard—his action films such as the Lethal Weapon series and others, as well as his depiction of the battles and death of William Wallace as Braveheart. He was considered as too bloodthirsty. Some reviewers referred to his "zealot's rapture" for the Passion and as indulging in sadomasochism.

This is what many saw: because they felt that the violence was over the top, it seems to have prevented them from seeing so much more that was in the film. The caption at the opening of the film is a quotation from Isaiah 53, the suffering Servant of Yahweh. The Servant songs of the Book of Isaiah are the peak of redemptive theology in the Jewish scriptures: the innocent Servant who is prepared to be the innocent lamb led to the slaughter bearing the sins of others in vicarious suffering. Vicarious suffering has always been acknowledged and admired as complete self-sacrifice. The Jerusalem Bible translation includes the phrase to describe the impact of the suffering Servant on those who witnessed his suffering: "they were appalled on seeing him."

"Appalled" is the biblical word, and that is what Gibson wanted in his audience. Jesus' suffering and death are shocking. Perhaps too long an easy spirituality and sanitized art has prevented us from being appalled.

It is surprising to read the Passion account in Matthew's Gospel and note how much detail of the screenplay is taken from that text. Dramatically, many sequences are just as effective: Peter and his protestations, his drawing of his sword, his denials in the jostle of the courtyard, and his weeping and confession to Mary; the significance of Judas, his going to the authorities, Gethsemane, his bewilderment in the courtyard, his torment by the children, and the rotting corpse of the donkey as he hanged himself; the support of Simon of Cyrene, who is taunted as being a Jew.

Caviezel's screen presence is strong, a well-built man who could endure so much suffering. His quiet gentleness, smiles, and humor in the flashbacks are a welcome counterbalance to the suffering. Morgenstern's performance and presence as Mary made a great impact originally and retain their power, both her strength in grief and the moment when she weeps.

SAN PIETRO

San Pietro (Saint Peter) is a 2005 Italian television production with Omar Sharif as Peter. It's a film reverent in tone that opens with Peter's Gospel encounters with Jesus and then moves into the early decades of the spread of Christianity. Running for three hours, it received better reviews from Catholic countries whereas some Protestant and evangelical viewers from the United States complained that the film was too Catholic, especially in its treatment of Peter's leadership and the place of Rome in the church. Director Giulio Base had also made television movies about St. Maria Goretti and St. Pio, better known as Padre Pio.

During the opening credits, Jesus is glimpsed on the cross, with John and a howling Mary Magdalene at the foot of the cross. The early part of the film goes back to the Last Supper (da Vinci again) and a discussion about Peter and his life. With Peter absent from the Passion except for his three-times denial (seen later in flashback), the film shows Jesus' burial process and the work of Mary, mother of Jesus, and Mary Magdalene. However, Peter goes to the tomb and sees the light of the risen Jesus. He is the strength of the apostles who are full of fear and confusion after the death of Jesus.

A great deal of attention is given to the episode in John's Gospel, chapter 21, when Peter and others are out fishing on the Sea of Galilee and Jesus appears. Peter leaps into the water to greet Jesus. The episode of Peter's commission to feed Jesus' lambs and sheep is highlighted. At the end of Peter's life, there is a flashback to the scene in Matthew 16, where Peter is called the rock on which Jesus will build his church. Peter dies crucified like Jesus.

COLOR OF THE CROSS AND COLOR OF THE CROSS 2: THE RESURRECTION

Advertised for U.S. distribution in October 2006, *Color of the Cross* indicates a new direction for the Jesus film: Yeshua as black with issues of racism behind his Passion and death. As Mary asks Joseph after Yeshua is taken, "Is it because he is black?" Joseph gives his answer: "No, it is because he is the Messiah." The staging of the Gospel sequences follows the visual tradition of the American Jesus films, and they are recognizable. The difference is in the way that the camera tracks and focuses on the black Jesus.

The information on the film's website, along with a trailer, states:

> This powerful, epic film vividly portrays the last 48 hours of the life of Jesus Christ and challenges commonly held assumptions about Him. With moving performances from Jean-Claude LaMarre (*Malcolm X*) and Debbi Morgan (*Woman Thou Art Loosed*), this stirring film is a triumph!
>
> The first depiction of Jesus as a black man, *Color of the Cross* is also the first to suggest that the Crucifixion could have been racially motivated. A compelling script and astounding interpretations of The Bible make this daring masterpiece an achievement not to be missed. With its inspiring, unconventional approach to an emotionally volatile issue, *Color of the Cross* presents a fresh perspective on the history of Christianity and delivers as moving a portrait of His life as has ever been put to film!
>
> By portraying Jesus as a black Jew, this movie may appear controversial to some. However, it stands to be the single most positive image of a black lead character in a film to date. This film will undeniably resonate in the hearts and minds of the black community and strike a chord of inspiration in the hearts of Christians of all ethnicities around the world.
>
> *Color of the Cross* tells a story that is familiar to most. The movie addresses four areas: Jesus and his disciples, the state of mind of the Romans occupying Judea, the issues facing the Rabbis in the Sanhedrin, and the family life of Joseph, Mary and their remaining children as they were affected by Jesus' persecution.[1]

The movie opens with Jesus and the disciples approaching Jerusalem for the Last Supper and the film unfolds with the events leading up to Jesus' capture and Crucifixion. This extensively researched film remains true to Biblical and historical facts.

The claim that this is the first black Jesus is not accurate. The South African *Son of Man* was released in 2006.

The reactions to *Color of the Cross* were mixed. Some alarming condemnations of making Jesus black can be found on the Internet Movie Database (IMDb). They come from bloggers. These commentators do not seem to be aware of the tradition of adapting the figure of Jesus to the culture of those re-telling the story. In the twentieth century, especially as a reaction against the white representations of Jesus and Mary, an abundance of Jesus images and Madonnas could be found—Aboriginal Madonnas, Japanese Madonnas with local features and garb, holding the baby Jesus similarly dressed.

There were also vehement comments about the liberties taken in the screenplay in diverging from the Gospel texts. The comments on moving away from Gospel detail were just as strong for *Color of the Cross 2: The Resurrection*.

The Resurrection opens with the Agony in the Garden and Jesus severely criticizing Peter's inability to pray with him. During the credits there is a note that Yeshua is a radical interpreter of the Torah. In the background are voices recapitulating events of Yeshua's life. In the Crucifixion sequence, shown at quite some length, Jesus is tied by rope to the cross, not nailed. He is alone (although reference is made to the two other men crucified). There is no one at the foot of the cross. His mother, Mary, returns home to find Joseph and her two sons, James and Jude, arguing whether Jesus was really the Messiah or had deluded himself, referring to 132 texts from the Torah that he had to fulfill. Mary challenges them by reminding them that Yeshua had given to them land that was his by right. Later, on the road to Emmaus, the disciples encounter a wise man who opens their eyes to the Resurrection.

Jean-Claude LaMarre's Jesus is black but there is less emphasis in the screenplay on race as a political issue. On the cross, he is bearded. Risen, his head is shaven and he is beardless.

The running time of the film is comparatively short but there is quite some repetition from the first film. Jesus rises forty minutes into the film.

However, the writers, including LaMarre, have drawn on many texts, and they have a variety of characters (apostles, priests, and Pharisees) quote and explain them. Mary Magdalene offers a voiceover commentary as well as a flashback to Jesus' kind treatment of her. Pilate features with the priests and the tomb guards and remarks to his wife that he wished he had washed his hands of the whole affair.

Judas features quite strongly, especially in the suicide sequence. When the other apostles come across his hanging body, they condemn him harshly.

The Resurrection is suggested by some hand movement under the burial cloths, then an earthquake and sight of the stone rolled away. Many of the Gospel Resurrection texts are used: the burial of Jesus by Nicodemus and Joseph of Arimathea; the fear of the soldiers; Magdalene's encounter with the angel at the tomb and with Jesus; much discussion among the apostles about what they should do; the apostles' fears and Thomas's disbelief. There are warm scenes where Yeshua's mother and the Magdalene converse.

Production values and re-constructions are limited but often effective. During the final credits, the director takes the opportunity to go through key scenes yet again.

THE CROSS: THE LAST HOUR OF JESUS

A sixty-minute animated film by Cy Bowers (2005), which can be used as an installation experience. The technology is explained in the promotion material:

> For the first time ever, an animated digital portrayal of Christ on the Cross has been created by DigiArt LLC.
>
> This moving painting with optional sound tracks creates a unique and compelling experience of Christ's suffering on the cross.
>
> Two years in the making, *The Cross* is the result of the intense labors of a team of animators and digital artists. Virtually all animation sequences are seven or eight seconds long, while *The Cross* is an astounding one-hour shot containing 87,000 files.
>
> The work began with digital paintings of the elements, and the figure of Christ was then wrapped like a skin over a three dimensional wireframe. Every wire in the wireframe was controlled by animation software, making it possible to convey even the slightest change of position. The figure, the cross, the clouds and the backgrounds were then all deftly composited into this extremely complicated digital work. The subtle movement creates an intense dynamism. The result is a new way of enjoying art, a living painting that moves. Glance at it and then return a minute or an hour later, and it's a slightly different perception. Or watch it like a movie and be drawn into the almost mesmerizing real time experience.

Video artists of great skill have been supplying museums and wealthy patrons with digital video art for years. But this is first time a work of digital art is available at a very modest price for a wide range of consumers. *The Cross* plays on any DVD capable computer or through any DVD player to any video screen.

For a museum-like display, all that is necessary is a flat panel screen and a DVD player. If it is set up with a dedicated playback system, *The Cross* creates a jeweled renaissance style alter wherever it is placed.[2]

LA SACRA FAMIGLIA

Raffaele Mertes, who directed the Italian television series *Gli amici di Gesu* (The Friends of Jesus), also made a television film *The Holy Family* (2006), covering the infancy stories of the Gospels. This was the same year as the release of Catherine Hardwicke's *The Nativity Story*. The show has a strong cast with Allessandro Gassman as Joseph, Ana Caterina Morariu as Mary, Franco Nero as Zachary, and Angela Molina as Elizabeth. It runs for two hundred minutes.

THE PASSION

This version of *The Passion* is the 2008 BBC/HBO series, an ambitious series which was shown during Holy Week 2008 in the United Kingdom and repeated on Easter Sunday afternoon before the last episode screened that evening. As with so many biblical films, it was made in Morocco, taking advantage of the Mediterranean locations, the desert, and buildings, which easily stand in for Judea. Directed by Michael Offer and written by Frank Deasy (who had a Catholic background), *The Passion* in fact did not focus solely on the events of the Passion as did Mel Gibson's film. Rather, it opens with Jesus riding into Jerusalem on the donkey, and the first half of the film covers Jesus' preaching and actions until the Last Supper. The second half begins with the Last Supper and has forty minutes on the Passion. The final thirty minutes are on the Resurrection. The cast would have been known to viewers of British television or the London stage. Jesus was played by Joseph Mawle (who was thirty-three when the film was in production).

Adapting the Gospels for Television

As with any version of Jesus' life, it is "based on" the Gospels rather than an exact following of them; not even Pasolini's *Gospel according to St. Matthew* did this. As the early Christian communities did, the filmmakers omit, add, and create dialogue and incidents. They interpret. This is the interesting point for the viewer, the challenge to the viewer's ideas and presuppositions. *The Passion* screenplay certainly picks and chooses. It also creates some incidents and coincidences.

The style of the film is determined by television conventions using a great many close-ups, but the backgrounds add a touch of the spectacle without dominating. In most ways, the filming is visually traditional. The actors speak in a variety of British accents, although James Nesbitt's Pilate has the actor's natural Ulster accent, which is more than a little disconcerting and distracting. Pilate was a foreigner in Judea, but with such an accent?

In many ways, there is too much in the first half of *The Passion*. Many of the things that Jesus does did not take place in the Gospel texts during his final days. To that extent, the action seems crammed. Added to that is the inclusion of so many of the sayings of Jesus that preceded this week. It is a value to have these teachings spoken on-screen, but they come, one after the other, without enough time to absorb them and their meaning.

While the presentation is in the line of *The King of Kings* and the *Jesus* Project, what is always interesting and worth watching is what the filmmakers do with the familiar texts and how they interpret Jesus and the principal characters.

Here Jesus is very ordinary. At first, he does not stand out. In fact, he is only moderately charismatic or magnetic. The actor relies on an inner conviction and strength rather than dramatics, except when he throws the money changers and sellers out of the Temple, but this episode stands out in the Gospels themselves as not "typical" of Jesus. At first it is difficult to distinguish Jesus from the apostles, and the apostles, except for Judas, are not quite distinct until the Last Supper. The impact that Jesus makes is not instant. Rather, it is a cumulative effect until he is dying on the cross.

With the focus on the last week of Jesus' life, the characters of interest are Judas, Pilate, and the religious authorities.

Pilate, Caiaphas, and Judas

Sequences with Pilate give some background to the Roman occupation, the contempt of the Romans for the Jews, and their lack of understanding and tolerance for Jewish religious beliefs and practices. Yet, Pilate has to keep the peace as well as watch his back at the court of the emperor. The spirit of Zealot revolt is also on Pilate's mind. Barabbas, called Jesus Barabbas, is shown with his followers with their violence and rioting. Pilate's wife is a strong influence on Pilate, and the film emphasizes the

Gospel story where she has the dream of Jesus and tries to dissuade Pilate from executing him. But Pilate is capable of executing criminals without any compunction as we see when many are brought before him and he, almost offhandedly, condemns them to crucifixion.

This version presents a much more rounded portrait of Caiaphas than most Jesus films. He is played by Ben Daniels as a dominating religious leader who prides himself on walking the difficult path between his people and the Romans and keeping the peace in Judea. In that light, Jesus is a threat to peace. His followers are potential rioters who will antagonize the Romans. Jesus constantly refers to the Temple, speaks of destroying it and rebuilding it, and throws out the buyers and sellers. Caiaphas says that the only way Jesus can be saved is by his renouncing everything.

Caiaphas is shown as money preoccupied. His pregnant wife is the person who reminds him that Jesus is only one man and, therefore, expendable. Caiaphas is shown as acting according to his intuition for the political good (and, therefore, the religious good). He has many advisers in the Sanhedrin, some of whom challenge his stances, especially Joseph of Arimathea. His father-in-law, Annas, is much more conniving. Ultimately, Caiaphas is shocked by Jesus' claims and uses all his diplomatic skills and cunning to persuade Pilate not to antagonize Emperor Tiberius and to crucify Jesus.

As with Zeffirelli's *Jesus of Nazareth*, there is a fictional character who represents those who plotted against Jesus. This character is played by John Lynch as part police, part thug, part rabble-rouser. His vicious hitting of Jesus after his response to Annas is far more brutal than the "slap" of the Gospel.

Judas (Paul Nicholls) fits into this plan. He is caught up in the same ideas as Caiaphas and is presented as seriously concerned about Judea and what Jesus is doing. Judas has personal conversations with Jesus. He tells Jesus that they all believe. They want to. But Jesus answers, "When you look into your heart, what do you see?"

Judas says, "Forgive me, Lord."

"You are forgiven. Now tell me what do you see inside?"

Judas has no answer. And Jesus says, "I'm, sorry, Judas."

Judas feels that he is a true disciple but that he needs to speak with the authorities. With his role as the purse keeper and his rebuke of Mary anointing Jesus with the expensive ointment, his motives are mixed. When he betrays Jesus, he spits on those who give him the silver. They say they do not want to be in his debt and that he can give the money to the poor. At the Last Supper, Jesus sends him away before the breaking of the bread. "Judas, you have to go." Judas hurries out, but in a surprising dramatic moment, he suddenly vomits in the street. Resigned to what he has done, Judas kisses Jesus in Gethsemane with some force but then collapses morally, drinking, encountering Barabbas, wandering the streets, finally coming to a well and using the rope for the bucket to hang himself down the well.

Disciples, Men and Women

These are the characters around Jesus who make much more dramatic impact than the apostles who appear as his group of followers and have more prominence at the Last Supper, with the washing of their feet and Jesus giving them the bread as his body—with some of them muttering that they do not understand what Jesus is doing. They join in the melee with swords in Gethsemane but, afterward, are shown fearful in the upper room, some wanting to go back to Galilee where they say they had a life, others sympathizing with Jesus' fate. John rushes with Mary, Jesus' mother, and Mary Magdalene to the foot of the cross.

The women play a not insignificant role during these days. Jesus' mother is shown as aging and matronly, talking with Jesus privately after he comes out of the room where he is preaching. This invented sequence places Mary in her role as mother but also as stepping back. Jesus says that God asks everything of him and she touches him, "Is there anything I can do?" She is given some lines that led to controversy, indicating that she didn't know what was happening until she felt the child in her womb: "I never asked for you. What if Joseph had said no?" She is seen in the upper room and, on the news of Jesus' Crucifixion, hurries to Calvary. Her line is, "My beautiful son." She screams and rushes to the cross, kissing Jesus' feet. Jesus' line is, "John would you look after her as your own mother. Mother, this is your son." Jesus also adds, "Love one another."

Mary Magdalene is shown as a close friend of Jesus, always present and supportive, especially as she says farewell to him after the Last Supper. The earlier part of *The Passion* has Jesus pass a brothel and encounter the "woman who was a sinner in the city." She taunts but is struck by Jesus' sincerity and is able to leave her work, feel affirmed, and follow as one of the disciples. When one of the apostles taunts her as Jesus is dying, saying that she will soon go back to work, she says strongly that she will not. She has a new life.

A Portrait of Jesus

And the portrait of Jesus himself? We first see him with the group and then riding triumphantly into Jerusalem, the crowds acclaiming him. He quotes many of the Gospel teaching passages, almost as conversation pieces in passing—the filmmakers presuming knowledge of these texts and their being able to absorb them as they are reminded of them, passages especially from the Sermon on the Mount about the law. Jesus also speaks of his Father and that the Father will never abandon him.

At times, he glimpses crosses already on Calvary. His character and mission are seen more forcefully when he encounters the prostitute and there is a raid on the brothel. The woman is initially defiant, saying "Plough, not preach." But Jesus says to the woman, "You have suffered enough already, your sins are forgiven. Your faith strengthens mine." He is also forceful in the Temple, calling the merchants a nest of criminals: "Is this how you honor God?" And then he goes into action against them.

Familiar episodes are introduced. A dwarf comes to challenge Jesus about paying the tax. Jesus kneels below the dwarf's eye level and gives him the answer of rendering to Caesar and to God. When he tells the parable of the lost sheep, someone remarks that a shepherd would guard the ninety-nine and the lost one would come back. Joseph of Arimathea admires him, and Jesus asks him what is the greatest of the commandments. He speaks the parable of the vineyard while holding a child. Jesus also begins to attack the religious leaders along the lines of the condemnations of Matthew 23. He also begins to speak about destroying the Temple and raising it up again.

The Last Supper and the Agony in the Garden

As the week is coming to an end, Jesus is anointed by Mary with ointment and Judas makes his criticism. But then the time of Passover approaches, and Jesus sends Judas to buy a lamb for the sacrifice and for the upper room to be prepared for the supper. As they gather, there is a lightheartedness and jokiness about Galilee that we do not usually associate with this solemn meal. Jesus says, "I wanted to enjoy this last meal together." He first washes the feet of the apostles with Peter protesting. The screenplay offers a précis of Jesus' words after the supper: love one another, learn from me. But Jesus suddenly speaks in a more theological language: "This will be your sacrament. This will be how you will bring me back to you when I am gone." Yet some of the apostles say, "I don't understand" and "the wine can't be his blood." Jesus also tells them not to be too hard on themselves. They have to let him go. He adds, "Don't hunt for the traitor."

In his agony, Jesus first holds on to the trunk of a tree: "Is there another way? . . . Release me from this pain. Can you forgive me if I refuse this path? Your will. You give me nothing. No sign? Silence. I am begging you, release me from this." After going to the disciples who excuse themselves for sleeping—"Forgive us, we're just tired"—he prays again, this time face to the ground: "Give me strength to do your will, to be light to the world." When Judas comes, Jesus greets him, "Peace be with you" (which he also says to Barabbas when they pass each other in the cells).

Passion, Death, and Resurrection

During the trial sequences, Jesus is silent, the camera focusing on his face. He is like a patient icon. While Pilate tries to save Jesus—"Truth is what men make it"—Caiaphas persuades him to condemn Jesus after the stirred-up crowd cry for Barabbas' release. Jesus is scourged (only two strokes heard and the camera on Jesus' face). He carries the crossbeam to Calvary, where a bystander tries to smooth his face and is thrust away by the soldiers. Jesus falls and there is a brief flashback to his triumphant entry into Jerusalem. He is nailed through his wrists. Again the camera focuses on Jesus' face and his scream. He is taunted by one thief, comforted by the other. Jesus is shown as semiconscious. He refuses the wine, though the soldier tells him that it is easier to die when drunk and that he will be screaming for it later. When Jesus does scream later, the soldier says that he told him so.

The sky darkens. Mary, Mary Magdalene, and John arrive. When Jesus cries out, "My God, why have you abandoned me?" his mother cries out, "Jesus, no." Joseph of Arimathea looks on. Jesus' final words are, "Father, I give you my spirit. I love you with all my heart."

After Jesus' death, a considerable amount of attention is given to the burial of Jesus: Joseph of Arimathea, ashamed of not coming forward that morning and asking Pilate's permission to bury Jesus; Caiaphas confronting Pilate about this; the taking of Jesus from the cross; the procession to the tomb; the guards (at whom Mary sneers as they warn her away) and the closing of the tomb. The drama of the faithless apostles is interesting and striking, bringing home just how weak their loyalty to Jesus was. With Mary Magdalene at the sepulchre, Peter and John running to the tomb, and the disciples walking and talking on the way to Emmaus, the drama uses the device of having a different actor portray Jesus when he is not recognized and Joseph Mawle appearing once Jesus is recognized. The final words of Jesus, spoken principally to Peter (an arresting theological emphasis), take place as Peter is caring for the sick and the poor where the infirm gather.

In some ways, this is a more reserved presentation of Jesus than an extroverted American drama or a more baroque and emotionally exuberant Italian version.

MORMON JESUS FILMS

The Church of Jesus Christ of Latter-Day Saints, the Mormons, have treated communication and communications as an important part of their ministry and evangelization. Although the Book of Mormon has some character and thematic links with the Jewish and Christian scriptures, it moves away from mainstream understanding of Jesus, his life, and his mission. It is not surprising that Mormon directors should make Jesus films.

- *The Lamb of God* is a twenty-five-minute film of Jesus last hours and Resurrection, produced by the Church of Jesus Christ of Latter-Day Saints itself.
- In the 2000, *The Testaments: Of One Fold and One Shepherd* was made by Kieth Merrill (who won an Oscar in 1973 for a documentary, *The Great American Cowboy*). It is a sixty-seven-minute film, best introduced by the plot summary from the IMDb:

  Although in America, Helam witnesses the star heralding the birth of Christ, and 33 years later he faithfully awaits the promised coming of The Messiah despite persecution for this belief. Helam's son, Jacob, is interested more in the ways of the world, including the lovely Laneah, and when his abilities as an artisan bring an offer to work for the wealthy and powerful Kohor, he jumps at the chance and is estranged from his father's house. Kohor is plotting to destabilize the existing government and become the absolute ruler. In contrast, Amaron, a holy man, preaches to people of Christ, whose ministry and miracles are concurrently taking place across the seas in The Holy Land. As Jacob becomes more immersed in the secular life of Kohor's house, Laneah becomes more interested in the humble faith he is forsaking. Her conversion to Christ, and the death of Amaron at the hand of Kohor's men, brings Jacob to his senses, but he knows of Kohor's plans and is imprisoned when he refuses to join the conspiracy. In Jerusalem, Jesus is crucified and the far away city of Zarahemla is plunged into darkness and destruction as Helam pushes through the crowds and ruins to help his son. All seems hopeless when he is blinded, has not found Jacob, and thinks his quest to see The Messiah has failed.[3]

  Clearly, this is not a film that mainstream Christians or evangelical Christians would understand or approve of. It does not relate to known church history. However, it is very instructive to read the blog comments on the IMDb—mostly from the United States and specifically Utah and Salt Lake City, and mostly from Mormons or those sympathetic to the Mormons. As with some mainstream churches who use the Jesus movies in their services, a writer warns that some churches are doing this with *The Testaments*.

- In 2003, *The Book of Mormon, Volume 1: The Journey* was released. It went back to ancient Israel and the story of the ancestors who left Israel and journeyed to America. Among the cast list can be found both Joseph Smith and Jesus Christ. Once again, the comments on the IMDb are interesting, all except one from the United Kingdom coming from the United States, most from Utah or Americans who declared their Mormon faith. However, the reviews are mixed, to say the least, both enthusiasm for the project and complaints that the film was not well produced.

NOTES

1. Fox Connect, "*Color of the Cross*: Description," www.foxconnect.com/color-of-the-cross-dvd-widescreen.html.

2. PRWeb, "Digital Art Breakthrough by DigiArt LLC," May 28, 2005, www.prweb.com/releases/2005/05/prweb245382.htm.

3. Brian Greenhalgh, "Plot Summary for *The Testaments: Of One Fold and One Shepherd*," Internet Movie Database, www.imdb.com/title/tt0258247/plotsummary.

13

THE JESUS FILMS:
JESUS IN OUR WORLD TODAY

At the end of *Jesus* (1999), Jesus tells the apostles that he will be with them always. He then walks toward the wall and out into the sunshine of the twenty-first century, wearing modern dress, having a contemporary hairstyle, being greeted by children, and going off with them. It shows that one way of creating a Jesus-figure is to incarnate him in the present. Two films did this in the early in the first decade of the twenty-first century: *Joshua* from the United States and *Son of Man* from South Africa.

THE BOOK OF LIFE

While it was released in 1998, *The Book of Life* is a millennium film. It takes place on December 31, 1999. This is the same date for the action in the Arnold Schwarzenegger apocalyptic thriller *End of Days*. Interestingly, both films are set in New York City with the countdown to the beginning of the millennium, ignoring the reality of New York being nineteen hours behind the international dateline time.

Hal Hartley is a writer-director who has built up a cult reputation with his offbeat stories, his rather more intellectual approach to cinema, and his extensive dialogue. His visual style is often experimental with washes of color across the screen. He also uses a group of actors in many of his films, which include *Trust*, *Simple Men*, and *Henry Fool*. *The Book of Life* stars Martin Donovan, who appeared in most of Hartley's earlier films, as well as several members of the *Henry Fool* cast, which he made at this time. The film is brief, only sixty-three minutes, but it is quite substantial in its imagining of Jesus confronting Satan as the world comes to an end.

One of the difficulties with Donovan as Jesus is that the actor generally looks morose, sometimes impassive. That is the case here. He first appears in New York City with his assistant Magdalena. He has been given a task by his Father to prepare for the apocalypse and the judgment. Four of the seven seals have been broken, and the Book of Life has the names of the 144,000 who are to be saved. This time the Book of Life is on a laptop computer, which Jesus wants to save from any enemies. In his Second Coming, Jesus reacquaints himself with the human race and is moved again with pity. He says his Father is too vengeful and he cannot live up to that. Jesus now wants to go against his Father. "My Father is an angry God. He likes lawyers."

The film dramatizes the struggle between good and evil by having Satan also in New York City trying to gain souls. He is located in a bar where the symbolic human being is a compulsive gambler and his girlfriend tends the bar, although she is rich and manages a soup kitchen. The bar becomes the location for discussions in the Hartley style about human nature, about the soul being only a material phenomenon, a biological accident—yet Satan says he will snatch souls from the All-Knowing until the last day. "As long as there are hopes and dreams, I'll have my work to do."

While Satan talks in this vein, Jesus fears the breaking of the fifth seal: with the souls of the those slaughtered for the word of God who cry for vengeance. It is the darkest hour of the dark night of the soul, the time of the divine callousness. Jesus asks himself about the comfort of dreams of vengeance and why he had not revolted: "I rose to the occasion and lied. . . . Love is only a survival defence mechanism." He tosses the laptop into the Dumpster but it is rescued by his assistant.

The gambler loses money but is willing to sell his girlfriend's soul to Satan on a long shot. Satan describes her as "terminally good." The gambler discusses atheism with Satan.

In the meantime, Magdalena has explained her love and loyalty to Jesus. She is the woman of John 8, the woman caught in adultery. Without benefit of flashback but with the camera focusing on her face, she recounts the event using the words of the Gospel text. It is a moving recitation. She finishes by saying that she thought he had fallen in love with her—"he's that kind of guy!"

Eventually Hartley sets up a verbal confrontation between Jesus and Satan in the bar. Jesus has borrowed a quarter from the rich woman (who offers him soup) to make an appointment to meet Satan. Their initial interchange is about Jesus working for someone who makes rules. Satan said he did too, but he quit because he wanted to make his own rules. Jesus retorts that Satan didn't quit. He was fired.

Jesus does not want to complete the apocalypse. Jesus inveighs against Christians who speak of love and forgiveness but who believe in divine vengeance, "a closed door policy." They have distorted the soul of humanity—and with references to Faust and Frankenstein. Jesus says he imagined that the truth of the Gospel was self-evident and had no idea it would be perverted by people who preached it in his name. He also says that he is addicted to human beings, the allure of free will, the thrill of possibilities, human persistence in inventing, the developments of artificial intelligence and cybernetics. Yet, humans will become obsessed with themselves in new ways.

Throughout the film, there is talk in the background, radio talk of an Armageddon variety and quotations from the Psalms: "Fall on us rocks and protect us from the wrath of God."

While Satan persists in his stances and the gambler listens to the arguments, Satan gets hold of the laptop.

Jesus continues his outburst, his rant, about his Father. He sees himself as an exile, an outcast, a man without a country. He thought the apocalypse was a good idea, but nobody learns. But God has a weakness for sacrifice, and, Jesus says, "I know I can work that angle."

As Jesus moves to a lawyer's office and then back to the hotel room, he continues to reflect on the Incarnation—"not a good idea to have God made flesh, messy. . . . I'm a victim of my own history, a pawn."

The irony of Satan having the computer is that all the experts and hackers he takes it to find it too difficult to open: "It's a lockout." "We don't service that brand." "It's an ancient warranty and it's expired!"

Apocalypse does not happen and the world moves on to January 1, 2000.

The new year, the millennium, is "just another day in the lifetime of similar days, filled with the possibilities of disaster and perfection. To be there amongst them was good, the innocent and the guilty, all perfectly helpless, lost and all deserving of forgiveness." Jesus sees a Salvation Army musician and speculates on the future, test tubes, and computers and wonders whether in a hundred years people will remember what he said and did or whether someone else will come along and say the same thing.

In an ominous scene in retrospect because of the Manhattan skyline with the Twin Towers prominent, Jesus throws the laptop into the water. Does it matter? Do we matter?

The Book of Life is a contemporary philosophical/theological morality play with Jesus posed against Satan for the salvation of humanity. Since Hartley is not giving official doctrinal positions or concerned about church sanctions, he speculates about the nature of God and opts for the commonplace condemnation of the God of vengeance. His Jesus is an earnest Son of God who wants to do the best for the human race to which he says he has become addicted. Satan is still the seducer, the smart talker full of self-confidence who never recognizes when he is defeated.

This film is not a crowd-pleaser but it offers enough provocative thinking to make it worthwhile.

LAS AVENTURAS DI DIOS

Spanish-born, Argentinian writer-director Eliseo Subiela is always interested in religious themes and the transcendent in his films, especially his classic *Man Facing Southeast*. In 2000, he made a surreal cinema adventure of Jesus on earth in the present. It was filmed on digital video, trying to blend dream with reality. He offers

> a Jesus who questions the identity of people that meet him, and that pawns his crown of thorns to taste a coffee with a slice of bread and butter . . . a lottery reminds Jesus over and over that he has to save the world. At the end of the movie the protagonist emerges from the sea . . . alienated from his grey existence. . . . In the middle of the road, Jesus is hitchhiking and gets a ride in a car that disappears at great speed.[1]

Subiela draws on his Iberian cultural heritage and its Catholic Christian imagery and imagination.

JOSHUA

What if Jesus were to come to earth now and live his mission among us all over again?

We need to ask further questions. Where would he live? Would he preach in the way that he did two thousand years ago? Would he work miracles now, even raise the dead? What about challenging the religious authorities as he did with the scribes and Pharisees? If you have ever wondered about these questions—or even if you haven't—then *Joshua* will provide some answers.

Father Joseph Girzone has written a series of Joshua novels, and he creatively answers all these questions. The books show how Jesus preaches more by example and living amongst ordinary people than by teaching. It is by sharing in their lives that Jesus wins people to himself. He affirms them as the persons they are with their particular gifts and talents.

Father Girzone holds that Jesus' miracles would be much more low-key than in the past, and they would drain the power out of him (as he said when, in Mark 5, he healed the woman with the hemorrhage and felt power go out of him). He would be "ecumenical" and would test the faith of many who preach the Gospel in his name but fall short of the ideals or misinterpret them: tent-show healers as well as of fear-of-God parish priests. And, in the case of Joshua, he would be living in the United States.

This is all to be found in this first film of Father Girzone's Joshua stories.

It should be said that it is made for those who like their good messages clear and positive with a minimum of ugly confrontation. It does not take a very sophisticated approach and, yet, underlying the entertaining story, there is quite some serious reflections on following Jesus and on faith.

Tony Goldwyn, who showed he could be quite a villain in *Ghost* and in *The Sixth Day*, is much different here. His playing of Joshua is of a man who is both outgoing and quiet, down to earth yet insightful, speaking the truth yet compassionate. Like the Jesus of the Gospels, he is a listener as well as a man of action. It is a subdued but pleasing interpretation.

The filmmakers had to make decisions as to how Joshua would be credible in modern times let alone in the film. Questions they had to face concerned his age, his appearance, and his manner. How could the actor portray him as reserved yet friendly? Who could convey the impression that he was grounded in the real world as well as able to communicate deeply about realities beyond day-to-day human experience? When Joshua first came to the town, appearing out of nowhere, there was initial antagonism toward him, but eventually, he began to make friends. The writer took Father Girzone's lead and showed Joshua doing "Gospel" things. He was able to move into the workshop of her husband by a woman in the parish. After all, Jesus was a carpenter. Joshua made carvings—and gave a heart to the woman.

And the local church? He was there to help pull it down in order to build it again. When you see the film, you will appreciate how Joshua was, like Jesus, all things to all people—his growing friendliness with the various people that he met: the boy and his guitar and his clash with his father; Maggie and her grief for her dead husband and wanting to move; Father Pat and his difficulties in the church (who becomes something of a Peter-figure); the Baptist minister, Theo, and the congregation; Joan and the difficulties with her husband; Father Tordone, the parish priest, and the clashes people have with him. A dramatic highlight is the raising of the church bell and Theo falling off the roof—and his being brought back to life. Joshua goes to the revival tent and a woman gets her strength back, he challenges the preacher about his lack of faith and quietly heals the blind woman. And, like Jesus of old, Joshua felt the strength going out of him as his enlivening power went into those who were healed.

Kurt Fuller is genial as Father Pat and F. Murray Abraham is not so genial as the pastor. Giancarlo Giannini appears at the end as the pope receiving Joshua in audience and listening to his message. Audiences who prefer their messages to be less explicitly inspirational will find the film too sweet for their taste.

The screenplay is too simplistic for many, with much happening too fast and without the dramatic and psychological impact that would have given it more depth. Father Tordone's literal change of heart was rapid in the extreme. Father Pat (who may drive more staid parishioners up the wall) is very genial. And, yet, it made me reflect on how Jesus would be incarnated today, what his manner would be like, how he would heal, how he would affirm and challenge.

SOUPERNATURAL

This punning title does not sound like a candidate for a Jesus film. It is in the vein of *Joshua* insofar as the Messiah comes to the United States and takes up work in a parish soup kitchen—the pastor cannot believe that this is what Jesus would do, especially as he is referred to as the man with spikey blond hair with the look of a drugged-out, sex-crazed rock star! Perhaps the title of the film should have been *Souperman*.

However, despite the satirical tone and the point being made that if Jesus came back into today's world it's questionable if he would be recognized or acknowledged, a TV reporter goes on a mission to find him, and she does. She is told to look for the Jesus-looking guy with a soup ladle in his hand. The channel boss is not so reverent. He asks whether the Messiah is the smelly guy.

Once again, audiences are interested in the question, what would it be like if Jesus came into today's world? How would he cope? How would we cope? The film has quite an elaborate website, which includes a trailer so that net surfers can see and hear actor Kevin Max as the Messiah.

MAN DANCIN'

This film is indebted in concept to *Jesus of Montreal*.

In 2003, British director Norman Stone released *Man Dancin'*, the story of a political prisoner in Northern Ireland who returns home; resists the pressures of the local gangsters, thus endangering his life; but also works with a parish priest to put on a Passion play involving the locals and some of his friends. Like Daniel in *Jesus of Montreal*, the main character undergoes something of a passion himself while bringing the Gospel message to people in a down-to-earth way.

What begins like a British gangster film of the late 1990s/early 2000s moves into a piece of Christian filmmaking, an effort to spread the Gospel message by means of popular entertainment, an effort in entertainment-proselytizing in a good way. The film has the courage of its convictions.

The original story came from the director, Norman Stone, and was written for the screen by Sergio Casci, who wrote the screenplay for another offbeat Scottish gangster comedy-drama, *American Cousins*. What Stone and Casci have attempted is what might be called a variation on Denys Arcand's Jesus of Montreal, a kind of Jesus of Glasgow.

EastEnders' star Alex Ferns does a good job as Jimmy Kerrigan, released from a Northern Ireland jail after nine years for gun-running. He is older and wiser and has a mind to move away from the criminal gang of his youth. We get an inkling of his heroism to come when he offers to take a beating from some young thugs instead of his addicted brother. He shows how to turn the other cheek.

He does not remain long free from his past. He is called by the chief (James Cosmo), who runs protection, prostitution, and other rackets in the city, as well as by the corrupt police officer (Kenneth Cranham), who works in cahoots with the chief. Jimmy stands his ground; tries to get his brother away from the drugs; visits his ailing mother in the hospital; befriends Maria, a prostitute who wants to get out of the game, and assorted other criminals, club managers, and dealers. His life resembles that of Jesus in some ways (like the contemporary story of 1916 in *Intolerance*). He also has his Judas-figure, Terry, who betrays him to the chief.

But he also gets caught up in the activities of the parish priest, Father Flynn, to save his parole, and he has to go to anger management sessions. The parish is putting on a Passion play and soon Jimmy is running it and rewriting it, and Maria and her friends, his brother, and an old blind singer (Tam White, who wrote the songs for the film) are all involved. It is clear that there are analogies with the Passion of Jesus. Jimmy is brutalized. His brother betrays him, and the audience is left to get the Gospel message, especially as the troupe take to the streets for performances after the chief has the parish hall burned down. Stone is able to mix streetwise conventions and a tough world with Gospel basics.

It is risky ground, making a tough gangster film with a Christian message. It is not the kind of film the "converted" usually go to see. *Man Dancin'* also hoped to bring some Gospel meaning and credibility to the cinema multiplex audience.

SON OF MAN

After the worldwide success of Mel Gibson's *The Passion of the Christ* in 2004, one might well ask what direction the Jesus film could move in. An answer came very quickly from South Africa. The film is *Son of Man* (2005). It is a contemporary rendering of the Gospel story, spoken and sung in Xhosa and English. It opens the way to what many small groups were doing in the 1990s with their video cameras, making the Jesus story relevant to their own cultures.

A popular word used these days, when critical comments are offered about the lack of vision in so many film classics being remade, is *re-imagining*. In 2001, publicity told us that we were being treated to Tim Burton's "re-imagining" of the 1968 *The Planet of the Apes*. It is a good word. All of us do our re-imagining of so many stories. It is only right because the Gospels have been re-imagined in all art forms over two millennia and in film during the twentieth century.

Distinctive

What is distinctive about *Son of Man*?

In February 2006, *U-Carmen e-Khayelitsha*, a contemporary version of Bizet's *Carmen*, set in a South African township near Cape Town, won the Golden Bear at the Berlin Film Festival. It was a fresh experience of Bizet's classic story, a dramatization of the intense characters and interactions with South African images and South African voices. The local language, Xhosa, was used. The same company, with the same director, Mark Dornford-May, is responsible for *Son of Man*. Pauline Malefane, who played Carmen, is now Mary, mother of Jesus.

Given the role of music and dance in the South African tradition, *Son of Man* is filled with song, chant, humming, and a wide range of instruments, all offering exciting variety as the film moves into its different moods. The cast are always ready to sway, stomp, dance; to fill the scenes with motion and emotion. *Jesus Christ Superstar* and *Godspell* had already brought contemporary melodies and rhythms to the Gospel in the 1960s and 1970s. Both of them (as with *He Who Must Die*, *Jesus of Montreal*, and *Corpus Christi*) are about putting on a play about Jesus, the re-enactment of the story. *Son of Man* is showing us what the Incarnation could be like if it happened now. This is the Jesus story in our times.

With this film, African audiences have the opportunity to appreciate the relevance of the Gospel to their own situations. Those from outside the African tradition are offered a chance to look at familiar stories with new eyes, with different perspectives.

The running time of the film is quite short, only eighty-six minutes. Clearly, not every Gospel episode can be included. The social and political dynamic behind this re-imagining of the Gospels means that the selection of events and the emphases are to be of a piece with the "good news for Africa." Jesus' encounters are limited here. There are no parables. While there is an emphasis on healings, the core of the Sermon on the Mount is what Jesus preaches.

On first viewing, Jesus may seem less charismatic than we might hope for, sometimes more unassuming than we might think he ought to be. However, on further viewing, the portrayal of Jesus by Andile Kosi combines a quiet compassion with earnest determination to carry out his mission of peace and justice. The character who makes a profound impact is Pauline Malefane's Mary. She is a big and strong woman, an earth-mother figure, with a powerful singing voice. The Magnificat after her experience of the Annunciation is dramatic and memorable. At the end, she is the strong figure who stands up for the meaning of Jesus' life and death.

The Infancy Stories

The infancy narratives comprise a quarter of the film's running time. However, the film opens immediately with the temptations of Jesus and then flashes back. The Satan figure (as with *The Greatest Story Ever Told* and the 1999 *Jesus*) reappears frequently throughout the film. He is a blend of the charming appearance and the sinister attitude. He arrives at crisis moments. He observes. We know that he is there and has his eye on Jesus.

The setting for the temptations is sandy and rocky desert terrain, but it is on the coast. The rock for bread is picked up from the ground. Satan's invitation to accept the kingdoms of this world are on a cliff top where Jesus pushes Satan away (quite vigorously). They sit on a sandy slope while Satan asks Jesus to worship him. This time Jesus roughly shoves him down, telling him, "Get behind me, Satan." Satan says it is his world. Jesus retorts that it is his world, and he repeats this later. The appearance of Jesus for non-Africans is arresting. He is covered in white paint, which, fifteen minutes later, we find is part of his initiation ceremony as a man. The imagining of the temptations as part of this initiation rite makes good sense.

Suddenly, a voice speaks in English. We see a broadcast from Channel 7 from the kingdom of Judea, Africa. Herod is king. People are shown shooting and looting. Militia groups jog and chant. In this civil uprising, Mary is seen running for safety, the camera tracking along a school path, past empty classrooms. Mary takes refuge, dismayed at the dead bodies lying on the floor. She pretends to be dead and survives the gaze of a black-cloaked machete holder.

Suddenly, an angel appears.

There are many angels in *Son of Man*, most of them adolescents or young boys—with suggestions of feathers on their backs. It is interesting to see how easily angels can appear in this kind of African context, a context of myth, lore, and song, a far cry from Western logic and reason for everything. The angel speaks the text of the Annunciation in some detail. There are close-ups of Mary (this happens frequently throughout). She is puzzled. However, at the end of the angel's speech, she breaks out into a beautiful aria of the Magnificat (sounds of shooting in the background), which continues into the transition of seeing her pregnant, with Joseph; walking along the beach; and arriving in a village where men with megaphones are summoning the population to register. The scene is still chaotic with military chasing citizens. Mary and Joseph are offered a stable room.

The re-imagining of the Nativity is delightfully local. Young children wander about, goats and goatherds, music and whistling and a chorus of angels chanting about the sun rising from the mountains—"today we are united, one people." Then the baby appears. Mary hums. Joseph looks on. A "Gloria" breaks out with angels sitting on the rafters. A child brings the gift of a young goat. Mary cuddles and plays with her son.

Music signals that the Magi are on the way, a long journey—and Jesus is seen wearing a paper party hat crown. Some time has passed, and Mary is hanging out the clothes on the line. Jesus is now walking and talking. Mary is washing Jesus in a tub when the wise men are let through a roadblock and arrive with their gifts. Mary presents her son. And the angels are smiling.

But Herod urges the troops to look for the boy. Joseph is in the fields when he hears the megaphone announcing the registration of the infant males. Then it is night. Satan arrives and smiles. Gabriel stares at him. Day comes, and people are running scared. The soldiers search the shanties but the people are gone, walking an exodus in silence. They are set upon by the soldiers. Mary and Joseph have been at the end of the line and hide in the vegetation, Mary putting her hands over Jesus' eyes as the soldiers begin to kill the children with machetes. There is music of lamentation and Satan says, "This is my world."

In giving so much time to detail of the infancy narratives, *Son of Man* takes the audience into the African world—its violence and unrest, its language, its music and movement, its settings, its clothing, its sense of the transcendent—all of which prepares us for the mission of Jesus.

Jesus' Ministry

The infancy flashback is now over. Young men are washing in the sea. They emerge and are painted white as part of the initiation ritual. Suddenly we are back to Jesus pushing Satan down the slope. The initiation is complete as Jesus has successfully confronted evil. An elder announces to the community that now they are men. They wash—and the film makes the transition to Jesus dressing for the road, saying farewell to his mother, and leaving home. She sits and contemplates. Jesus walks through towns and villages, through factories and coal mine assembly lines, choosing disciples (whose names come up on-screen). During the film, they are not particularly delineated except for Peter and, of course, Judas. Times are still violent with hooded men running—from these come James the Less and Philip. There are also women apostles, Andie and Thadea. Judas is shoveling coal for a train, but he also supplies guns to two men who arrive in a car—and their names come up on-screen, Annas and Caiaphas.

As with Franco Zeffirelli's *Jesus of Nazareth*, some devices are found to give the political background. Once again, we have Channel 7, which announces the death of Herod. The army of the Democratic Coalition, under Governor Pilate, announces an interim government, which is at the service of the people and is to support democracy.

In the meantime, Jesus is seen with his followers in a room. He is teaching. They are responding, sometimes loudly and argumentatively. This is one of two key scenes where Jesus speaks his message. He highlights the evils of poverty and overcrowding. But he warns that his followers are not to be corrupted. They are not to be violent. They have a right to their beliefs but they must never kill. As night falls with a curfew, he invites his disciples to hand in their weapons—as one of the apostles does so, he has a visual memory of his mother desperately urging him as a child to shoot.

Satan appears again, watching. The screenplay takes the story from John 8 of the woman taken in adultery as a key event for Jesus' message. Here the accusers pour petrol over her and want Jesus to give an answer so they can burn her. In this episode, Jesus is less emotional than one would expect. He does not accuse the woman and lets her go. He sternly tells her to "go." There is a puzzling moment when her jewelry is returned to her—but then we see her going to a pawnbroker, then to a merchant where she buys some fine ointment and then enters into the banquet room and pours the ointment over Jesus' feet as she weeps. While Jesus rebukes the host (a woman) about his not receiving the courtesy of washing when he arrived, it is Judas who makes a scene and complains about the money and how it could have been used for the poor of the country. He says Jesus is corrupt and his behavior inappropriate. Jesus tells Judas he wanted to offer a lesson of peace.

This is exemplified as the hostess takes the sinful woman, caringly sits her down, and sings to her, joined by a chorus of women. Judas sits at his table, frowning.

Video Cameras

From this point on, *Son of Man* uses not only the device of television news, but also a video camera with which Judas films Jesus. This material is then viewed by Caiaphas and Annas and is taken to Governor Pilate as evidence of Jesus' political ambitions. This device works well as it uses contemporary technology (as Judas notes in *Jesus Christ Superstar*, in 4 BC there was no mass communication) and enables us to observe Jesus from Judas' viewpoint.

Judas has complained to the bosses that Jesus has focused in his teaching on "invisible morals" and ideals. Yet, Jesus' sayings are particularly strong and pointed. While he says that authority is divinely instituted, he tells his disciples that they are to follow him. He says that he has not come to disrupt the law (in a paraphrase of Matthew 5:17–18) but to be creative. He wants to do away with all hate. Then he is more specific. He attacks the tribalism and corruption of Africa, people being beaten and tortured in the Middle East, the child labor scandals of Asia, the unjust trade subsidies of Europe and the United States, and the restriction of necessary medicines because of patent disputes. People disappear. We are lied to. "Evil did not fall."

Miracles follow.

The first is a brief rendition of the paralytic (here a young boy) who is lowered through the roof in front of Jesus. Jesus is speaking of the innate goodness of human beings and warning that his followers are not to be a suspicious group. He holds the boy, who is jolted into health. Next, there is a scene in a funeral parlor (videoed). Jesus arrives and asks for the coffin to be opened—and the comment is made about the stench. But Jesus prays and touches the dead man on the forehead, and he too is jolted back into life. The choir chants and there is a panorama of a rainbow. Then, on the road, Jesus hears a child's cry. Again the scene is videoed for evidence, a greenish and swirling picture of a child in a fit. Jesus calms the child, raises the child, and smiles—and we see Annas and Caiaphas watching the television monitor. They demand of Judas proof of Jesus' political ambitions.

Jesus is now an acclaimed leader and stands on a high, makeshift plinth (again recorded). He urges "collective dialogue," for them to act as a group and to treat people with dignity, to unite. The people are excited and dance but military personnel turn up and declare the gathering illegal and force the people to disperse. Jesus gets down—and stops Peter from throwing stones. Judas runs the length of an abandoned building and declares that he has "got him," handing over the camera to Annas and Caiaphas while extending his hand to receive money.

Riots get worse. Citizens are beaten and the governor goes on television to impose martial law: to protect democracy requires hard decisions, to impose order one must be strong, to achieve peace, we must use force. Women protest in the streets and lay their babies on the road. The men do a sit-in cradling the children.

As the crowds in the township raise Jesus aloft and carry him in triumph in Palm Sunday exhilaration, the authorities tell Jesus that he is a minority and they will not allow him to disrupt what they have worked for years. In the meantime, Mary packs and leaves home, arriving in the busy city with its cars and freeways and overpass steps.

We see Annas and Caiaphas watching the video of Jesus on the plinth and realize they are watching it with Pilate, who says it is not evidence. He pours himself a glass of water, accidentally spilling it on his hands. He tacitly allows Annas and Caiaphas to act against Jesus.

The Passion

Jesus is in a house with Mary at the sink, a microwave next to it. The Last Supper sequence follows. As Jesus hands around a big can from which the apostles drink, they see in the base of the can, in blood-colored tones, images of torture, killing, and lamentation, a front-end loader scooping up a corpse. He does not need to (and does not) say, "This is my blood." Jesus says he will be betrayed while Judas collects the used plates. Jesus tells him to go. He also warns Peter that he will deny him.

The agony sequences take place in a sandy area with large open pipes for a pipeline. The apostles watch Jesus—"Brother, you're troubled"—but do not really support him. Jesus goes apart. Satan is present again but Jesus asks a small angel if this suffering can pass. He begs the apostles to be with him but the noisy crowds approach. Satan watches. Once again there is the video camera, catching Jesus say, "I am he," while Judas looks straight to camera and kisses Jesus.

The filmmakers said they wanted the Passion sequences to be relevant to South African experience, especially the torture and death characteristic of the apartheid regime. So, Jesus is hustled down to a secret place in what looks like an abandoned factory and bashed. Judas exits from this hidden torture room and vomits. When Annas and Caiaphas offer Jesus a share in power, Jesus urges them to talk because they cannot beat him into agreeing. There is a grim long shot of Jesus being bashed again. His body is then bundled into the trunk of a car.

Judas looks dismayed as vivid lightning flashes. Peter, hiding in a pipe, is accosted by military who say they have seen him with Jesus. He denies Jesus by saying people look alike. Nothing happens to him as the soldiers are summoned away by walkie-talkie.

Jesus' body is driven out into the countryside and, in images familiar from torture films from many countries, his body is carried in a blanket to a place where a hole is dug and he is tipped in. In the meantime, back on television, Annas and Caiaphas are being interviewed. They will work in collaboration with the government and work out a timeline for withdrawal for the occupying forces.

Mary does not know of Jesus' death. A grieved young man from the burial party finds Mary amid a group of protesters chanting against the occupiers and holding photos of Jesus as they burn effigies of Annas and Caiaphas on upraised crosses. Mary screams and laments.

It is interesting at this point to wonder how the film will treat the Resurrection. Mary and the women go to the burial hole, and Mary starts to remove the branches and dig for the body. We cut to her holding the body of Jesus in Pietà fashion. We are then invited to contemplate this tableau as the camera follows Mary holding Jesus on the back of a utility truck, moving along a modern freeway with its overpasses.

What follows is surprising. Mary ties the arms of Jesus to a cross with scarves. Jesus is lifted up on the cross for all to see, and in the words of John's Gospel, he draws all people to himself. This is the sign of the cross. People are going about their everyday work and chores but they see Jesus and approach. Mary stands at the foot of the cross and sings a chant previously heard: "The land is covered in darkness." A helicopter flies over. Mary and Peter begin to dance, stomp, and chant: "Unity, freedom fighters, strength, comrades."

However, soldiers approach with guns and the people scatter as they are given two minutes to disperse. Mary stands her ground, looks at Jesus on the cross, and slowly approaches the military, a shot of her with rifles framing her and Jesus crucified in the background. She sings and she dances, "The land is covered in darkness." The women join in.

That is not the end. A bright wall painting of a cross is seen. Silence. Then the empty grave and slowly a silhouette of Jesus appear. This time the chant is of the sun rising: "We are united." The shadow cast by Jesus grows and the angels smile. And now, Jesus walks up the sand hill, happy, followed by what can only be described as a multitude of angels. He raises his arm in the gesture of defiant hope.

Jesus is risen.

During the end credits, after a quote from Genesis that we are made in God's image, there is a sequence of photos of a range of ordinary people. This Gospel is good news for everyone.

In this overview of *Son of Man*, we can see where there are similarities to the previous Jesus film. But, we can also discern many ways for the future in re-imagining the Gospel narrative, of appreciating what the Incarnation might entail and mean were it to happen in our time, society, and culture. This opens the way to many more, and varied, Jesus films.

MARY

Abel Ferrara's career has been a strange mixture of violent films, films where characters were drug dependent, but also a number of films that dealt with religious themes: *The Addiction*, *Bad Lieutenant*, and *Mary*. *Mary* won the Grand Jury Prize in Venice, 2005, as well as the Catholic SIGNIS Award. The Mary of the title is Mary Magdalene. Juliette Binoche plays Mary in a film called *This Is My Blood*, directed by Matthew Modine's character, who also plays Jesus. When the filming has finished, she remains in Jerusalem to sort out her life. He returns to New York and encounters an atheist journalist (Forest Whitaker) who is preparing a television series on Jesus. This gives Ferrara the opportunity to offer some scenes for his Jesus film, familiar enough in style, focusing on the disciples, Mary Magdalene, and Judas, as well as some discussion about the claims of Jesus.

In a sequence at the television station, there is a comment on the commercial success of *The Passion of the Christ*. There are also connections with *The Da Vinci Code* and its perspective on Mary Magdalene. *Mary* was made when *The Da Vinci Code* was a best seller, the film being released in the year following *Mary*. This film has suggestions about Mary Magdalene's relationship with Jesus. It opens with the Resurrection sequence, the rolling back of the stone, the absent body, the angels speaking. Mary sees Jesus and hears him telling her not to touch him because he has not yet ascended to the Father. Mary is given various monologues with a Gnostic emphasis on the "nous," the mind, and the spirit. Peter and the other apostles are called by Jesus with Mary present on the shore with later suggestions of a rivalry between Peter and Mary. We also see Jesus at the Last Supper, the washing of the feet, Jesus' words, and his legacy of love, unconditional love.

By way of comment on Jesus as a holy person, the actor, Tony (played by Modine), who portrays him, is vain with a high estimation of himself. In real life he is no Christ-figure but the point is made that it is he who wrote the screenplay and was quite aware of the themes that were expressed in the dialogue. This contrasts with Ted, who questions his TV show guests about Jesus, historicity, the Romans and the Crucifixion, the blaming of the Jews, the Jews seeing Jesus as the Messiah and not wanting to kill him. There is a variety of experts who include actual scholar Elaine Pagels, with her feminist approach and her comments on the Gnostic Gospels of Thomas, Philip, and Mary Magdalene. There is also a French theologian who emphasizes Mary as a woman as the first disciple, along with an archaeologist and historians.

Thematically, Ferrara makes a comment through atheist Ted's poor treatment of his wife and missing the birth of the child. However, after arriving at the hospital and speaking with his wife, he goes to the chapel, prays a desperate outburst and the acknowledgment of his sinfulness, asking to be punished. The crucifix is glimpsed. He invokes the sacrifice of Jesus for his son and wife to live. There is a strong parallel between Harvey Keitel's outburst in the church in *Bad Lieutenant* with that of Ted's prayer and the iconography of Jesus. Ferrara offers a theology of punishment, love, and sacrifice, something of a Mel Gibson theology.

WE ARE ALL CHRISTS

Polish sensibility has deep Catholic roots. This is evident in a grim and graphic film about alcoholism, *We Are All Christs* (2006), directed by Marek Koterski. The central character is a professor of art who takes students on guided tours of churches. We see him standing against the station of the cross where Jesus falls the first time. He explains the sufferings of Jesus with some forcefulness. Interspersed amongst the scenes of family conflict because of alcohol are brief sequences of Jesus carrying his cross, but against the background of a modern high-rise apartment building.

Not only that, but various characters are depicted as being on the cross and their sides pierced, like that of Jesus, by a spear wielded by another member of the family who is being cruel. So, we are all Christs. Toward the end, when father and son attempt reconciliation, we see the two of them, dressed in white robes, carrying a heavy cross like that of Jesus, each helping to bear the other's burdens. The Jesus-figure and the Christ-figures bring Jesus into the harsh contemporary world of addictions where people suffer like Jesus. They fall. But Jesus has been there before them.

TUTTA COLPA DI GIUDA

Maybe Italy would not be the first country, with its deep-seated Catholic traditions (along with some anti-clerical heritage), to make a film about putting on a Passion play, rethinking the meaning of expiation and sacrifice. But, by 2009, here was *Tutta colpa di Giuda* (*It's All the Fault of Judas*). The reason that Judas gets his name in the title rather than Jesus is that the film is set in a Turin prison with inmates performing the play. And no prisoner wants to take on the role of Judas.

Writer-director Davide Ferrario was a volunteer for work in a prison for ten years. The experience led to this idea of prisoners doing a religious play and prisoners, in fact, play the main central roles in the film.

The setting up of the situation is ordinary enough. A young director, Irene (Polish actress, Kasia Smutniak), is allowed to come into the prison to work with a special section, not considered dangerous, and do theater work with them. They are interviewed on video, so we have some inkling of their past and their personalities (although they do not become particularly clear as distinguishable characters throughout the film). The prisoners are wary, especially when asked to perform choreographed dance movements. However, they eventually give it a go. The chaplain is very enthusiastic. The warden does not want prisoners too excited and agitated. The nun who works in the prison presents the puritanical and sour face of the church.

It is the chaplain who has the idea of doing a Passion play for Holy Week. Irene, the director, is agnostic and does not know the Gospels. She buys a copy, reads and studies it, and has to come to terms with an interpretation of Jesus. A first passage puts her off, Jesus cursing the barren fig tree (which is briefly but effectively shown as a black and whitewash animation sequence). But, this gives her the idea of Jesus as obsessed with his salvific mission rather than genial and gentle: tough talker, hard on his disciples, and halfheartedly working miracles.

The priest urges her to consider further the human element in Jesus. This gives rise to quite an effective modern dance interpretation of Jesus on her part, especially in gesture, with Irene finally leaping over the cross. The prisoners cannot make much of this performance.

The prisoners choose roles, avoiding Judas. They are fitted with costumes and a big solid cross is built and set up (which sets them wondering how Jesus ever carried his cross). By now, used to dance, they sing a vibrant song about Judas, about trials and judges, about imprisonment—a song and dance routine with verve.

Irene begins a secret affair with the warden. With her support, the inmates decide to get rid of the big cross and their block letters and substitute "expiation" (*espiazione*), which they turn so that facing the audience is "freedom" (*liberta*). They want to emphasize Jesus' passion for life and that everyone should have exuberant life through him. This lively song and dance routine, "Come and Dance," has Jesus finally coming down from the cross and joining everyone in the dance. It is too much for the chaplain, who tells Irene she has gone too far with her human element and this is a blasphemous interpretation. He declares that it goes against faith and the role of the church. She, on the other hand, speaks against religion.

With a performance planned for Good Friday, two events complicate the issue. First, the prisoners discover Irene's affair with the warden and refuse to perform. She has to choose and, of course, in a sacrifice of her own, chooses them. The second is an amnesty announcement, which means that almost all of the prisoners will be released on Good Friday. The play will not go on because they choose life.

How to resolve the drama of the film? The prisoners set up a table, dress formally in suits and ties, and sit for a last supper with Irene. The actor playing Jesus takes on the role and speaks the Gospel words over the bread and wine. They all share the loaves and, with the wine, toast Irene. The supper is a celebration, and Jesus' saving of the world, with a sacrifice, is so that they might live.

This is a Jesus film in the tradition of the Passion plays, of *Jesus of Montreal*, of *Corpus Christi*, of *Man Dancin'*. It is a presentation of Jesus and selected Gospel episodes, not to give a theological interpretation but to explore some spirituality aspects of Jesus' life and mission. Using contemporary rhythms, songs, and dance, it suggests questions and evokes feelings about the Gospel message.

This pattern of Jesus film has the potential for all kinds of modern settings and question raising. As Davide Ferrario said about this type of exploration and not knowing where it will lead, Columbus set out to find India but didn't; he found interesting alternatives.

ALMANYA: WILLKOMMEN IN DEUTSCHLAND

There is an intended shock toward the latter part of Yasemin Samdereli's *Almanya*, a serious though often gentle and funny tale of Turkish immigrants in Germany, when the little boy at the center of the story has a nightmare. He is Muslim and is finding German culture and way of life puzzling and sometimes alienating. He has been told that the Germans are Christian and that Jesus is God. In his nightmare the boy sees Jesus on the cross and cannot understand why the Christian God has to die. The sequence highlights quickly and effectively how difficult it is to understand what others take for granted, the meaning of Jesus and his death, when all one has is unexplained information.

NEDS

Toward the end of this very Scottish story of John, a young lad who becomes a vicious delinquent (NEDS means Non-Educated Delinquents), John is glue sniffing. He looks up and sees a statue of Jesus on the cross. Then Jesus steps off the cross and begins a physical fight with John, punching and kicking. Director Peter Mullan has a Catholic background—and said that mere social realism bores him, so he likes to use his imagination and go beyond the merely real and functional. This vision puzzled many audiences and alienated those who could not appreciate the meaning of this moral struggle.

NOTE

1. Ricardo Yanez, "The Son of Man (Facing Southeast): Jesus Christ in the Films of Eliseo Subiela," in *Through a Catholic Lens: Religious Perspectives of Nineteen Film Directors from around the World*, ed. Peter Malone (Lanham, MD: Sheed & Ward, 2007), 112.

14

THE JESUS FILMS:
VERBAL JESUS-FIGURES

While we expect the Jesus films to portray Jesus visually, there are several films that talk about Jesus, creating a portrait from the verbal descriptions.

One of the difficulties for Christians in cinema of the last thirty or more years is that "Jesus" and "Jesus Christ" have become frequent unnecessary and unthinking expletives. Sometimes, these uses of the name *Jesus*, *Christ*, or *Jesus Christ* are considered blasphemous. However, blasphemy is an offense with intent. The casual use of sacred names is more a profanity of something held sacred.

With the offense taken by Muslims concerning the publication of cartoons in Denmark and other countries, it can be seen how profanity (in this case labeled "blasphemous" by many who were offended) strikes deep into the religious psyche. Commentators have pointed out that many Muslims have declared that the Prophet was never insulted and, therefore, it should never be done. Other commentators say that he was insulted and mocked in his lifetime. There is quite a contrast with Jesus in his lifetime, with insults and abuse culminating in his Passion and death. Throughout the centuries, Jesus has been insulted (and there are mocking images on YouTube to corroborate this). Christians are often upset and draw on the treatment of Mohammad and Islam compared with that of Jesus and Christianity. The right of freedom of speech was invoked to justify the publication of the cartoons. Little was said about obligations for respect.

It would seem that the battle against prolific profanity has been well and truly lost. However, the issue of humor and mockery in good faith and bad faith is still an issue. A small example: In the romantic/sex comedy *My Best Friend's Girl*, the obnoxious central character takes a Christian girl for a date to a pizza parlor, Cheesus Christ, where the menu has religious references and the waiters look like and are dressed like Jesus pictures. A joke that anyone ought to be able to take? Offensive humor? Something incidental with religious reference in a secular world? The girl in the film is offended and the man apologizes. What are the limits of humor, freedom of speech, respect, and good taste?

However, it is worthwhile considering some serious presentations of Jesus verbally.

LILIES OF THE FIELD

An easy example of the verbal Jesus-figure is the ending of Ralph Nelson's *Lilies of the Field* (1963) for which Sidney Poitier won the Best Actor Oscar. After helping a group of refugee East German nuns build a church, Baptist Homer Smith joins them in singing "Amen." The verses, sung with verve by Poitier and the sisters, take us through the life and death of Jesus.

WISE BLOOD

John Huston made a striking version of a bizarre novel by Catholic author Flannery O'Connor, *Wise Blood* (1979). She has referred to the southern United States as the "Christ-haunted South." She brings this observation to life through a negative experience. Hazel Motes (Brad Dourif) is a strange, ambitious young man. Disillusioned by organized religion, he decides to form his own version of Christianity, "The church of Christ without Christ"—"and it does not cost a dime." Aided by a simple young man (Dan Shor), he preaches his Christless church in the streets and on top of a car, attracting disciples, a blind preacher, con men, and religious charlatans who argue for the commercialization of religion. Hazel is an anti-Christ figure, whose obsession with religion leads to his own destruction, passion, and death. *Wise Blood* is a powerful film.

Jesus is a fact, says the blind preacher, you can't run away from that. Hazel spits and retorts,

> I don't believe in sin. . . . I come a long way since I believed in any-thing . . . nothing matters but that Jesus don't exist. Maybe you think that you ain't clean because you don't believe. I tell you every one of you is clean and it's not because of Jesus Christ crucified. I ain't sayin' he wasn't crucified. But he wasn't crucified for you. I don't need Jesus. What do I need Jesus for?

Hazel says he is preaching his church without Christ

> where the blind don't see and the lame don't walk and what's dead stays that way, where the blood of Christ does not foul it with redemption. . . . There was no fall, no sin, no judgment. Nothing matters except that Jesus was a liar.

He reflects on the Crucifixion and how it does not means anything for people. There is no peace. He goes on to say that the Church does not need Jesus . . . but it needs something in place of Jesus.

Hazel ultimately goes through his Passion and death.

The challenge of *Wise Blood* and this talk about Jesus is to ask what true religion is and what the real meaning of Jesus' life and sacrifice were for.

AT CLOSE RANGE

This film has a brief but effective use of Jesus' name for expressing feeling when Sean Penn's character is being threatened with, "I'll beat the Jesus out of you," and he answers, "I haven't any Jesus in me."

THE NAME OF THE ROSE

The film version of Umberto Eco's *The Name of the Rose* (1987), directed by Jean-Jacques Annaud, offers verbal figures. William of Baskerville (Sean Connery as a medieval Sherlock Holmes) arrives with a novice trainee. The occasion is an assembly of Franciscan friars and Roman church authorities at a Benedictine monastery in northern Italy in the winter of 1327. The topic of dispute is, did Jesus own his own clothes? (This, of course, is not as trivial or as silly as it might sound—the Franciscans urge that Jesus did not own his own clothes and, therefore, the church should not own property, a view that is vigorously, if not theologically, argued by the bishops.) The dispute sequences dramatize comically but effectively how images of Jesus can be used and misused. But there have been some bizarre murders in the monastery and the representative of the Inquisition comes to investigate. The murders also have theological implications. It is alleged that a book of Aristotle's *Poetics* has been discovered, which discusses laughter. Another seemingly trivial question is raised: did Jesus laugh? This is definitely a Jesus-figure question. However, there is a deadly political point. If Jesus did laugh, then Christians would feel free to laugh. This would lead to frivolity, the faithful not taking their power structures as seriously as they should—authority would be undermined.

MATEWAN

Matewan was one of John Sayles' social concern films, looking at coal mining companies, scab labor, and attempts to form unions in 1920s West Virginia. He uses the device (as have other directors) of inserting a sermon that offers a Gospel basis for social justice, speaking about Jesus and quoting parables like that of the laborers in the vineyard. What makes Sayles' use of the Gospels and the sermon more effective is that he counterpoints two sermons—one a fire-and-brimstone harangue (from a preacher played by Sayles himself), the other spoken by a young miner who is also a lay preacher whose words blend Gospel justice with compassion.

THE DARK SIDE OF THE HEART

A symbolic story of a poet, this 1992 film by Argentinian director Eliseo Subiela (*Man Facing Southeast, Aventuras de Dios*) has a brief conversation between the poet and an artist. The artist raises a daring question: did Jesus experience physical love? The artist believes that he did and that the church has separated natural behavior and functions from religion. He speaks of Jesus in a series of sculptures, making love and, finally, confronting death and overcoming death in love.

ALIVE

Alive (1993) is the story of the football team who crashed in the Andes in 1973. Their survival dilemma turns on whether they can eat the flesh of those who have died. They discuss ethics, civilized behavior. They also pray. However, there is prologue and epilogue to the film, spoken by John Malkovich, who uses the imagery of Jesus and the Last Supper as well as the text of John 6, of eating the flesh of Jesus to have life as the basis for their decision. He speaks of the cross that was planted on the burial site later and that is photographed at the end of the film while the Ave Maria is sung. "We were brought together by a grand experience."

As one of the survivors says, "It's like communion. In their death, we live."

THE BIG KAHUNA

The Big Kahuna (1999) is based on a play opened out for cinema. It takes place over a twelve-hour period, from evening until early morning, as three salesman meet in a Wichita hotel to promote contracts for oil lubricants. One of the salesmen is a neophyte who looks on one salesman (Danny DeVito) as a role model and falls foul of the verbal attacks of the other (Kevin Spacey). One of the issues is that of Jesus, in whom the young man, a Baptist, believes and about whom he thinks he should proselytize. Instead of seeking a large contract with a prospective executive, he spends the evening talking about Jesus. He comes under fire when he returns and defends himself by talking about his faith in Jesus, backing up his arguments quoting St. Paul: "It is important to me that people hear about Jesus." The senior salesman's attack includes some hard talk: "What kind of lubricant would Jesus have endorsed?"; he acknowledges Jesus dying for our sins but asks the young man, who declares he believes what Jesus said, how he knows what Jesus said because he wasn't there and others wrote it down. The other senior salesman tries to instruct the younger man about character. He also makes the point that the desire to proselytize in the name of Jesus is no different from trying to sell lubricant: "Once you lay your hands on a conversation, it's not just a conversation. It's a pitch." Even in talking about Jesus in this way, he becomes a sales rep.

DOGMA AND RED STATE

Dogma (1999) is Kevin Smith's contribution to the millennial films about religion and the church. Smith had previously made *Clerks*, *Mallrats*, and *Chasing Amy*, full of pop culture. Smith sees himself as a new generation Catholic, not educated in the more dogmatic styles of the past, feeling free to speculate about doctrine and practice, to mock, and to use profane and scatological images and language. A critic commented that it was the *South Park* of religious films.

Smith introduces Rufus, the thirteenth apostle who literally falls from the sky, interrupting the mission given to Bethany (Linda Fiorentino)—who, it seems, is descended from Mary of Nazareth—to stop two fallen angels from being absolved of their sins and so bringing the world to an end. Rufus is played by Chris Rock and is black. This gives rise to a lot of Smith humor about the early church concealing the fact that Jesus himself was black and the racist omission of Rufus altogether from the Gospels. He speaks of Jesus as a buddy, a good leader, a good friend. (And Smith has his characters refer to God as she, although God is beyond gender—but she finally appears in the form of Alanis Morissette.)

Just over ten years after *Dogma*, Smith made another film with religious themes, *Red State* (2011). It is quite a savage parody of evangelically fundamentalist church communities who impose a rigid biblical morality on all who are outside their privileged, "saved," family, using entrapment to lure "sinners," whom they torture and execute during prayer services. They are led by a charismatic leader, played by Michael Parks, who is given one of the most terrifyingly bigoted sermons, a call to judgmental violence, all in the name of Jesus and the Bible.

DELIVER US FROM EVA

Watching some films like *Life of Brian* and *History of the World: Part I*, one asks the question whether Jesus himself might enjoy the tongue-in-cheek humor. There's a particular line in *Deliver Us from Eva* (2002), a black updating of elements from Shakespeare's *The Taming of the Shrew*. One of the characters, trying to describe how hard Eva is, remarks that someone gave her a present of a crucifix—and the next day Jesus was gone!

SAVED!

After the success of *The Passion of the Christ*, some publicists rushed articles to the press about religious films being popular again and headlined *Saved!* Either they had not seen it, or they had their tongues firmly in their cheeks. Yes, the film is about Christianity, but the film is light-years away from *The Passion*—except that most of the characters in *Saved!* would have been the first to buy tickets for *The Passion*. It is about born again Christians. It targets the more-righteous-than-thou kind of Christians, parodies their behavior, and makes quite a few satiric digs at the double standards of many professing believers who justify whatever they do (good deed or bad whim) by attributing it to Jesus. There is quite a deal of "Jesus language" as well as images of Jesus, including the crash of one when the upset prom queen drives recklessly into it. *Saved!* is a mixture of comedy, critique, and some serious questioning of what it is to be a true Christian.

THE DA VINCI CODE

The Da Vinci Code became something of a second bible (or a first for many!) in the first years of the twenty-first century, a reading phenomenon, creating an industry for supporters and for critics alike. It presented its own Jesus-figure, generally limiting it to Jesus' relationship with Mary Magdalene. For the film, which toned down some of the more outlandish claims of Dan Brown's novel, there were not major visual Jesus-figures (more suggestions from traditional art). Rather, the presentation of Jesus was verbal.

The hypotheses about Jesus veer away from the four accepted Gospels (except in some discussions about the Last Supper) and put all the narrative emphasis on apocryphal and Gnostic Gospels of the second or third centuries (or later) without acknowledging that it was a common enough practice in the early church for writers wanting to fill in the traditional Gospel stories with more colorful detail to invent their own Gospels and ascribe them to a New Testament personality. They often gave names to unnamed Gospel characters—it is only in this period that names like Salome, Dismas, and Longinus first appear. Some writers wanted to illustrate their particular spirituality of hidden knowledge being revealed to them by the Holy Spirit or to advance the status of particular Gospel characters. These latter were Gnostic Gospels.

The hypothesis that Jesus was merely human, certainly a great prophet, and that this was the thinking of the early church until the fourth century ignores the writings of John and Paul, many of the early writers like Justin or Iranaeus, and the records of theological disputes before and leading up to the Council of Nicaea, where Constantine did not impose the divinity of Jesus on the participants. (Actually, the fourth-century church was still divided for many decades on whether Jesus was equal to the Father or subordinate—the widespread heresy of Arianism—and not a Constantine-unified Christianity throughout the Roman Empire.)

The hypothesis that Mary Magdalene was married to Jesus, pregnant at the time of the Crucifixion, and fled to France where she gave birth to a daughter is all much later speculation.

Stories of the Grail—which did not emerge until the early Middle Ages with the tales written by Chretien de Troyes—became popular and encouraged several more books on the Grail and locations where it was taken (to Spain, to Glastonbury in England, where Arthur's knights could go on quests). The screenplay suggests that Christian faith is centered on the Grail as the cup of the Last Supper—which would be news to most Christians. The development of the code of the Grail, that it be interpreted not as *san grael* (the holy vessel) but as *sang real* (the holy blood). Sir Leigh Teabing explains this with a PowerPoint illustration in the film.

This discussion has led to the hypothesis that Mary Magdalene was the Grail, holding the child of Jesus in her Grail-womb, the vessel of the holy blood royal. This is where Leonardo da Vinci comes in with the speculation that John in his painting of the Last Supper is really Mary Magdalene, linked to Jesus in a feminine V space, thus establishing the Sacred Feminine—which means that Mary Magdalene's story was suppressed in favor of Peter's authority in the early church. She should have been the leader of the church—which, of course, means male cover-up and a two-thousand-year-old lie.

For those who would like a clearer exposition of this, the film does supply one: the speech that Ian McKellen, as Sir Leigh Teabing, makes in the middle of the film. He truly believes it. Robert Langdon keeps offering cautions. Sophie is a skeptical listener.

The Da Vinci Code created a market for avid readers and television and DVD viewers. A 2008 novel purporting to tell the true story (and the author acknowledges that it is not the biblical story) of the "greatest love story ever told," that between Yeshua and Miriam (known as Mary Magdalene). Yeshua was king but Miriam was the unknown queen. The book is *King and Queen* by C. A. Thomas—but, in this digital and You-Tube age, there is a video promotion of one minute highlighting the dramatics of this story.

THE OXFORD MURDERS

During a small scene in a hospital, an eccentric father hoping for an organ to become available for a transplant for his daughter engages the young student at the center of the film in a conversation about not believing what you read in the paper: "It's all lies." This leads him to ask if the student reads the Bible and then explains that when Jesus died his body and soul rose from the dead but that he spent the forty days in visions and conversations with Peter. But his main point is that Jesus was a terrorist, a revolutionary expelling buyers and sellers from the Temple, and that the reason he rose from the dead was to avenge himself against his murderers. This seemingly marginal character later plays a key role in the Oxford murders and illustrates his further madness.

CHOKE

While the film based on novelist Chuck Palahniuk's *Fight Club* was about macho violence, the 2008 film of his novel *Choke* is about sex addiction, particularly male addiction. The central character, a promiscuous tour guide ("history interpreter") is also constantly visiting his institutionalized mother wanting to know the identity of his father. The film takes a humorous and sardonic tone toward its subject and includes an inmate's invention that Jesus' "sacred foreskin" was taken from Rome in the 1970s and used for cloning experiments, the only successful procedure being that of the hero. He begins to perceive himself like Jesus, thinking (as does Linda Fiorentino's character in *Dogma*) that he is a son of Jesus. He emulates his gestures, tries to be kind and compassionate toward people, and talks about Jesus and how he is descended from Jesus and must be like him. Eventually, he realizes that this is not his lineage.

THE WRESTLER

Has-been wrestler The Ram is making a comeback. His sympathetic stripper friend asks him if he has seen *The Passion of the Christ*, telling him about how much Jesus suffered laying down his life for others. He was the sacrificial Lamb of God. She makes the connection with the wrestler's pain and his professional name, The Ram.

TALES FROM THE MADHOUSE

In Holy Week 2000, the BBC presented a series of short programs, dramatic monologues, that were made for Lenten viewing. Unfortunately, they were screened very late in the evening. The public that might have appreciated them found that they were unable to stay up to see them, although it was reported that two million people watched the programs.

The series had what might be an alarming title, *Tales from the Madhouse*. The basic idea was that in each episode, an inmate of an asylum would tell his or her story to the camera. Each of them had encountered Jesus in some way, and their lives had been changed because of him. The characters included the serving girl who heard Peter deny Jesus, the centurion, the thief on Calvary, the rich young man now grown older, Pilate's wife, and the widow of Nain. Better known characters included Barabbas and Judas himself.

Each of the stories is about thirteen minutes, just enough to watch at a short viewing. The producer is Norman Stone who has worked extensively with the BBC—Religion. He also directed *Man Dancin'*. Stone directed more than half the episodes. One of his celebrated productions was the original television version of *Shadowlands*, with Joss Ackland and Claire Bloom. Both these actors are back for *Tales from the Madhouse*. The other actors are from the best of British performers. James Cosmo is the centurion. Joss Ackland is Barabbas. Claire Bloom is Pilate's wife. Other actors in the series include Eileen Atkins as the widow of Nain, Jonathan Pryce as the thief, Helen Baxendale as the servant girl, Peter France as the rich young man. Tony Robinson wrote and performed "The Best Friend: The Judas Story." Writers include playwrights Nigel Forde ("Pilate's Wife"), Arnold Wesker ("Barabbas"), and writer of *The Miracle Maker*, Murray Watts ("The Mourner: The Widow of Nain").

The introduction to each story is straightforward. A coach drives into the madhouse grounds. The camera is welcomed indoors. It then picks out the subject of the story who immediately starts to tell us what it was like to have seen and experienced the presence of Jesus. The asylum itself has the décor and atmosphere of an eighteenth- or nineteenth-century English country house. The costumes are of the period as are the set decoration and props. The setting suggests a cross-centuries, cross-time approach to the characters.

As the characters move about the asylum, they reflect on what happened to them. Some of the stories are very emotional. The audience, who know something of the characters from the Gospels, are able to share their feelings at once.

What do these characters tell us about Jesus? The first story is that of the centurion. Now he is a carpenter, making crosses. He recalls his military duties and his young assistant, Anthony. When Anthony was ill, he approached Jesus for help. He speaks with great emotion of the kind reception he had from Jesus. When Anthony is healed, he goes off to follow Jesus. We finally realize that the centurion, who had done his duty with regret in crucifying Jesus, is now preparing a cross for Anthony.

The Judas story follows. Judas describes himself as a very efficient public servant with a skill for ferreting out information for those in charge. He was assigned the task of infiltrating the followers of Jesus. He despised Jesus but was touched by his appearance and his voice. However, he disguised his mission and was responsible for handing Jesus over. We then realize that Judas is tidying up his premises, commenting on documents and his public service life. He is tidying everything up so that he can hang himself.

The servant girl takes the audience into her confidence and chats about her friend, Malchy. She is no better than she should be, but she too has encountered Jesus who has looked at her, looked into her. Consoling Malchy after his ear was sliced and seeing Peter in the crowd, she realizes that things were different for her after that look of Jesus. She mentions to the audience that he was crucified but that she didn't go to look. None of her business. But yet . . .

Barabbas is reminiscing about the boots that he acquired over forty years earlier, the most comfortable boots he ever had. They remind him of his revolutionary days, the idealism, the hopes, the songs. He then tells us of how he despised Jesus and his rebelling against Jewish society and how ineffectual he was. Barabbas describes Pilate (abhorring him) and the whole episode of his being freed while Jesus went to death. This is a jaundiced Barabbas view of Jesus but vividly describing the familiar story nonetheless.

It is something the same with Pilate's wife. A very refined lady, she genteelly remembers the same past, her life with Pilate in the provinces, as a granddaughter of Augustus. She also remembers her dream and the effect that Jesus had on her.

Particularly fascinating as a fiction is seeing the rich young man tell us why he approached Jesus and wanted to be a disciple but couldn't face it. Now he is a lonely old man surrounded by his wealth and his gourmet table, but full of regrets.

Perhaps the most moving of all the stories is that of "The Mourner," the widow of Nain. Dressed somberly in black with a black bonnet, she confides in the audience, telling her life story, her marriage, her barrenness, her resorting to magic herbs and then to prayer. The plea to God is to conceive just one little baby before it is too late. She rejoices in the birth but when the boy was five, his father suddenly dies. Twelve years later, her grief is compounded as her son dies. She beautifully describes the sudden appearance of Jesus, the stranger from the hills, how he wept and grieved. She recites verbatim what Jesus said to her and tells how this story spread throughout the countryside. Jesus raised her son to life. He then left home to be a disciple of Jesus. Tragedy followed. A rock dislodged in a quarry where the disciples were, and her son was buried under rock and uprooted trees. Her son had died twice in one year.

Now the mourner rails against Jesus, no soft words but great bitterness. She describes how she went to confront Jesus about her son dying again but could not find him until she saw him on the cross, his face unrecognizable from the beatings. She knows that he is a charlatan and is glad that this is where he ended his life. On the way back home at a dingy inn in the hills, she heard rumors of Resurrection. As she says, no reasonable person would believe them. Nor did she. But she still mourns with her regrets.

The last character is the thief. He seems the epitome of self-confidence as he describes his life and career, giving a positive gloss on all that he did. He had encountered Jesus and had stood in crowds, always at the back, to listen to Jesus and see what a deceiver he was, playing with people's minds so that the crowds believed in his miracles. It came as something of a shock to find himself arrested and, worse, incarcerated in a squalid prison. When he was taken out for execution, the thief found that Jesus was to be crucified with him. There are taunts and shared experiences on the crosses—with Jesus saying something to him. But, says the thief, that was private, between Jesus and him.

Although the audience never see Jesus, they learn a great deal about him from the testimonies of these eight people, the impact that Jesus made on each of them, their emotional responses, their understanding of who Jesus was, for better or for worse.

One of the difficulties with verbal Jesus-figures is that the name *Jesus* or *Jesus Christ* means that Christians can feel ultra-sensitive about what they often refer to as blasphemy. It is probably better to hear this expletive use of Jesus' name as "profanity" rather than blasphemy—which is deliberately offensive. However, one might notice that there can be effective use of Jesus' name. As in *At Close Range* where Sean Penn is threatened, "I'll beat the Jesus out of you," and he answers, "I haven't any Jesus in me."

One of the most effective was the telemovie *Peter and Paul*, where Paul spends some time with Peter in Galilee and recounts much of the teaching of Jesus.

15

INTEREST IN JESUS AND FILM BEYOND CHRISTIANITY

AU NOM DU CHRIST—COTE D'IVOIRE

*A*u *Nom du Christ* (*In the Name of Christ*, 1993) was directed by Roger Gnoan M'Bala from Cote d'Ivoire. It was received well, especially at the biennial Fespaco festival in Ougadougou, Burkina Faso, winning the main prize. Screened in competition at the Festival of Locarno, it won the Young Audience Award. M'Bala's central character is a Christ-figure, a figure who resembles Jesus quite significantly. He has a dream and a vision of black baby Jesus, who commissions him to his ministry. He also claims to be a son of Christ and is a preacher and healer like Jesus. In *New Image of Religious Film*, Francois Voukama refers to Magloire I as having Christ as his "cousin." This is a portrait of a character with the traits and qualities of Jesus but is seen, by his name Magloire I, meaning My Glory, to be disreputable and promiscuous as well as doing some good. He desires crucifixion and puts himself in front of shooters—but not with savior results. This is a film from a Muslim director who is making a film critical of the Christian sects (referred to as "shyster religion" and "aberrant sects" by Deborah Young in her *Variety* review of the film) that were proliferating at the time of making the film, late 1989 and the first half of the 1990s.[1]

The synopsis indicates plot and themes:

> Gnamien Ato, an occasional pig man who also works as a welder, is the odd-job man in the village of Bali Ahuekro which has a population of three thousand. One day, alone in the forest Gnamien Ato experiences "hypnotic convulsions." In a vision he sees a child and hears a heavenly voice telling him what his mission in life is. Taking this dream for reality

the pig man goes to the village square one morning to preach his new faith, he performs several "miracles" thus gaining the trust of the villagers. Amazed and convinced of the coming of a "messiah," the inhabitants of Balo Ahuekro all join the new faith. Now named Magloire 1st, the former pig man embarks on his mission as a "Liberator" appointed by God . . . Magloire 1st, who also claims to be the son of Christ, acquires great fame. From all over the country people come to see him: would-be politicians, shopkeepers who want to make more money, sterile women, paralytics, blind people and poor people.[2]

JESUS, THE SPIRIT OF GOD/
THE MESSIAH—IRAN

Western film buffs were surprised at the Fajr Film Festival in Tehran in 2005 to find a Jesus film. It was Nader Talebzadeh's *The Messiah*, a two-hour film cut down from a ten-hour miniseries. This should not have been completely unexpected since there had been a film/miniseries called *Saint Mary* (2002), a portrait of Mary, mother of Jesus, based on the Koran.

Talebzadeh continued to work on his Messiah, especially engaging in dialogue with Christian audiences. By 2007, he had filmed a second ending using Christian sources. It was inserted preceding his original ending based on Islamic sources and the Gospel of Barnabas. Screenings of this film, now titled *Jesus, the Spirit of God*, followed by discussions, took place in Europe and North America during 2007.

Jesus, the Spirit of God stands as an interesting version of the Gospels as well as having its Muslim perspective, especially in the role of Jesus as a Prophet who was not the Son of God but a great prophet who foreshadowed Mohammad. The quotations that follow are taken from the English subtitles for the film.

Pilate and Caiaphas

Sets, décor, and costumes are quite lavish, enough to rival other Jesus films. However, the director was influenced by European and American Jesus films, and his Jesus is a tall, dignified figure, long haired and clad in white. However, he is also presented as a Middle Eastern figure, a teacher and a leader, a charismatic prophet in bearing and speech.

In this film version—the miniseries was to undergo more work during 2008—the Roman occupation of Judea is important. The film opens with

Pontius Pilate returning from Rome (and wanting to go back there as he says he hates the faces of the Judean people). He holds court, discusses the phenomenon of Jesus of Nazareth, and is, at first, impressed. The Romans are cruel and are putting down riots violently, crucifying Zealots on Golgotha. Pilate, who is shown in one scene having a haircut and inquiring about the massacres, wants crucifixion to be a means for intimidating the people.

Caiaphas, the high priest, also looms sinisterly in the film, holding talks with Barabbas, who is a vicious leader (seemingly connected with the now beheaded John the Baptist) and who wants a Jewish king, not the Son of God. Caiaphas commissions Barabbas to get the people to find Jesus so that Jesus will make a declaration about himself. Caiaphas tells Barabbas that Jesus is the best opponent he will ever have and to investigate the claims that he is a sorcerer and that he was fatherless.

Caiaphas is not above other scheming and meddling, uniting with Pilate and Herod. Ultimately, Caiaphas wants to bribe Pilate to kill Jesus with the offer of chests of money.

Jesus, Preacher and Healer

The portrait of Jesus is dignified and quite serious. Jesus does not laugh. A voiceover commentary introduces him as he walks through green hills with a staff and a choral background. We are told that the Prophet of Galilee is beginning his mission. He calls some of the apostles, especially by the Sea of Galilee. Philip is a shepherd. Barnabas comes from Cyprus and John from eastern countries. Judas is chosen and described as not benefiting from being blessed with faith. Jesus speaks of worship and gives the beatitude concerning mourners, concerning the poor who have turned from worldly enjoyments to eternal enjoyments, and concerning wayfarers. People flock to Jesus.

Included is a healing story, a woman coming to Jesus pleading and weeping, asking for a cure for her deaf and mute sister. Jesus is silent, quietly bows. He is like an icon and watches. After the cure, the people crowd around to touch him. Jesus goes into the Temple, raises his arms in the manner of the familiar statues, and praises God the Creator and the holy name of God. He praises Moses the mediator of the law. But he condemns the heads of the priesthood and reproaches the scribes and Pharisees for their false interpretations of the law.

Another miracle follows. A hunchbacked woman is presented. Jesus raises his hand in blessing. The apostles watch silently. Gradually, the woman unbends and rises. Jesus is referred to as adopted son of Joseph, healer of Mary Magdalene, and the Savior of the world.

At this point a story based on the Acts of the Apostles is inserted—an argument in the Sanhedrin where Gamaliel, against Caiaphas, advises not doing battle with Jesus or killing him but instead letting time pass for it will reveal the truth.

A different kind of miracle occurs out in the desert with the disciples asking for food from heaven. Now Jesus speaks directly and in his own voice. He kneels and prays, quoting God as sending food down and warning that those who do not believe will be chastised. This echoes the manna in the desert as well as Jesus' references to food from heaven in John 6 and is an anticipation of the condemnation of Judas. After a long gaze at the skies, Jesus sees a lavish banquet laid out on the ground and the apostles eat. Judas does not (and the screenplay adds a rare touch of humor when one of the apostles urges him on, reminding him that he does not have to pay). While Jesus prays thanksgiving, Judas runs away calling it all a mirage.

Another miracle occurs when the widow of Nain comes to Jesus with the question whether his birth was a miracle and whether God had given him great power: "I beg you, son of Mary." Jesus urges no tears since the boy is sleeping and he invokes "the Lord of the two worlds." At this stage a large idol, already shown being carried to the entrance to Nain, topples as the boy rises from the dead.

Jesus Not God, Son of God, or the Prophet

A key discussion sequence follows when the people find Jesus and Caiaphas worships him, appealing to Jesus to quell the dissension he has roused. Jesus says he is not God, nor the Son of God, nor the Prophet. He says he is a human being but "my consolation is in the coming of a prophet who will correct wrongs. His teaching shall spread over the world. His teaching will have no end and God shall keep it safe."

The encounter with Nicodemus follows with Jesus invited secretly to a meal. In reminding Nicodemus that he had initially suspected Jesus of wanting to abolish the law, Jesus condemns the distortions of the Torah and the corruption of later prophets, the difference between preaching and practice. In referring to the slaying of the prophets, he asks, "What religious man have they left to die a natural death?" They are the children of Satan and do his will.

Mary Magdalene is identified with Mary, the sister of Martha and Lazarus. She comes weeping to Jesus as her brother is dying. We see the mourning, the sisters' plea to Jesus, and Jesus raising Lazarus from the dead by the God of Abraham, Isaac, and Ishmael. A Palm Sunday sequence follows with tambourines, palms, and cloths laid on the path before Jesus, who declares that he has come to complete the religion of Moses.

The Woman Taken in Adultery

As with so many Jesus films, the story of the woman taken in adultery receives quite some prominence. As in other films, it is made part of the high priest's plan to trap Jesus. They arrange a setup. The point is that they can condemn Jesus either way: he refuses to obey the law of Moses by stoning the woman or he betrays his own teaching of mercy. The woman proclaims her innocence (witnesses testify against her) and says she had come from Samaria in search of her husband. Jesus listens, makes the statement about the stoning, and withdraws and traces a square. This becomes a mirror and the first stone thrower looks into it and sees a distorted, ugly reflection and then runs away. Interestingly, the woman speaks again and says that, if she is pardoned, she will sin no more. Jesus says God has not sent him to condemn her.

Toward the Crucifixion

A long section follows where Jesus goes into the Temple on the eve of Passover—a roasting lamb is shown. There are accusations that Jesus lies. He defends his telling of the truth. Once again, he speaks of Mohammad, the final prophet who is descended from their great ancestor, Ishmael. He will tell the truth. Jesus asks why they rebuke him as an enemy rather than as a brother; "If I work iniquity, reprove me." The elders of the Sanhedrin ask him whether the great ancestor is Isaac or Ishmael, the father of the Arabs. Jesus says that the Messiah must be descended from Ishmael and that he is his messenger. Uproar ensues as they pick up stones to hurl at Jesus. He passes from them and, blinded, they throw the stones at each other.

It is at this stage that Caiaphas tries to buy off Pilate. Pilate rejects the claim that the Jews and Romans have common interests and taunts Caiaphas, "The unseen God you are always talking about is greed." The whole proposal is a good bargain but a bad deal: "You want me to incriminate someone who has not broken Roman law." Pilate says there will be a permanent stain on them.

The next scene is somewhat surprising for Christian audiences. In the woods, Jesus tells the apostles he will be leaving them soon and that they should keep faith during his absence. He adds (in the words of John's Gospel), "I will ask the merciful God to send the Comforter. He will remind you of all I have said and bear witness to the truth of my teachings." Here is an interesting area for discussion between Christians and Muslims on the Comforter (the Spirit).

At the Last Supper, Mary Magdalene brings the perfume and liberally showers Jesus with it. Judas shakes his head and claims that thirty people could have been fed with its cost. Jesus tells Judas that he knows what is in his heart. Judas now goes to Caiaphas and is announced, "His Excellency, Judas son of Iscariot, is at your service." Caiaphas offers thirty silver coins. The voiceover at the supper says that this year was different for the apostles. As Jesus washes the feet, it continues that it was destined that Jesus have a Last Supper.

The Christian Ending

It is at this point that the screen states, "Continuation of events according to the Christian narrative."

This is quite brief. The Romans come to the supper room, manhandle Jesus, and take him to the court where there are cries of denunciation: "The cure for this accursed man is the lashings of the Romans." Jesus is silent as Pilate speaks, saying that he does not want to crucify him, that he does not want to be blamed for Jesus' murder. The guards spit at Jesus. He is scourged. And scenes of the treasure bribe being carried in for Pilate are intercut. Pilate says he thinks people will change their minds when they see Jesus' broken body.

They do not. Jesus carries his cross, and women follow him. In a brief sequence he is seen raised from the dead.

The Islamic Ending

Now, at this point, the screen states, "Continuation of events according to Islamic sources and the Gospel of Barnabas." There are some great surprises now for audiences not familiar with these sources.

Jesus reflects on people wanting to kill him and prays to God that he may be saved from their snares. The angel Gabriel appears and explains God's plan for Jesus' suffering: "Son of Mary, I shall take you from this world and purify you." Jesus sees a bright light and hears, "Your appointed time has come." Jesus walks into the light.

Now Judas returns and the apostles are sleeping. The bright light turns on Judas, who screams and is transformed "in speech and face" into the form of Jesus.

The film returns to the Romans coming to the door. Judas/Jesus is arrested, protesting that Jesus has escaped. He is mocked, called a "heathen," struck, and lashed. (There is a short interlude where a soldier accosts the terrified Peter, "Have you seen a jinn?" Peter says, "I am still his disciple but that man in not my teacher.")

When Judas/Jesus is with Pilate, Pilate's officer says he is talking nonsense and is an idiot. Pilate says that his eyes testify but his inner conscience says this man bears no resemblance to Jesus. The people cry out for his death. Pilate expresses the dilemma when Judas says he has been transformed by Jesus' sorcery: that if this is truly Jesus, then he has lost his understanding and it is cruel to kill a mad man; he deserves pity. However, the Sanhedrin declares it is Jesus and that they take full responsibility.

The Crucifixion follows with the voiceover comment, "God set a seal on the cruel hearts of the people of Israel because they killed (not him but who appeared so) the Messenger of God, Son of Mary." Jesus/Judas cries out from the cross that God has abandoned him.

There is a Resurrection epilogue with a reference to a Koran sura that God raised Jesus—and we see the risen Jesus, in the company of his disciples.

Jesus, the Spirit of God (and the miniseries) is a different contribution to the Jesus films and opens up avenues for interfaith theological dialogue.

ROBIN—IRAN

Robin (2006) is an extraordinary story to come from Iran. It is an interfaith story directed by P. Sheikh-Tadi, a story of Muslim and Armenian Christian children and a faith in Jesus.

The film portrays a remote mountain village, the villagers going about their ordinary way of life—although taking recreation in a struggle between bulls locking horns and crowds urging them on in their fight. However, the focus is on the boys of the village. One of the boys is persecuted by the others—suggested in surreal-like pursuit that audiences might imagine is a dream but is a boy disguised as a scarecrow. In the background of the village is the religious coexistence of Christianity and Islam. The priest brings a huge new crucifix to adorn his church, very proud of it, and the crowds gather to watch. In the meantime, the imam gives advice in the village and the custodian of the Islamic shrine laments that there are not more relics.

The focus of the film is on the death of one of the boys. The persecuted boy wants to frighten his tormentor, who falls from his donkey and down the mountainside to his death. The persecuted boy is shocked and goes to his friend who is a Christian because the boy had understood that the breath of Jesus could bring people back to life. The second half of the film is about the Christian and Muslim boys carrying of the cross down to the river, as well as going to the Islamic shrine and taking one of the relics, a helmet with green cloth attached. There is a lot of discussion about Jesus as Son of God, his death by wicked people, the possibilities of miracles, the nature of life after death. The priest has his views. The imam gives his advice to the boys. The film ends with the miracle—coming through the clouds and down into the valley a huge sigh that is the breath of Jesus bringing the boy back to life.

The film is very interesting in terms of interfaith collaboration especially in Iran. The 1999 film *Son of Mariam* is another example of peaceful coexistence between Catholics and Muslims. The 2007 film *The Sun Shines on Everybody Equally* is about an Armenian Christian woman who has lost her faith because of her sense of responsibility for a death. She leaves to find herself and is contacted by a Muslim friend and asked to participate in a mission: to abduct her terminally ill husband from the hospital and drive toward a shrine. Ultimately, they come to a Muslim shrine in the woods where the Christian woman has a profound religious experience, talking to a nun who is a symbol of God—all in a dream. The Muslim continues in prayer and the husband is healed. They then continue to a major Muslim shrine. Iranians are very strong on belief in miracles. These films also shows the traditions of spirituality in the two faiths and how they can coexist and collaborate.

There have been several films from India with Jesus as their subject. Some of them have raised passionate controversy. Descriptions of the films and articles about the controversy are included here.

KARUNAMAYUDU—INDIA

India's best-known film of Christ's life, from 1978, is also widely known as *Daya Sagar* (Hindi for *Ocean of Mercy*). *Karunamayudu* (Teluga for *Man of Compassion*) is a tale of encountering Jesus set against the backdrop of Roman oppression of the Jews and woven together into a fairly standard harmonization of Jesus' life. Five main characters—Barabbas (Thagyaraju), Judas, Mary Magdalene, the disciple John, and a blind man named Malachi—discover that in a world of despair and injustice, Jesus offers hope and an alternative to violence as the solution to their desperate situations. Each has a life-changing encounter with Jesus, moved by his compassion and grace. Barabbas and Judas, leaders of a small band of Zealots, are bent on overthrowing their Roman oppressors by violent means. Although they initially share a common interest in joining forces with Jesus to accomplish their objective, their stories take very different turns. Judas leaves Barabbas early on to join Jesus' band of disciples, but his story eventually recovers the biblical script and ends in suicide. Barabbas, on the other hand, eventually experiences a change of heart, running toward the site of Jesus' Crucifixion in the closing scenes, crying "Prabhu! Prabhu!" ("Master! Master!"). Mary Magdalene finds hope in observing Jesus' gracious forgiveness of an adulterous woman. John's quest for a Messiah is satisfied, and his friend Malachi is released from both physical and spiritual blindness by Jesus. Following his Resurrection, Jesus commands his disciples to live the way he did and then ascends into a galaxy of stars, growing ever larger before disappearing from view.

The Jesus of this film is the antithesis of violence. The crowds sing to him during his triumphal entry into Jerusalem, "Your eyes are the pools of mercy . . . are the signs of love and equality." It is a blend of the Western biblical epic and the mythological, devotional, and historical genres of Indian cinema. It presents a "hybrid" Jesus, a god for India's poor. The film was produced by Vijaya Chandar, who also played Jesus, but directorial responsibility is shared at least three ways. According to the credits, the film was officially directed by A. Bhimsingh, one of Telugu cinema's more prolific filmmakers. He died before production on the outdoor scenes could begin, however, and was replaced by A. Thirumalai, who directed the remainder of the project under Chandar's watchful eye. Christopher Coelho, OFM, is a third official contributor to the direction of the film. He was responsible for the screenplay, but also technically held directorial rights over the whole project and is formally recognized as co-director.

The film's popularity has earned it a regular spot in Good Friday programming on Doordarshan, Indian's national television network, and on regional networks like Gemini in Andhra Pradesh. The film also spawned a made-for-TV serial titled *Daya Sagar* that was produced by Chandar and ran for approximately a year on Doordarshan in the 1990s.

It is not the only film about Jesus to be released commercially in India. In 1969, production began on a film entitled *The Life of Jesus Christ* that was to star the well-known Tamil actor M. G. Ramachandran, but may not have been completed. Reports of numerous locally made films of Jesus' life circulate particularly in South India, but other than *Karunamayudu*, only the following are well documented: *Jesus* (directed by P. A. Thomas, 1973); *Shanti Sandesham* (Telugu for *Gospel of Peace*, directed by P. Chandrasekhar Reddy, 2004), and *Mulla Kireetam* (Telugu for *Crown of Thorns*, 2006).

This overview is drawn from Dwight Friesen's study of the film in which he compares the film with the Western Jesus films and offers all kinds of interesting detail: the accusers of the woman taken in adultery running away shouting that Jesus is writing their sins on the ground, an amalgamation of Matthew and Zacchaeus, and the presence of an owl, an Indian omen of bad luck. And Jesus takes his place alongside the pantheon of Indian deities. The film has its own site, www.dayasagar.com, which offers background information, stills of audiences watching the film, and references to commentaries. Selected scenes are also available on YouTube.

JESUS COMES TO INDIA—INDIA

In 2000, *Jesus Comes to India* was screened at the Calcutta Film Festival. It explicitly links Jesus to a visit to India and to Hindu teachings. The film did not have extensive release outside of India, although it did win an award at the Religion Today Festival in Trento, Italy.

The following excerpts from press releases and letters from 2000 and 2002, courtesy of Father C. M. Paul, SDB, indicates some of the issues and the potential for controversy:

11th December 2000
Bengal Church Silent on Film on Jesus
Pinky Vincent, Calcutta: (UCAN)

Two controversial films, based on Christianity, were screened at the sixth Calcutta Film Festival from 10–17 November. One of them,

The Adventures of God, an Argentine production by Eliseo Subiela, was screened as the inaugural film of the festival. However, the Asian premiere of the docu-drama *Jesus Comes to India* evoked more interest among the film buffs of Calcutta. Directed by Mumbai-born Preeti Chandrakant, who now resides in Switzerland, the film investigates whether Jesus did come to India.

The Bengal Church, however, was quite indifferent and even ignorant about the films that were screened at the festival. Though Chandrakant claimed that the Church could have got her killed in Protestant Switzerland, the Church raised not a whiff of protest.

Trained in filmmaking in the US, *Jesus Comes to India* is Chandrakants's second feature film. "The film was inspired by a chance remark by my mother that Jesus had come to India," said Chandrakant. The film takes off from the view that Jesus came to India during his travels. It poses the question about Jesus' whereabouts between the age of 12 (Jesus' visit to the temple) and 30 when he appeared in a desert. "Very few people know that the biblical lifespan of Jesus is only three years. The Gospels talk about the 12-year-old Jesus and then his sudden appearance in the middle of the desert at the age of 30. No one knows what happened to him during the intervening 18 years. My film tries to trace these years," she says.

The film explores the obscure belief that Jesus visited India during this period to visit places of Hindu interest and study religious doctrines.

Chandrakant weaves the docu-drama around a foreign tourist traveling to India and his chance encounter with a mystic woman Kali, enacted by the director herself. While the tourist explores the myth surrounding Jesus, the elusive Kali gives him leads but remains out of reach like "maya." The director also wonders that if Jesus did come to India, then "anyone coming to India with its strong 'shakti' worship culture cannot but be influenced by it."

Chandrakant, who is influenced by the teachings of revolutionary and mystic Sri Aurobindo, asks, "If Jesus came to India, how could he go back to Palestine as a male god?"

It took almost nine years for the 37-year-old director to complete the film.

"Financing was difficult to arrange. The film was completed with funds from public and private institutions in Switzerland," she said. Shot mostly in Tamil Nadu, India, the film was controversial enough to generate heated debates in Switzerland. But she said, "I never attempted to generate any controversy. Controversy usually comes when you are looking for it and I didn't."

Chandrakant said that since she was dealing with "a religious icon and four religions," her script had a difficult time looking for a producer.

What created ripples in Calcutta media were her comments on the Vatican. "It was a cat-and-a mouse game with the Church. The Church wanted to finance the film but it wanted to make the necessary changes to the script to which I did not agree. Many do not know that the Church in the West keeps a close tab on films and other aspects of public life. When the film reached Italy, critics tore the film to bits. It seemed that the Vatican scrutinized every dialogue and scene because it questioned the very existence of Western civilization," she added.

"The Church could have killed me but I still live. It proves that people have begun to look at art from a different light," Chandrakant said.

Christians in Bengal have been muted in their reaction to Chandrakant's film. Brother T. Carlo of Chitrabani, a media center here, refused to comment on the heat generated by the film. "I haven't heard about the film," he admitted.

Robin Behura, chief coordinator of the interdenominational Bangiya Christiya Pariseba (BCP, Bengal Christian association), admitted that Christians have not shown any interest in the events at the film festival. "The BCP cannot comment about the film, because we have not seen the film," he said.

Arun Biswas, president of the All-India Minority and Weaker Sections Council, a non-political organization for minorities and rights awareness, said Chandrakant was "purposely creating mischief." "If someone had a made a film like this on Prophet Mohammad, Muslims would have raised hullabaloo by now," he said.

"On one hand the chief minister of Bengal, Buddhadev Bhattacharjee, tries to appease the minorities, on the other, he allows the screening of such films at a prestigious festival," Biswas added. "I will demand an inquiry into the matter," he said, while admitting that he was not aware about the film.

However, Chandrakant clarifies, "I am not trying to prove Jesus did come to India. For me travel is an inner journey. To find oneself is the most important thing."

When asked for some comment by Father Paul, I replied (at that time as president of the International Catholic Organization for Cinema [OCIC]):

12th December 2000

I do not know the film at all. The comments of the director sound sensationalist with death threats and Vatican intervention.

Festivals are a challenge to the Church to be present in local cultural events and to dialogue with film-makers and other film professionals. OCIC wants to be part of such festivals and to promote dialogue about films like those screened in Calcutta. The festival offers an opportunity to the communications office of the diocese to take initiatives in this regard (which OCIC wants to support).

As regards the director experiencing death threats in Switzerland, and by Protestant groups, this seems highly unlikely and seems like an exercise in rhetoric rather than reality.

From the earliest centuries of Christianity, there have been speculations about Jesus' hidden life and a great desire to know more detail about Jesus, his family and his life. The apocryphal gospels have provided Christians with names of Gospel characters: Joachim, Anne, Salome, Dismas the Good Thief, the centurion Longinus.

It is the same with Christian art, especially that of the Renaissance. This tradition is especially strong amongst some groups in the West who are devotees of mystical writers like Anne Catherine Emmerich or with some charismatics, The Poem of the Man God. These are "meditative visions," like imaging prayer but which have been often interpreted as more authentic than the Gospels.

Some of the silent films, for example the Italian film, *Christus*, made in 1914–16, and shown recently at the Venice film festival has Jesus travel in Egypt (going to see the Pyramids as well as the ruins at Luxor). In *Jesus of Montreal*, it is suggested that Jesus travelled in the east and absorbed much of the culture, especially that of the contemporary magicians.

For the director to speculate on Jesus going to India, it is an interesting device (and in the line of Christian inventive storytelling about what the Gospels do not tell us). Since our evidence on Jesus is the New Testament and the early Christian writings, there is no evidence there of Indian influence.

We would need to hear some accurate detail about who was interested in financing the film. There are so many groups in the Church, from fundamentalists to middle of the road to liberals that to talk about "the Church" is of no help whatever. The director's comments on the church keeping tabs on films are a surprise. To speculate that Jesus visited India hardly questions the very existence of Western civilisation.

As regards death threats, these are the stuff of fiction rather than reality. Novelists who write about the Dead Sea Scrolls or about documents in the Vatican Library introduce this kind of sub-plot—a bit like the film, *Stigmata*.

The Vatican scarcely intervenes in comment on western films let alone those from the East.

As far as I know, the film has not had a release in my part of the world, so I cannot comment on it. As with so many issues, Christians are more tolerant of interpretations of Jesus than Muslims are with Mohammad. This is a strength in openness—and not seeing conspiracies where there are none.

20th December 2000
India Unorthodox Film on Jesus "Finding Himself" Largely Unnoticed by Christians
Calcutta, India (UCAN)

A film about Jesus making a spiritual journey to India so as to "find himself" has evoked such little response from Church people that its Indian director says she is surprised.

Preeti Chandrakant told UCA News that the Church in Calcutta was "quite indifferent and even ignorant" about her film "Jesus Comes to India," which was screened during the sixth Calcutta Film Festival Nov. 10–17.

The Mumbai-born director believes that screening the film in Switzerland, where she resides, could have gotten her killed, but Salesian Father C. M. Paul, a Church media official, said he doubts such a claim.

Father Paul also told UCA News that the indifference of Indian Christians should not be taken as ignorance. Rather, he said, it shows they are tolerant about interpretations of Jesus and his life in art and culture.

According to Father Paul, film festivals challenge the Church to be present in cultural events and to dialogue with filmmakers.

The priest, president of Unda/OCIC-India, is based in Calcutta, some 1,400 kilometers southeast of New Delhi. Unda is the International Catholic Association for Radio and Television, and OCIC is the International Catholic Organization for Cinema and Audiovisuals.

Chandrakant's film, her second, depicts Jesus visiting places of interest to Hindus to study religious doctrine and suggests that he traveled to India between the ages of 12 and 30, a span that the Gospels do not chronicle.

She weaves this into the story of a foreign tourist who travels to India and encounters a woman mystic, Kali, played by the director herself.

The film took nine years to complete and was shot mostly in the southern Indian state of Tamil Nadu. Chandrakant says it is part of a tradition of speculation about Jesus' "hidden life" in the desire to know more about him.

She explained that the film does not try to prove Jesus went to India but instead deals with an "inner journey to find oneself." The film, she added, was "never meant to generate controversy."

According to Chandrakant, *Jesus Comes to India* evoked much interest among Calcutta film buffs but critics "tore it to bits" when it reached Italy.

The director maintains that "the Vatican scrutinized every dialogue and scene as (the film) questioned the very existence of Western civilization." But Father Peter Malone, OCIC world president, views Chandrakant's claims that the Church monitors films as "a surprise." The Sacred Heart priest, a member of the Pontifical Council for Social Communications, observed that speculating that Jesus visited India hardly questions the "very existence" of Western civilization. "The Vatican scarcely comments on Western films, let alone those from the East," Father Malone told UCA News by e-mail.

Jesuit Brother Thomas Carlo of Chitrabani (sound and voice), a Jesuit-run media center in Calcutta, said he had not heard about the film, even during the film festival.

Robin Behura, coordinator of the interdenominational Bangiya Christiya Pariseba (Bengal Christian association), commented that Christians are not interested in the film.

8th April, 2002
India: Church Scholars See Distortion in Film Depicting Jesus as Hindu
Kochi, India (UCAN)

Some Church scholars in southern India have claimed that a film depicting Christ as a Hindu is a distortion of Biblical truth and Christian theology.

However, film critics and newspaper reviewers hailed Indian filmmaker Preeti Chandrakant's *Jesus Goes to India* as "a good work of art" that probes the mind of Christ.

The film was screened at the March 29–April 4 International Film Festival in Thiruvananthapuram, the capital of Kerala state.

"The film is a distortion of Biblical facts and Christian theological positions," Jesuit writer Father Abraham Adapur told UCA News April 5. He lamented that some filmmakers and researchers now try to portray Christ "as a man of different religion and of different geography."

However, Chandrakant denied her film was an attempt to prove that Jesus came to India, or to "carve" his geographical movements.

She told an April 3 press conference in Kochi, Kerala's commercial capital, that she was not "bothered about the theories that Jesus came to India" but wanted to tell the world that Jesus displayed every tenet of Hinduism.

Chandrakant, who also plays the central female character of Kali in the 82-minute film, describes it as "a spiritual odyssey transcending religions and faiths."

Actor Romano Fasciati, a Swiss of Italian origin, is its screenplay writer and producer.

The film depicts a young Western tourist arriving in Chennai, the capital of neighboring Tamil Nadu state, in search of Christ. He meets a Hindu woman Kali, who has been following the studies of an Israeli researcher in India. For many years, the Israeli had been trying to prove that Jesus had visited India.

Kali's persuasiveness impresses the tourist, who is depicted in the film accidentally meeting Jesus on board an aircraft. He begins to believe the theory of Kali and the Israeli that Christ lived in India.

In the scene on the aircraft, the tourist asks Jesus why he said: "I am the way, the truth and the light; only through me does one reach the Father." Jesus replies: "Repeat it to yourself, go on repeating it."

Chandrakant claims Jesus' declaration is "basically a Hindu notion" and her film attempts to integrate "the finest tenets of Hinduism in what Jesus said and did." She said she read the Bible several times before embarking on the film and spent nine years on its preparation.

Shot in Tamil Nadu and the adjoining federally ruled unit of Pondicherry, the film won an award at the Trento International Film Festival of Religion in Italy last year.

The filmmaker said her quest to know more about Christ started from her days as a student in a Catholic school.

"I felt that the Catholic Church basically existed to detect the small sins that we students committed. So I had this desire to look beyond Christianity and probe into the life of Jesus," she added.

V. K. Somashekar, a film critic, hailed the film as "a fine work" that probes Jesus and his philosophical leanings to Hinduism, besides portraying him in a different setting.

Although the film uses the myth that Jesus Christ came to India, it does not try to prove it, Somashekar told UCA News April 3. "It is about how his teachings have vital bearings and similarities with Hinduism," he added.

However, Father Adapur said people made "various mad theories about Jesus Christ to distort Christianity" although they have no "scholarly recognition."

Church historian Father Thomas Mundadan said the film is "a mutilation of facts and truths about Christ and the formation of Christianity." The Carmelite of Mary Immaculate priest told UCA News that people spread such rumors "with commercial interests."

However, Chandrakant denied the film aims to insult the Church. She said she made it because she finds Christ's preaching on love and compassion in the central precepts of Hinduism. "For me, Jesus is a Hindu, a Hindu of the highest order," she added.

THE UNTOLD STORIES OF JESUS—INDIA

The following article appeared in the *Times of India*:

> Jesus Christ, it is said, spent a part of his life in India. This isn't news. Speculation such as this has abounded. But that there could be some historical basis to this contention is perhaps not known to many. A film made by city film-maker Shubhrajit Mitra now throws light on the controversy.
>
> It's fabled that Christ reached Kashmir, preached and even breathed his last there. *The Unknown Stories of the Messiah* (2006) deals with this hazy phase of Christ's life in India. Soumitra Chatterjee plays an archaeologist in the film and Aparna Sen a novelist. The plot unfolds through a conversation between them. *Unknown Stories . . .* picks up Christ's story days ahead of his crucifixion. It takes the viewer on a Bharatdarshan—to Ladakh, Kashmir, Varanasi, Kerala to and Puri, where he reportedly studied Hinduism for many years.
>
> "Stories of a Jesus-like man travelling across the country in the first century AD figure in the scriptures. I have worked on theories of experts such as Holger Kersten and Nicolai Notovich, proponents of the theory that Christ spent years in India," says Mitra.
>
> The film-maker claims: "There's evidence in Hindu, Muslim, Islamic and Buddhist scriptures of Jesus staying in India. A Jesus-like man finds mention in the holy books of Jerusalem, Alexandria, Turkey, Persia, Afghanistan, Pakistan, Tibet and India. These mentions date back to around the first century AD. Despite being so distinct in terms of culture, philosophy and geography, texts in all these countries talk of this Christ-like man."
>
> The theory that Christ came to India was propounded by Russian scholar Nicolai Notovich. "During one of his several journeys to the Orient, Notovich was at Zoji-la. Here a monk at a monastery told him of a "bodhisattva" saint called Issa. Notovich found parallels between Issa's teachings and martyrdom with that of Christ's life, teachings and crucifixion," the film-maker says. Notovich claims Christ traveled extensively—for about 16 years—through Turkey, Persia and Western Europe. He finally arrived with Mary to a place near Kashmir where she died and was buried in a tomb there.

The first step in Christ's trail after the Crucifixion is found in Persian scholar F Mohammed's work Jami-ut-tuwarik, which talks of Christ's arrival in the kingdom of Nisibis, now known as Nusaybin in Turkey. This is reiterated in Imam Abu Jafar Muhammed's Tafsi-Ibn-i-Jamir at-tubri. Kersten found that in both Turkey and Persia there are ancient stories of a saint called Yuz Asaf, whose behaviour, miracles and teachings are remarkably similar to that of Christ.

Several Islamic and Hindu historical works record local history and legends of kings, noblemen saints of the areas thought to be travelled by Jesus also bearing evidence of a Christ-like man. Mitra says his docu-feature "is an assimilation of these theories and stories."

Talking about some of the evidences which he would be screening, Mitra said in Vavishya MahaPuran, a text dating back to second century AD, there are references of interaction between King Shalibahan, the grandson of Vikramaditya. and Jesus in Kashmir.

"Several scholars even confirm the reference and say it to be the only one after Christ's post-resurrection phase in any Hindu religious text," he said. "Tibetan Buddhism holds a special mythical place for a Jesus-like man both in the pre and post resurrection period," he said.

Ashim Maharaj, the publication department head of Ramakrishna Mission (Golpark) said, "The issue is quite serious and sensitive. There are two contradictory theories about Jesus Christ living in India. More research should be done on the topic so that some day or other there will be the light on the controversy." The Maharaj, however clarified that the Ramakrishna Mission was in no way involved in the "contradictory aspects" of the theory.

Father Broyleantus, a Jesuit, told TOI that they did not subscribe to the "alternative theory" regarding Jesus' life in India. "There's no historical or scientific evidence to the theory."

The film evolves around a discussion between a novelist, played by Aparna Sen and an archaeologist, played by Soumitra Chatterjee.[3]

THE AQUARIAN GOSPEL—INDIA

As a 2007 article, "Hollywood Takes Action Hero Jesus to India," published in *The Guardian* indicated, the fascination with the idea that Jesus spent some of his 'hidden years' in India continues:

New Delhi: Hollywood is to fill in the Bible's "missing years" with a story about Jesus as a wandering mystic who travelled across India, living in Buddhist monasteries and speaking out against the iniquities of the country's caste system.

Film producers have delved deep into revisionist scholarship to piece together what they say was Jesus' life between the ages of 13 and 30, a period untouched by the recognized gospels.

The result is *The Aquarian Gospel*, a $20m movie, which portrays Jesus as a holy man and teacher inspired by a myriad of eastern religions in India. *The Aquarian Gospel* takes its name from a century-old book that examined Christianity's eastern roots and is in its 53rd reprint.

The film's producers say the movie will be shot using actors and computer animation like *300*, the retelling of the battle of Thermopylae, and will follow the travels of Yeshua, believed to be the name for Jesus in Aramaic, from the middle East to India. Casting for suitable Bollywood and Hollywood actors has begun.

The article highlighted quotes from the director, Drew Heriot, and the producer, William Sees Keenan. According to Keenan:

> We think that Indian religions and Buddhism, especially with the idea of meditation, played a big part in Christ's thinking. In the film we are looking beyond the canonised gospels to the "lost gospels" . . . We are looking at new themes.

Perhaps one of those hinted at themes would be manifested by the appearance of a beautiful princess in the film, though it wasn't mentioned if a love interest for Jesus would be depicted in the movie. The article did suggest that the film would be "a fantasy action adventure account of Jesus' life with the three wise men as his mentors." At the time of the article, casting had begun for roles to be played by both Indian and Hollywood actors.

Though the movie was scheduled for a 2009 release, by 2012, there was no indication that the film ever got off the ground. The search for more information on the film reveals practically nothing about it, not even if any footage had been shot.

Although the film is listed as forthcoming in a number of review websites like Rotten Tomatoes and movies.nytimes.com, it is not listed on the Internet Movie Database (IMDb.com). Nor do the IMDb credits for William Sees Keenan and Drew Heriot include the film. While the Wikipedia entry on Keenan notes a number of links with India, there is no mention of *The Aquarian Gospel*. There is no reference at all on Drew Heriot's website, www.drewheriot.com. One might speculate that the project lost its financial backing. One might also speculate that it raised sufficient controversy that it lapsed.

EKATTORER JISHU—BANGLADESH

Film lists include a Bangladeshi production, *Ekattorer Jishu*, released in 1993, based on a story by Shahriar Kabir, directed by Nasiruddin Yousuff, and starring Humayan Faridee as Desmond. The Internet Movie Database has the running time at one hundred minutes. Practically no information comes up through a Google search. However, the short story is to be found in full. The following edited version gives an indication of the Christian themes and the Jesus focus for the central character, the eighty-two-year-old church bell-ringer, Desmond, and his experience in the war of 1971 with Pakistan and the references to the passion of Jesus for his own experiences.

> The Punjabi soldiers slowly headed north, burning down towns and villages as they went. Since the beginning of May, the villagers had started moving further north towards the woods . . . those who were intending to go left for good. Only a few collaborators of the Jamaat-e-Islam and the Muslim League stayed back, along with a few old men. Desmond de Rozario, who tolled the church bell, was one of those few old men. Father Martin used to be in charge of the church. When he heard that the Punjabis had killed missionaries at Jessore, he too left for the city.
>
> "They are killing missionaries as well. I am going to the city. If you sense trouble, go to India. The Indians have given shelter to our people. God will take care of them," Father Martin had said as he drew the sign of the cross. . .
>
> Desmond was only twelve when the church was founded. Father Nicholas had been the priest then. It was he who had baptised Desmond. "Don't leave the House of God. He will protect you," he had said. Desmond had been living in the church ever since. . . . . He spent most of his time there and tolled the church bell. He believed that the Lord had endowed him with holiest task of all. . . . In the evening, he would play with the children, whom the Lord loved. So many times the fathers had read out to him from the Bible, "But Jesus said, Suffer little children, and forbid them not to come unto me: for of such is the kingdom of heaven."
>
> When it became unbearable, Desmond read the Gospel of Matthew that Father Ganguly had given him. He could not read well. The words kept fading out. Still, he would continue, spelling every word and reading out loud, "Now Peter sat without in the palace: and a damsel came unto him, saying, Thou also wast with Jesus of Galilee. But he denied before them all, saying, I know not what thou sayest. And when he was

gone out into the porch, another maid saw him, and said unto them that were there, This fellow was also with Jesus of Nazareth. And again he denied with an oath, I do not know the man. And after a while came unto him they that stood by, and said to Peter, Surely thou art one of them; for thy speech betrayeth thee. Then began he to curse and to swear, saying, I know not the man. And immediately the cock crew. And Peter remembered the words of Jesus, which said unto him, Before the cock crow, thou shalt deny me thrice. And he went out, and wept bitterly."

He wept every time he read about the Crucifixion. Yet, he would go on. He felt the holy words drove away the silence, deadly as the devil. He kept reciting from the Bible till nightfall. One rain-soaked night in late August, they came to Desmond. He was cleaning the crucifix in the dim light of the hurricane. He heard footsteps at the doorway, looked up and saw three young men, drenched to their nails, standing there. Water rolled down their hair like pearl drops and their eyes sparkled in the faint light. He kept staring at them for a while. They seemed like three angels from heaven. Desmond became so overwhelmed that he could not speak. . . .

Desmond chatted with the boys late into the night. The angels had brought divine words for him, he thought. They knew why the birds did not sing and the butterflies did not dance any more. . . . Desmond lost track of time. In the mornings he would walk down to the river bank. Sometimes he would go all the way to the city. The Punjabi soldiers ignored or teased him.

Often Desmond visited the village across the river. The villagers still had not abandoned the village, believing the Punjabis would not raid this remote area. Desmond had asked the villagers to move in with them and not live in the church alone. He had only nodded with a pale smile. He knew that an uprooted plant never survives.

One night the small village across the river too was in flames. The screams and wails of helpless people filled the air. Desmond became restless in desperation, unable to do anything. Within the walls of the church he felt like a trapped mouse. Sometimes he knelt before the crucifix and mumbled something. Moments later he flung out of the church hearing the faint, desperate cries drifting through the air. A raging fire was burning houses and trees to ashes and killing innocent people ruthlessly. Desmond helplessly watched the destruction. It was as though he had been nailed to a cross. . . A little later, he decided to bury everyone. If left unburied, the bodies would be devoured by wolves, dogs, and vultures. He decided to pray for the departed souls. He believed all men and women were equal in the eyes of God. . . .

While Desmond dug the graves and buried the charred bodies, the little girl stayed in his house. At night she accompanied him to light candles at, the graves and pray for the dead. He believed the souls of those killed by the brutes would go to heaven. . . .

He buried his face in the Holy Bible and uttered again and again, "No, my Lord, no. . ."

The words of Jesus on the cross rang in Desmond's ears, "My God; my God, why hast thou forsaken me?" Desmond wept silently. The uproar outside the room dragged him out The brutes were hastily making something against the wall with wooden planks. His heart seemed to shatter. What were they doing?

In a short while the gang had made three crosses and mounted them on a pile of earth. The three angels! (These were freedom fighters whom Desmond had sheltered and responded to as angels.) The faces of the three angels turned blue in pain but they did not utter a sound. Desmond lifted up his head from the ground and looked at the sky against which three huge crosses were silhouetted. The sight of the crucifix in the courtyard had instigated the gang of scoundrels to plan this killing.

The three freedom fighters, who had blown away the enemy camp the night before, became Christs that morning. Against a cloud, Desmond saw the apparition of Christ on the cross. "Eli, Eli, lama sabachthani? . . . my God, my God; why hast thou forsaken me?"

The gang of brutes left noisily. The boys mumbled something, their heads drooping to one side. Blood dripped from their hands and bodies and formed a red pool on the green grass. Desmond rushed towards a cross and collapsed underneath it. Now he could hear the words clearly, not once but thrice. They embedded themselves in his heart. "Independence, my independence."

At that instance a terrifying sound of thunder rocked the heavens and the earth.

Three days later, while Desmond was reading about the Resurrection of Jesus, he was suddenly distracted by the sound of footsteps at the door. Three angels stood there with smiling faces, shining eyes and pearly beads of sweat, three freedom fighters like the ones before them. The face of the mute little girl lit up again. The final words from the Gospel of Matthew flashed before Desmond's eyes, "And know, I am with you always, even unto the end of the world." Gradually each word turned into millions of crucified Jesuses.

"We've come," said one of the angels. Desmond broke into tears. Through blurry eyes he stared at thousands of Jesuses.[5]

NOTES

1. Francois Voukama, "Recent Developments of the Religious Film in Africa," in *New Image of Religious Film*, ed. John R. May (Kansas City: Sheed & Ward, 1997), 269–70; Deborah Young, "Au Nom Du Christ," *Variety*, October 10, 1993, www.variety.com/review/VE1117907760?refcatid=31.

2. The Pirate Bay, "Roger Gnoan M'Bala—*Au nom du Christ* (1993)," thepirate bay.se/torrent/5496156/.

3. Saumyadipta Chatterjee, "Film-Maker Traces Christ Steps in India; Soumi-tra-Aparna Starrer Kicks Up Controversy Over 'Alternate Life' of Jesus," *Times of India*, Kolkata edition, November 2, 2005, p. 5.

4. Randeep Ramesh. "Hollywood Takes Action Hero Jesus to India." *The Guardian*, November 18, 2007.

5. A précis of "Ekattarer Jishu" (Jesus '71), by Shahriar Kabir, trans. Mahjabeen Hossain. "Ekattarer Jishu" is also included in Husne Ara Shahed's *Muktijuddher Shatagatpa*, vol. 1 (Dhaka: Globe Library, 2001).

16

THE REVERENT/SERIOUS

GOING TO GLORY . . . COME TO JESUS

The Internet Movie Database (IMDb) refers to this as a lost film. It quotes the advertising tagline: a fight with the devil. It also notes that it is referred to in *That's Black Entertainment*, an hour-long 1990 documentary on black cinema from 1929 to 1957.

WHISTLE DOWN THE WIND

This film (1962) is a moving British allegory, directed by Bryan Forbes. A group of children, led by Hayley Mills, come across an escaped convict in a barn. As they approach him, he mutters the expletive, Jesus. They think he is Jesus and show their love and devotion by sheltering him and bringing him food.

SEDUTO ALLA SUA DESTRA

This is an Italian film from 1978, directed by Valerio Zurlini and starring Woody Strode, Jean Servais, and Franco Citti. This is principally a dialogue between a prisoner, a former black leader of an African country awaiting execution, and a guard and another prisoner. The Italian title translates as *Seated at the Right Hand*, the suggestion being made that the prisoner is a Christ-figure martyr.

LE MARTYRE DE SAINT SEBASTIEN

Based on a miracle play by Gabriele D'Annunzio with music by Claude Debussy, this is a German production (1984) for French television with an international cast, Michael Biehn as Sebastian and Nicholas Clay as Augustus. With the transposing of the life of Sebastian from the fourth century to the time of Jesus, it allows for Jesus to appear. (Derek Jarman's homoerotic *Sebastiane* [1976] is set in the correct period so no presence of Jesus.)

SEOUL JESUS

In *Seoul Jesus* (1986), a mental patient escapes from an institution, calls himself Jesus, and goes to Seoul to warn the city of impending disaster. The director, Sun-Woo Jang, stated his intentions:

> I co-directed *Seoul Jesus* with Son-U Wan because my police record made it hard for me to sign it myself. Also, I had no confidence about handling the technical aspects, and needed someone with more experience alongside me. The film was a simple work of imagination: what would happen if Christ appeared in Seoul today? My feelings about the Christian church (especially but not only in Korea) are strongly sceptical; there has been enormous deviation from what I understand to have been Christ's teachings. The original idea was to end the film with the protagonist's crucifixion, but we had to change that to a happy ending. Actually, we had two problems throughout the production: no money, and no cooperation from the authorities, who saw it as an anti-government film.
>
> We made *Seoul Jesus* independently because we couldn't find a producer. I did find a producer for my next film, and so I made it within the film industry. There are sometimes negative aspects to working with a producer, but on the whole it's an easier way to make films. I don't think there's any significant creative difference between what I did in *The Age of Success* and what I'd done in *Seoul Jesus*: this time, I set out to satirise society's commercial and economic development. The story is a satire on commercial exploitation, advertising and so on. In the 1970s, materialism from America conspired with Korean fascism to deform society, and I wanted to register a protest, that's all.[1]

THE MAGIC BOY'S EASTER

This is an inspirational story of a magician (Bernie Kopell) who visits a hospital (1989). One boy doesn't find his performances funny because of his bone illness. However, he has a dream that takes him back to Gospel times. A twenty-five-minute film for religious education using a format often employed for a biblical lesson (as in the 1998 *Stephen's Test of Faith*).

THE GARDEN

Derek Jarman was an idiosyncratic filmmaker, a designer, and an artist. Jarman died from complications from AIDS. He was outspoken about his sexuality and this pervaded his films beginning with the strange, Latin-spoken, homoerotic *Sebastiane* in 1975. In the poetic *The Garden* (1991 and winner of an ecumenical commendation at the 1991 Berlin Film Festival), he makes a parallel between the persecution and Passion of Jesus and the treatment by contemporary secular and religious societies of a homosexual couple. It is special pleading for understanding and for tolerance and an appeal to Gospel understanding. As with Terence Davies (*The Long Day Closes*) and Paul Verhoeven (*The Fourth Man*), the point of reference is Jesus and his Gospel message of peace, love, and compassion.

In Isaac Julien's 2008 documentary *Derek* on Jarman, his life, and his work, Jarman reminisces on how he spent a year, aged eight, at a Catholic school and was versed in Catholic imagery—and during the film Tilda Swinton remarks that he should have been a Catholic (especially with his love for costume and ritual). Jarman eschews the church and Jesus but sees him as a rebel, a social justice stirrer, and, therefore, an icon for homosexuals, someone who willingly accepted the lepers, the unclean of his day. Because of this, Jarman uses images from the Passion of Jesus to make his point in *The Garden* and in *Caravaggio*, in which the artist's religious paintings are from models from the streets. At one point in *The Garden* (shown in *Derek*), Jesus, with his side pierced, stands in an artificial landscape and a sports referee follows him, seems to accost him and blow his whistle. Jarman remarks that authority blew the whistle on Jesus.

LA VIE DE JESUS

This 1997 somber film by French director Bruno Dumont (Cannes winner for *L'Humanite* and *Flandres*) is about working class young men, unemployment, and the mundane details of their day-to-day lives. It leaves it to the audience to make the Jesus' connections.

LES DEMONS DE JESUS

Set in 1968, *Les demons* (1997) is a story of a family of gypsies, one of whom is called Jesus.

STEPHEN'S TEST OF FAITH AND RESURRECTION

Tom Newman appears as Jesus in both these short inspirational films (1998, 1999, respectively). *Stephen's Test of Faith* focuses on a boy who is bullied and has a dream in which he goes back into the past and encounters Jesus, Stephen, and Saul. *Resurrection* is a story of early Christians.

JESUS 2000

This is a 1998 thirty-minute satirical short involving television reporting about Jesus' last week if he had come in our time.

JESUS' SON

A not so bright but very good-natured young man tells his story. However, he interrupts himself to explain his relationships with his friends and the dangers he found himself in as he fell in love with a sympathetic drug addict and became dependent himself. Gradually he makes contact with addiction groups and finds work in a home for the elderly and senile. It emerges that he has a gift for reaching people—but he is not self-consciously aware of it. A nurse urges him to touch people and he pacifies them. He also listens to a young Mennonite woman singing. This soothes him, and he repeatedly goes back to listen. Looking through her window, he sees that she is blind. He reaches through the window and touches her. She regains her sight. He also befriends a woman who sees herself as the cause of the illnesses and deaths of husbands and lovers. When he invites her to dance at a social, she leaves her cane behind. Without his intending it, he becomes a means of healing. He is like Jesus' son.

Jesus' Son won the International Catholic Cinema Organization's award at the 1999 Venice Film Festival. The citation stated that it was a film of healing. It is the journey of a confused but good young man who is imperceptibly transformed into a man of compassion who literally and spiritually touches people and changes their lives. The film makes compassion and grace visible.

DA JEG TRAFF JESUS . . . MED SPRETTERT

The title (which translates *When I Hit Jesus . . . with My Slingshot*) refers to a small boy in Norway in the 1930s who wants to find out more about Jesus and God. The film is based on a memoir by poet and jazz musician, Odd Borretzen. This is a pleasing reminiscence about childhood, growing up, and religion (2000).

IN JESUS' NAME, JESUS WEPT, AND BABY JESUS

These are three short experimental films on images of Jesus and painted light by lecturer and filmmaker Stan Brakhage (2001).

DAS JESUS VIDEO

A television version of a German novel in the "What if . . . ?" vein. A young student of archaeology finds a Sony video camera instruction book in Jerusalem where it was buried two thousand years earlier. Did a time traveler photo-record Jesus? The film has some tongue-in-cheek adventure and quest (2000).

SUPERSTAR

Perhaps a bit of the irreverent and the bizarre, but this is a 1999 comedy about a Catholic schoolgirl, Mary Katherine (Molly Shannon) and her ambitions to be a star. It has light poking fun at the church and school, with Will Ferrell as the heartthrob but appearing in fantasies as Jesus—and supporting Mary Katherine's hopes.

DRACULA 2000

It may be something of a surprise to find a Dracula film in this list but there are some brief Jesus moments when the screenplay reveals who Dracula actually is.

This is a Dracula for the beginning of the twenty-first century. While it opens with memories of the Bram Stoker novel and Dracula being transported to England, it moves to the end of the twentieth century with Van Helsing (Christopher Plummer) keeping himself alive by the help of leeches. However, a group of American criminals decide to raid the safe that Van Helsing owns, thinking that it will provide wealth. However, it unleashes Dracula (Gerard Butler) again—to their detriment and their being transformed.

Jonny Lee Miller is the hero of the film, a reformed drug addict, who gets help from Van Helsing, who is an antiques dealer. Johnny then has to help Mary Heller, Van Helsing's daughter, who does not know the secret of her ancestry. The action takes place in England but moves to the United States and to the city of New Orleans during Mardi Gras.

The particular point of interest—and quite surprising—is that at the seventy-seventh minute it is revealed that Dracula is, in fact, Judas. There is a flashback to Judas and his betrayal of Jesus, the kiss, the pieces of silver, the Crucifixion, Judas hanging himself—and the rope breaking, which means that he has roamed the earth since then. The final confrontation with Dracula by Mary is to hang him, with the rope not breaking this time—and she taking up the Van Helsing tradition as safeguarding humanity from vampires. Not exactly the Gospels, but arresting nonetheless.

SECONDO GIOVANNI

This 2000 Italian experimental film, fifty-two minutes, combines a modern story of a young man who committed murder and wanders the city with an encounter between a modern Pontius Pilate and Jesus. It has digital camera work and elaborate editing with text and images, as well as a nonprofessional cast.

THE CROSS

The Cross is a twenty-minute short film on the Passion using the technique of the camera being the point of view of Jesus himself, something that was developed in the 1970s for the film on Mohammad, *The Messenger*, since the prophet could not be portrayed face-on. It is a reverent film by a director, Lance Tracy, whose family have been missionaries in Indonesia since the early 1990s. It is worth checking an interview by Matt Page of the director who indicates similarities in the filming of the Crucifixion with *The Passion of the Christ*. Tracy also speaks of an ambition to make a feature on

Jesus (in the *Gladiator, Lawrence of Arabia* vein). In the meantime, he mentions that he is making a documentary on the adult industry in the United States! (The interview can be found on the *Bible Films Blog*, along with a longer review by Matt Page.)[2]

WHAT WOULDN'T JESUS DO?

In this fifteen-minute short (2002), an interviewer goes to the home of Jesus in contemporary Los Angeles to get his views on how he sees modern society. God is also in the cast list.

THE BOY WHO SAW CHRIST

This is a debut short film (2003) from an African American writer-director, Kenya Cagle, who then went on to a series of feature films and a television series raising social issues, especially concerning children, like *Thug Kidz*.

JESUS, DU WEISST

Jesus, du Weisst (*Jesus, You Know*, 2003) is a feature-length documentary from Austrian director Ulrich Seidl (*Dog Days, Import/Export*) in which six Catholics go to different churches and are filmed expressing their prayers and personal intentions to Jesus. They include a woman cleaning the church whose husband is a Muslim, a woman angry at her husband's adultery, and a young man whose family ridicule his faith.

SCREEN DOOR JESUS

Not quite as odd as it sounds, it is the story of people in east Texas and their religious responses, faith, and eccentricities when someone detects an image of Jesus on a screen door (2003).

DE ARM VAN JEZUS

Translated *Jesus' Arm* (2003), this is a Dutch film about a search by a son for his father. It involves migrating from Rotterdam to the United States, with the son later returning to find his father. The film includes footage of the bombing of Rotterdam in World War II.

SEARCHING FOR THE WRONG-EYED JESUS

This documentary film (2005) takes a close-up look at the culture of some small towns in the American south—rural, poor, disadvantaged regarding education, and strongly Pentecostal in religious belief and practice.

JESUS CAMP

Oscar-nominated documentary (2006) focusing on Becky Fischer, who runs a summer camp for small children that, she says, is based on the methods of the Islamic Madrasas. Enthusiasm and commitment to Jesus is what she claims. Brainwashing is the view of critics, especially when the children see themselves as part of the Army of God, proclaim their faith loudly, are crusaders for moral issues like abortion, and absorb a political agenda that is supportive of the stances of President George Bush.

GAS STATION JESUS

This was the working title of a film, also known as *Miracle Baby*, which was released in 2006 as *False Prophets*. A young woman experiences a miraculous conception and decides to abort the child. A fundamentalist Christian group intervene and persuade her to join an adoption scheme. She becomes suspicious and ends up at a service station, where she meets a wise radio preacher and his son, Manny, who becomes her guide. Attacked, she prepares to undergo a difficult birth and a possible miracle. The question is whether Manny is a Jesus-figure or an incarnation of a Jesus disciple. (Bloggers' comments on the IMDb are generally favorable and see the film as a parable and serious minded.)

WORLD TRADE CENTER

Oliver Stone's 2006 re-creation of the collapse of the Twin Towers focuses on two New York firemen buried in the rubble who are finally rescued. They give each other moral support. One is Hispanic and, at one stage, has a kind of "vision" of Jesus. For many audiences (and film critics) the vision looks particularly kitsch, but it is one of those very popular devotional images of Jesus—brightly colored, predominantly yellow—of the Sacred Heart. It gives the man some strength to survive.

WHAT WOULD JESUS BUY?

This is a sometimes raucous but telling documentary (2007) about the commercialization of Christmas in the United States. It includes many sequences of frantic shoppers and interviews, as well as some comedy with an actor who, with a growing entourage of singers and performers, pretends to be a protesting reverend, picketing stores like Walmart, and getting arrested for his pains. The spirit of Jesus is there in this critique of very un-Jesus-like commercialism.

THE PRIESTESS

Armenia was the first nation in the world to accept Christianity as its state religion. This happened in 301 AD. Armenian director Vigen Chaldranyan created a fictional story about a priestess of Mithra who became a pivotal figure in foretelling the rise of Christianity and who succored Gregory the Illuminator in his imprisonment. As she makes a prophecy, Jesus is seen in the background carrying his cross, a moving icon indicating a spirituality that was to pervade the nation. The director himself plays Jesus in the brief sequence (2007).

THE PERFECT STRANGER AND ANOTHER PERFECT STRANGER

With the interest in religious films after the success of *The Passion of the Christ*, these two films (2005, 2007, respectively) were popular amongst Christian niche audiences in the United States. Based on books by David Gregory, the films introduce a stranger who, in the first film, comes to dinner with the Cominsky family. He is Jesus who talks about issues of faith and religion. In the second film, which takes place ten years later, the little girl, Sarah, of the first film, is now nineteen, going to college, and facing spiritual questions. She meets a traveling stranger for more discussions.

TERESA, EL CUERPO DE CRISTO

One of the saints who had visions of Jesus was Teresa of Avila (1515–1582). Filmmakers took more interest in her because of the erotic undertones of her experiences, best known from the statue by Bernini. There was a straightforward film from Spain about her in 1961, *Teresa de Jesus* (available on YouTube); a television series in 1984, *Teresa de Jesus* (a complete and reverent look at her life); and a telemovie in 2003, *Teresa, Teresa.*

The sexual motifs are to the fore in Ray Loriga's *Teresa, el cuerpo de Cristo* (2007), with Paz Vega a rather unlikely choice for portraying the saint. There is a focus on her visions and ecstasies and an actor credited with playing Jesus.

There had been some controversy in the 1990s with Nigel Wingrove's *Visions of Ecstasy* (1989), an eighteen-minute film on Teresa and her visions that was banned by the British censors. When the distributors appealed in 1996, the European Court of Human Rights upheld the British ban for blasphemy. In 2000, Wingrove made a salacious sex film, *Sacred Flesh*, about a convent where the superior had visions of Mary Magdalene and discussed sexuality, the Catholic Church, and its attitudes toward sex—Mary Magdalene's views were not those from the Gospels.

NOTES

1. Sun-Woo Jang interview with Tony Rayns appears in Rayns' book *Seoul Stirring: 5 Korean Directors* (London: Institute of Contemporary Arts, 1993).

2. "Interview with Lance Tracy," *Bible Films Blog*, February 19, 2007, biblefilms .blogspot.com.au/search/label/Cross%20%28The%20-%202001%29; Matt Page, "*The Cross* (2001)—Review," *Bible Films Blog*, February 7, 2007, biblefilms.blogspot .com/2007/02/cross-2001-review.html.

17

THE BIZARRE

PLASTIC JESUS

This is a banned film (1971) about a filmmaker in Belgrade who is against the powers that be. It includes controversial footage of Hitler and Tito.

THE JESUS TRIP

Prolific television director Russ Mayberry made this feature (1971) in the vein of so many bikie culture films of the period. The religious connection is that a bikie gang involved with heroin hide in a convent and abduct a nun who has to make a decision about her vocation.

SWEET JESUS, PREACHER MAN

This is a "Blaxploitation" film (1973) with William Smith and Roger E. Mosley about a hit man who poses as a Baptist minister. The director, Henning Schellerup, moved to more respectable telemovies in the late 1970s and directed a number of religious documentaries: *In Search of Historic Jesus* (1979), *Ancient Secrets of the Bible* (1992), and *The Incredible Discovery of Noah's Ark* (1993).

THE THORN

This is reportedly a poorly produced feature film (1974) that is a parody of the life of Jesus, played by John Bassberger, with a young Bette Midler as a Jewish mother, Mary. The film is also titled *The Divine Mr. J.*, though *The Thorn* was the original title. (Bette Midler apparently dropped it from her list of performances; however, there are some comments on the IMDb regarding the rights and wrongs of Bette Midler's attacks on the film and her dropping it from her list of performances.)

JEG SA JESUS DO

This crass, technically poorly made pornographic Danish film (translated *I Saw Jesus Die*, 1975) concerns the disciples of Jesus and Jesus' Crucifixion. (See appendix 3 on films concerning Jesus' sexuality.)

EL ELEGIDO

In a Mexican village, the inhabitants celebrate Holy Week by putting on a Passion play. The film 1977 has been interpreted as anti-religious, showing the villagers as deformed and stupid.

STRIDULUM

This Italian horror film was popular at the time (1979) and concerns mothers, babies, and strange births—with an international cast including John Huston, Shelley Winters, and at the end, Franco Nero as Jesus.

DEUX HEURES MOINS UN QUART AVANT JESUS-CHRIST

This French comedy (1982) starred and was directed by Jean Yanne. Fortunately, Jesus comes only into the title, which is a humorous point of reference for a story about ancient Rome before the coming of Christ.

DAS GESPENST

The Ghost (1983) is an odd drama by iconoclastic German director Herbert Achternbusch. It caused some controversy in its time, a petition of two thousand signatures with the public prosecutor in Munich confiscating the film because it "injured human feelings and human dignity" and "slandered a religious community."[1]

It was also confiscated in Australia.

> This is the tenth film in eight years from writer and director Herbert Achternbusch and is radically out on its own limb. The premise is that Jesus Christ has returned as a fairly palpable ghost behaving in a slightly less than saintly manner, and no one knows how to react to him. He lives on bread and wine, teases the Mother Superior, and has a crown of thorns that nettles him at times. Achternbusch aficionados will readily enthuse about this latest creation though other reactions may vary from amusement to objection.[2]

ASI EN EL CIELO COMO EN LA TIERRA

God decides to send another son to the earth to save the world. Jesus Christ disagrees because in such a case the history should be rewritten. To solve the dispute they decide to organize the apocalypse. This Spanish tongue-in-cheek farcical comedy (1995) is set in heaven with an attempt to have a second Incarnation to fix up troubles on earth. It has some respectability with Francisco Rabal (veteran of many European classics, including Bunuel's *Nazarin* and *Viridiana*) as St. Peter.

SOUTH PARK

The Spirit of Christmas is the name of two different animated short films made by Trey Parker and Matt Stone, two shorts which anticipated the South Park series. They are often referred to as *Jesus vs. Frosty* (1992) and *Jesus vs. Santa* (1995).

Jesus vs. Frosty

In 1992, Trey Parker and Matt Stone, students at the University of Colorado, made *Jesus vs. Frosty*, part of Avenging Conscience Films. Parker and Stone used only construction paper, glue, and an 8 mm film camera. It featured four boys very similar to the four main characters of *South Park*. The Jesus reference in this story of an evil Frosty who disguises himself as Santa occurs when two boys run away and then find a Nativity scene with a baby Jesus, who flies to the evil snowman and kills it by slicing off the magic hat by throwing his halo.

Jesus vs. Santa

In 1995, Fox executive Brian Graden paid Stone and Parker two thousand dollars to make another animated short as a video Christmas card he could send to friends. It was *Jesus vs. Santa,* a version of *The Spirit of Christmas.* Jesus descends to South Park where he meets the kids. He asks them to take him to the local mall, where he finds Santa. It turns out that Jesus is angered with "Kringle," because, according to Jesus, Santa diminishes the memory of Jesus' birthday with his presents. Santa, insistent that Christmas is a time for giving and not merely to remember Jesus' birthday, claims that "this time" they will "finish it." They fight in a manner reminiscent of martial arts video games like Mortal Kombat, accidentally killing various bystanders (including Kenny) in the process. Jesus pins Santa down, and they each ask the boys to help them. Stan hesitates, and wonders, "What Would Brian Boitano do?" The figure skater miraculously appears and delivers a speech about how Christmas should be about being good to each other. The boys transmit the message to the ashamed fighters, who agree and decide to bury the hatchet over an orange smoothie. In 1997, *Jesus vs. Santa* received a Los Angeles Film Critics Association Award for best animation. (*Spirit of Christmas: Jesus vs. Santa* can be found on the *South Park the Hits: Volume 1* DVD.) In *Red Sleigh Down,* Jesus and Santa unite as friends to kill Iraqis.

South Park has never been noted for its reverence. There have been many religious references that have brought protests. Another Jesus connection is that the kids of South Park listen to a program called *Jesus and Me,* in which Jesus is a television talk-show host similar to the sensationalist Geraldo Rivera (who toned down as he grew older).

WHO KILLED BABY JESUS?

An American feature film (1992) about a psychopathic mother and her relationship to her daughter as they hire a hit man to commit a robbery. The synopsis offers no explicit Jesus connection.

JESUS VENDER TILBAGE

This 1993 Danish film (translated *The Return*) has a history, perhaps indicating why some Christian audiences around the world are suspicious of announcements of Danish films about Jesus.

Shortly after his 1970 success with the film *Stille Dage i Clichy* (*Quiet Days in Clichy*), director Jens-Jorgen Thorsen started trying to get *Jesus Vender Tilbage* (*The Return*) made. For the next twenty years, he kept at it when the money was available but had to cope not only with short-ages of money, but an legal ban on the film in his native country of Denmark which was not revoked until 1990. In the face of these obstacles, he has put together a smoothly professional-looking film which seems to be intended to offend the religious sensibilities of a great many people. This satirical drama follows Jesus' career after he returns to earth to save it from environmental pollution. After a little exploration, he decides that Paris suits him just fine as a base of operations. When he gets entangled with a group of terrorists attempting to hijack a plane, he gets into serious trouble with the authorities, but one compensation for his troubles is that Jesus, the still-virgin Demiurge, finally gets to sample feminine carnal delights, which are offered to him by a lovely hijacker (Atlanta). When the authorities capture the hijackers, they assume that Jesus is their leader, and he is condemned to death. However, somehow the Pope (a despicable child molester) and Billy Graham (a bewildered fool) hear of his presence on the planet, and they scheme for his release, in return for a few miraculous favors.[3]

JESUS OF JUDSON

This is a New Jersey short film (1996) about an army brat, his charismatic friend, and coming-of-age issues.

STRIPPING FOR JESUS

A provocative title for a sixteen-minute film (1998) written and directed by actress Anne Heche, which is the memoir of the daughter of a hypocritical Baptist minister.

HYAKUNEN NO ZESSHO

In this Japanese film (translated *Jesus in Nirvana*, 1998), a young man who works in a used record store hears voices and sounds of the past urging him to return to his home, a village that had been flooded years before. He wreaks revenge but also dies. There is no immediate link to the name of Jesus and its use in a Japanese religious or cultural context.

MENSCH JESUS

This is a twenty-three-minute film (1999) about the return of Jesus to Stuttgart to evaluate their spirituality and his disappointment by their evil. He is also confronted by Satan. He prepares a judgment day and warns the people about the impending apocalypse. However, he relents when he meets a sympathetic widow (with the symbolic name of Christa). There are similarities in theme to Hal Hartley's *The Book of Life*.

SUPER JESUS

This is an American short film (1999) about a young child, his strange aunt, and an out-of-control cat. (Needing Jesus' power to control it?)

JESUS IS A PALESTINIAN

This is a Dutch spoof about a young man who becomes involved in an obscure cult in Holland that is waiting for the coming of a Messiah (1999).

JESUS AND HUTCH

This is a short satire (2000) derived from the television series *Starsky and Hutch*. This time there is action in New York City with Eric Stoltz as Jesus (in biblical dress) and Tate Donovan as Hutch pursuing criminals with guns blazing. Writer-director Paul Harrison's short can be seen on a trailer on Filmsewer.net.

CAN'T DRAG RACE WITH JESUS

This is a two-minute animated short by Bill Plympton in which a choir sings an ode to Jesus and to drag racing (2000).

TERRORAMA

Edwin Brienen from Holland saw and sees himself as a radical and pro-vocative media personality, Dutch-style. This feature (2001) has a group of young adults rebelling against society—which includes some irreverent sequences with Jesus and sexuality.

THIS FILTHY EARTH

This small-budget British film (2001) is more of an experiment than an entertainment, directed by Andrew Kotting. It is based on a novel by Emile Zola, with the setting transferred to Yorkshire and a grim, ugly experience of life on farms and the earthiness of this life. One of the characters is called Jesus Christ, who is an alcoholic and also an idiot savant. As the other characters descend into their own madness, he becomes wiser. It is allegorical and difficult.

THE TERMINATOR (JESUS PARODY)

This rather cleverly done five-minute video (2004) screened on YouTube is probably a sign of things to come. YouTube and other websites provide open access to everyone to place their videos for all to watch.

The video is a take on *Terminator 3* as well as the Jesus films: *The Greatest Action Story Ever Told*. The Cyborg terminator appears naked in the street in Bethlehem. The date is 0000. With his inbuilt detector he finds the Magi and asks one for his robe. He refuses, and the Terminator asks whether he is some kind of wise guy. He replies that actually he is. That sets the tone. As does the signature saying, "Hasta la vista, baby Jesus."

The video then focuses on Jesus with the Terminator intervening to save him: mowing down Roman soldiers as he interrupts the Sermon on the Mount.

During the Last Supper, the Terminator continually tries to save Jesus by shooting Judas, explaining that Judas is to betray Jesus. However, Jesus keeps reviving Judas. Finally, the Terminator tricks Jesus by calling out, "Pontius Pilate at 10 o'clock." Jesus automatically looks up and the Terminator shoots Judas.

On the way to Calvary, the Terminator comforts Mary, playing on his catchphrase, "He'll be back!"

JESUS CHRIST VAMPIRE HUNTER

I came across the producers of this film at the Cannes Film Festival of 2001 and was prevailed on, out of a sense of duty, to see this film. No, the title and film have not been invented as a hoax.

This is one of those B-budget (or Z-budget) films beloved of companies like Troma. Genres are taken over and the conventions subverted in blunt, unsubtle ways. Aficionados of this kind of film enjoy the extremes and the desperation.

When vampires roam the city by day, some priests call on Jesus to come and destroy them before the last day and final judgment. Some are lesbians. We get the idea from the poster: The first testament says "an eye for an eye"; the second testament says, "love thy neighbor"; the third testament "Kicks Ass." And another: The power of Christ impales you. The film is said to be a combination of Kung Fu, action, prophecy, humor, and musical.

Jesus is said to be the ultimate action hero, a super Messiah. The theme song is "Funky Jesus, Super Dude."

It is from Canada (2001), directed by Lee Demarbre, and runs for eighty-five minutes. It is too silly to be blasphemous. But, it would be offensive to many and in bad taste for all.

ULTRACHRIST

The popularity of screen heroes larger than life was at its peak in the early years of the twentieth century. Here Jesus is imagined as returning to earth and unable to relate to youth. So, he becomes the comic book–style hero Ultrachrist, spandex costume and all, and, tongue in cheek, combats evil enemies like Hitler, Nixon, and even Dracula. It is a low-budget and corny spoof comedy (2003).

JESUS HENRY CHRIST

This is a short film about a questioning young student in a strict Catholic school (2003).

JESUS CHRIST SUPERCOP

This is a series of five-minute short films for New York Channel 102 by Austin Bragg. Like the *Vampire Hunter* film, the series takes police action conventions and subverts them by having a supercop whose name is Jesus Christ, who has authority problems, and whose girlfriend has Tourette's syndrome; again, a question of taste (2005).

JESUS CHRIST SERIAL RAPIST

There are solid grounds for a libel case for this one released in 2004. Fortunately, Jesus does not enter it at all, except in the mind of the central character, someone certifiable who imagines he is Jesus with a mission to persecute and destroy his enemies. It has no dialogue, has loud music, and is the "work" of what one commentator called a "demented guy from New Jersey" who calls himself Bill Zebub. You get it?!

JESUS CHRIST THE MUSICAL

This bizarre video clip of seventy seconds' duration, directed by Javier Prato, has a camp Jesus in a loincloth, walking down a city street miming to Gloria Gaynor's "I Will Survive" (1978), and then he is hit crossing the street by a bus. It is available on YouTube (2005).

JERRY SPRINGER: THE OPERA

Audiences familiar with television's *The Jerry Springer Show* will know that the parade of characters appearing with the host have all kinds of social and sexual problems that are meant to arouse curiosity and some prurience about how the other half live. In composing an opera centered on Springer, clearly there had to be shock elements. And there are. The stage performances elicited protests. The BBC's screening of the television version roused controversy over whether it was obscene and blasphemous. *The Opera* is following in the tradition of the freedoms of the 1960s where any topic was fair game for objection or ridicule. Since some of the show's guests have religious problems and manias, it was inevitable that religion would offer targets.

Jesus appears. An actor who has previously appeared in a loincloth is seen again as Jesus in a loincloth. There are discussions and debates (and a song with a confrontation between Jesus and the devil) with Adam and Eve confronting Jesus. The Virgin Mary also appears (and is given some salacious language) and, with Jesus' somewhat camp behavior, there are questions insinuated about his sexuality.

Blasphemy is always an intended insult to religion. With this kind of satire, the authors, Richard Thomas and Stewart Lee, are not intending blasphemous insults but are taking religion as a phenomenon that has its limitations, even its scandals, as well as its mysterious teachings and beliefs. The authors would agree that this kind of material is clearly offensive to those who feel targeted—but would say that this is what satire is about. And satire, through its mockery (depending how clever and telling it is), raises questions that need answers.

THE TEN

This is a mainstream American spoof film (2007) in the vein of *Saturday Night Live* offering modern illustrations of the Ten Commandments. Reverent they are not, religious they are not. There is something to upset or offend most audiences in one or other of the stories. A host, Paul Rudd, who is involved in his own commandment problems, is the link. In the story about taking the Lord's name in vain, the filmmakers do that precisely. A devout churchgoing woman (Gretchen Mol) travels to Mexico and her horizons open, especially when she discovers Jesus, this time Jesus H. Christ (Justin Theroux), a hippie-looking guitar player and singer whose doctrine of loving one another is of the physical variety rather than the spiritual. Later in the film in another commandment, the woman, now married, encounters him once again. Jesus looks like the traditional holy card—long hair, beard, and white robe—but his behavior is less than divine. This is one of those spoof films that use broad and generally unsubtle humor that enjoys upsetting its audience. And does.

JESUS ON YOUTUBE

With the growth of the Internet and the range of websites, there are more Google references to Jesus and films than one can deal with. As streaming video has become more accessible and of better quality, subscribers to YouTube are placing their favorite clips on the net. When searching *Jesus*, *Christ* or *Jesus Christ* on YouTube, pages and pages of entries emerge.

Some of the images of Jesus on YouTube are from the classic films, especially Franco Zeffirelli's *Jesus of Nazareth* with the face of Robert Powell; many are from The *Jesus* Project with the face of Brian Deacon; and, more recently, many are from Mel Gibson's *The Passion of the Christ* with Jim Caviezel. Some are direct clips from the film. Others are compilations of scenes edited together. Others are really slide shows accompanied by pious and/or theological graphics or are accompanied by religious songs. There are many from the 1973 as well as the 2000 version of *Jesus Christ Superstar* and a number of the songs from this show in other languages. Some of the more effective are in Spanish with Alberto Sogorb. As with music videos in general, there is an industry of religious and Christ-centered music videos.

Other clips on YouTube are up-front evangelical and proselytizing videos. Some are effective and eminently usable in talks and workshops, including a series of anime Jesus with such episodes as Jesus walking on the water.

A number of clips are simply the reading of the Gospels, sometimes with the person filmed, sometimes with captions or with still images. This is also true of readings of apocryphal Gospels like those of Philip, Mary Magdalene and Jesus, Judas, and Thomas.

Since YouTube is open to everyone, many aspiring filmmakers (at best) and uninspired amateurs (at worst) do not hesitate to file their clips. One of the surprising aspects is not so much how many references there are to Jesus but how many parodies of the Gospels there are, or clips that put Jesus into contemporary and often compromising situations. While some people are being overtly offensive, most assume that Jesus is in the public domain and can be used without any threat of copyright and that he is so sufficiently well known that their serious or comic short films will be understood by most surfers who hit on their clip. The films are not necessarily intended as blasphemous. They may be intended as offensive to some Christians but they are also intended to get a bit of a giggle. Religious people may well feel hurt if Jesus is reduced to a parody, a spoof, or a bit of a giggle, but the question to be raised about the compassionate, understanding, and tolerant Jesus is whether he would be able to put up with them, even smile, more than some of his single-minded followers.

While most of the YouTube entries are not meant as insulting to Christianity—they merely accept the Jesus of culture without any faith commitment—there are quite a number of offensive sites that mock, if not the person of Jesus, then the images, especially those of popular piety. Referencing Zombie Jesus on YouTube will bring up collages of images, for example, the Sacred Heart of Jesus with Hitler moustache added and other alterations and distortions. One image has a person with a foot jammed into his mouth with the caption that religion will try to make us swallow anything.

One of the alarming aspects of Jesus on YouTube is that modern-day evangelists claiming to be Jesus Christ incarnate in his Second Coming get plenty of tubespace. One of those who turns up with some frequency is Jose Luis Miranda, a Miami-based preacher who says he is Jesus in his Second Coming. He had a 1973 epiphany when the risen Lord "integrated himself" into Miranda. His clips speak for himself although he has an alarming number of completely dedicated followers. He says sin no longer exists, that Satan is a Hollywood character, and that prayer is a waste of time. Critics note that he is not against that important aspect of religion: the collection.

A few examples that may inform as well as satisfy (or provoke) curiosity follow:

Jesus vs. Hitler

This is one of those to be seen to be believed: a wrestling match in Salt Lake City (animation over live action) with long commentary, American-style ("Mel Gibson's was worse than this because of the pain"). It is literally Jesus versus Hitler, who begins by winning, but after a violent intervention from Gandhi with a chair, Jesus wins.

Jesus Cristo Funny

This is an unfunny clip with a man on a cross, Spanish speaking, calling out "blasphemy."

Funny Jesus

This has a song with an icon animated in eyes and mouth.

Oh Jesus

In this animation, a crucified Jesus is singing and wiggling. It is attributed to sickanimation.com.

Comedy Jesus

Jesus does stand-up comedy.

Jesus Goes on a Blind Date

Jesus arrives to take a girl out in the present day, though he is dressed as in art. He can't eat meat on Friday, talks about Lent, discusses his Jewish upbringing, turns his glass of water into wine, and goes bowling (and is quite good). Then the guards from the mental institution come to take him back.

Modern-Day Jesus

This is about another date, but one that is more lascivious in tone.

Christ's A-poppin

This one takes place in modern day and involves a very hard birth for the mother, husband beside her and three men outside dressed like the Magi. The soundtrack is the "Christ Is Born" hymn. It does finish with an ironic joke. When the Magi give their gifts, the Joseph-figure remarks that future generations might turn this event into something commercial. "As if that would ever happen," says Mary.

★ ★ ★

A more recent feature of YouTube and other Internet channels for distribution is the popularity of the web series. We may expect to see more appearances of Jesus in a range of situations and contexts, especially that of spoof or satire. The 2008 series Fun with War Crimes (which has its own website with a great deal of information about the makers and the issues) sets George Bush and his inner cabinet (Dick Cheney, Donald Rumsfeld, Condoleezza Rice, and Karl Rove) in a hearing where Abraham Lincoln and Harpo Marx are on the panel. The series (each episode just over three minutes) is both serious in its critique of Bush and, especially, the war in Iraq, and funny in its mockery of the political celebrities.

In episode 5, "That Certain Feeling," Jesus is called as a witness. He delays answering a question as he is on his mobile getting a ticket for a Frank Sinatra concert. However, he is serious in telling President Bush to stop believing in himself. Bush counters that he believes because he talks with Jesus. Jesus agrees that he talks but does not listen. Jesus also declares firmly that he is not a Republican because he turns the other cheek, lives among the poor, and is a Jew. At this stage, Dick Cheney is getting a rifle loaded and cocked to shoot Jesus. Jesus leaves with a warning that global warming is true and is coming sooner than they think—with Harpo Marx playing with the thermostat of the heaters causing panic to the accused.

While the episode is political and satirical, it is of interest how a group with secular intent chooses to include the figure of Jesus and the particular Gospel attributes that the filmmakers see as contrary to the values of the Bush administration.

By the time this book is published, the entries will have increased and multiplied and surely will continue to do so, both the good and the edifying and the bad and the offensive.

NOTES

1. Case involving Herbert Achternbusch found on the File Room website: www.thefileroom.org/documents/dyn/DisplayCase.cfm/id/782www.thefile room.com.

2. Eleanor Mannikka, "*Das Gespenst* (1983): Synopsis," All Movie Guide, www.allmovie.com/movie/das-gespenst-v152200.

3. Clarke Fountain, "*Jesus Vender Tilbage* (1992)—Synopsis," MSN Entertainment, movies.msn.com/movies/movie-synopsis/jesus-vender-tilbage/.

18

AFTER *THE*
PASSION OF THE CHRIST

Before *The Passion of the Christ* was released at the beginning of 2004, most commentators did not foresee it as a box-office success, let alone bonanza. Some wished Mel Gibson well. Some thought he was just aiming for a tax loss. Others were concerned about its alleged anti-Semitism. Word had gotten around about its graphic depiction of Jesus' suffering and the violence.

Within a week of its American opening, it was clear that audiences wanted to see the film. Whether he had intended it or not, Mel Gibson had alerted the industry to the potential for religious films. It also alerted the independent filmmakers that Jesus and other Christian stories were worth considering for their films. The satirists saw a theme that was worth mining. It was possible to use Jesus language and Jesus images much more readily than before *The Passion of the Christ*.

In the chapters on the reverent and the bizarre images of Jesus, films, especially short and student films, were listed with some brief comment. In the IMDb (Internet Movie Database) page on Jesus as a character, there have been 126 entries since *The Passion of the Christ* (for only seven years, up to 2011). There seems to be a rush on Jesus films. Looking at the list, one finds that they are mostly short films, with an emphasis on comedy, spoof, and horror.

It should be noted that this was reinforced by the release of *The Da Vinci Code* in 2006 with the controversy that preceded it because of Dan Brown's novel. There was much less controversy after the film since the screenplay watered down the expression of some of Brown's claims about Jesus, Mary Magdalene, the Knights Templar, the Priory of Sion, and Opus Dei.

We can ask if there are some discernible trends in production as listed in the IMDb since 2004. Here are some examples:

DOCUMENTARIES

Almost immediately after the release of *The Passion of the Christ*, documentaries appeared on *The Making of . . .* , interviews with Mel Gibson (one of the most useful is that by the traditional Catholic network, EWTN [Eternal Word Television Network], in which Raymond Arroyo interviewed Gibson during production before the anti-Semitic discussion really got under way, a calmer, more objective discussion), and with Jim Caviezel. Gibson's theology and that of his father, who holds some extreme views, and his personal spirituality were explored.

Some key examples:

- *Time Machine: Beyond the Da Vinci Code* (2005)——Shown on the History Channel and including discussions with authors who have written on Rosslyn Chapel, the Templars. It includes re-enactments of Jesus' episodes, according to *The Da Vinci Code,* rather than according to the Gospels.
- *The Life and Passion of Christ* (2005)——An earnest look at the Gospels with the aim of highlighting, if not proving, their historicity. The film has a literal approach to the scriptures. The film is hosted by the devout Pat Boone and includes re-enactments.
- *Science of the Bible* (2006)—A television series looking at relics of the period and discussing their authenticity. It also includes re-enactments of Gospel episodes.
- *Unlocking Ancient Secrets of the Bible* (2006)—Another search for biblical secrets released at the time of *The Da Vinci Code* movie.
- *Secrets of Mary Magdalene* (2006)—Plot summary from IMDb: "Secrets of Mary Magdalene strips away the veils of history to reveal the flesh and blood woman who served as Jesus' foremost disciple and possibly the love of his life. Based on the nonfiction book, *Secrets of Mary Magdalene,* by bestselling authors Dan Burstein and Arne de Keijzer, this documentary special uncovers the latest information on one of the world's most controversial religious figures."[1]
- *The Gospel according to Caesar* (2007, 115 minutes, Holland)—Dan Brown did not think up this one. A priest and a linguist discuss and come to the conclusion that Julius Caesar is the real Jesus. There were some difficulties in production as the program was seen by

executives as possibly alienating audiences because of their faith in Jesus.

- *The Lost Tomb of Jesus* (2007)—An old topic given a contemporary gloss.
- *Shroud of Turin: Material Evidence* (2008, 60 minutes, United Kingdom)—There have been many documentaries about the authenticity of the Shroud of Turin. After *The Passion* and *Da Vinci*, the shroud has the potential to stir renewed interest.

TELEVISION SERIES

It is now more acceptable (and doable) to introduce Jesus or characters resembling Jesus into television programs and series. The *South Park* creators had no difficulty in introducing Jesus satirically—which set a precedent for many followers and imitators.

Animation series which allude to Jesus or introduce him:

- *Robot Chicken*
- *Cavalcade of Cartoon Comedy*
- *Family Guy*

Serious series:

- *Rescue Me*—The stories of firefighters and their work and personal struggles.
- *The Book of Daniel*—A more interesting example, which was taken off the air after some protests. Aidan Quinn plays a pastor who is involved in current moral issues and dramatized crises. The screenplays introduce scenes where the pastor discusses some of the matters with Jesus (Garret Dillahunt). This was an attempt at a more serious introduction of Jesus and religious and moral themes.

HORROR

Jesus Christ Vampire Hunter had already made an appearance soon after 2000. Two titles from 2003 are *Necromaniac: Schizophreniac 2* and *Zombiegeddon* with special effects man Tom Savini listed as Jesus and a cast that included horror directors (acclaimed and ridiculed) Uwe Boll and Lloyd Kaufman from Troma films. YouTube provides a site for some images (many scurrilous) of

Jesus and the horror genres. It seems inevitable, given the continued popularity of horror and slasher movies, especially amongst younger male audiences, that Jesus will be associated with horror films. Already some examples have appeared:

- *Beaster* (2004)—A ten-minute short with Jesus resurrected after three days as a flesh-eating zombie.
- *Scarlet Moon* (2006)—A ninety-minute Z-budget horror with Satanists, vampires, and conflict, and the presence of Jesus.
- *Zombie Jesus* (2007)—Again Jesus returns as a zombie for immortality. Zombie associations with the living dead and resuscitation will occur to filmmakers when they consider the Resurrection.
- *The Becoming* (2012)—Satan rules the world.

SATIRE AND SPOOF

Quite a number of the examples of the bizarre in the earlier chapter are spoofs. In a time when there is immediate access to sites to add easily and inexpensively made clips, and where reverence toward traditional Christianity has disappeared in many areas, then satire and spoof of religion and of Christianity are to be expected while not welcomed.

- *Outtakes of the Christ* (2004, United States)—Spoofs that use footage from Mel Gibson's film.
- *Kvetchin' of the Christ* (2004, United States)—Another spoof of Mel Gibson. The film has its own poster on the IMDb.
- *Alfa y Omega* (2004, Spain)—Adam and Eve, God, and a discussion about creation.
- *Parabola* (2004, Italy)—Jesus, Lazarus, and his sisters; noted as a comedy/history.
- *Not My Religion* (2005, Canada)—Jesus encounters a mermaid.
- *Passion of the Crust* (2005, United States)—Uses a recurring joke of wordplay with Christ and crust (used also in the feature film *My Best Friend's Girl*, 2008).
- *The Greatest Story of All Time* (2005)—"God appears to two friends as a talking van and gives them a sacred mission."[2]
- *TV the Movie* (2006, United States)—Satire on TV programs. Includes a skit on Jesus, asking him questions about living with his father for three thousand years, and questions about Mary's virginity. This film had some theatrical release and DVD release.

- *Ultimate Remote* (2007, 78 minutes, United States)—Another skit compilation where two friends are sent by their remote into another dimension where political correctness is not important. The casting lists an actor as Jesus/That Darn Jesus.
- *Drake Beckett: The Devil's Newest Threat* (2007, United States)—A DJ lives a worldly life but is then transferred to the religious broadcasting department and has to face his life.
- *Welcome to Reality* (2008, United States)—A professor helps six men who play games to have a more historically accurate and involving adventure, while meeting new characters, including Jesus.
- *Prop 8: The Musical* (2008)—Direction by Adam Shankman (*Hairspray*) and music by Marc Shaiman. A group of actors, including John C. Reilly, Neil Patrick Harris, and Allison Janney, join in a four-minute song and dance to protest the loss of the law to permit gay marriages. Suddenly Jesus appears onstage in the form of Jack Black—it is Jesus as Jack Black, patter, jokes, and quips, condemning religious attitudes of hate rather than love and reminding the audience of the separation of church and state. It is readily available online.
- *For Christ's Sake* (2009, United States)—Listed as a drama about an institute, which, to survive, is cloning characters from history using DNA. The cast list includes as an actor The Clone of Jesus.
- *What If God Was One of Us?* (2011, United States)—Jesus is too comfortable in heaven and God sends him down to earth.
- *The Jesus Workout* (2011, United States)—A three-minute "infomercial parody."

SERIOUS FILMS

- *Reconciled/Reconciled through Christ* (2004, United States)—A feature film directed by a one-time horror exploitation filmmaker, Tim Ritter (with titles like *Killing Spree* and *Dirty Cop No Donut*), who seems to have had a conversion experience, "a testament of my own faith that I integrated into the movie." While drawing on some of his techniques in his former style, he tells the story of a man pursuing his wife with vengeance but meets a stranger who tells him the story of Jesus with some visualising of Gospel sequences. "This is a Tim Ritter Christian horror film, so it shouldn't be surprising that it comes off like one of his old exploitation flicks remade through the lens of his more recent Christian conversion."[3]

- *Messiah: Prophecy Fulfilled* (2004, 50 minutes, United States)—The synopsis seems to raise issues for Jews and Christians:

  Nick Mancuso plays Rabbi Yehudah an excellent teacher who knows the Holy scriptures. . . . After following and studying Yeshua (Jesus) the Rabbi knows with out a doubt Yeshua, is the Son of the living God that has come to fulfil all the prophecies relating to the Messiahs coming foretold by the prophets. . . . During the Jewish observance of Passover, Rabbi Yehudah and his family share a Seder meal in a traditional Passover sitting. . . . Rabbi Yehudah in a superb teaching explains in detail how the Seder itself, as well as the prophecies of the Torah, have been fulfilled in Yeshua (Jesus). However, during the teaching the Rabbi is challenged by two younger brothers, for his acceptance of Yeshua as the Messiah.[4]

- *Matthew 26:17* (2005, United States)—This film has its own poster on the IMDb entry. It is a conversation at the Last Supper with serious tone. Mary Magdalene is present with some intimations of her friendship with Jesus.
- *Quitting Is for Losers* (2005, United States)—A fifteen-minute short about a man who has to face his life.
- *Forgiving the Franklins* (2006, United States)—A drama in which an American fundamentalist family are involved in a car accident and have to re-appraise their lives, the potential for good as well as bad. Well received by many religious audiences.
- *Hitler Meets Christ* (2007, United States)—What seems an unlikely title for a serious film is, in fact, the title for a film about the embodiment of good in Jesus and the embodiment of evil in Hitler and the confrontation between the two. The film is based on a play by actor Michael Moriarty, *Hitler and Christ Meet at the Port Authority Bus Terminal* (1991). Moriarty says that it focuses on polar good and evil and shows the tenacity of Christ and his love.
- *Passions of the Christ* (2007, United States)—An eight-minute film about a couple with marriage difficulties who pray for help.
- *Teenage Christ* (2008)—An attempt to show that Jesus is not only relevant but became incarnate in his own time. What about our time? The synopsis was written by the director: "This story chronicles Jesus Christ in a modern-day high school. In addition to the typical adolescent problems of girls, puberty, school, and family, he has to manage newfound abilities that might not be normal, and face the truth about his biological father. Weaving together drama, comedy, and a Biblical background, audiences may discover that Jesus' coming of age is not unlike their own."[5]

- *The Godening* (2008, United States)—A forty-minute morality play about a Christian who descends into hedonism and is in need of redemption.
- *Crucifixion* (2008, United States)—A 120-minute television film of the Passion and death of Jesus. (Difficult to trace information about the film.)
- *JC in tha Hood* (2008, United States)—A seventy-minute gangster and drug film with a Jesus character.

> *JC in tha Hood* is a story of religious redemption, following four lost souls in the inner city of Los Angeles. A prostitute, a gang-banger, an alcoholic and a drug addict are all in need of spiritual guidance from big brother Jesus Christ. JC roams the hood unnoticed but ever present. All four people are eventually given a second chance to redeem themselves by accepting God into their everyday lives. JC; An uplifting story of hope and redemption proposing that everyone deserves a second chance to find and worship God.[6]

- *Forgiven* (2008, United States)—Only a six-minute short but the synopsis has interesting aspects.

> *Forgiven* is about a man named James who has an encounter with Jesus Christ during His walk with the cross to the crucifixion site. It turns out that James is the one who nails Jesus to the cross and as he does so, he starts to remember the bad things in his life that are affecting it and the people around him. He begins to realize that his sins are what nailed Jesus to the cross. This encounter gives James forgiveness, hope, and a second chance to live a better life then the one he was living previously.[7]

- *The Sindone* (2009, Spain)—While this film, with Gospel scenes as well as a modern story about the presence of Jesus, was in production, a *Making of . . .* short appeared on YouTube along with a trailer and other promotional clips.
- *Ben-Hur* (2010, United Kingdom)—A new version of *Ben-Hur* was in production in 2009, a British production with some excellent credentials: director Steve Shill who has worked in the United Kingdom and the United States, especially for television; a script by veteran Alan Sharp (*Ulzana's Raid, Rob Roy, Dean Spanley*), a British cast including Joseph Morgan as Ben-Hur and Stephen Campbell Moore as Messala, and a supporting cast including Ray Winstone as Arrius. Audiences will be keen to see how the film handles the presence of Jesus in Nazareth and on the way to Calvary compared with the previous versions and their reticence.

- *The Road to Emmaus* (2010, United States)—A thirty-minute dramatization of Luke 24, the road to Emmaus after the Resurrection. Bruce Marchiano is Jesus as he was in *The Visual Bible: Matthew* and *The Visual Bible: Acts*.
- *The Encounter* (2010, United States)—A modern story where Jesus encounters a young woman on the road.
- *The Lion of Judah* (2010, United States)—A full-length animation film about animals and the story of Jesus, especially a lamb who grazes near Jerusalem at the time of the Passion. The voice of Jesus is that of Bruce Marchiano, who was Jesus in *The Visual Bible: Matthew*, *The Visual Bible: Acts*, and *The Road to Emmaus*. Other voices include Michael Madsen and Ernest Borgnine.
- *City of Gardens* (2011, United States)—Full-length feature film about a surfer thrown into a Peruvian jail in the 1980s. True story.

NOTES

1. Anonymous, "Plot Summary for the *Secrets of Mary Magdalene*," Internet Movie Database, www.imdb.com/title/tt0892428/plotsummary.

2. "*The Greatest Story of All Time*: Storyline," Internet Movie Database, www.imdb.com/title/tt0488395/.

3. Steve McNaughton, "Well Worth a Look by Horror Fans and Beyond," *Reviews & Ratings for "Reconciled*," Internet Movie Database, www.imdb.com/title/tt0386737/reviews. McNaughton has made a documentary on a 1980s film by Ritter, *Crimson Carnage: The Making of Truth or Dare* (2009).

4. Ken James, "Plot Summary for *The Messiah: Prophecy Fulfilled*," Internet Movie Database, www.imdb.com/title/tt0368025/plotsummary.

5. Julie Sesnovich, "Plot Summary for *Teenage Christ*," Internet Movie Database, www.imdb.com/title/tt1347385/plotsummary.

6. Zmovie.tv, "*JC in tha Hood*," www1.zmovie.tv/movies/view/jc-in-tha-hood.

7. Hans Hernke, "*Forgiven*: Storyline," Internet Movie Database, www.imdb.com/title/tt1307445/.

AFTERWORD: MORE THAN
A HUNDRED YEARS OF
JESUS FILMS

In the late nineteenth century, audiences were eager to see devout representations of Jesus in the new medium of moving images. Short biblical and Gospel films were shown everywhere and were often used for religious instruction and inspiration.

With the coming of feature films and feature length in the second decade of the twentieth century, films like *From the Manger to the Cross*, *Christus*, and the Gospel sections of *Intolerance* drew on a reverent tradition and on the popular religious art styles of statues, pictures, and cards to dramatize Jesus, his life, and his preaching. With the silent filmmaking, actors relied on declamation for the captions and an overdramatic presentation. The theological and spiritual underpinning of these films was based on quite a literal reading of the biblical texts, with an emphasis on Jesus' divinity underlying his humanity. This was the perspective of Cecil B. DeMille with *The King of Kings* in 1927, although he allowed himself and his writers some liberty in inventing facets for the familiar stories.

For whatever reason that national industries shied away from representing Jesus face-on and speaking from 1927 to 1961 (*King of Kings*), more than three decades of reticence followed, especially in the era of the development of sound, of color processes, and of wide-screen photography. Was it an overemphasis on Jesus' divinity and not wanting to represent his ordinariness and humanity? This theology and spirituality kept audiences at a distance from Jesus when he reappeared in the 1950s, partially seen in films like *The Robe* and *Ben-Hur*.

However, away from the studios in the United States, members of evangelical churches and some Catholic producers were working on more direct presentations of Jesus, using the text rather literally but also being inventive on how to fill out details not included in the Gospels.

While the 1960s were a time of turmoil and change, Jesus at last was seen on the big screen, in color, and he spoke. This provided filmmakers with opportunities to be creative in their characterization and in their storytelling as well as to indulge in spectacle with "biblical-sounding" scores. However, the reading of the texts was still fairly literal, emphasizing the divine Jesus but opening up different ways of looking at him as a human being (though European rather than Semitic). Even Pier Paolo Pasolini's *Gospel according to St. Matthew* uses a very literal reading of the text, using it as a screenplay, which makes it a stylized piece no matter how "realistic" it was intended to be in its stark black-and-white photography.

With the rethinking of Christian doctrine and practice in the 1960s, movements like the Jesus movement, and groups of charismatic prayer in mainstream churches and not solely in Pentecostal communities, there was room for a different kind of Jesus, the rock opera Jesus of *Superstar* and *Godspell*. These plays and films moved quickly into the audience consciousness (the films only twelve years after *King of Kings*), although many traditional Christians found it hard to come to terms with this singing Jesus.

But, it was the 1970s that saw the landmark films on Jesus. Franco Zeffirelli made his *Jesus of Nazareth* for television (and an edited version for the cinemas). This was not a literal interpretation of the Gospels. The background of Judea at the time was explained. The writers took note of biblical scholarship during the twentieth century and interpreted the texts according to the different literary forms and drew on their Hebrew references. *Jesus of Nazareth* was particularly popular in Catholic countries.

On the other hand, the Jesus film from The *Jesus* Project, which was released at the end of the 1970s, stayed with the more traditional image of Jesus and the literal use of the text. This interpretation has lasted for almost three decades and has had many new leases of life in its original form, in the many subtitled versions in Asian and African languages and in sections being used for particular focus versions, for instance, for children.

But, the freedom for filmmakers to present Jesus in different ways led to some arresting images (like those of Ken Russell in *The Devils*) or the possibility of humor (as in the Pythons' *Life of Brian*). This was also the period of the early 1980s when VHS copies and machines were becoming more readily available. This also meant that more challenging images of Jesus could appear on-screen, testing beliefs concerning humanity and divinity, creating some uproar for those who thought these attempts were blasphemous, but stimulating, on the other hand, for those who wanted to study the Gospels in more depth. This was the impact of *The Last Temptation of Christ* and *Jesus of Montreal* in 1988.

The 1990s saw a proliferation of films and videos that were less for commercial entertainment than for edification and teaching. Anyone could operate a video recorder. This meant that there was a range of theology available from the most fundamentalist reading of the texts to imaginative interpretations.

The millennium, however, brought a new impetus to Jesus films in the mainstream. The television *Jesus* with Jeremy Sisto caught the imagination of many audiences with its more humane Jesus. Animation had been used at this time and *The Miracle Maker* showed how entertaining and instructive animation films could be.

Then, *The Passion of the Christ*. What was a personal enterprise (personally and professionally) for Mel Gibson became a byword for Gospel films and their impact on audiences (and on the box office). While many European commentators criticized the film for a seeming lack of attention to the Resurrection (and, therefore, an incomplete theology that emphasized the suffering and death of Jesus), audiences around the world responded and many, especially older audiences who were brought up in this kind of expiation spirituality, felt at home with the film despite the brutality of the scourging. Younger audiences also seemed to value a strong and suffering Jesus. With the release of *The Da Vinci Code* two years later (and with the millions who read the book), discussion about Jesus, whether grounded or not in the scriptures or in history, was open to everyone.

Mel Gibson has offered filmmakers not only a liberty to go in whatever direction they wish (for example, several films since with an African American Jesus) but an ever more alert audience of both believers and unbelievers (including many who are interested financially rather than because of faith). High-definition cameras and digital editing mean that almost anyone can make a Jesus film. Considering the Internet Movie Database list for Jesus as character and the entries since 2004 reinforces this. And with website outlets from YouTube on, some exhibition is the least of the filmmakers' worries.

This book has suggested that directions already taken include documentary, presence in television series, a growth in horror films, satire, and spoof, as well as many serious films. Many of these films and clips are from independent filmmakers and student directors.

All of this means that, if these trends persist, there could be a need for another larger chapter on Jesus films before many years have passed.

APPENDIX 1: THE MAJOR JESUS FILMS

THE SILENT ERA

1898   *La Vie et la Passion de Jesus-Christ* (France, d. Georges Hatot, Louis Lumiere)

1905   *La Vie et la Passion de Jesus-Christ* (France, d. Lucien Nonguet, Ferdinand Zecca)

1913   *From the Manger to the Cross* (United Kingdom, d. Sidney Olcott)

1916   *Christus* (Italy, d. Giulio Antamoro)

1916   *Intolerance* (United States, d. D. W. Griffith)

1923   *The Wandering Jew* (United Kingdom, d. Maurice Elvey)

1923   *I.N.R.I.* (Germany, d. Robert Wiene)

1925   *Ben-Hur* (United States, d. Fred Niblo)

1927   *The King of Kings* (United States, d. Cecil B. DeMille)

THE SOUND ERA

1933   *The Wandering Jew* (United Kingdom, d. Maurice Elvey)

1935   *The Last Days of Pompeii* (United States, d. Ernest Schoedsack)

1935   *Golgotha* (France, d. Julien Duvivier)

1939   *The Great Commandment* (United States, d. Irving Pichel)

1946   *Maria Magdalena, pecadora de Magdala* (Mexico, d. Miguel Contreras Torres)

1948   *Reina de reinas* (Mexico, d. Miguel Contreras Torres)

1949   *The Lawton Story* (United States, d. William Beaudine, Harold Daniels), re-issued as *The Prince of Peace*, 1951

1949	*The Pilgrimage Play* (United States, d. Frank R. Strayer)
1951	*Quo Vadis* (United States, d. Mervyn LeRoy)
1952	*El martir del Calvario* (Mexico, d. Miguel Morayta)
1952	*I Beheld His Glory* (United States, d. John T. Coyle)
1953	*The Robe* (United States, d. Henry Koster)
1954	*Day of Triumph* (United States, d. Irving Pichel, John T. Coyle)
1959	*The Big Fisherman* (United States, d. Frank Borzage)
1959	*Ben-Hur* (United States, d. William Wyler)
1961	*King of Kings* (United States, d. Nicholas Ray)
1962	*Pontius Pilate* (Italy, d. Irving Rapper, Gian Paolo Callegari)
1962	*Barabbas* (United States/Italy, d. Richard Fleischer)
1963	*Acto de primavera* (Portugal, d. Manoel de Oliveira)
1964	*Il Vangelo secondo Matteo* (Italy, d. Pier Paolo Pasolini)
1965	*The Greatest Story Ever Told* (United States, d. George Stevens)
1969	*The Milky Way* (Spain, d. Luis Bunuel)
1971	*Pilate and the Others* (West Germany, d. Andrzej Wajda)
1971–1972	*Jesus, nuestro señor* and *Jesus, el niño Dios* (Mexico, d. Miguel Zacarias)
1972	*Jesus, Maria y José* (Mexico, d. Miguel Zacarias)
1973	*Jesus Christ Superstar* (United States, d. Norman Jewison)
1973	*Godspell* (United States, d. David Greene)
1973	*The Gospel Road* (United States, d. Robert Elfstrom)
1975	*Il Messia* (Italy, d. Roberto Rossellini)
1976	*The Passover Plot* (United States, d. Michael Campus)
1977	*Jesus of Nazareth* (United Kingdom/Italy, d. Franco Zeffirelli)
1978	*Karunamayudu* (India, d. A. Bhimsingh)
1979	*Jesus* (United Kingdom, d. Peter Sykes, John Krish)
1980	*The Day Christ Died* (United States, d. James Cellan Jones)
1982	*Cammina, cammina* (Italy, d. Ermanno Olmi)
1982	*Cercasi Gesu* (Italy, d. Luigi Comencini)
1985	*The Fourth Wise Man* (United States, d. Michael Ray Rhodes)
1986	*L'inchiesta* (Italy, d. Damiano Damiani)
1986	*AD* (d. Stuart Cooper)
1987	*Un bambino di nome Gesu* (Italy, d. Franco Rossi)
1988	*The Last Temptation of Christ* (United States, d. Martin Scorsese)
1989	*Jesus of Montreal* (Canada, d. Denys Arcand)
1991	*Incident in Judaea* (United Kingdom, d. Paul Bryers)
1991	*The Garden* (United Kingdom, d. Derek Jarman)
1992	*Bad Lieutenant* (United States, d. Abel Ferrara)

1993	*The Visual Bible: Matthew* (South Africa, d. Regardt van den Bergh)
1995	*The Visual Bible: Acts* (United States, d. Regardt van den Bergh)
1996	*Kristo* (Philippines, d. Ben Yalung)
1998	*I giardini dell'Eden* (Italy, d. Alessandro D'Alatri)
1998	*The Book of Life* (United States, d. Hal Hartley)
1999	*Mary, Mother of Jesus* (United States, d. Kevin Connor)
1999	*Jesus* (United States, d. Roger Young)
1999	*Jesus* (France, d. Serge Moati)
1999–2001	*Gli amici di Gesu* (Italy, d. Raffaele Mertes)
2000	*Tales from the Madhouse* (United Kingdom, d. Norman Stone and others)
2000	*Jesus Christ Superstar* (United Kingdom, d. Gale Edwards, Nick Morris)
2000	*The Miracle Maker* (United Kingdom/Russia, d. Derek W. Hayes, Stanislav Sokolov)
2001	*The Body* (United States, d. Jonas McCord)
2002	*San Giovanni—l'apocalisse* (Italy, d. Raffaele Mertes)
2002	*Joshua* (United States, d. Jon Purdy)
2003	*The Visual Bible: The Gospel of John* (Canada, d. Phillip Saville)
2004	*Man Dancin'* (United Kingdom, d. Norman Stone)
2004	*The Passion of the Christ* (United States, d. Mel Gibson)
2005	*Son of Man* (South Africa, d. Mark Dornford-May)
2006	*L'inchiesta* (Italy, d. Giulio Base)
2006	*Color of the Cross* (United States, d. Jean-Claude LaMarre)
2006	*La sacra famigilia* (Italy, d. Raffaele Mertes)
2007	*Jesus, the Spirit of God/The Messiah* (Iran, d. Nader Talebzadeh)
2008	*Jesus Christus Erloser* (Germany, d. Peter Geyer)
2008	*Color of the Cross 2* (United States, d. Jean-Claude LaMarre)
2008	*The Passion* (United Kingdom, d. Michael Offer)

TELEVISION, VIDEO, AND DVD DOCUMENTARIES

Jesus Christ Movie Star (1990), fifty-four minutes, is a quite comprehensive documentary film produced by Britain's Channel 4 in conjunction with Anglicans in Britain. It traces the history of the Jesus film with a generous selection of clips and interviews.

E voi che dite che io sia: I Gesu' del cinema (1999), Associazione Cattolica Esercenti Cinema, thirty minutes, contains a great number of excerpts from the Jesus films, especially several from Italy that are not available in other documentaries.

The Passion: Films, Faith and Fury (2006), Zigzag (UK) Productions, was screened on Channel 4 in the United Kingdom and on the History Channel in the United States. It contains many clips from the Jesus films as well as a wide range of expert commentary. I am one of the contributors.

APPENDIX 2:
JESUS AND THE CRUCIFIX

FAITH AND CULTURE

The use of the crucifix in films has become more prevalent since the 1980s. It was frequently part of the set design as a quick indication of Christianity or belief. However, in the latter part of the twentieth century, more secular times, the cross and the crucifix have been used by Christian and non-Christian directors alike to give some religious depth to their films. Steven Spielberg is a striking illustrator of this in his *Amistad* (1997).

Gospel stories and Gospel images are an intrinsic part of world culture, especially Western culture. The metaphors of crucifixion, resurrection, son of God, and miracles are used by believer and nonbeliever alike. A distinction can be made between the "Christ of faith"/the "Christianity of faith" and the "Christ of culture"/the "Christianity of culture." The former is lived Christianity, commitment (however minimal), belief, and an acknowledgment of Jesus as Lord and Savior, usually in a church community. The latter is an understanding and use of the tenets and stories of Christianity that does not necessarily involve any personal commitment. Christian stories, images, and metaphors are available to everyone as part of world cultural heritage. Filmmakers generally use aspects of the Christianity of culture.

However, there has been, since the middle of the nineteenth century, a terminology related to biblical interpretation and theological study. It is associated with rationalist scholar, Ernest Renan. A distinction was made between the "Jesus of history" and the "Christ of faith." Attempts were made, in the name of historical accuracy, to establish the facts about Jesus of Nazareth, or the Jesus of history. The commitment of believers in the Gospels was to the Christ of faith. This distinction is still used, but, with the developments in biblical studies and the growth of a personalized spirituality centered on Jesus, it is less useful and helpful than it was. It is not useful in reference to understanding Jesus-figures.

In cinema, writers and directors present Jesus-figures and Christ-figures. One might ask how the distinction between faith and culture relates to these figures, to "faith/Jesus-figures" and to "culture/Jesus-figures," to "faith/crucifixes" and to "culture/crucifixes." (A suggestion has been made that the latter might be represented in type in lower case: jesus-figures.) However, it is difficult to assess faith and/or culture in popular cinema since the director may be drawing on faith experience while asserting the portrait is cultural. A useful example is *The Last Temptation of Christ* based on Greek Orthodox Nikos Kazantzakis' novel, Calvinist Paul Schrader's screenplay, with Catholic director, Martin Scorsese. Is this "fictional" portrait a faith/ Jesus or a culture/Jesus—or both?

THE CRUCIFIX, ICON AND SYMBOL

Some examples of films from the 1980s and 1990s that offer images of the crucifix in popular films can be found in my essay, "Jesus on Screen" in John R. May's collection *New Images of Religious Film*. The films included there are *Lilies of the Field*; some films that use Catholic images in connection with a homosexual orientation (*The Fourth Man, The Long Day Closes,* and *The Garden*); and dramas like *The Penitent, A Prayer for the Dying, Twinkle, Twinkle Killer Kane, The Lawnmower Man,* and *Born on the Fourth of July*. The use of the crucifix also includes the graphic use of the cross in connection with the Dracula myth in the prologue of *Bram Stoker's Dracula* and in the hallucination scene, discussed earlier, in *Bad Lieutenant*. The crucifix can also make a judgment about the characters and situations. In the corridors of *The Nun's Story* (1959), there is a very large crucifix dominating the space, the sisters, and the stern formation the novices are undergoing. In *Christopher Columbus* (1991), Torquemada (played by Marlon Brando) interrogates Columbus about his expeditions, quoting St. Augustine to query the efficacy of the voyages. Once again, a crucifix looms large over Torquemada.

One of the best films for discussing the role of the crucifix is *Leap of Faith* (1992) with Steve Martin as a phony, but big-time traveling evangelist in the American South (Jonas Nightengale). As the assembly tent is set up, a huge crucifix is raised. It dominates the charismatic meetings and the song-and-dance routines and the showbiz pizzazz. But the figure of Jesus on the cross is a mournfully dying figure, quite a contrast to Jonas' antics. Jonas also uses earphones from his controller to urge people forward, to comment on the drought situation in the area (information gleaned from the ushers who note where the individuals are sitting and the data passed on to Jonas onstage). There is even an alleged healing.

However, in his quieter moments, Jonas goes into the tent and contemplates the crucifix, as does the camera for the audience to reflect on the true Christian meaning of what they are watching. However, ever the charlatan, Jonas puts some liquid on the eyes of Jesus and later claims the statue is weeping.

Where this thematic of the crucifix comes to a challenging climax is a scene where the young boy from the local restaurant, whose legs are crippled, believes that the faith-healer can actually heal and comes into the tent, full of faith, for a cure. Jonas hesitates—only to find that the boy is cured. While he makes another song and dance routine of the experience, he gives up his ministry.

FREEDOM AND HUMAN DIGNITY

Steven Spielberg highlights the plight of African slaves in *Amistad* (1997). Spielberg, with his Jewish background, powerfully uses Christian symbols, especially the cross, to dramatize the suffering of the African slaves and offer a means for interpreting its meaning. They were the new Christs. This was a new Crucifixion. The slaves identified with the Judeo-Christian stories, composed their Negro spirituals, and took so readily to literal and evangelical Christianity.

Amistad has a moving sequence in which the imprisoned slaves are looking at one of those books of stories of the Gospels and the history of the early church, which are illustrated by sketches. As they look with wonder at the life of Jesus, his miracles, his preaching, and then his suffering and death, the audience watches the slaves pondering the Crucifixion and the crosses on Calvary. They identify their suffering with that of Jesus. They also look at his Resurrection in a symbolic way rather than a scientific, analytic way and appreciate that this heaven might be a good place to go after suffering. This sequence reminds us of how readily the African slaves took up a Gospel-style Christianity. Spielberg intercuts with this sequence another in which the judge appointed by President Van Buren to condemn the slaves and who has hidden his Catholic identity goes into a church and prays before the crucifix. The next morning, as the slaves walk in chains to the courthouse, Spielberg shows the three masts of the ship *Amistad* (which means "Freedom") outlined above the roofs like the three crosses in the sketches of Calvary.

Spielberg, not a Christian, is using the inherited cultural symbols from Christianity to focus a discussion on slavery using Christian insights. Spielberg also used images of the cross in *Saving Private Ryan* (1998). This shows the power of cinema analogies for moral discussion.

In films taking an anti–capital punishment stance, the criminal to be executed is shown with arms outstretched evocative of Jesus on the cross. This is true of *The Execution of Raymond Graham* (1982) with Jeff Fahey and Morgan Freeman. It is seen in *Last Dance* (1996) as Sharon Stone goes to her death. A Catholic context is important for the death scene of Sean Penn as Matthew Poncelet in *Dead Man Walking* (1995). Sister Helen Prejean had ministered to Matthew in prison when he asked for a spiritual companion before his execution. Listening to him, praying with him, singing "Be Not Afraid" with him, she virtually heard his confession, helping him perceive God's forgiveness and love for the sinner before he died. With capital punishment, even the guilty person reminds us that Jesus died as a criminal on the cross for us all. On the cross, Jesus asked the Father to forgive his executioners, "for they know not what they do." He forgave the repentant thief.

The end of *Dead Man Walking* reminds the audience of the repercussions of this kind of forgiveness. The camera tracks around the outside of the church. We see inside. Sister Helen is praying with Mr. Delacroix, who could not bring himself to forgive Matthew Poncelet. He had attended the execution. But, now he is praying with the nun, whom he differs from so profoundly. In death there can be reconciliation.

A film that audiences responded to, especially many clergy, was *Priest*. It began its life as a modest television film for the BBC, written by Catholic author Jimmy McGovern, who had recently moved back to the church following the death of his father and was appreciative of the help given by the priests at that sad time. McGovern was interested in the role of priests in the 1990s, the issues of celibacy and of sexual orientation, and the role of confession and its protection of secrecy for the privacy of the penitent.

The two central priests raised the celibacy issues very clearly. The parish priest was a zealous man who had spent time in Latin America as a missionary. On his return to Liverpool, he was conscious of his experience abroad, that a man was expected to be with a woman otherwise he was not truly a man. He was living in his presbytery with his housekeeper in what was formerly and technically called a "concubine." This came as a shock and a scandal to his new assistant, Father Greg Pilkington (Linus

Roache), one of the group of more traditional young men being ordained in the 1990s. However, he was tormented by his homosexual orientation. He spends the night with a man he meets at a club, then refuses him communion at Mass. When the priest meets him again, he is arrested for lewd behavior, is shamed, and attempts suicide.

One sequence is powerful in its use of the crucifix. Father Greg has become concerned over the confession of a young girl whose confession he hears and who reveals sexual abuse by her father. The priest is threatened by the father in the confessional and his own behavior attacked. Father Greg is overwhelmed and, in a very moving scene, prays desperately before the crucifix, with a strong visual focus on the crucified figure of Jesus, about God's seeming inaction in painful experiences. He wants a miraculous intervention. He does not realize it, but because of the bickering at a parish meeting, he had ended it before time, enabling the mother of the abused girl to return home earlier than expected and discover what was happening.

Father Greg brought to the screen for the first time in a major film the issue of a priest's sexual orientation, something that was discussed during the 1990s by the churches. The basic principle of a priest leading a celibate life no matter what his orientation had been a long tradition in the church, though one that had not been openly acknowledged in many countries. *Priest* surfaced questions within the context of prayer, parish ministry, and personal decisions and anguish.

While Steven Spielberg uses crucifix images again for the Ryan family and their prayer and faith during World War II in *Saving Private Ryan* (1998), crucifix imagery can be used as a comment on the violence and pain of war. In *The English Patient* (1996), Kip, the bomb disposal expert, takes the nurse Hana up in the church to look at the beauty of the religious frescoes. World War II films often move the action into a church, still standing or destroyed, to evoke a more religious response to war.

An intriguing example of the crucifix literally in the middle of war action is seen in Samuel Fuller's *The Big Red One* (1980). The sergeant, played by Lee Marvin, fights during World War I in Flanders Fields. In the middle of a ravaged and desolate field is a more-than-life-sized wooden crucifix. It is old and weathered. It is marked by bullets. Fuller shows the cross, evoking rather than asking for an emotional response to the battle and for audiences to reflect on the Gospel message in the context of war.

The sergeant returns to Flanders in World War II after fighting with his young soldiers in North Africa, in the invasion of Italy, and at Normandy. The crucifix is still there. But a German sniper uses the crucifix as a cover to hide behind and to kill. The shadow of the cross is cast over the dead men lying on the ground. Now there are insects in the eyes of the figure of Jesus. Jesus is dead. Is God dead—or, at least, absent? What is the meaning of Christianity and the message of Calvary in the wars of Christian Europe? The use of the crucifix in cinema continues to offer insights into the role of Jesus and his Passion as interpreted for contemporary cinema audiences.

APPENDIX 3: THE ISSUE OF
FILMS ON JESUS AND SEXUALITY

THE ISSUE OF A FILM OF A GAY JESUS:
RUMORS AND CHAIN LETTER PETITIONS

For many years, Christians around the world received, and many sent on, a letter petitioning the powers that be to prevent the making of a Jesus film in which Jesus was presented as gay and as being in relationship with one or other of the apostles. This occurred in the 1980s and 1990s. However, with the Internet and e-mail, it was more widespread from 2000 on. A useful website chronicling some of this activity is www.truthorfiction .com/rumors/g/gayjesusmovie.htm?ref=3b.org.

Corpus Christi

There was a further complication because of the controversy concerning Terrence McNally's play *Corpus Christi* (1998), which was the story of a gay group putting on a play with a modern Texas setting in which issues of homosexuality, Gospel role models for homosexual men, and the issue of gay marriages were presented. The treatment is clearly controversial, but much of the writing and the dramatizing of Gospel incidents were done with reverence for the Gospels. While it has been performed internationally in theaters, *Corpus Christi* was filmed on video.

The actual play is not what the vigorous protesters outside the theaters suggested. It is not saying that Jesus or the apostles were homosexual. Rather, it uses the style of *Godspell*, *Jesus Christ Superstar*, and *Jesus of Montreal*. It is a kind of modern "mystery play" deriving from the tradition of the Middle Ages.

First of all, there is the play about Joshua and his friends in Corpus Christi, Texas. The friends then put on a play about Jesus from their perspective, their interpretation of the familiar Gospel stories. As with *Jesus of Montreal* or *Man Dancin'*, it is a "What if . . . ?" interpretation of the Gospels.

It shows actors putting on a play about young men in *Corpus Christi*, whose lives are made to resemble something of Jesus and the Gospels, and so, there are suggestions of "What if some of the apostles were gay?" The perspective is of people with a homosexual orientation (including Terrence McNally, the writer of the play) asking the churches about their place in the larger church and in following Jesus. They feel themselves discriminated against but want to know how they can commit themselves to Jesus. In fact, while the mood changes with some farcical moments and some very serious moments, with a range of hymns and songs ("Panis Angelicus," "Ave Maria") as in *Godspell*, there are some very reverent moments with respect for the Gospels and the Gospel characters. The recitation of the Lord's Prayer is very moving. The most controversial section has Joshua (the Jesus parallel character) blessing a union between two of the apostles. The play is one of special pleading rather than one wanting to scandalize and exploit. It is the parallel between making Jesus an African slave or feminist interpretations of the Gospel story.

A thoughtful review by Roy Ames appeared in the *Tablet* in November 1999. He concludes, "I don't even believe that McNally is suggesting that Jesus was gay, but rather he asks: If Jesus had been gay, how would we have treated him. How can the Church as his representatives on earth preach a Gospel of Love when it rejects loving gay relationships?"

The phenomenon of the chain letters concerning the making of a film about Jesus as gay predates *Corpus Christi*, but the appearance of the play may have confounded (and confused) the issues.

Further information about protests comes from Snopes.com:

Terrance [sic] McNally's dramatic offering *Corpus Christi* began previews at the Manhattan Theater Club in New York. As described by *The New York Times*, it "retells the Biblical story of a Jesus-like figure—from his birth in a Texas flea-bag hotel with people having profane, violent sex in a room next door, to his crucifixion as 'king of the queers' in a manner with the potential to offend many people."

And it did. The Manhattan Theater Club's announcement of the play as part of its fall season was greeted with bomb threats promising to "burn the place to the ground" if the production opened. In May 1998 the theatre announced it was pulling "Corpus Christi" from its line-up. A week later it changed its mind, reinstating the play to its fall roster. Caught between cries of censorship on one side and outraged sensibilities on the other, the theatre had to make a choice.

Additional security measures were taken during the play's run to protect both the actors and the audience. The Catholic League for Religious and Civil Rights (self-described as the nation's largest Catholic civil rights group) planned an opening-night protest at the theatre involving busloads of people from as far away as Baltimore and Philadelphia as well as nuns, priests and lay people from Long Island. "Hopefully we'll send a message that this is basically unacceptable," said William A. Donohue, the league's president.

Corpus Christi continues to play various theatres from time to time. It completed a four-week engagement at London's Pleasance Theatre in late 1999, and in March 2001 it became the subject of a brouhaha at Florida Atlantic University in Boca Raton when several state lawmakers threatened to cut funding for FAU because its theatre department staged the play. *Corpus Christi* is undoubtedly the "play that went on for a while but never stopped" referred to in the current petition, but there are still no plans to make a film of it.[1]

Material from Websites with Examples and Background to the Chain Letters

One cannot vouch for the truth or authenticity of all the following material, but it may be of interest to those who have experienced the chain letter and its urgency.

There is no movie coming out in 2001 that we can find featuring a gay Jesus or gay disciples. This appears to be a new, Internet version of a rumor we investigated more than 15 years ago when an article in a magazine in the state of Illinois in the United States claimed such a film was being proposed. The movie project was authentic, but never got off the ground. A rumor about the movie was circulated far and wide, however, and multitudes of letters were received by an Illinois state agency which, for some reason, became the focus of the protest. The movie never had anything to do with Illinois but had merely been mentioned in a publication from Illinois. The rumor as it is currently appearing on the Net is very weak. It doesn't give any specific information as to who is producing the movie or where anyone could write to effectively protest it. Additionally, the encouragement to add a name to the list and forward the email is useless. Who is going to send the final version and to whom?

There is a stage play titled "Corpus Christi" that has created contro-versy wherever it has been presented. It features a lead character with the name Joshua, which is a variation of the name Jesus. In the play, Joshua is a young gay man who fled from his home town of Corpus Christi, Texas, because of persecution over being homosexual. He returns, assembles a group of disciples, with whom he has sex, faces violent opposition, is betrayed by his friend Judas, and is crucified.[2]

The Snopes website cites an example of the letter writing:

I can't believe it. There is a movie that is coming out in 2001 saying Jesus and his disciples were gay! There is already a play that went on for a while, but never stopped! Maybe we can all do something! Please send this to ALL of your friends to sign to stop the movie from coming out. Already certain areas in Europe have started to ban it from coming to their country and we can stop it too! We just need a lot of signatures and you can help!

Please do not delete this! Deleting it will show your lack of faith and a lack of respect for our Lord and Savior Jesus Christ who died for us!

Please help!

Variations:

- Sometimes the publication news of this upcoming film was gleaned from is said to be *Modern People News*; at other times it's *Modern Film News*.
- Protest letters are directed to the Attorney General of either Illinois or Alabama.[3]

Origins

This piece is one of those examples that demonstrates a good petition never goes away, even when the issue it addresses has long since been settled (or was never really an issue in the first place). The "gay Jesus film" petition first hit the fan in 1984, and by the end of 1985 more than a million Christians had written protest letters in an attempt to have this non-existent movie banned.

Yes, non-existent. There never was such a film in production, but this petition continued to circulate anyway:

Modern People News has revealed plans for the filming of a movie based on the SEX LIFE OF JESUS in which Jesus is portrayed as a swinging HOMOSEXUAL. This film will be shot in the U.S.A. this year unless the public outcry is great. Already a French Pros-titute has been named to play the part of Mary Magdalene, with who Christ has a blatant affair. We CANNOT AFFORD to stand by and DO NOTHING about this disgrace. We must not allow this perveted world to drag our Lord through the dirt. PLEASE HELP us to get this film banned from the U.S.A. as it has been in Europe. Let us show how we feel.

Detach and mail the form below to the address shown. Make a few copies and give them to your friends. Only one name per copy.

Attorney General Scott,
301 South Second Street,
Springfield
ILLINOIS 62606
Dear Attorney General Scott,

I would like to protest, in the strongest terms possible, the production, filming, and showing of any movie that supposedly depicts the sex life of JESUS CHRIST by MODERN PEOPLE NEWS, 11030 West Addison Street, Franklin Park, Illinois 60181.

Such a movie would be blasphemous and would be an outrage and contrary to the truth. We urge you to take proper action against this moral corruption.

In the early incarnations of this call to arms, people were asked to fill out an attached form letter of protest and mail it to the Attorney General of Alabama. The message often contained the following postscript:

> Evangelist Jimmy Swaggart recently reported that the above mentioned movie HAS BEEN COMPLETED!!! According to Brother Swaggart, the movie company has released word that the movie is scheduled to be shown in various locations around the country during the Christmas Season. So, the time is short to put a stop to it. We sincerely hope that all spiritually and morally minded people will band together and keep this UNGODLY type of filth out of Alabama.

Many fell for it, including a radio station, which happily passed the story along to its listeners and later had to retract it. According to folklorist Jan Brunvand,

> By later the same day the radio station [in Gadsen, Alabama] personnel had attempted to contact Modern People News and had been in touch with the Alabama Attorney General's office. Following these efforts at verification, a statement was read on the air saying that although the attorney general had received between two and three thousand letters over a period of several weeks concerning the supposed gay-Jesus movie, no evidence could be

found that such a project ever existed. Modern People News, it was stated, seemed to have either gone out of business or changed their name.

In January 1985 Ann Landers published a letter from the attorney general's office of Illinois, which tried to set the record straight. Now the publication was given as Modern Film News, which supposedly had its offices in Illinois (which is how that state got dragged into this issue). People were exhorted to write to Attorney General William J. Scott . . . a man who had last held that office four years earlier:

Dear Ann Landers:

The office of the Attorney General of the State of Illinois respectfully requests your assistance in combating an international chain letter that is distressing hundreds and thousands of Christians and those of other faiths as well.

The chain letter is a plea to protest "in the strongest possible language" the making of a movie in which Jesus Christ could be depicted as a swinging homosexual. Both this office and the Associated Press have chased down every possible clue and cannot find a shred of truth in the story that such a film was ever in production.

Modern Film News, which reported the film plans, has been out of business for more than two years. Moreover, 90 percent of the protest mail that has been overwhelming our staff is addressed to the former attorney general, William J. Scott, who has been out of office longer than four years.

Despite our efforts to get the word to the public that the chain letter is a hoax, we continue to receive approximately 1,000 protests every week and at least a dozen phone inquiries each working day. The inquiries and protests have come from 41 states, Canada, Puerto Rico, New Zealand, Australia, Cambodia, Spain, Brazil, the Dominican Republic, India, the Philippines, Guatemala, Costa Rica and Portugal.

We have concluded that the "Jesus movie" rumor originated in 1977 when a suburban Chicago publication, Modern People News, reported that certain interests in Europe were planning such a film and requested that readers express their opinion of the purported project. The result was the chain-letter protest, which, for some unknown reason, has been revived and is again sweeping the world.

We are appealing to you, Ann Landers, to help us get the word out. The scope of your readership and impact on millions of newspaper readers around the world cannot be overestimated.

The postage and phone calls, not to mention the valuable time of employees, run into a great deal of money that could be used for so many worthwhile purposes. Will you please help us?

—Neil F. Hartigan, Attorney General, State of Illinois

Dear Attorney General Hartigan:

Hoaxes die hard and the zanier the hoax, the more difficult it is to convince people that it is not true.

If any of you, my readers, receive a copy of that wacky chain letter, take my word for the fact that there is not an iota of truth in it. And please tell friends that chain letters are illegal and should be tossed into the handiest wastebasket or fed to the nearest goat.

The only such movie that seems to have been planned or made when this petition originally began circulating decades ago was the 1974 film *Him*, described briefly in Harry and Michael Medved's 1980 book, *The Golden Turkey Awards*, as an "everything you ever wanted to know about bad movies, but were afraid to ask" offering:

This innovative film, designed exclusively for gay audiences, goes into excruciating detail concerning the erotic career of Jesus Christ. The ads for the film show the face of The Savior (with a cross glistening in one eye) while the headline inquires "Are You Curious About HIS Sexual Life?" Filmmaker Ed D. Louie satisfies that curiosity by showing us that the Son of Man was a voracious homosexual. (After all, why did he spend all that time hanging around with the Apostles?) The central character of the film is actually a young gay male in contemporary America whose sexual obsession with Jesus helps him to understand the "hidden mean-ing" of the Gospels.

Contrary to common belief, the entry for *Him* in the Medveds' book was not a hoax concocted by them. However, this minor, low-budget film was so obscure even after its release that it's hard to imagine it could have triggered a massive outpouring of petitions to stop its production.

The non-existence of a "gay Jesus film" did not stem the ire of those who heard about it. Blasphemy—even the hint of it—is enough to mobilize good Christian soldiers everywhere. In 1988, Martin Scorsese's *The Last Temptation of Christ* reaped massive publicity—and long lines at the box office—after fundamentalist Christians picketed theaters. The uproar wasn't over a gay Jesus, merely one who both questioned his fate and who had a dream about a sexual relationship with Mary Magdalene. The film remains controversial to this day.

We take our religious icons seriously, as Denis Lemon, editor of the British publication *Gay News*, found out in 1978. He lost his appeal against conviction for blasphemous libel involving poem he had published about a Roman centurion's homosexual love for Jesus. Though the nine month suspended sentence was set aside, the $900 fine against him and $1,900 fine against his magazine were upheld.[4]

And from a different website:

Be warned, some of the stuff I quote here is kind of distasteful—it's not excessively graphic, but it may plant unwelcome thoughts in your head—but I think I may have finally resolved a mystery that goes way, way back to my early teens and possibly even to my pre-teens.

Anyone here familiar with *The Golden Turkey Awards*? It's a 1980 book that Michael Medved and his brother Harry co-wrote back when Michael was known mostly as a bad-movie buff and had not yet become a religious culture warrior. The very first page of this book declares . . .

A Challenge To The Reader:
Over 425 actual films are described in this book, but one is a complete hoax. Can you find it?

. . . and I have long wondered if the hoax film in question might be *Him*, the alleged 1974 gay-porn film about Jesus and/or a present-day man who obsesses over him sexually. This is how it is described on page 165, where it is listed as one of the nominees for "The Most Unerotic Concept in Pornography":

This innovative film, designed exclusively for gay audiences, goes into excruciating detail concerning the erotic career of Jesus Christ. The ads for the film show the face of The Savior (with a cross glistening in one eye) while the headline inquires "Are You Curious About HIS Sexual Life?" Filmmaker Ed D. Louie satisfies that curiosity by showing us that the Son of Man was a voracious homosexual. (After all, why did he spend all that time hanging around with the Apostles?) The central character of the film is actually a young gay male in contemporary America whose sexual obsession with Jesus helps him to understand the "hidden meaning" of the Gospels.

And then, on page 168, when it is declared the winner in its category, the Medveds write:

For sheer tastelessness, this film has no equals. In one scene, our homosexual hero goes to his local priest to confess his erotic fixation on Jesus Christ. The priest sits in the confessional, listening to the young man breathlessly elaborating his perverted fantasies, while taking advantage of the situation to reach under his cassock and masturbate grotesquely on camera. This charming episode surely marks one of the absolute low points in the history of American cinema. Those pathetic few who might want to see *Him* ought to come to the theater dressed in plain, brown paper wrappers, that hopefully cover their eyes along with the rest of their faces.

Now, like I say, I have often wondered whether *Him* might be the hoax film in question, but since it's the one that won the "Golden Turkey Award" in its category, I kind of assumed it wasn't; that is, I assumed that only one of the also-rans would be the hoax film. The possibility that this film actually existed was given a boost when I came across a reference to it in Roy Kinnard & Tim Davis's *Divine Images: A History of Jesus on the Screen*, which lists all the Jesus films made up to 1992 and has this to say at the end of the intro on page 18:

> Dramatic films that contain only fleeting glimpses of Jesus, but do not otherwise concern themselves with the subject, are also excluded; among them, *The Birth of a Nation* (1915) and *Sparrows* (1926). Otherwise unrelated films that use brief appearances by Christ or Christ-like figures merely for shock or satirical effect are not examined; this category includes such diverse titles as *L'Age D'Or* (1930), *Gas-s-s-s* (1970), *A Clockwork Orange* (1971), *The Devils* (1971), *Savage Messiah* (1972), *The Trial of Billy Jack* (1974), and *The Visitor* (1980). Sub-professional, amateur productions like *The Sin of Jesus* (1961) and *Multiple Maniacs* (1970) also are excluded. So are animated films such as *The Star of Bethlehem* (both 1921 and 1969 versions) and pornography like *Him* (1974) and *I Saw Jesus Die* (1976).

But today I chanced upon this comment at the Snopes urban legend site:

> We've been unable to turn up anything to confirm this purported film's existence, however—we've never found a copy of it, anyone who has seen it, or a review of it, nor have we located any other reference to the film or "filmmaker Ed D. Louie" anywhere other than this one entry in the *Golden Turkey Awards* book.

And this reminded me of how it had always seemed a little suspicious that *Him* did have one of the shorter write-ups in the Medveds' book, and that it was one of only three award "winners" that did not even have a photo (the others being *Rat Fink a Boo Boo* and *Attack of the Mushroom People*—both of which have IMDB entries, BTW, which

Him does not). And I suppose it's possible that Kinnard & Davis's only source of info re: *Him*, which they evidently felt no desire to track down, was the Medveds' book. Running a Google search for more info, I came across a site (http://www.truthminers.com/truth/gay_jesus_movie.htm) that states even more definitively:

> Michael Medved, a well-known film reviewer, wrote a book with his brother that was published in 1980 called the "Golden Turkey Awards." It reviewed bad films. Medved claimed that it was a review of over 425 actual films, but that he had included one hoax and asked readers to spot it. The hoax was a review of a non-existent 1974 film called "Him" which supposedly portrayed Jesus as a homosexual. The film never existed.

I have no idea if this is something that Medved himself has confirmed in more recent years or if this is a conclusion that the site in question reached for itself.

In any case, I would be interested to know what Medved has to say about this now. I was only 11 or 12 when I got this book as a birthday present from someone in my Sunday School class, and just reading those paragraphs excerpted above bothered me a fair bit at the time. (To this day, I cannot hear the word "cassock" without thinking back to the first time I saw it in this book.) If it turns out Medved was planting those thoughts in minds like mine just as part of some stupid hoax, then I think he's got some 'splaining to do—especially if he is now promoting himself as some sort of defender of pious Judeo-Christian sensibilities.[5]

For readers wanting a Christian perspective on this story (and commenting on the preceding material), see Peter Chattaway's article "The Gay Jesus Movie—Hoax or Fact?" on his *Film Chat* blog.[6]

Update 2007

After all the controversy, finally a pornographic gay film on Jesus has been produced. The information comes from the website.

Passio: The Gospel According to Matthias von Fistenberg
Studio launches PassioTheMovie.com to introduce the provocative movie trailer
For Immediate Release
   September 20, 2007 (New York). Dark Alley Media's Matthias von Fistenberg, never one to shy away from controversy, is now taking on perhaps the biggest institution of them all—Jesus Christ himself—in his latest movie, Passio.

With films known for bringing a biting wit and kinky gay sex edge to current events (including the award-winning Mutiny and political parody Gaytanamo), the notorious director has gone back 2,000 years to re-imagine the Son of God as Dark Alley Exclusive Danny Fox, bring love to all mankind. Whether tied to the cross or turning the Last Supper into a Feast of Flesh, he's sure to inspire legions of men to kneel in worship.

"Passio depicts a selection of incidents from the life of Jesus," von Fistenberg explains. "The Latin word 'passio' means 'suffering,' and commonly it's translated into English as 'gospel.' The original Passio texts tell the story of Jesus according to his Disciples—one of them being Matthias. Since my name is also Matthias, this movie is a gospel—a Passio. A version of the story according to me."

When the current Pope calls gay people "satanic," and the Anglican church is tearing itself apart over gays, the time is right to throw a different light on the subject, something von Fistenberg is only too happy to do.

"The Last Temptation of Christ explored the humanistic aspect. Mel Gibson proved in Passion of the Christ that the naked body, whether suffering or not, is sexually attractive. Priest showed a gay priest lusting after Christ on the Crucifix. All of these are a prelude to my Passio," says von Fistenberg. "I just took it one step further: if Jesus has feelings, needs and wants aside from the ones God supplied him, why can't he also lust?"

http://www.PassioTheMovie.com, the exclusive site featuring trailers and pics from this sure-to-be-talked about film. The site will be updated on an ongoing basis, so check back often.

[In fact, the director has a long director's statement about film influences (Priest) and the history of art, religion and sexuality quote various Italian artists. The stills on the site do not tend to confirm his statement.]

Dark Alley Media, 451 Communipaw Ave, New Jersey, NJ 07304, ph 212-380-1010 (New York), fx 646-201-5549, darkalley.com, darkalley .tv, darkalleydirt.com.

The Corpus Christi Protest Continues

The following e-mail was circulated widely, especially in Asia, in 2009:[7]

Shocking info about JESUS—Please fwd don't ignore
Date: Thu, 22 Jan 2009 19:24:25 +0900
Hi ALL,
The movie *Corpus Christi* is due to be released this June to Aug.

I totally agree with the message below.

Let's stand for what we believe in and stop the mockery of Jesus Christ our Savior. If the Muslims do what they believe to be right against their religion, where do we stand as Christians?

At the risk of a bit of inconvenience, I'm forwarding this to all I think would appreciate it too. Please help us prevent such offenses against our Lord. It will take you 4 minutes! If you are not interested, and do not have the 4 Minutes it will take to do this, please don't complain when God does not have time for you, because He is far busier than we are.

A disgusting film set to appear in America later this year depicts Jesus and his disciples as homosexuals! As a play, this has already been in theatres for a while. It's called Corpus Christi which means "The Christ Body." It's revolting mockery of our Lord. But we can make a difference. That's why I am sending this e-mail to you. Will you please add your name to the bottom of the list at the end of this e-mail? If you do, we will be able to prevent this film from showing in America and South Africa.

Hey, it's worth a shot! Apparently, some regions in Europe have already banned the film. All we need is a lot of signatures!

Remember, Jesus said "Deny Me on earth and I'll deny you before my Father."

Hit forward, and when it comes up, delete any e-mail addresses, fill in whom you want to send it to, scroll down to the last name and add your to the list. When it reaches 500 please send to mailto: homasg@ softhome.net

IF WE WORK TOGETHER WE CAN DO THIS.

NOTES

1. Barbara Mikkelson, "Gay Jesus Film," Snopes.com, updated June 2010, www.snopes.com/politics/religion/gayjesus.asp.

2. Truth or Fiction, "A Movie Coming Out That Features a Gay Jesus—False," updated June 21, 2010, www.truthorfiction.com/rumors/g/gayjesusmovie .htm?ref=3b.org.

3. Mikkelson, "Gay Jesus Film."

4. Mikkelson, "Gay Jesus Film."

5. Peter T. Chattaway, "Michael Medved and Gay Jesus Movie," *Arts & Faith* (blog), October 7, 2003, artsandfaith.com/index.php?showtopic=879.

6. Peter Chattaway, "The Gay Jesus Movie—Hoax or Fact?" *Film Chat* (blog), May 13, 2005, filmchatblog.blogspot.com/2005/05/gay-jesus-movie-hoax-or -fact.html.

7. Chain letter sent to author.

APPENDIX 4:
INTERVIEW WITH THE
DIRECTOR OF *JESUS,*
THE SPIRIT OF GOD

What follows is a conversation between Nader Talebzadeh, Iranian director of *Jesus, the Spirit of God* (*The Messiah*), and me.

What interested you in making a film of the Messiah or about Jesus?

Very simple. It was the fact that the Muslim culture knows so much about Jesus and he's one of the most important prophets. And, most important of all, we are awaiting the return of Jesus as Muslims. We believe in the end of times and we believe in God's justice at the end of world history, and it will happen once two companions come back. This is the belief of Muslims. One is Jesus and the other is Matthew, the grandson of the prophet.

So this is an ordinary common belief and I think that Christians do not know that the Muslims have this belief about Jesus nor the fact that, especially in a country like Iran, Christians have been living among us all through the centuries. In fact, the first Christian church was built in Iran. The very first church was built in Yerevan, presently in Armenia, which was part of the Persian Empire. It existed within Iranian boundaries and after Islam they continued to exist in peaceful coexistence.

So you took as a basis for your screenplay the verses in the Koran about Jesus? And how much did you create from the text for the film?

Well, I took history and I used what is known in history—I incorporated the four Gospels and the Gospel of Barnabas, which I think is an interesting Gospel, and what is said in the Koran which is not contradicted by the Gospels—that is very important—I used that as the basis for the story.

Basically, it's the same traditional story up to the end and I did not deviate from the main story, from the main storyline. There's some different events that happened, there are different interpretations of some of those same chapters of the Bible. However, it's the same storyline. And at the end, I put two endings: one, which is the Christian belief about the end of Christ and the other is the Muslim belief as interpreted by the Koran.

That was the interesting thing for me, that as I looked at the film and the Last Supper scene, and then Jesus goes into glory. And then am I right in thinking that Judas assumes the person of Jesus and goes to the Passion? But would you say a bit more about that, because that is new for us.

Yes. First of all, you saw the version that was in the Fajr festival in 2005. That has changed. Basically the same line, but at the end I first present the Christian ending where Christ is crucified. After that, I do the Muslim version of the end of Christ. And as you mentioned, yes, the person who betrays Jesus is the one who assumes the face of Jesus and he screams out that he is not Jesus, he is Judas, but no one listens to him and he's taken into captivity and you have the rest of the story up to the Crucifixion.

I wanted to point to the fact that Jesus in the Bible mentions the fact that he who digs the well for me will fall into that well—will fall into that pit. And it's also emphasized very strongly in the Koran that he was not killed. It appeared this way to people who thought that who they crucified was Jesus.

The Gospel of Barnabas clarifies this, saying it was Judas. Islamic interpretations are different—about ten or twelve different interpretations of who that person was. Some say he was a good disciple; some say he was a bad disciple. Different interpretations, but in this cinematic version, I used the Gospel of Barnabas. I mentioned this in the subtitle: according to the Islamic narrative and the Gospel of Barnabas.

In the main part of the film, leading up to the Passion, you portrayed some of the miracles of Jesus and an amount of his preaching which I suppose Muslims and Christians could easily identify with.

Yes, of course. Let me elaborate that in the television series which is coming after the feature is released—in ten parts—you will get in great detail the sermons of Jesus, the different sermons, the different teachings, different miracles that Jesus performs, in great detail. I think that will be very, very interesting.

The cinematic style you used—how Iranian is it and how much influenced by other cinema traditions?

I don't think it's very Iranian—at least that's what people tell me. I shot a lot of it myself—did a lot of the camerawork myself, a lot of hand-held shooting. It's influenced by European film directors whose films I saw as I was growing up. There's also my documentary background. I've been doing documentaries a long time.

I really didn't want to make a festival film. I wanted to make a film that would connect Christians and Muslims, or create dialogue between them. And I filmed it the best way I knew how to shoot.

There is a difference between this film and other films, according to people who have seen it. I have not put the film out yet in any festival because the film is, as we are speaking, being processed in the lab. I refused to let the early copy be released because it was not complete. What we added to the version you saw is the Christian ending, where we say it: this is what Christians believe. It is a more interesting way to do it.

In talking with people, I found that was precisely the thing they were interested in, the comparison. I want to ask about your actor who performed the role of Jesus and his style. It reminded me a bit, say, of Cecil B. DeMille's King of Kings, *much less of the more recent Jesus films which tend to emphasize his humanity. What were your perceptions on the character of Jesus and your direction of the actor?*

The actor is from a mountainous area of Iran. He has been a hard-working artist all his life, a hardworking man, also a very ardent religious Muslim. He prays—as soon as there's a call for prayer, he rushes to his prayer rug. I like that aspect of him. He's a man who likes to pray. Also he's never been seen in any film in Iran and he made a vow to himself that he would not act in any film afterwards. He is a nonprofessional actor.

We searched among the professional actors and we felt that his face looked very much similar to how the face of Jesus appears in church paintings and in the history of Western paintings of Jesus. Maybe that was a mistake; maybe I should have used a different actor with different complexion, for more drama. Instead, I chose something more documentary-like. The way he feels, the way he walks, the way he moves—I think he presented himself in a convincing way. I have never talked to anyone who is not convinced by his acting. They might not like the style, but I felt that he was the proper actor for this sort of contentious filmmaking.

In a way, that's what Pasolini did with the Gospel according to St. Matthew. *He took the amateur actor who gave an intense non-professional performance. Had you seen Pasolini's film?*

Yes, and I enjoyed that film very much. I still think it's a classic film among religious films in world cinema.

When you spoke of your actor being a prayerful man, I was reminded of Mel Gibson's choice of Jim Caviezel for Jesus. He is also a praying person. There seemed to be an intensity about Jim Caviezel, perhaps from his own personal life. Did you see The Passion of the Christ?

Yes, I not only saw *The Passion of the Christ*, I talked about it on television—four or five different programs, live and recorded. I spoke about it in different religious circles. I admired the film, even though it's not the right story in Muslim belief. But it was done so passionately and with such conviction, it's admirable.

Two or three nights ago I recorded an interview with guest, a very famous Ayatollah, an authority on cinema, and we talked about *The Passion* again and we were intercutting it with some images of the film. So *The Passion* is still a very live subject. I admire it. I think Gibson did something for Christianity and religion. He brought the subject alive again, which I think is an admirable thing.

You're right, because one of the members of our jury in 2005 from Bangladesh said when he saw The Passion, *it was the first time he understood the Christian interpretation.*

The favorite image of Jesus on-screen, at least with Catholics is Zeffirelli's Jesus of Nazareth *with Robert Powell.*

Yes, I also admire that film. I'm a fan of Franco Zeffirelli. I think he's a great director and his *Brother Sun, Sister Moon* is a masterpiece. His *Jesus of Nazareth*, I thought, was a very good film, you know, made with conviction, and it was the longest film made in the West about Jesus. I like Zeffirelli's style and tone. It affected me very much.

Now, this is prime time to interject with a different film, coming from Iran. Right now Iran is a controversial country and being blamed for many things, but I think a lot of people will be surprised that Iran has made a film about Jesus. It's not a short film—it's almost eight hundred minutes. Basically, we're talking about creating an opportunity for talk between Christian and Muslim people and scholars.

It's important for a film to be able to talk about it. I think that it is an effective enough film and I think due to the collaboration of a lot of artists it's a strong enough film to create a backbone for a serious discussion.

SELECTED
BACKGROUND READING

Baugh, Lloyd. *Imaging the Divine*. Kansas City: Sheed & Ward, 1997.

This is a scholarly work examining the principal Jesus films as well as films that have characters who parallel Jesus. Baugh is sometimes severe in his judgments on the Jesus films, theologically critiquing them as if they were to be considered the equivalent of inspired Gospels rather than as films based on the Gospels.

Butler, Ivan. *Religion in the Cinema*. New York: A. S. Barnes, 1969.

This book is indebted to Butler's research on the early films of the silent era. Much of Butler's information comes from a book from the 1920s by Terry Ramsaye, *A Million and One Nights*. New York: Simon & Schuster, 1926; reprinted, Frank Cass & Co, 1964.

Ford, Charles. "The Tragedy of the Life of Christ." *International Film Review* 1, no. 3 (1949): 12–14, Belgium.

This article provides an eternal subject for the cinema. It is an example of surveying the Jesus films of the previous fifty years (going back to the earliest years of cinema) with some more explicit details from these films than are found in later articles. The periodical was founded and sponsored by the Organisation Catholique Internationale du Cinema, Brussels.

Friesen, Dwight. "Karunamayudu: Seeing Christ in Indian Cinema" (unpublished dissertation).

This is a study of the 1978 film *Karunamayudu* and comparisons in content and style with Western Jesus films and the distinctive Indian styles of filmmaking it uses.

Hess, Brian. "A Brief History of Christian Film: 1918–2002." http://www.avgeeks.com/bhess/christian_film_history.html.

This is a useful and interesting overview of Christian film, especially with reference to the United States and to evangelical filmmakers like James Friedrich and Cathedral Films in the 1930s–1950s.

Kinnard, Roy, and Tim Davis. *Divine Images: A History of Jesus on the Screen*. New York: Citadel Press, 1992.

I am indebted to the research and detail in this book. Kinnard and Davis have cataloged all the major Jesus films and noted many minor ones in chronological order, including the credits, a brief synopsis and commentary, some selected quotations from reviews, and a large number of stills.

Malone, Peter. *Movie Christs and Antichrists*. New York: Crossroads, 1990.

This is my Jesus-films book, an overview of films that portray Jesus as well as Christ-figure films that portray characters who resemble Jesus significantly and substantially. There is also a section on evil, Antichrist-figures.

Malone, Peter, ed. *Through a Catholic Lens: Religious Perspectives of Nineteen Film Directors from around the World*. Lanham: Sheed & Ward, 2007.

Directors include Luis Bunuel, Denys Arcand, Mel Gibson, Kevin Smith, and Terence Davies, whose films are discussed in this book.

Marsh, Clive, and Gaye Ortiz. *Explorations in Theology and Film*. London: Blackwells, 1997.

This book contains a collection of chapters on popular films and religious and theological meanings. The chapter by William Telford offers a survey of Jesus films and their significance. I wrote a chapter on *Edward Scissorhands* and Christology.

Martin, Malachi. *Jesus Now: How Jesus Has No Past, Will Not Come Again, and in Loving Actions Is Dissolving the Molds of Our Spent Society*. New York: E. P. Dutton, 1973.

The book offers the basis for the use of Jesus-figure to describe all images of Jesus himself.

May, John R., ed. *New Image of Religious Film*. Kansas City: Sheed & Ward, 1997.

This book contains a collection of chapters on cinema and theology (generally from a continental European perspective) with chapters on Jesus on-screen by Peter Hasenberg and myself.

Nicolosi, Barbara. "Christ Figures in the Movies." *Ligourian*, Missouri, USA, February, 2003.

Taking her lead from the focus of Vatican II, Barbara Nicolosi suggests the framework of Jesus as Priest, Prophet, and King for understanding the mission of Jesus and how Christ-figures live these models.

Plate, S. Brent. *Re-Viewing "The Passion": Mel Gibson's Film and Its Critics*. New York: Palgrave Macmillan, 2004.

This collection of essays was written in the immediate aftermath of the release of *The Passion of the Christ* and the controversies. Topics include reviews, theological assessment, and the anti-Semitism issues.

Reinhartz, Adele. *Hollywood Jesus*. Oxford: Oxford University Press, 2007.

The author combines biblical research and the Jesus films, focusing on the members of Jesus' family, his friends, and foes and drawing on scholarly and popular reflection. (See also her contributions to *The Routledge Companion to Religion and Film*, "Jesus and Christ-figures," and to *The Continuum Companion Religion and Film*, "Jesus Movies.")

Shafto, Sally. "Artist as Christ/Artist as God the Father: Religion in the Cinema of Philippe Garrel and Jean-Luc Godard." *Film History* 14, no. 2 (2002): 142–57. This lengthy article is of interest in placing Philippe Garrel in his historical/cinema setting.

Stern, Richard C., Clayton N. Jefford, and Guerric Debona. *Savior on the Silver Screen*. Mahwah, NJ: Paulist Press, 1999.

The authors have run courses on the principal Jesus films from Cecil B. DeMille to *Jesus of Montreal*. This is the expanded course with a thorough rationale for studying these films.

Tatum, W. Barnes. *Jesus at the Movies: A Guide to the First Hundred Years*. Rev. ed. Santa Rosa, CA: Polebridge Press, 2004.

This book offers a comprehensive overview and study of the history of the Jesus films with information about the making of the films, the reaction on release, and theological reflections on the portraits of Jesus.

Note: This list is limited to books and articles in English. Extensive research into Jesus on-screen has been done by European scholars such as Reinhold Zwick, Peter Hasenberg, and Charles Martig. Their writings are in German.

INDEX

ABOUT THE AUTHOR

Peter Malone is an Australian Catholic priest, a Missionary of the Sacred Heart. He studied at the Australian National University in Canberra for an arts degree in history and at the Gregorian University in Rome for a licentiate in theology.

After teaching in secondary schools and the seminary in Canberra, he taught in the Yarra Theological Union, part of the Melbourne College of Divinity, Old Testament Studies, Fundamental Theology. He also worked at the National Pastoral Institute and the Heart of Life Spirituality Centre in Melbourne, specializing in media studies as well as Australian theology.

He edited *Compass*, a review of topical theology, from 1971 to 1998.

He was elected president of OCIC (Organization Catholique du Cinema) in the Pacific in 1989 and served on the international board of OCIC until his election as world president in 1998. With the merger of OCIC and Unda, he became the first president of SIGNIS, the World Catholic Association for Communication (2001–2005). He now works for the cinema desk of SIGNIS.

He has reviewed films since 1968 and has published books and articles including *The Film, Films and Values, Movie Christs and Antichrists, Can Movies Be a Moral Compass?* and the Lights Camera Faith series. He edited *Through a Catholic Lens: Religious Perspectives of Nineteen Film Directors from around the World*.